Downward Mobility

Downward Mobility

The Form of Capital
and the Sentimental Novel

KATHERINE BINHAMMER

Johns Hopkins University Press, *Baltimore*

Printed in the United States of America on acid-free paper
9 8 7 6 5 4 3 2 1

Johns Hopkins University Press
2715 North Charles Street
Baltimore, Maryland 21218-4363
www.press.jhu.edu

Library of Congress Cataloging-in-Publication Data

Names: Binhammer, Katherine, 1962– author.
Title: Downward mobility : the form of capital and the sentimental novel / Katherine Binhammer.
Description: Baltimore : Johns Hopkins University Press, 2020. | Includes bibliographical references and index.
Identifiers: LCCN 2019031250 | ISBN 9781421437606 (hardcover) | ISBN 9781421437613 (paperback) | ISBN 9781421437620 (ebook)
Subjects: LCSH: English literature—18th century—History and criticism. | Capitalism in literature. | Social mobility in literature. | Sentimentalism in literature.
Classification: LCC PR448.C34 B56 2020 | DDC 823/.5093553—dc23
LC record available at https://lccn.loc.gov/2019031250

A catalog record for this book is available from the British Library.

Special discounts are available for bulk purchases of this book. For more information, please contact Special Sales at specialsales@press.jhu.edu.

Johns Hopkins University Press uses environmentally friendly book materials, including recycled text paper that is composed of at least 30 percent post-consumer waste, whenever possible.

CONTENTS

ILLUSTRATIONS

ACKNOWLEDGMENTS

For thousands of years, across geographical regions, humans have recorded their debts. The debts entered in the ledger below cannot be balanced and are myriad in form, from financial and social to intellectual and institutional. In other words, they constitute the œconomy of this book.

The anonymous readers whom Johns Hopkins University Press recruited provided spectacularly generous and rigorous readings of my manuscript, for which I am infinitely in their debt. I thank Catherine Goldstead, my editor at the Press, for her engagement with the book as well as her savvy suggestions moving forward. Steven Baker deserves a prize for his invisible copyediting work in making my prose appear seamless. Sue Lanser went from being an anonymous essay reader to identifying herself as the demanding reviewer who pushed me to improve my work; I thank her for caring enough to be hard at a crucial moment in the project's development. Dianne Chisholm, Alison Conway, and Corrinne Harol read embarrassingly rough drafts and always helped me see where the kernel of the argument was buried; their long and diverse support of the project has been transformative. Eugenia Zuroski's and Eddy Kent's important and timely feedback improved the manuscript.

I have benefited from conversations with and questions and comments from many colleagues, both local and international, in specialized and nonspecialized ways, at home and abroad, including: the late Srinivas Aravamudan, Susan Carlile, David Cooper, Isobel Grundy, Nick Hudson, Suvir Kaul, Sarah Krotz, Beverley Lemire, April London, Devoney Looser, Julie Murray, James Phelan, Mary Poovey, Chris Roulston, Betty Schellenberg, Norbert Schürer, Ann (Rusty) Shteir, Peter Sinnema, Stephen Slemon, Mark Simpson, Helen Thompson, and Chris Wiesenthal. The audiences and session organizers at the annual meetings of the Canadian and American Societies for Eighteenth-Century Studies where I presented this project have provided countless scenes of productive scholarly insight.

The project germinated and then bloomed in multiple graduate classrooms, and I thank the students in "Capitalist Realism," "The Novelization of Money, 1714–2014," and "Trading Stories" for keeping up with the reading and for thinking collaboratively. The conceptualization of capital's chronotopes that appears in chapter 4 owes everything to these class discussions. Ben Neudorf provided graduate research assistantship, including much technical support. Nakita Valerio came through with important last-minute quote checking.

Thanks to Peter Sinnema, who as chair invited me to deliver the department's annual Broadus Lectures, which are meant to serve the larger university and general-public communities. The challenge of translating my research for such an audience was meaningful and confirmed for me the debt scholars owe to the public that supports them. My own research productivity depends on a university budget balanced through the use of contract teaching staff; their precarious employment introduces social and intellectual inequities that must be resolved. I would particularly like to thank Leslie Robertson, Laura Schechter, Lucinda Rasmussen, Kristine Smitka, and Ahsan Chowdhury. During the final years of this project I served as a faculty representative on the University of Alberta's Board of Governors; the opportunity to learn how such a complex public institution shares its resources was one I value and I am grateful to Board Chair Michael Phair, President David Turpin, and all my fellow members for their service. An Insight Grant from the Social Sciences and Humanities Research Council of Canada provided financial support; I am fortunate to live in a country that values humanities research in this way and I hope it continues to do so.

My life is sustained in these "end times"—indeed, it flourishes—thanks to the intellectual and emotional camaraderie of Beau Coleman, Alison Conway, Judy Davidson, Mo Engel, Nat Hurley, Ada Jaarsma, Catherine Kellogg, Susanne Luhmann, Katja Pettinen, and Heather Zwicker. Bob and Beverley Binhammer gave me life, love, and the confidence to have a voice in the world; my sister, Kris Savage, and her children, Emily and Nicholas, continue to bring fresh perspectives to my ivory tower views. Dianne Chisholm is so much more than the person with whom I share a domestic economy; her unaccounted work in reproducing my intellectual life can never be repaid.

Sections of this book were revised from essays previously published. The introduction and chapter 5 include portions of "Narrative Exchange in *David Simple*," *The Eighteenth-Century: Theory and Interpretation*, 56, no. 1 (spring 2015): 1–19. Chapter 5 also includes material from "The Economics of Plot in *Camilla*," *Studies in the Novel*, 43, no. 1 (spring 2011): 1–20. A condensed version of chapter 2 was published as "The Story within the Story of Sentimental Fiction," *Narrative* 25, no. 1 (January 2017): 45–64. I thank the Debtor's Relief Funds Charity, also known as the 1772 Debtor's Relief Fund, for permission to publish images from minute books of the Society for the Discharge and Relief of Persons Imprisoned for Small Debts, held at the London Metropolitan Archives.

Downward Mobility

Introduction

Over the course of the eighteenth century, money changes its form. With the rise of financial capital, money shape-shifts from gold coin into paper currency, a transformation that launches its narrative form. From symbolic value to fictitious capital, from metaphor to metonymy, money after the advent of financial speculation is defined by its narrative temporality, by its ability to store value between investing and then selling for a profit. This narrative temporality turns money into capital since it is not the bill of exchange in itself that changes money's form. The fact that the bill can be transferred from one person to another for profit is that which gives it a story.[1] What aligns fictitious capital with fiction is not only a parallel abstracted distance from the "real" but also a shared reliance on a temporal series, on a beginning, middle, and end. In this book, I argue that money's transformation into capital prompts its novelization since the novel, with its complex temporal structure and interpretative webs, is the narrative genre that renders capital's epistemological and temporal contradictions comprehensible. The fiction that the future can be one of infinitely compounding economic growth acquires purchase in our imaginative "real" partly through the novel.

While the book details how capital novelizes money by turning it into a temporal dialectic, it is equally invested in thinking about the inverse—how the novel capitalizes on money's new story. To do so, I investigate financial and narrative exchanges in a particular genre of fiction, the sentimental novel in Britain in the latter eighteenth century, because financial crisis fuels the genre's development. By focusing on narrative form, I show how sentimental stories of downward mobility surprisingly align with capital's plot of infinite growth and, as such, provide a counterintuitive illustration of the relationship between economic and literary history. Ever since Ian Watt's *The Rise of the Novel*, novel studies has assumed a link between the progress narrative of mercantile capitalism and the upward mobility plot of *Homo economicus*, paradigmatically illustrated by Daniel Defoe's *Robinson Crusoe*.[2] By taking as my object of study sentimental tales of loss, such as Sarah Fielding's *The Adventures of David Simple* and Oliver Goldsmith's *Vicar of Wakefield*, I propose that downward mobility is as important a myth as upward mobility to the literary and economic history of capitalism and that financial failure performs a crucial structural role in both the business cycle and the novel's genealogy. Why, I ask, do stories of downward mobility become popular at the same moment that Britain's net wealth begins increasing annually, initiating the continuous economic growth on which capitalism depends? The answer suggests that the relationship between economic and literary history is less about mutually reinforcing discourses of empiricism, bourgeois individualism, and progress than about the emergence of the "financial imagination," that is, the new form of understanding that the novel and finance both depend upon to make the contradictions of capitalism comprehensible.[3] By *narrative* I refer both to prose that tells a story, and, with Peter Brooks, to a "mode of human understanding," a fundamental way of making meaning and determining value that is central to our social being.[4] The novel's mode through which it shapes meaning and capital's system of value are homologous; their roots lie in the same historical tree. By reading downward mobility, this book maps the overlaps between how novels capitalize on new financial epistemologies and how capital novelizes money to tell a particular story of infinite economic growth.

The Myth of Downward Mobility

Downward mobility narratives in sentimental fiction help us understand capital's form for reasons of both literary history and theory. This book began with my observation that financial loss prompted the telling of story after story in the latter eighteenth century, and I wanted to think about why everyone was losing money in fiction and what this phenomenon might explain. The presence of loss acts as the central "*narrative goad*" in the sentimental novel, the phrase Jeffrey Williams uses for "a catalyst that spurs or elicits the telling of a narrative."[5] I noticed that, while financial failure catalyzes stories, it was a particular kind of loss. The appearance of a character in financial distress does not elicit the desire for narrative in itself, but a downwardly mobile genteel character does because *they were once rich and now are poor.* The reader's desire for the story stems not from a curiosity about poverty per se but from the presence of "status inconsistency," to use Michael McKeon's term for the mismatch between a person's class or financial position and their rank or birth status.[6] The lowest common denominator of all stories is to account for "What happened?" and status inconsistency immediately presents itself as an event requiring explanation. Downward mobility is often analeptically introduced on the first page of sentimental novels, with the past loss constituting the lack that the narrative will fill. Charlotte Lennox's *Sophia* (1762), for instance, begins: "Harriot and Sophia were the daughters of a gentleman, who, having spent a good paternal inheritance before he was five and thirty, was reduced to live upon the moderate salary of a place at court."[7] Because of her father's past profligacy, Sophia is economically and thus erotically vulnerable on the marriage market, and this is the conflict that the narrative will resolve. In the first pages of *David Simple,* David is cheated out of his inheritance by his brother, an event that sets off the picaresque narrative, prompting him to leave home in search of a true friend to replace blood ties.

Although many central characters experience financial loss—Cecilia, Camilla, the Vicar of Wakefield, Sidney Bidulph, Amelia, to name only a few eponymous ones—much of the economic loss comes from secondary characters who tell their stories in embedded tales. Stories-within-stories, or shifts in narrative level, are ubiquitous within the sentimental genre, and in the majority of cases they are prompted by downward mobility: the man or woman of feeling encounters a person in financial need whose appearance indicates that they were once wealthier. The first thing David Simple notices when he initially encounters Camilla and Valentine in the garret is that Camilla is wearing a silk dress that was once quite fine and the spoiled dress signifies a story: David "longed to know their Story" for he "was certain by their Manner, and Behaviour, they could not have been bred in very low Life."[8] When Emily Montague in Frances Brooke's novel encounters the "fair cottager," she instantly recognizes that she "is not in the station in which she was born," and the figure "excite[s] the most lively curiosity."[9] In *Man of Feeling,* Harley takes a tour of Bedlam and notices an inmate "whose appearance had something of superior dignity," which elicits his desire to know the poor woman's story.[10] Sidney Bidulph is drawn to the flower seller on the street because she looked as though she "had not been bred in poverty"; curious to discover "what misfortunes" she experienced, "I [Sidney] desired her to sit down, and relate to me the particulars of her story."[11] In *Millenium Hall,* Mrs. Thornby notices that Louisa Mancel "had not been born for the station she was then in, and [I] begged a particular account of her whole life."[12]

Over and over, downward mobility prompts a scene of storytelling as the character in financial distress always satiates the spectator's curiosity with their tale. To what effect? Interestingly, the opposite mobility narrative, that of a lower-class person raised up, does not prompt the same narrative desire. Figures of upward mobility are also sartorially marked: Burney's novels, for example, are littered with uppity characters from Madame Duval to Mr. Hobson to Mr. Dubster whose mimicking of gentry manners is evident in their tacky and inappropriate appearance. But the overdressed fop's gaudy silk does not register as narratable in the way that Camilla's spoiled silk does. The difference between the narrativity of downward but not upward mobility in the sentimental novel is the literary historical event that this book aims to explain.

My hypothesis is that the value of these stories is linked to the cultural history of capitalism not only in *what* stories they circulate but in *how* they tell their stories, and that by concentrating on narrative techniques, we can learn about the contradictions at play in early financial discourse. The frequency of financial failure as plot, event, and theme points to how the novel thrives on the boom-and-bust cycles of speculative capital but not in any simple mimetic or ideological way. James Kim observes the increasing popularity of what he calls "romances of downward mobility": "After mid-century or so, one begins to find what might be called 'romances of downward mobility,' narratives in which the protagonist loses his or her class position only to regain it by articulating, maintaining, or vindicating the logic of class stratification."[13] Kim's essay concentrates on *David Simple*, reading Fielding's incessant "anguishing . . . over the plight of genteel folk wrongly cast down" as a conservative melancholia for a lost gentry class.[14] I read the romance differently, in part because not all loss is restored in these novels (David Simple's losses in *Volume the Last* exemplify this point) and the gentry are not always vindicated; but also because I see downward mobility negotiating, on the level of form, a logic of crisis that is central to the culture of infinite growth and to the emergence of the financial imagination. In other words, downward mobility stories are not simple "lost princess" fairytales critiquing an emerging commercial economy; rather, they play a central role in novelizing money as speculative capital by the way they manage the temporal and structural contradictions behind capital's logic of infinite and compounding growth. Downward mobility stories significantly dominate fiction in the latter eighteenth century at the same time as economic history witnesses the empirical rise in Britain's wealth. What explains this mimetic inversion?

The majority of economic historians concur that Britain's overall wealth began to increase annually around 1760, though the percentage of that increase remains variable and the rate initially estimated by Phyllis Deane and W. A. Cole in *British Economic Growth* has been lowered.[15] While these scholars concur that Britain's gross domestic product (GDP) begins its constant march upward in the period, they debate whether people's standard of living actually increased in symmetrical ways. Some argue that the "consumer revolution" was evidence that more people had more money to spend on luxuries, whereas others argue that poverty did not substantially decrease and that inflation in prices actually lessened the buying power of the laboring classes.[16] Whether or not people's lives were materially improving, the cultural belief that the future will be wealthier begins to take form in the second half of the eighteenth century. Infinite economic growth may not be fully naturalized within the British cultural imagination until the nineteenth century, but its genealogy can be traced within the period studied here. Anthony Brewer notes the significance of this emerging belief: "The idea that (capitalist) economies normally grow over time was a major change of perspective, part of a wider change in which people ceased to think of past, present, and future as essentially alike."[17] In other words, economic growth requires people to understand their lives in ways similar to the plots of novels, as having a future not predetermined by birth. The change in phenomenological time introduced by infinite economic growth also invests the plots of novels, including the plot of downward mobility, with its complex temporal dynamic.

The material and cultural history of growth that starts to take form in the latter eighteenth century relies on a series of prior events known collectively as the "financial revolution."[18] Before the industrial revolution in the nineteenth century, Britain develops the financial infrastructure that allows capital to launch a productive cycle and that results in the accumulation of vast imperial wealth. Signal developments in Britain's eighteenth-century financialization include the founding of the Bank of England and the introduction of a national debt to finance colonial wars; the birth of insurance through underwriting risks of maritime trade, including the trade in human lives; and the evolution of the modern stock market with the introduction of financial instruments such as bills of exchange, bonds, mortgages, and annuities all of which provide the liquidity (along with the Atlantic and Indian Oceans) for global trade. Ian Baucom has called the shift to a speculative economy with the introduction of paper credit "the central epistemological drama of the long eighteenth century," and many literary studies have taken up the "crisis in value" that ensued, reading literature symptomatically, as registering both anxiety and anticipation concerning the historical emergence of a credit economy.[19] My book adds to this body of work both by thinking about how the novel form embeds the contradictory logic of infinite growth and by reading loss rather than gain, debt rather than credit.

While the economic history reviewed above forms the background of this study, my hypothesis that downward mobility stories negotiate the logic of growth on the level of form, not content, means that I am less invested in the material history of capitalism than I am in the forms of capital.[20] Like David Harvey, I make "a clear distinction between *capitalism* and *capital*," between the particular machinations of the economy at any one time and the general structure that defines money as capital.[21] In approaching the sentimental novel from this point of view, I read into the history of the novel the *structure* of capital's narrative, not its *history*, in order to provide a reading of what I call the *novelization of money*. If, as Bakhtin theorizes, the novel's rise can be traced to its "novelization of other genres," or the way its dialogism and heteroglossia embed themselves in other forms, capital's rise can be traced in its novelization of money, the way it takes over money to give it novelistic form.[22] "To think finance capital is to develop new forms of narrating it," Mathias Nilges posits, and I transpose his claim from its contemporary context back into the eighteenth century to argue that the narrative form of the novel develops as a space to think capitalism's new financial instruments.[23]

My methodology for reading the plot of downward mobility as an effect of money's novelization lies somewhere between new historicism and new formalism insofar as it unravels a particular moment in the history of capital and thus is grounded in its specific historicity while it reads that historicity through the formal narrative techniques of characterization, voice, and plot. I see this book as part of a critical school that Anna Kornbluh, in her work on Victorian fiction, *Realizing Capital*, has called "financial formalism."[24] At the crossroads of critical finance studies and literary criticism, I hope to denaturalize our current discourse of late capitalism's financialization by unraveling the formal properties under which such financialization comes to appear as commonsense, a process I read into stories of crisis and downward mobility in the late eighteenth century. The term *financialization* most often denotes the ever-increasing proportion of the economy's profits that come from buying and selling financial products, the ever-greater reliance of households on financial markets through debt and equity (from mortgages to pension funds), and the increasing sophistication of financial instruments, including the collateralized debt obligations largely responsible for the 2008 crash and any of the endless derivatives that package and repackage risk and time through computer algorithms.[25] Critical finance studies takes as its object of study the cultural and social impact of financialization. When wealth unleashes itself from material production, when political or ethical valuation is replaced with a numerical calculation that monetizes time, financialization fixes all forms of value to a rate of return. The work of critical finance studies is to register the costs of forgetting that economics is not about mathematical models and maximizing profits but about *oikonomia*, that is, determining the best way for the household to manage its shared resources.

Critical finance studies, at the same time, performs its own forgetting, assuming that financialization is a wholly contemporary phenomenon and that the scale of today's financial abstractions makes the current context radically different from earlier moments in capitalism's history. Max Haiven, for instance, is one of a number of critics to date financialization to the rise of neoliberalism, Reaganomics, and the collapse of the Bretton-Woods accord in 1971 (which effectively ended the gold standard and loosened regulations on Wall Street).[26] The forms of understanding that generate our twenty-first-century financialization, however, are readable in the historical moment when financial instruments begin their compounding growth, and I wager that it is easier to read capital's form through the defamiliarizing gaze of history than it is today. It may be the case that late capitalism is so fully globalized and universalized that, as the saying goes, "it is easier to imagine the end of the world than to imagine the end of capitalism."[27] And if, as Mark Fisher proposes, we are living in a moment of "capitalist realism," when the global saturation of financial capitalism in a post–Berlin Wall era has made any alternative not only not viable but *unimaginable*, it may be worthwhile to revisit the moment when both capitalism and realism emerge.[28] My hope is that by studying the eighteenth-century financial imagination, the end of capitalism—or at least a mitigation of the vast social and political inequities global financial wealth generates—might be easier to imagine. The myth of downward mobility, I further propose, provides a critical frame for demystifying our current naturalized assumption that more wealth *overall* translates into more wealth *for all*.

While I return to the historical moment when a financialized epistemology emerges and economic growth begins its compounding rise, I do so with the "formalism" of "financial formalism," not with historicism, and I attend to the formal narrative techniques developed in the sentimental novel to highlight how sentimentalism and capitalism converge. Critics have long observed the way sentimentalism redefines virtue in ways that correspond to the displacement of wealth from land to capital, but they disagree on how and to what effect sentimentalism and capitalism are intricately related.[29] On the level of content, sentimental fiction appears explicitly opposed to emerging commercial culture in its insistence that money does not buy happiness. For this reason, Janet Todd has defined the movement as "ardently anti-capitalist."[30] Donna Landry goes so far as to call *David Simple* a "proto-communist" text.[31] Another scholarly current reads sentimental literature as a bourgeois genre propping up commerce by providing "the icing on the materialist cake of capitalism" and as adding feminine virtue to soften the masculine greed of the marketplace.[32] In beginning from the homologous genealogy of capitalism and sentimentalism, I read the narrative structure of downwardly mobile fictions for the ways their form is generated by the new cultural scripts of finance capital, including such assumptions as that debts are purely financial, that wealth is infinite, and that future risks can be managed. Not only does financial capital take narrative form, but, analogously, novelistic narrative flourishes with fictitious capital's circulation. I show how the novel's signature deployment of narrative techniques—from complex characterization to plausible plots to shifting perspectives—profits from capital's temporal dynamics. This is particularly the case in the sentimental novel, with its stories of financial insolvency and crisis. In arguing that the novel thrives on capitalism, I pursue the interconnectedness of our forms of storytelling with capital's logic of economic growth to suggest how we might tell the story of downward mobility differently, as not always about loss.[33] We talk about social mobility most often in terms of raising up the poor, not of decreasing wealth.[34] An undercurrent of this book is that contemporary culture might need to embrace downward mobility for some in order to combat our addiction to a growth economy and to make the global distribution of wealth more equitable.

The Novelization of Money

My argument that downward mobility narratives reveal the historical and formal homology between capital and the novel—between money's novelization and the novel's financialization—rests upon the theoretical claim that capital's form is narrative. This claim is not new. Beginning with Lukács, critics have proposed formal links between the novel and the history of capitalism, and many critical finance scholars since Fredric Jameson emphasize the centrality of narrative in understanding the temporal logic of capital.[35] For Jameson and others, the narrativity of capital is linked to how it shapes time to produce infinitely accumulating surplus value. Marx's "General Formula for Capital" famously distinguished simple commodity exchange (C-M-C) from capital's production of surplus value through M-C-M′, buying a commodity only to sell it later for more money. The historical drive of capital, as scholars such as David Harvey and Giovanni Arrighi detail, is toward freeing itself from the commodity to achieve M-M′, when money breeds more money without material production, a drive that is possible only by keeping money in motion.[36] Joshua Clover outlines capital's narrative roots: "It is in this most basic of Marxian formulations (the 'general formula of capital'), that one sees narrative's most primitive relation on the logic of capitalism. . . . Narrative requires motion and change, not simple replenishment; motion and change are exactly what constitute the general formula . . . the increase from M to 'M′.' There is no coming to rest for narrative until it ends. Equally, capital is capital in that it moves."[37] Late capital moves across global stock markets at unprecedented speed, generating profits through automated algorithms that monetize milliseconds such that it is hard to trace its movements as profits appear instantaneously. This collapse of space and time, the dematerialization of surplus value through mathematical equations, leads Clover to suggest that capital's contemporary form is poetry, but others, including Max Haiven and Mathias Nilges, continue to highlight narrative precisely in order to resist the material erasures of financialization.[38] Nilges writes, "The temporal and structural episteme of finance capitalism . . . presents itself as a problem of narrative," and thus he turns to novels as a way to analyze the problem of what is at stake in capital's increasing abstractions.[39] Other critical finance scholars, such as Leigh Claire La Berge, Annie McClanahan, and Alison Shonkwiler, similarly foreground narrative. Shonkwiler proposes that since we have arrived at a moment of totalizing M-M′, reading fictional narratives of finance may help demystify speculative sublimities and reveal strategies of disruption that remember the narrative circulations behind M-M′: "The novel recapitulates the representational logic of this [financialized] imaginary but adds friction, slows it down, expands it, subjectivizes it, adds data and history. The novel aims to resituate finance's logic within its own formal terms."[40] For Shonkwiler and others, the scale of "capitalist realism" today renders the connections between social and financial relations difficult to make visible, and these critics see contemporary fiction as helping to materialize those hidden and abstracted connections. Reading eighteenth-century sentimental fiction, I suggest, allows us to slow the financial narrative down even more, revealing capital's narrativization in a raw and rough form, before its logic evaporates with absolute liquidity in the twenty-first century. Representations of financial crises within sentimental novels show us how the temporal dynamics of narrative form allows capital's infinite sequence of accumulation to imaginatively cohere.

In taking up critical finance studies' interest in the narrativity of capital, I highlight the analogous structure of capital and narrative over that of money and language, thus reading from a different angle than much of new economic criticism.[41] New economic criticism has tended to focus not on the temporal nature of money but on how money functions as a medium of exchange and thus as a symbol and metaphor, as a representation within a system of exchange. Money and language are then viewed as analogous semiotic systems; Marc Shell's and Jean-Joseph Goux's germinal work on "[t]he remarkable structural parallel between money and language" has been influential in understanding money as metaphor.[42] Money as a representational system provides the focus of Mary Poovey's *Genres of the Credit Economy*, in which she persuasively argues that money is naturalized in the eighteenth century such that its history as a genre of writing, as representation, disappears. Contemporary ideology normalizes money as a simple numerical abstraction, and money's origin as writing, she importantly argues, needs to be remembered in order to recognize how all representational systems are grounded in value judgments that have political and material effects. I think about money's origins in a particular form of writing, the novel, to emphasize the narrativity of capital, the way it requires money to be understood metonymically, as part of a sequence within the script of infinite economic growth. Capital's novelization of money signifies a particular passage of time, a repetition of a sequencing of events: buy first, then sell for a profit, then buy, then sell for more ad infinitum. The logic of infinite accumulation and the logic of narrative shape value and meaning within a fictional temporal dynamic in which the future's profits can be realized in the present. Narrative meaning, like speculative value, profits from compounding instabilities.

Time, then, is what novelizes money, and fiction is what narrativizes infinite growth; both work through a temporal dialectic that combines chronological sequencing with nonchronological temporality to build coherent unity out of scattered series. Wrestling provisional wholes out of nested sequences, sequences that are themselves in motion, requires a dynamic process, one in which meaning is realized only in the act of interpretative or transactional evaluation. Narrated events come to a close, stocks are sold, but the process of evaluation—of determining the ending's meaning or the stock's price—can never be fixed. In this way, both novels and capital work through a productive tension between abstracting general value and concretizing meaning in a particular material and individual form. Fictional plotting is the narrative process that best registers how the interpretative act combines diachronic and synchronic or linear and circuitous patterns of thought, patterns that, I argue, allow temporal contradictions to cohere. Paul Ricoeur's philosophical insight into the way narrative captures "the human experience of time" is helpful in understanding time as a dialectic between linearity (the clock time of material existence) and "true historicality" or "the plural unity of future, past and present," the time in which we make connections and make sense of our lives.[43] This "temporal dialectic," for Ricoeur, is "the basic operation of eliciting a configuration from succession," that is to say, of creating narrative, of connecting multiple threads into a meaningful whole and of simultaneously representing that which exists and that which will and has existed.[44] Novels may have beginnings, middles, and ends but their meanings are realized only in the configurations that constitute the interpretative process, that is, in the infinite dialectic between reader and text, between what is written and what could be understood. Analogously, capital takes a material form as it cycles through financial instruments, but its value lies not in the fixity of those instruments but in the historical processes through which wealth is realized and distributed. Financial markets and financial fictions generate webs of meaning in which value is neither fixed nor stable but determined through the act of configuring futures that have not yet arrived.

The dynamic instabilities and contradictions within the form of capital—of time, of value, of meaning—generate narrativity. Characters engage interest, time takes shape as a dynamic of plot, and voices shape meaning in ways that map capital's circulations and that are not immediately readable on the level of content, a fact particularly relevant when interpreting stories of downward mobility. Financial crisis in fictional narrative can be read as embedding the narrative logic of capital. On the surface, sentimental stories of downward mobility betray an empathy toward the victims of a market economy and present a challenge to capitalism, yet I argue that on the level of form, we can read the way the story of loss captures the contradictory logic of compounding growth. "Crises are essential to the reproduction of capitalism," Harvey notes, and yet each stock market collapse appears as if it is an unexpected surprise, as if it could have been avoided.[45] As Harvey and Giovanni Arrighi, among others, have pointed out, the temporality of infinite growth, the endless quest to increase surplus value in the quickest way possible by reverting to "more flexible forms of investment," leads to a cyclic historical pattern in which a so-called economic collapse, like the 2008 subprime mortgage crisis, is a predictable and necessary event.[46] Speculative busts are the logical outcome in the drive to reduce the time of profit by freeing capital from a productive cycle and turning M-C-M′ into M-M′.[47] Crisis, in other words, is built into capital's temporality, especially in its fictitious form, and financial failure is not an aberration but the rule. The internal contradiction within capitalism between use value and exchange value produces the necessity of crises such that, far from shocking and unpredictable, stock bubbles or market collapses are necessary events within the history of capital accumulation.[48] In seeking out faster ways of breeding money from money, capital moves from car factories to subprime mortgages to the revelation of the Ponzi scheme, at which point one cycle ends and another begins. In other words, crisis and loss are inevitable events in capital's circulations. Narrative's temporal dynamic, I suggest, configures the inevitability of crisis within a story that never ends.

Downward mobility narratives help us imagine the sequencing of capital's cyclical logic of crisis and compounding growth in myriad ways. In reading for the ways character, plot, and voice are animated by the instabilities produced by capital's contradictions, I return to the following tensions: between use value and exchange value; between endless compound growth and finite resources; between abstraction and materialization; and between debt and equity.[49] These contradictions are moving and dialectical and, as such, produce dynamic modes for attributing value and meaning. How particular novels use their narrative form to represent financial loss depends on how these contradictions are embodied. For instance, I argue that the formal device of narrative embedding or stories-within-stories—a defining feature of sentimental novels—displaces financial exchanges onto narrative ones that negotiate the tension between use value and exchange value. By reading specific scenes of storytelling in which characters tell their tales of downward mobility for their form, not their sympathetic content, we can read the way they may mystify or challenge or make visible the shifting dynamic between exchange and use value. Novels, in other words, do not simply reflect their economic context; their form produces interpretive modes in which capital's contradictions can both make sense *and* be reframed and denaturalized. I attend to the specific way individual novels manage, plot, characterize, and negotiate the contradictions not to suggest one monolithic narrative but to highlight their heterogeneity.

The purpose of reading the multiple and specific forms narrative takes in different novels is, then, to mine novels for alternative dynamics that might defamiliarize capitalism's scripts, in particular the script of infinite economic growth. I animate the relationship between economic crises and the logic of compound growth in order to trouble the common sense that the wealth of nations can infinitely increase. I suggest that fictional stories of downward mobility contribute to the naturalization of economic growth, a crucial shift in cultural attitudes that emerges in the late eighteenth century. In this way, my book does for downward mobility what Bruce Robbins has done for its opposite in *Upward Mobility and the Common Good*; he argues that "rags to riches" stories in nineteenth- and twentieth-century American texts are not simply fairy-tales of self-sufficiency and individual hard work but, counterintuitively, that they support the welfare state and the collective sharing of resources.[50] Analogously, I argue that "riches to rags" narratives are not only sympathetic tales about the losers of early capitalism, nor that they function simply as cautionary fables to warn readers against speculative risks; this book illustrates how they shape meaning to conform to a growth economy and how they render narratively comprehensible the epistemologically incomprehensible speculations of infinite growth.

Fictional Dynamics, or Why *The Wealth of Nations* Fails to Novelize Money

Insofar as I center the rise of the novel as an event in the history of economic growth, I claim the value of literary knowledge for economics. In "What Is Literary Knowledge of Economy?" Christopher Newfield provides a persuasive account of the ways literature produces economic insight, one of which is that "literary knowledge of economy will analyze and express the economy's internal contradictions."[51] Infinite economic growth is one of these contradictions. The importance of literary knowledge cannot be underestimated given the extent to which economists resist humanist methodologies, preferring to shroud their financial modeling under the guise of science and mathematical complexity, as incontestable fact, and the extent to which popular discourse reduces "the economy" to financial metrics.[52] However, a few economists would agree with my most general claim that narrative holds the key to capitalism's history, though the difference between their use of narrative and my own defines why I remain committed to the literary text. Proving the value of narrative to understanding economics was the topic of Robert J. Shiller's 2017 presidential address to the American Economic Association.[53] Shiller finds a direct link between the stories popular culture circulates and the state of the financial markets. He claims that expectations of what the future will hold rely on the stories we tell and that those expectations are central in shaping what mutual funds will be worth tomorrow. In other words, he uses narratives rather than numbers as the predictive mechanism, but he remains attached to an epistemology of modeling, of foretelling the future based on the past in order to profit from selling time. Our need to manage future risk to produce greater profits is not the problem that narrative theory should help us solve.

A more productive encounter between economists and literary scholars has come from historians of economics, such as Deirdre McCloskey and Emma Rothschild, who have been using literary critical skills to read the history of political economy for decades. They do so in order to uncover economists' rhetorical production of meaning and to demonstrate the nonempirical foundation of a discipline that often resists the fact that its basic method of modeling is itself an imaginative thought experiment.[54] Reading the literariness in the rise of economics as a discipline in the eighteenth century, we can see how thinkers such as Daniel Defoe, David Hume, and Adam Smith rely heavily on rhetorical devices to persuade readers that the "the wheels of commerce" will expand wealth infinitely, a crucial component of the "culture of growth" (Joel Mokyr's designation of this period).[55] It is hard to imagine capitalism rising to dominance without the water imagery that pours out of early economic writing. From the "Ocean of Commerce" to "Trade as a spring" to the "fountain of wealth," liquidity is imagined as the key to growth long before "liquid modernity" takes hold.[56] The figurative language in early economic writing is telling, but my project concentrates on narrative because of its centrality to the culture of growth.

Whereas new economic criticism often reads political economy as literature, I read literature to show the economic function that stories of downward mobility perform at a particular moment in the history of capitalism. Ultimately, I make a claim for the importance of literary interpretation to demystifying late capitalism's financialized imagination. To demonstrate why the novel is more important to emerging speculative epistemologies than political economy, I end my introduction with a discussion of why the kinds of narratives we find in early economic discourse—primarily those about the origin of capitalism and the history of money—fail to novelize money, that is to say, fail to capture the contradictory and dynamic energy of financial capital's form. Reading Adam Smith will help illustrate this point.

The story Smith tells in *The Wealth of Nations* is a classic adventure tale of upward mobility.[57] Its plot follows a quest narrative in which its central heroic characters—a merchant trading across the globe and an entrepreneur efficiently producing pins—set out on a path to happiness through commerce. Events are sequenced in such a way that the merchant's investments and the entrepreneur's increased efficiencies through the division of labor are causally linked to their rising wealth, with the climax reached when capital is realized and the risks pay off. For Smith, the expansion of wealth lay in global commerce, not in agriculture or in firm national borders, and thus the setting is not only Britain but substantially North America and the East Indies.[58]

Smith's narration of stadial or conjectural history, that highly persuasive Enlightenment theory of the four stages of civilization, best captures how political economy tells the story of capitalism's origins. Stadial theory charts the history of mankind as one vast teleological plot, beginning with the age of hunting, advancing to pasturage, then agriculture, and finally arriving at its denouement with the great Age of Commerce in the eighteenth century.[59] Money, in this narrative, arrives on the historical stage during the transition from an agricultural economy to a commercial one, when the division of labor produces excess goods such that "every man . . . becomes in some measure a merchant," exchanging his corn for another's cut of meat. In Smith's chapter "On the Origin and Use of Money," he narrates money's origins as evolving naturally out of barter to solve what economists call the problem of the "double coincidence of wants." Once upon a time, there was a butcher who had more meat than he could consume and a baker who wanted his meat, but the butcher did not want what the baker had to sell. Enter money as a medium of exchange to solve the problem of finding a seller of meat who wants bread just when the bread seller is looking for mutton.[60] Money here provides the "grease" for the wheels of commerce, allowing commodities to circulate across greater stretches of time and geography and lubricating the ever-expanding networks of wants. This origin story of money is retold throughout eighteenth-century economic texts, as well as appearing in fiction (Henry Brooke provides a near-verbatim version in *Fool of Quality*, which I discuss in chapter 2).

The story is so compelling and often repeated that it has become virtually irrefutable, circulating as common sense in many economic textbooks today. But, as the radical anthropologist David Graeber argues in *Debt: The First 5,000 Years,* this oft-told tale lies on shaky historical ground. For Graeber, it rests on a historical fallacy in that no culture in documented history matches the narrative: "We did not begin with barter, discover money, and then eventually develop credit systems. It happened precisely the other way around."[61] Long before money existed as currency or as a medium of exchange, Graeber's anthropological evidence suggests, cultures recorded debts and kept accounts of what was given and owed. Barter was what people did with strangers; debts were how economies were managed among friends. Why it matters whether the origin story of money lies in debt rather than in barter is significant for our understanding of capital, and I unravel the difference between the two stories in this book's first chapters, focusing on the shift in the characterization of debt in the eighteenth century from sin to necessity. I introduce the origin story of money here to illustrate why the sentimental novel and not political economy is the best location for my investigation of capital's narrative form.

Smith's narrative about the triumph of commerce is full of plot holes and blind spots in its upward mobility tale of infinite economic growth. While he celebrates global commerce as the cause of wealth's monumental expansion, he is unable to account for wealth's uneven development or the violence in its imperial exploitation of resources.[62] Smith contradicts his stadial narrative of history when he collapses time into space and places eighteenth-century North American indigenous populations at the beginning of mankind's history: "[T]he natives of every part of America . . . were only hunters" and are caught in a colonial time warp in which British merchants arrive as the heroes of progress.[63] Smith's barter story of money's origins leads to his liberal optimistic theory of global trade as "reciprocal gain" in which everyone benefits equally.[64] Free trade economists see the exchange of the world's resources and a global division of labor—known as the doctrine of universal economy—as the most capacious answer to the problem of the "double coincidence of wants": the people of Britain have cotton but no spices and Indonesians have spices but no cotton and thus trade occurs to the mutual benefit of both countries.[65] The "reciprocal gain" theory imagines trade as an equal exchange of use value and, for this reason, is unable to account for the way wealth expands through the production of surplus value, through financialization and through violence, indeed, through the "violence of financial capitalism."[66] In other words, *The Wealth of Nations* cannot narrate the way money works as capital, mostly because it is unable to capture capital's fundamental contradictions. It imagines the world through C-M-C whereas capital requires M-C-M′. Enter the novel—in particular, stories of downward mobility in sentimental fiction—as the form best suited to capture these structural contradictions.

Early eighteenth-century realist novels are closer to Smith's narrative than the sentimental novel, and they help clarify the role of downward mobility. Like *The Wealth of Nations*, early novels often profit from the fantastical promise of a newly emerging global commerce and most often narrate upward mobility. Defoe's famous representation of *Homo economicus* in *Robinson Crusoe* glosses over the ethical question of where the *more* of economic growth comes from by emphasizing that the value of Crusoe's wealth originates in the seed of corn he plants on his island plus his labor and ingenuity in turning that corn into bread. The novel explicitly celebrates a theory of value as based in commodities, understood as use value plus labor. Yet Defoe undercuts his celebration of commodity exchange by ultimately tracing Crusoe's wealth to speculative capital since, in the end, his riches come not from his island but from the surplus value that his South American plantations have accrued in his absence or, more precisely, through the reinvestment of that surplus value into the plantation, including buying more slaves, to continue the flow through compounding expansion. I relate the lack of closure in Defoe's novels, the picaresque circularity that has Crusoe setting off on more adventures at the end, to the contradiction that requires infinite motion. Like capital, Crusoe cannot come to a stop. Latter-eighteenth-century sentimental culture cannot be as blunt in its mystification of capital accumulation, of making money from money, as Crusoe's upward mobility plot, in part because different economic events have had very different ends. After enough speculative bubbles like the South Sea scandal, after wrenching periods of high inflation, after fortunes have been lost and gained overnight, such a progressive narrative was no longer as imaginatively viable.[67] Characters are often rewarded with speculative wealth in sentimental novels, as the number of East Indian fortunes that coincidentally arrive in the final pages attest, but they first circulate through downward mobility. For example, Emily Montague must first reject financial gain in Canada and marry for love-without-money in England before she is reunited with her long-lost father and rewarded with his East Indies fortune, acquired "by a train of lucky accidents."[68]

This narrative journey through downward mobility coincides with a moment in the developing culture of growth that sees the discursive separation of matters of finance from matters of morality, a moment when fictions of loss often exchange moral for economic capital by turning narrative into currency. By the end of the eighteenth century, heroes and heroines must reject financial gain as a precondition for moral goodness and wealth.[69] David Simple explicitly states the incommensurability of financial and moral ambition: "[A] contempt for Money . . . he esteemed necessary to make a good Character."[70] Novels narrate over and over again how money cannot buy happiness. Sir Charles Grandison affirms, "Riches never made men happy," though the novel repeatedly rewards moral good with money after it has first circulated through storytelling as loss.[71] In Burney's *Camilla*, Mr. Westwyn, hoping his son will marry the penniless heroine, declares that "[m]oney goes but a little way to make people happy; and true love's not a thing to be got every day."[72] Happiness and true love, in sentimental fiction, require characters to first actively reject and show an abhorrence of financial gain. (The chiasmatic formula in which money is rejected to accept love in order for love to be rewarded with money is explored as a gendered phenomenon in chapter 5.)

Sentimentalism's moral economy, the way rejecting financial ambition is a precondition of having wealth, engages the long history of the debate between commerce and virtue and normalizes the division of economic labor that separates social from financial valuation.[73] The cliché that money does not buy happiness presumes commerce and virtue inhabit separate and opposed realms: the love of money and that of virtue are incommensurable. In this way, the status of the disavowal as a fictional convention in the late eighteenth century confirms Mary Poovey's argument that by the 1790s the discursive separation of economic and moral theory was solidified.[74] The "Adam Smith problem"—

the perceived contradictions between *The Wealth of Nations* and *Theory of Moral Sentiments*—succinctly captures this emerging discursive divide. Smith's "invisible hand" has become *the* metaphor for laissez-faire capitalism but only by relegating his moral theory to philosophy departments, having no import on financial markets.[75]

The disavowal of wealth, however, also weaves together, through necessary negation, commercial and moral exchanges, revealing their ongoing mutual constitution. In "Forms of Capital," Pierre Bourdieu diagnoses this formal link when he claims that "by reducing the universe of exchanges to mercantile exchange, . . . [economic theory] has implicitly defined the other forms of exchange as noneconomic, and therefore *disinterested*."[76] Sentimental culture plays a central role in introducing "disinterestedness" as the defining feature of moral economies. Nick Valvo describes "disinterestedness" as that which constitutes sentimental philanthropy insofar as it requires the object of charity to be an anonymous stranger in order to prove that the giver has nothing to gain.[77] (Chapter 1 addresses the tensions within the "disinterestedness" of sentimental philanthropy in relation to the Society for the Discharge and Relief of Persons Imprisoned for Small Debts). The effect of the discursive division is that we do not organize our economies, our common land, around ethical exchanges within specific social relations but around anonymous abstractions and what makes the best "business" sense.[78] If Bourdieu's concept of cultural capital sought to demonstrate how so-called disinterested moral and cultural exchanges have financial implications (a liberal arts education, for example, pays off), my book provides a cultural genealogy of how pure financial exchange and numerical calculations come to dominate economic discourse, a genealogy that paradoxically requires us to read novels. Sentimental fictions, as I show in chapter 2, are less about learning how to trust strangers in the anonymous marketplace than about teaching readers how not to trust friends, that is, how to negotiate the marketplace as if economic relations were only a matter of financial calculation. Never loan money to friends is a commonplace that sentimental fiction ends up consolidating for modern capitalism. Essentially, downward mobility narratives retell the story of money to replace its origins in debts between friends with barter between strangers.

The novel's amorphous form—its play between general abstraction and particular detail, between invoking types and celebrating descriptive specificity—provides abundant space to think through speculative temporalities. To unravel the place of the novel in rendering capital's epistemological forms commonplace, I have organized this book by pairing a narrative technique with a foundational contradiction. After a history of bankruptcy and debt in chapter 1, each of the following chapters illustrates how the novel and capital manifest parallel structures: characterization as financialized debt, embedded narrative as the story that generates infinite profit, the dynamics of plot as the temporal dialectic of compounding growth, and closure as the realization of capital.

The first chapter, "Fictitious Capital and the Social History of Debt," sets the contextual stage for my reading of fiction by first exploring the scripts of finance capital in discourses surrounding debt. In particular, it highlights both the transformation in attitudes toward bankruptcy (evidenced by the introduction of limited liability) and the late eighteenth-century campaign against imprisonment for debt in order to think about the normalization of debt in the period, the way debt is reconfigured as simply the cost of doing business. It presents original archival work on a philanthropic organization, the Society for the Discharge and Relief of Persons Imprisoned for Small Debts, to outline the tensions between the society's sentimental sympathy for individual debtors and capital's buying and selling of debt for profit, a tension readable in the charity's turn to statistical aggregation. I end with an analysis of the life and work of James Stephen, whom I identify as the first "debt resistor" (the Occupy movement's term) to show what his case illustrates about financial capital (Stephen was also Virginia Woolf's great-great-grandfather).

With the contradictions of capital's eighteenth-century debt economy laid out, I move to a fictional reading of "character" in chapter 2 involving specifically the plethora of debtors that appear in sentimental novels. Focusing on literary character as a dynamic between fixed and unstable meanings, I compare the ways debtors are characterized in Henry Brooke's *Fool of Quality* and Goldsmith's *Vicar of Wakefield*. Reading characterization as a dynamic akin to the circulation of financial instruments explains the plot lacuna that has the Vicar released from prison without paying his debts, whereas Brooke relentlessly accounts for and pays all debts in his didactic fiction. I read literary character from the perspective of debt, not credit, so as to query how sentimental characterization might be less about normalizing a trust in speculative futures where strangers behave in predictable ways, than about using insolvency as a way to divorce the claims of the past and of friendship from capital accumulation.

The narrative device of embedding is the subject of chapter 3, where I argue that the scene of storytelling, in which a character tells their tale to another character, is the signature narrative structure of sentimental fiction. By reading a range of scenes of storytelling—from *Man of Feeling* to *David Simple* to *Millenium Hall*—I depict how narrative replaces money as the currency of exchange and how, by reading narrative exchange, we can thus trace capital's circulations. Posing Roland Barthes's questions "*What should the narrative be exchanged for? What is the narrative 'worth'?*" I compare a variety of formal structures of embedding to read how they are valued within the novel's system of exchange.[79] Does the value of the story shift with differences in narrative level? Sentimental scenes of storytelling foreground social relations between teller and listener by dramatizing the narrative act. Different structures of embedding—whether the listener is also a narrator and the teller also the heroine, whether characters from different levels develop lasting social bonds, and whether these relations change the course of the plot—produce different narratives of an exchange economy. By representing scenes of storytelling as posing the problem of finding stable moral value in a world governed by the fluidity of capital, the narrative of sentimental narrative is infinitely catalyzed by capitalism's internal contradictions. In the end, what circulates through these scenes of storytelling—no matter what the novel's explicit politics may be—is the contradiction between use value and exchange value.

The final chapters highlight the dynamics of plot in Frances Burney's *Cecilia* and *Camilla*. Insofar as plot is the primary mode through which narrative's temporal dialectics plays out, these chapters argue that capital's time can be read into Burney's marriage plots. Indeed, it argues that her novels plot money, not marriage. Chapter 4 reads what I call the chronotopes of capital in *Cecilia* to demonstrate how plot functions as a form of risk management. Understanding plot not as the causal sequence of events but as generating multiple temporal worlds that circulate, coexist, conflict, and coalesce, I argue that plot mirrors the temporal complexity of capital. After laying out the chronotopes of capital, I show how Burney's specific deployment of the chronotopes in *Cecilia* resolves her plot through her heroine's diversification of risk. Cecilia must either retire from the world or learn to hedge her bets, diversify her pleasures, and save for a rainy day.

The last chapter turns to closure in *Camilla* to think about the endings of both capital and the novel. Sentimental romance plots often arrive at closure in marriage only after their heroines have suffered financial distress, a plot that registers financial risk as sexual. The particular overlap of the loss of money with the potential loss of virtue plots love as an effect of not having money. Through a reading of *Camilla*, the chapter argues that the discursive divide between virtue and commerce produces a marriage plot in which its heroine must go into debt. Sentimental fiction repeats the plot pattern in which a delay occurs between the heroine's marriage and the novel's ending; I take up this delay and read into it capital's nonnarratable, D. A. Miller's term for that which cannot generate more narrative and requires the novel's close. I see the nonnarratable of *Camilla* revealing the contradiction between production and realization, between the pressure for consumers to consume in order for capital to realize value and an equal pressure on laborers to save and not go into profligate debt. The cost of resolving this contradiction—which is the cost of inflation—is paid for by downwardly mobile heroines.

The homologous temporal dialectics of narrative and capital that I unravel through the eighteenth-century myth of downward mobility configures infinite economic growth as imaginatively real. In highlighting how the sentimental novel negotiates the contradictions that such compounding growth entails, the project dialogues with a history of the present to query our current cultural narratives and what they suggest about our continuing attachment to a growth economy. Despite knowing otherwise, despite the irrefutable scientific evidence of climate change, despite a refugee crisis that has laid bare structural inequalities of wealth, and despite growing wealth inequality, we continue to live as if infinite economic expansion for all is both desirable and possible. The genealogy of such a belief lies in the eighteenth century, but it remains intractable, sedimented into our imaginations and structured into our national economies.[80] The narrative of infinite upward mobility may be fraying; there have been anxious suggestions that millennials will be the first generation in the Western world, with some exceptions, to be poorer than their parents since "the great divergence" or "the great transformation" in the eighteenth century.[81] Of course, the narrative has always already been frayed in a non-Western or nonwhite context; for example, North American indigenous populations did not experience the Age of Commerce as progress. Whether the halt in Western upward mobility is empirically occurring, and whether we are, in fact, at the turning point in the "end of capitalism," is not the main question that concerns me here. What interests me is that despite everything climate scientists have proven, despite the 2008 financial crash, our culture continues to organize economies around an infinite economic growth that depends on fossil fuels, unremunerated labor, and the violence of financial capital. This book describes how literary narratives participated in the large-scale epistemological shift that made such a belief collectively comprehensible in the eighteenth century; by so doing, it suggests that a similar epistemological shift needs to occur today and that such a shift requires new cultural forms. Without valuing the importance of literary narrative in imaging a future without growth, we may be doomed to extinction. A revolutionary new story of money, I contest, will do more than science or facts or policies to change our culture of growth and to realize a world that distributes its resources in equitable and sustainable ways.

Fictitious Capital and the Social History of Debt

From Moral Sin to Business Risk: How Debt Changes Character

In a 2019 *New York Times* opinion piece calling for greater regulation of financial markets, Nobel Prize–winning economist Joseph Stiglitz turned to the eighteenth century to argue that capitalism can generate infinite economic growth and be socially progressive at the same time: "Standards of living began to improve in the late eighteenth century for two reasons: the development of science (we learned how to learn about nature and used that knowledge to increase productivity and longevity) and developments in social organization (as a society, we learned how to work together, through institutions like the rule of law, and democracies with checks and balances)."[1] This chapter complicates Stiglitz's progressive narrative of upward mobility by adding a third development—that of financial markets—and by turning to the history of debt in order to show that the problems of wealth inequality today may not be so simple as reinvigorating the social institutions that allow us to work together, as Stiglitz's suggests (though a renewed social contract that builds trust for legal, governmental, and educational institutions would help). When we complicate numerical calculations of economic growth, such as gross domestic product (GDP) figures or average income rates, with narratives of individual stories, we see how some people's downward mobility underwrites overall growth. How wealth is distributed is different from whether GDP increases. The "fictitiousness" of financial capital, the way buying and selling anonymous debt contracts for profit is a precondition of constant growth, needs to be part of the debate on how capitalism's inequalities are best addressed. The logic of crisis built into speculative finance means that some people will be caught paying for the losses (environmental, social, economic) when the bubble bursts, and this chapter turns an eye on some of those people in the latter eighteenth century. By focusing on the history of insolvency in the period, we can see how increased financial failure is an indispensable part of the story of infinite economic growth and that fictitious capital hides these downward mobility stories by what I call unfriending debt.

Unfriended debt is financial obligation divorced from the social calculation of what we owe one another. This unfriending began in the eighteenth century with the financial revolution and the normalization of debt as a simple matter of accounting. Unfriending is what happens when debt is turned into a financial instrument, that is, a contract bought and sold for profit between strangers; debt thereby becomes a numerical calculation abstracted from its material history and the specific situation in which individuals exchange risk for a cost. Assignability—the power to transfer ownership of a debt contract to someone else; for example, by signing over a bill of exchange—is part of the eighteenth-century financial revolution, and it is what gives debt its particular character under capitalism. When debt is normalized as a simple financial transaction and the cost of doing business, we forget the very real and material individual stories of economic suffering. One of the things that makes downward rather than upward mobility the "narrative goad," or what signifies a story, in sentimental fiction is precisely that, in being fiction, novels capture debt as "nobody's" story, part of the larger aggregate economic landscape but unattached to specific somebodies with real stories of economic loss, losses that society should be obligated to compensate. Debt can float in fiction when it becomes, itself, a detached fiction through financialization, the responsibility of a stranger somewhere else or in the future. Numbers—from credit ratings to mortgage amortization tables—help mask the social obligations that would be revealed if a debt's material history were remembered. As the saying goes, "Debt is a fiction," and as long as the fiction keeps circulating within financial markets, so too does the illusion that an aggregate wealth increase stands in for universal upward mobility. This chapter focuses on two particular episodes in the eighteenth-century material history of debt: the debates surrounding bankruptcy law and the campaign against imprisonment for debt. These two episodes illustrate how the introduction of fictitious capital changed the character of debt, producing the discursive shift of debt from moral sin to numerical calculation.

Debt has become, in the twenty-first century, a normal part of living. Despite occasional warnings against our historically high levels of household borrowing, contemporary Western societies have normalized debt as a fact of economic life (the US Federal Reserve Bank put the total figure of US household debt at $13.67 trillion in 2019; in 1980, household debt was equal to 43% of GDP, and at the end of 2017, it stood at 78%).[2] Taking on debt to buy a house or an education is understood as a good investment in the future, not a moral failing. In the seventeenth century, however, people with such high levels of debt would have been considered moral outcasts, doomed to hell for the sin of profligacy. The Quakers, for instance, had strict rules against debt, and not paying your debts "was seen to be a result of the moral failure of household virtue," as Craig Muldrew notes.[3] The social and cultural shift in attitudes toward debt that this contrast illustrates occurs over the course of the eighteenth century. Legal historian Bruce Mann describes the shift as "the redefinition of insolvency from sin to risk, from moral failure to economic failure."[4] By the end of the century, and partly through events described in this chapter, debt takes on its modern character as purely financial, a necessary component of commercial life and a smart investment. Debt as investment strategy came home to me when my partner and I submitted our household accounts to a national newspaper's weekly financial advice column: two university professors with over half a million dollars of mortgage debt were advised to borrow more money to invest.[5] The strategy makes perfect rational sense as a numerical calculation: since our equity was higher than our debt and interest rates were low, we could borrow money at a lower rate than we potentially could earn if we invested the money in the market, thus coming out ahead. As an abstracted financial calculation, with interest rates in one column and mutual fund returns in another, debt pays off. But what the calculation leaves out and what I hope this chapter documents is how such profits accrue only through leveraging equity—that is, by circulating the fiction that some people's futures are secure.

Debt as necessary risk, without which capital cannot accumulate, underlies the logic of economic growth: you cannot have one without the other, since expansion requires debt financing, or borrowing money against future profits.[6] Thus, the rise of commercial capitalism induces the new characterization of debt as a normal part of trading relations and not as moral sin. Outside these trading relations, however, and for individuals without equity, debt remains subject to moral judgment and the shame of consumer profligacy. The discursive division of good debt from bad is one I trace in this chapter within the history of bankruptcy laws and debates about imprisonment for debt. Significantly, debt forgiveness across the eighteenth century remained unavailable to those defined as "undeserving," mostly poor people with no social, financial, racial, or cultural equity to leverage (the very different bankruptcy laws applicable to commercial and personal debt today have institutionalized the divide). In the following two chapters, I use the phrase "capital's character of debt" to denote the historical shift that normalizes some people's debts while consigning others to debt servitude. Debt, as David Graeber polemically records, has at least a five-thousand-year history, and the particular form it takes within capitalist economies, where debt is bought and sold anonymously on financial markets, actively silences the differential power dynamics of debt's social relations.[7]

Whose debts require repayment and whose are forgiven as a "misfortune" of business became clear to many following the 2008 financial crash. Middle- and lower-class homeowners lost everything and were characterized as irresponsibly taking on too much debt, while Lehman Brothers' traders were just doing their jobs. Graeber opens *Debt: The First 5,000 Years* with this example and adds the observation that while leftist activists demanded jail time for the traders, they still believed that the homeowners should repay their debts. He complicates the assumption that "all debts must be repaid" by revealing the underlying politics of debt within a capitalist system in which debt's assignability and securitization (the financial term for breaking apart one debt contract to make "tranches," or collections of smaller pieces) justifies "things that would otherwise seem outrageous or obscene," like poor people losing their homes while stockbrokers cash in trillions.[8] Predatory student loan debt today provides countless obscene examples of an exploitation akin to serfdom.[9] This chapter begins by outlining changes to bankruptcy law and overviews the campaign against imprisonment for debt to introduce the historical genealogy of the reasons why some people's debts are forgiven. I then turn to two case studies that encompass stories of debt servitude: (1) the history of the Society for the Discharge and Relief of Persons Imprisoned for Small Debts, a charity founded in 1772 dedicated to freeing imprisoned debtors (herein referred to as the Society for the Relief of Small Debts or simply the Society); and (2) the contributions of James Stephen, Virginia Woolf's great-great-grandfather, who was both an imprisoned debtor and the first "debt resistor," that is, the first person to politicize debt under capital.[10] The case studies show the limits of a sentimental approach to debt forgiveness insofar as neither the Society nor Stephen was able to counter debt's unfriending. Wealth accumulates by estranging the costs of meeting our social obligations to one another, a political dynamic Stephen was the first to detail, yet his analysis disappeared into fiction.

The Birth of Limited Liability and the Campaign against Imprisonment for Debt

Changes to bankruptcy laws in the early eighteenth century register the increasing acceptance of debt and insolvency as normal parts of commercial life.[11] Legislation in 1706 added limited liability to the process of insolvency whereby a bankrupt's debts could be fully discharged after their estate was liquidated to pay off creditors. The first insolvency laws entered the books during Queen Elizabeth's reign, and they entirely favored creditors, defining all bankrupts as frauds and criminals. By introducing limited liability, the 1706 law acknowledged, as William Blackstone commented, that traders are "liable to accidental losses, and to an inability of paying their debts, without any fault of their own."[12] Blackstone saw bankruptcy legislation as "calculated for the benefit of trade" and since "[t]rade cannot be carried on without mutual credit on both sides: the contracting of debts is therefore here not only justifiable, but necessary."[13] The introduction of limited liability meant that bankruptcy was not the death Defoe described ("[b]reaking is the death of a Tradesman") but a rebirth, a new beginning.[14] Sheila Marriner notes that the old law "discouraged debtors from restarting their businesses after failure because all their future assets and income could be claimed to settle former debts," whereas full discharge "encourage[d] traders to restart their businesses and hence to maintain the nation's economic activity."[15] The reformed bankruptcy laws ultimately were a boon to economic growth. Economic historians partly attribute Britain's outpacing of other European countries in the period to the more liberal policy of full discharge, since limited liability encourages risk and thus allows capital to keep circulating, expanding, and seeking out new avenues of accumulation.[16]

That financial failure and economic growth are interdependent within capitalism is illustrated by the fact that rates of bankruptcy and imprisonment for debt increase in the latter eighteenth century at the same time as wealth accumulates. Bankruptcies rise from an average of 210 per decade in the 1750s to 762 in the 1790s.[17] Julian Hoppit's extensive research documents the interrelation of bankruptcy and growth; he notes that "[a]s the economy expanded and drifted into early industrialization bankruptcy became not less of a threat, but more of one," both because of increased competition and because of the increase in risk taking made acceptable in a growing market economy.[18] His research demonstrates a "clear relationship between growth and failure," with lower levels of bankruptcy in areas like Norfolk, where the cloth industry was stagnating, and higher levels in places like Lancashire, where the cotton industry was booming.[19] In other words, economic growth and increased financial failure go together because more risk taking increases the market's overall rewards.[20] But it also raises the number of individuals in financial straits. With capital circulating in larger commercial networks across greater stretches of time and geography, "decision-making became more risky" and the chances of something going wrong increased.[21] As Jill Lepore notes about the emergence of limited liability, "[B]ankruptcy protection makes taking risks less risky," but, I would add, it does not erase the risk; it simply displaces the costs of those risks onto others.[22]

If bankruptcy law reflects the social acceptance that financial failure was par for the course in a growing commercial economy and that, as Marriner writes, the "inability to meet debts was a normal occupational hazard," only a very small number of people counted as the rightful subjects of such accidental losses.[23] To be included as a person whose financial failure was considered accidental, one had to fit within a narrow definition of *trader*. Ever since Elizabeth I's time and until the middle of the nineteenth century, bankruptcy was restricted to those having "*used the trade of merchandize*, in gross or by retail, by way of bargaining, exchange, rechange, bartering, chevisance, or otherwise; or have *sought their living by buying and selling*."[24] Much ink was spilt in the eighteenth century on which occupations were included and how much someone had to buy and sell to count (for instance, many small craftsmen were excluded because they bought raw materials and sold manufactured ones).[25] However, the most restrictive condition on those who had access to a bankruptcy commission was not the *trader* definition but the fact that an action could be brought only if the debt was at least £100. The vast majority of debts were under that minimum. Hoppit calculates that there were 357 bankrupts in 1775; John Howard puts the number of debtors imprisoned at 2,437 for that year, many of whom were merchants whose businesses were too small to qualify.[26] Thus the majority of debtors remained subject to the law that allowed creditors to imprison them indefinitely. Since prisoners were responsible for paying their own fees for living in jail, they often incurred more debt while in prison, an obligation that often could never be overcome.[27] As with bankruptcies, the number of debtors imprisoned in the period increased and, as Joanna Innes determines, rose "steeply between 1760 and 1780," a temporal frame that corresponds with the emerging campaign contesting the law.[28]

Advocates for the abolishment of imprisonment for debt argued that all debtors, not just those with debts of more than £100, should have access to limited liability since such debts, too, were often "accidental" and were not, as Blackstone suggested, "the consequences of their own indiscretion."[29] Campaigners did not distinguish between those who counted as official bankrupts and those debtors whose debts were less than £100: both were considered victims of "misfortune." The campaign elided the difference between legal bankrupts and prisoners and replaced it with that between innocent and fraudulent debtors, claiming all innocent debtors should be forgiven. Josiah Dornford begins his 1786 letter on the inhumanity of imprisonment for debt with the following distinction: "It is not my design to plead the cause of Rogues, Swindlers, or fraudulent Debtors, but of honest, distressed, unfortunate men"; he then quickly collapses the "honest though unfortunate men" into "the honest unfortunate tradesman."[30] It is people in the "middle walk of life," the "tradesmen, mechanics and artificers," who concern Dornford, one of the founders of the Society for the Relief of Small Debts.[31]

While James Oglethorpe's 1729 parliamentary report on the state of imprisoned debtors had documented the need for reform, it was not until the 1770s that a sustained campaign was forged against the practice.[32] Peter Lineham, in his still-standard examination of the campaign, notes that "with the single exception of the comments of Samuel Johnson, nothing published before 1770 advocated new measures."[33] What I refer to as the campaign against imprisonment for debt includes a wide range of published texts, parliamentary reports, speeches, court cases, and newspaper coverage, along with the rise of charities dedicated to debt relief. Taken together, the material shows a wide cultural consensus that the law was evil and that debtors were sympathetic subjects, with only a few tracts arguing against the law's repeal. In fact, the arguments were so repetitive that the *Monthly Review*'s discussion of Edward Farley's influential 1788 tract complains: "The same objections are here produced, the same complaints are repeated, and the same remedies are prescribed."[34] A synthesis of the campaign's arguments includes the following points: persons in prison cannot earn money, thus, the oft-repeated saying "A prison pays no debts";[35] poor people who fall into debt out of illness suffer for what they cannot help and their imprisonment causes further misery to their wives and children; the law penalizes the innocent by ruining their livelihood and reputation with imprisonment for up to a year before their creditor has to prove the accusation; creditors are voracious, often refusing to accept payment by installment; debtors are housed in prisons with hardened criminals who corrupt and destroy the morals of people who would otherwise be pure; the only people who gain are lawyers and jailors; the nation as a whole suffers from the loss of labor that debtors would have contributed had they not been in jail; no other nation, especially Britain's commercial rival Holland, imprisons people for debt; and British liberty is denied to debtors as it is to African slaves.[36]

In repeating the same arguments, the campaign tracts underlined the crucial distinction between good and bad debtors, between the merely unfortunate debtor and the plotting swindler. The unfortunate debtor is our "poor fellow-creature, [who] perhaps for the immediate support of life, perhaps through sickness, unavoidable losses and disappointments . . . runs a few pounds in debt."[37] These debtors require our sympathy. But, as Margot Finn points out, they had always done so; the "misfortunate" debtor was a long standing trope in early modern culture.[38] "Pray remember ye poor debtors" had been the plea coming from Fleet Prison for centuries, a call frequently met in the sixteenth and seventeenth centuries by aristocratic bequests and royal jubilees.[39] It is in this spirit that Burney's Cecilia celebrates her coming of age by "pardoning many debts."[40] If imprisoned debtors had always been represented as "misfortunate," what is different about the late eighteenth-century campaign for debt relief?

The post-1770 call for sympathy for poor debtors did employ many of the same motifs and tropes that had circulated since early modern times—the 1793 sentimental poem *The Insolvent Debtor: A Simple Pathetic Tale* contains the clichéd tableau of sick prisoner, suffering wife, and starving infant, all imprisoned by an unfeeling creditor; but the tracts also extended the topography of suffering Innocence to include victims of the new commercial marketplace, and they added political and legal demands to their sympathetic feelings.[41] Significantly, the traditional division between the unfortunate and the fraudulent debtor was represented in this literature as the difference between trading debt and consumer debt. The question one needed to ask, according to A Liveryman's letter to the *Morning Chronicle*, was: "Did he lose his property by *misfortunes in a fair way of commerce*; or, like other profligates, by schemes of *riot* and *debauchery*, or pursuit of pleasure?"[42] *New, Candid, and Practical Thoughts on the Law of Imprisonment for Debt* poses a similar question: "[A trader] perceiving that his specific capital will not give employment to his industry, nor supply those channels of trade which his talents and experience suggest, is induced to enlarge his business beyond such capital," and then he fails because of "real losses and events not to be foreseen or avoided . . . can it be said that he has wilfully abused that credit?"[43] The answer is clearly "no." Debt incurred "from the casualties that are incident to the profession of the merchant" should be subject to limited liability, whereas the debt of men "with a disposition to pleasure . . . who spend more than their own, either in idleness or pleasure," should not be forgiven.[44] The difference between the honest and dishonest debtor is that between trading credit and consumer credit.

In fiercely sympathizing with honest debtors, the campaign assumed that it was possible to tell the difference between innocent trading debt and guilty profligate debt. But how can the law make such a distinction? The introduction of corporate limited liability in the nineteenth century drew the clear lines we have today with incorporated businesses subject to different bankruptcy laws than those covering personal debt. But all debt was attached to individuals, not businesses, in the eighteenth century. The writer of *The Case of the Creditors of Joseph George Pedley* identified the problem as the fact that the laws "in general are undiscriminating. They involve the worthless sharper and the unfortunate debtor in one common lot."[45] Ironically, the pamphlet outlines the case of Joseph Pedley, a Bristol bankrupt, in a way that makes it initially difficult to determine whether Pedley was himself a sharper or a victim. Pedley comes from a well-connected family, his mother is described as "a woman of character," and the writer acknowledges that his creditors have been overly aggressive. But, it turns out, Pedley took out loans to expand his brewery, bought goods for such an expansion, and then immediately sold the goods and cashed the bills of exchange. The writer describes complicated transactions in which Pedley played banks off against one another to exchange bills and liquidate assets. Such speculative schemes of buying and selling bills of exchange were central to the new market in financial instruments, and thus a constitutive part of the commercial networks that increase the risk of accidental losses. Hoppit points out that the practice of allowing one bill of exchange to circulate through multiple endorsements "meant that indebtedness and collapse could spread from one point in a credit network to another and perhaps distant one."[46] Are not Pedley's activities part of the misfortunes that constitute the regular accidents of commerce? When is transferring a bill honest commerce, and when does it become illegal? Once debt becomes a financial instrument, it is hard to draw a clear moral distinction.

Breakdowns in a merchant's trading and credit network were the prime explanations given by campaigners for innocent debt. Debtors were imagined as simply creditors who themselves had not yet been paid. In other words, the risk was someone else's, not their own. Edward Farley, a writer Lineham identifies as on the more radical end of the campaign's spectrum, gives the example of a retail grocer who raises a small sum to invest in goods from a wholesaler, paying for some and buying the rest on credit. When the bill becomes due and the retailer does not have the entire sum, because his customers have not yet settled their bills, the wholesaler refuses to accept payment by installment and has him arrested. The retailer is eventually bailed out by friends, but Farley points out the absurdity of the wholesaler paying £100 in legal fees to recover a debt of £20. Sudden accidents as well as unpaid trading debts interrupted the network flow and rose in number particularly with the greater risks of transatlantic trade. One critic adds cattle plagues, frequent in the period, to the list of possible misfortunes: "Losses by sea, disappointments in trade, during the War; and the mortality amongst the horned cattle, have been the ruin of many thousands, who are now confined in prison."[47] William Smith, the writer of *Mild Punishments Sound Policy; Or, Observations on the Laws Relative to Debtors*, saw timing or cash flow as so central in causing debt that he proposed a public fund be made available "for the timely assistance of the honest, unfortunate and industrious." For Smith, the problem of imprisoning the innocent was not one of debt but of liquidity since a trader's account books would show him to be in the black: "Many merchants have become bankrupts from an inability to answer a draught of fifty or a hundred pounds, at the very time that they were really worth some thousands."[48] From the rich merchant down to the lowly laborer, liquidity, not morality, was the problem. In a sermon preached for the benefit of the Society for the Relief of Small Debts, James Halifax notes the number of laborers rotting in prison because employers did not pay timely wages and "impatient creditor[s]" sent them to jail. Delays in receiving wages was an endemic problem, according to Finn, especially because coinage was in short supply.[49]

The metaphors used in the literature underscore that the campaign was not simply repeating older calls for sympathy toward unfortunate debtors but calling for a new understanding of debt to accommodate economic growth, with its anonymous financial marketplace and temporally complex trading networks. The translator of Beccaria's *Imprisonment for Debt Considered* commented: "[I]n the age we live in, when the wants of mankind . . . have opened up fresh sources of commerce, and divided the ancient stream into an infinite variety of new branches, a Debtor may fail without being fraudulent."[50] The metaphors of commercial relations as a tree with multiple branches or a stream with many channels imagine trade as a single organism, with traders as parts of a living whole. Other analogies for insolvency, noted by Hoppit, that were repeatedly used to illustrate the interconnectedness of trading relations include a drowning man pulling others underwater, a line of dominoes collapsing when one falls, a chain breaking when a single link fails.[51] Imprisoning every person who is a link in the chain is not only tragic but bad for business because nobody wins except the lawyers and the jailers. The most common cases described in the literature are those where both debtors and creditors pay more in lawyer's fees than the original debt. *The Public Monitor* describes the case of a tradesmen who was persuaded by attorneys to sue for "a trifling sum" of 2l. 7s. 5d.; litigation lasted sixteen months, and at the end the creditor had paid £70 in costs, and the defendant £15.[52]

The unanimity in defining the unfortunate debtor as a casualty of the new commercial world suggests that it should have been easy to reach a legislative consensus on extending the bankruptcy law to all debtors. It was not. Many of the tracts explicitly proposed this solution; for instance, Richard Bevan's *Observations on the Law of Arrest and Imprisonment for Debt* commends limited liability as putting debtors "in a way of honest industry" by giving them a second chance, and Bevan simply wants to extend the law to include debts less than £100.[53] Although many legislative reforms and committee reports were brought forward, all were ineffectual until the mid-nineteenth century.[54] Peter Lineham argues that the powerful merchant lobby vehemently resisted reform, arguing that imprisonment provided a useful mechanism for pressuring debtors to repay. In the majority of cases the threat of imprisonment was enough to produce payment, and thus creditors were hesitant to relinquish what they saw as an effective blackmailing tool that rendered it, as Paul Haagen has called it, "legalized extortion."[55] According to Joanna Innes, in 1791, twelve thousand bailable writs were issued (i.e., creditors filed a bailiff's writ that they intended to arrest) but only twelve hundred of those debtors were committed.[56] Ian Duffy observes that another obstacle to reform was the problem of landed estates: if all assets were subject to possession through bankruptcy commissions, aristocratic land would be threatened.[57] The government dealt with the problem through the stopgap of repeated but temporary Acts of Parliament for the Relief of Insolvent Debtors. Twelve such acts between 1755 and 1797 released debtors who disclosed their assets, and none of them distinguished between honest and fraudulent debtors. All debtors were offered the discharge indiscriminately and, though most writers emphasized the need to help honest debtors, public debate continued to voice concern that swindlers were benefiting as well. In fact, the temporary laws fed the anxiety over fraud as critics argued that their frequency had led debtors to anticipate them, purposely going into debt right before an expected act. Smollett's *Peregrine Pickle* contains a character who is an unrepentant debtor and fraudster and who explicitly uses Insolvency Acts to get out of jail. To address the concerns about the overly frequent Relief

Acts encouraging fraudulent debt, Parliament passed no such acts between 1781 and 1794.

The inability to stabilize the distinction between accidental forgivable debt and morally corrupt debt in either the law or public debate is precisely an effect of the Janus-faced character of debt under capitalism: from one perspective, it appears as equity, while from another, as a debt that requires repayment. In other words, it cannot be pinned down—a slipperiness that benefits those with the power to keep risk circulating. This chimera is an effect of capital's time: financialized debt introduces the "liquidity" that defines some debt as simply someone else's credit not yet repaid. The infinite temporal displacement hides the costs of risks by forgetting debt's origins in an individual social relation; instead, a social aggregate is held responsible for commerce's accidents. A case study of the Society for the Discharge and Relief of Persons Imprisoned for Small Debts illustrates the challenges in pinning down responsibility for the costs of commerce, including why some individuals' debts are not forgiven. The Society's Minute Books reveal that members ultimately discriminated between honest and fraudulent debtors with a political arithmetic that unintentionally shored up the unfriending of debt by defining the subject of their philanthropy as an aggregate, not an individual, and thus they deployed an accounting that left unchallenged the systemic inequality within capital's character of debt.

The Society for the Discharge and Relief of Persons Imprisoned for Small Debts

The Society is one of many public philanthropic organizations founded in the latter eighteenth century, a modern movement linked to both sentimentalism and capitalism through its underlying humanitarian ideals.[58] Rev. William Dodd, the famous clergyman who helped found the Magdalen Hospital for Penitent Prostitutes in 1758, preached the charity sermon that initiated the Society's activities in 1772.[59] As its name suggests, its purpose was to raise funds to free prisoners by buying their debts at discounted prices.[60] Information about the Society comes from two main sources: James Neild's *Account of the Rise, Progress and Present State of the Society* (first published in 1774, with fourteen editions before the end of the century) and the Society's surviving records, particularly its Minute Books, held at the London Metropolitan Archive.[61] Neild was the driving force behind the Society, its treasurer from its beginnings until his death in 1814, and a major proponent of prison reform. He had built up a highly successful business as a jeweler in London, which allowed him to retire early and focus on philanthropic activities.[62] Neild's *Rise, Progress and Present* begins by expressing outrage that a person with abundant resources can declare bankruptcy and resume his occupation, while the man who runs into debt for a few pounds is "cruelly arrested, torn from his home and his business." "Is this an equal distribution of justice?" he demands (iv). The Society's goal is to right this injustice by relieving those poor debtors, and to open "the Prison Doors to every industrious and deserving fellow creature" (24).

With the £80 collected after Dodd's sermon, members began "to search out proper Objects" by visiting jails and acquiring lists from jailors (24). They quickly disbursed all their money by releasing 34 prisoners, "most of whom had large families, and appeared to be useful members of society" (24). Seeing the need, the Society raised more funds, and the number of debtors they were able to relieve quickly increased, with an average of 717 prisoners released each year in the organization's first decade. Their criteria for determining "proper objects" included the following: prisoners' debts had to be under £10, with the Society always compounding, never buying up for full price;[63] prisoners had to fill out petitions, acquired free of charge from jailers,[64] that included their "age, business, family, name, where confined, the sums they are indebted, and the address of their creditors"; and prisoners had to provide two "names of persons who will vouch for the debtor's character for sobriety, integrity, and industry" (Neild, *Rise*, 3, 74). The Society prioritized prisoners starting with the aged and infirm, followed by those with the largest families, and then those who were "most likely to be useful to the community and appear to have lost their liberty by unavoidable Misfortunes, at least not by Fraud, Vice, or Extravagance" (Neild, *Rise*, 31–32). They specifically noted that women were included, and records show many single women were aided by the charity, though Neild almost universally speaks of debtors as male with wives and children.[65]

The Society accepted petitions every Wednesday and then sent a form letter to references stating that the prisoner had "referred them to you for a character; the Society request[s] the favour of a line, with your opinion of the petitioner's character for sobriety, integrity, and industry," and suggesting that references use the back of the letter to reply (Neild, *Rise*, 76). If the references were received, the prisoner would be placed on the list to be released the following Wednesday. When the work of sending these letters grew too much for volunteer members, the committee hired an administrator and rented an office on Craven Street to manage the correspondence. Unfortunately, none of the petitions or reference letters survive, and thus we do not know the extent of these references. But from the fact that a line on the back of a paper was considered a response and because prisoners were not asked for a narrative of how and why they fell into debt, the Society's mode at the beginning for identifying honest and industrious debtors relied on external markers of whether one had a social network that included two household heads (later on, when they began relieving prisoners outside London, the Society required a verification from local chaplains for rural debtors). The Society relied on these "characters," but, as the January 2, 1793, minutes reveal, references were not always prompt or responsive. At that meeting, they considered fifty-two petitioners, but "upon finding so many without characters resolved that the following N.B. may be added to the letters which may be sent in future for Characters 'Unless some answer is returned to this letter the Petitioner must remain in Prison totally unnoticed by the Society.'"[66] I cannot determine whether this plea was effective, but the tone of the resolution illustrates the Society's predisposition to assume prisoners' innocence. In the Society's initial years, its members universally default to characterizing imprisoned debtors as victims of circumstances, not fraudsters. Records show that they approved almost all of the petitions they received for the first six years. Starting on April 8, 1778, however, they begin regularly listing how many petitions were rejected out of the total number considered, with two out of thirty rejected that night.[67] As early as the 1783 edition of the *Rise, Progress and Present State*, Neild adds to the above forms a letter to creditors that "the Society have found it sometimes necessary" to send requests to the creditor asking them to inform the Society "of the manner in which the Debt was contracted: Whether in the common and ordinary course of Business, or by specious Pretences" (75). Why and on what basis do they begin to determine their "fellow creatures" are "undeserving"? Why do they become so concerned that the Society relieve "worthy object[s] . . . only" that they begin soliciting more information from creditors (75)? And why does the reporting of the number of petitions rejected become a standard component of meeting minutes?

The shift from accepting all applications to rejecting some and recording that figure occurs alongside another change in the content of the Society's minutes: the minute books shift from including lists of the individual names of prisoners released to providing only total numbers with no names. In the first years of the minute books, lists of "Benefactions" and "Disbursements" reported at each meeting are standard, and the disbursements not only include the specific names of the prisoners but also the amounts paid to acquire each petitioner's discharge, along with intermittent descriptive markers that individualize the prisoners, often with a sympathetic reference to their distressed circumstances: "Sarah Overton naked with 4 children"; "Susan Fletcher—maintained her mother"; "James Barter—old paralitick—2 chil"[68] (fig. 1). They also include information about employment, with the December 23, 1772, minutes listing a tailor, an undertaker, a shoemaker, a barber, a gardener, a weaver, a cook, a coach maker, a lighterman, a baker, and a laborer.[69] The minutes for June 10, 1772, take particular note of one Hannah Gyles who was relieved and given a special order for admission to the Lock Hospital for the treatment of venereal disease. The Society follows up, later noting when exactly she was removed "from Newgate to the Lock Hospital" and then again reporting, on August 12, 1772, that she was removed from the Lock Hospital and placed in the Magdalen Hospital for penitent prostitutes.[70] The call to universal sympa-

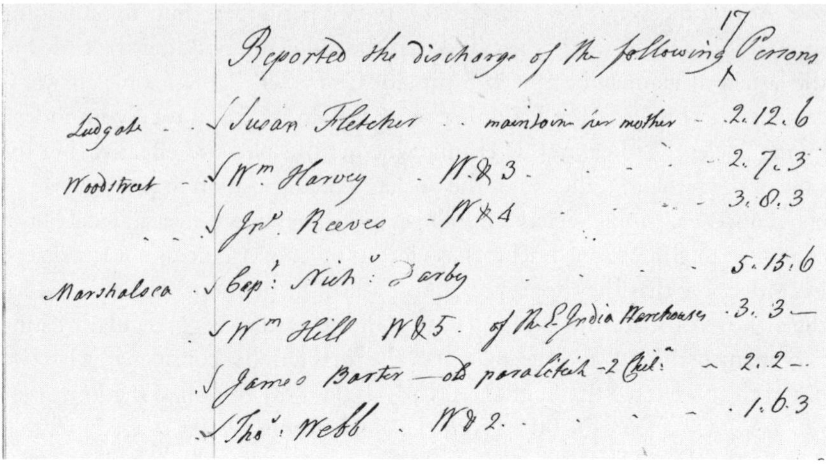
Reported the discharge of the following 17 Persons
Ludgate – Susan Fletcher .. maintain her mother – 2.12.6
Woodstreet – Wm. Harvey . W.&3 – 2.7.3
Jno. Reeves – W&4 – 3.8.3
Marshalsea – Capt. Nich. Darby – 5.15.6
Wm. Hill W&5. of the E India Warehouses 3.3.–
James Barter — old paralitick – 2 Chil. 2.2.–
Thos. Webb . W&2. – 1.6.3

Fig. 1. List of Persons Discharged from Prison, with Individual Description. Society for the Discharge and Relief of Persons Imprisoned for Small Debts, Minute Book, 1772–1773, October 7, 1772 (LMA/A/RSD/021/011). London Metropolitan Archives, City of London.

thy toward imprisoned debtors is individualized and concretized in these moments of naming real people with distresses and histories. But then, on June 8, 1774, the minute books cease naming individuals, providing only totals of numbers relieved.[71] Explanations for why the lists cease are not given. Increased numbers cannot be a justification, because the total number of prisoners released remains fairly constant; in the May 11 minutes, thirty-nine individuals are listed, but in June, even though only twenty prisoners are released, no names are provided.[72]

At the same time as the names of "proper Objects" disappear from the minutes, the names of swindlers begin to enter, with the details of petitioners who were rejected inserted irregularly (fig. 2). The June 12, 1782, entry includes details on individuals who failed to pass the character reference, along with the amount of their debt: "Evan Williams, 100—defrauded Lord Verney"; "Cha' Griffith 28—would have cheated Society"; "Daniel McNeal 68.7.0—a Swindler."[73] It is unclear how the Society obtained its information on rejected debtors, but one source was the Society of Guardians for the Protection of Trade against Swindlers. The first proto-credit-rating organization in Britain, the Society of Guardians, was member based, with merchants paying a subscription fee for access to a list of the names of high-risk debtors.[74] The Society for the Relief of Small Debts passed a resolution requesting that the Society of Guardians "acquaint this Society with the Names of such Persons as they may deem

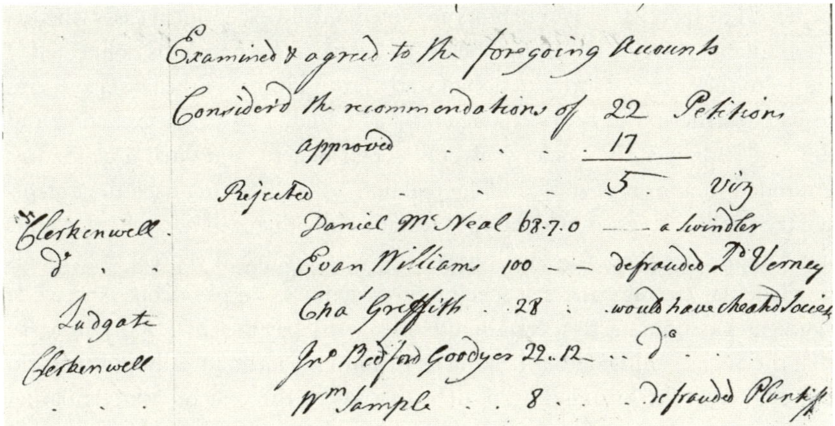
Examined & agreed to the foregoing Accounts
Consider'd the recommendations of 22 Petitions
approved . . . 17
Rejected - - - 5 viz
Clerkenwell. Daniel M^c^Neal 68.7.0 — a Swindler
do . . Evan Williams 100 — defrauded Dr Verney
Ludgate Chas Griffith . 28 . would have cheated Society
Clerkenwell Jno Bedford Goodyer 22..12 .. do . .
. . . Wm Sample . . 8 . . . defrauded Plantiff

Fig. 2. List of Debtors' Petitions Rejected. Society for the Discharge and Relief of Persons Imprisoned for Small Debts, Minute Book, 1778–1782, June 12, 1782 (LMA/A/RSD/1/6). London Metropolitan Archives, City of London.

unworthy of assistance from this Society," and the minutes later note the rejection of Christopher Metcalf for "being in the Swindler's list."[75]

While it is impossible to know the extent to which the Society relieved debts acquired through fraud and whether this number increased, the minute books reveal a growing pressure to acknowledge that "undeserving" individuals benefited from the charity. Copies of letters sent to the jail keepers at Hereford and Gloucester request that they emphasize to prisoners the importance of honesty and full disclosure in their petitions, which suggests they had discovered frauds among the petitioners: "[P]lease . . . order them," the letter to Hereford requests, "to fill up the Petitions now sent according to the directions. . . . I fear some persons in your Prison do not act faithfully."[76] Later minute books start recording the Society's mistakes, naming now-known swindlers who had been earlier relieved. A. J. Beart, who was released by the Society in 1786, was charged in 1788 with forgery for a bill of exchange worth 36l. 11s. A newspaper clipping inserted into the 1788 minute book recounts Vander Cruyson's elaborate scheme to steal £280's worth of gold watches with the following annotation underneath: "the above named Vander Curson was liberated by this Society on 9 Feb 1788 within 3 weeks after, the above appeared in the public papers."[77]

In general, the minutes increasingly individualize swindlers at the same time that they decreasingly name honest debtors. Some deserving specific cases are still discussed, but these tend to be sensational. Hercules Slade, for example, a thirteen-year-old boy imprisoned by his tutor for outstanding tuition fees was sought out and released by the Society after the case was reported in the newspaper.[78] The fact that honest debtors are noted only in exceptional cases whereas "fraudulent" or rejected debtors begin to be routinely named is connected, I argue, to the Society's introduction of statistics and its use of the law of averages in its construction of debt's character. The "swindler" was the exception and did not endanger the Society's overall social benefit, but such a claim was grounded in a form of statistical aggregation not unlike that used in contemporary credit ratings, in which types replace individualized narrative accounting. Credit rating reports constitute an aggregated subject, yet real individuals in particular circumstances at specific times acquire and pay debts. And while aggregates assume the risk, certain individuals still pay the costs, an asymmetry that the Society mitigated by helping those individuals financially, but they did not challenge the unfriending of debt that keeps the cost of risk circulating through the aggregate, allowing individuals with equity a free ride.

That the Society begins to characterize debtors through aggregation is readable by comparing their annual account statements for 1774–75 and 1776–77, when they introduce statistical averages. Previous statements (fig. 3) calculate totals of benefactions and disbursements, including numbers of debtors released and the total number of wives and children of those debtors. The 1776–77 account (fig. 4) provides all of the above plus a new statement averaging out the totals: "The Average for the total number of 4468 Debtors is £2.3.4 1/4 each; and the average for the 14007 individuals is nearly 14 each; It is probable the Public Benevolence has been diffused to twice that Number, because many Families of the Creditors who accepted composition for their respective debts, being in very necessitous circumstances, were also benefitted by the composition paid to them."[79]

Of what significance is the inclusion of averages? The rationale for the Society's work—and a major argument in the campaign against imprisonment for debt—became less about sympathy for the individual honest debtor who has experienced misfortune than about a numerical financial benefit to the public good, a form of William Petty–inspired political arithmetic that we might now identify with Foucaultian governmentality.

The average debtor replaces individualized descriptions of unfortunate debtors when the Society begins responding to negative critiques that it encouraged profligacy and crime. An argument against relieving imprisoned debtors was that, in doing so, fraud would be encouraged, and thus the Society was often challenged to explain how it avoided relieving dishonest debtors. Thomas Francklin, in his charity sermon in support of the Society, insists that "[e]very caution . . . hath been made use of to prevent fraud and imposture, and in the relief of objects the strictest attention always paid, and the fullest bounty always bestowed on those who were most deserving of it."[80] Yet the only evidence he provides is the claim that the vast majority of debtors are innocent: "[F]ew, very

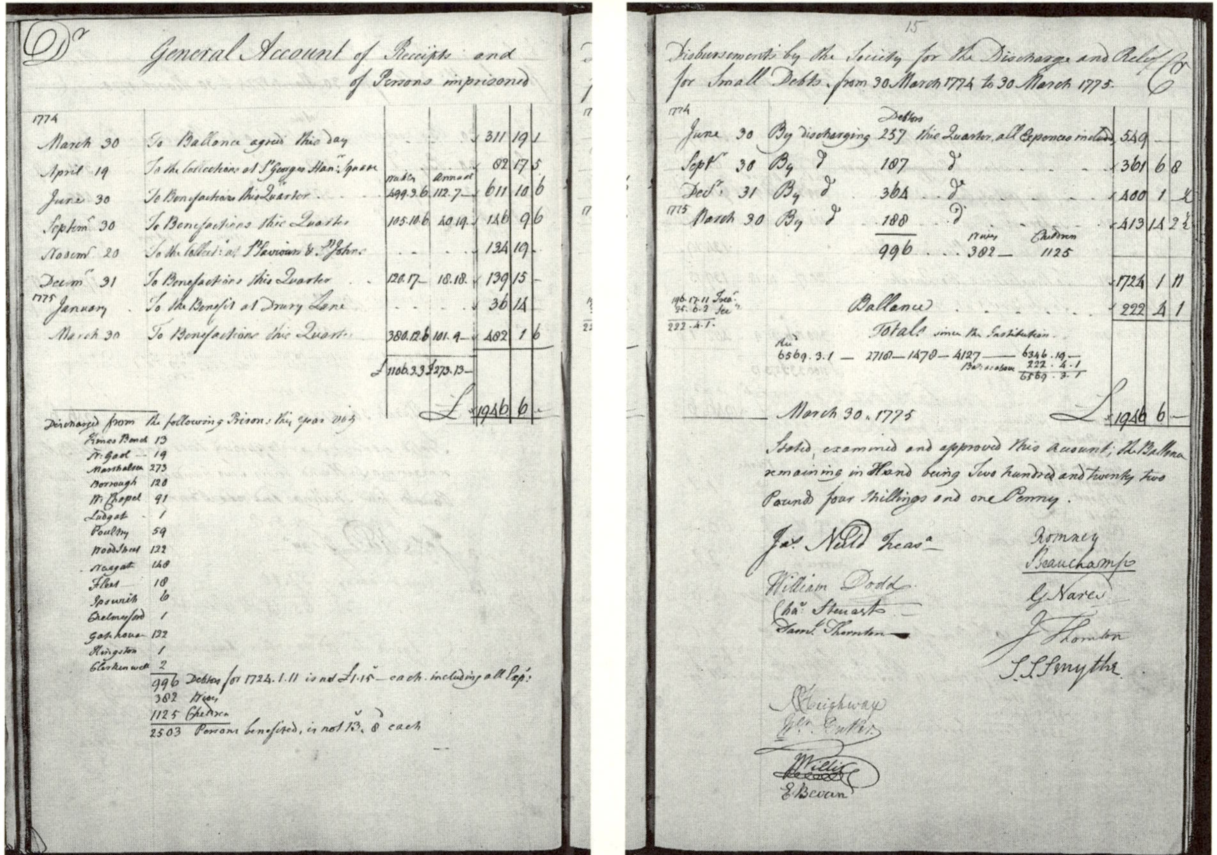
Dr General Account of Receipts and of Persons imprisoned

1774				
March 30	To Ballance agreed this day			311 19 1
April 19	To the Collection at St George Han: Square			82 17 5
June 30	To Benefactions this Quarter	499.3.6	112.7	611 10 6
Septem. 30	To Benefactions this Quarter	105.10.6	20.19	126 9 6
Novem. 20	To the Collect: at St Saviours & St Johns			134 19
Decem. 31	To Benefactions this Quarter	120.17	18.18	139 15
1775 January	To the Benefit at Drury Lane			36 14
March 30	To Benefactions this Quarter	380.12.6	101.4	482 1 6
		£1106.3.3	273.13	
				£1946 6

Discharged from the following Prisons this year viz.
Fleet 13, Wood Street 19, Marshalsea 273, Borough 128, Whitechapel 91, Ludgate 1, Poultry 59, Wood Street 122, Newgate 168, Fleet 18, Ipswich 6, Chelmsford 1, Gatehouse 132, Kingston 1, Clerkenwell 2

996 Debtors for 1724.1.11 is not £1.15 each including all Exp:
382 Wives
1125 Children
2503 Persons benefited, is not 13. 8 each

Disbursements by the Society for the Discharge and Relief for Small Debts from 30 March 1774 to 30 March 1775. Cr

1774		Debtors		
June 30	By discharging	257	this Quarter, all Expences included	549
Sept. 30	By do	107	do	361 6 8
Decr. 31	By do	364	do	400 1
1775 March 30	By do	188	do	413 14 2
		996	Wives 382 Children 1125	1724 1 11
	Ballance			222 4 1

Totals since the Institution
6569.3.1 — 2710 — 1470 — 4127 — 6346.19 / 222.4.1 / 6569.3.1

£1946 6

March 30. 1775
Stated, examined and approved this Account; the Ballance remaining in Hand being Two hundred and twenty two Pound four Shillings and one Penny.

Jas. Neild Treasr.
William Dodd
Chas. Stuart
Saml. Thornton
Romney
Beauchamp
G. Nares
J. Thornton
S. L. Smythe
E. Bevan

Fig. 3. Account Statement, 1774–1775. Society for the Discharge and Relief of Persons Imprisoned for Small Debts (LMA/A/RSD/1/3). London Metropolitan Archives, City of London.

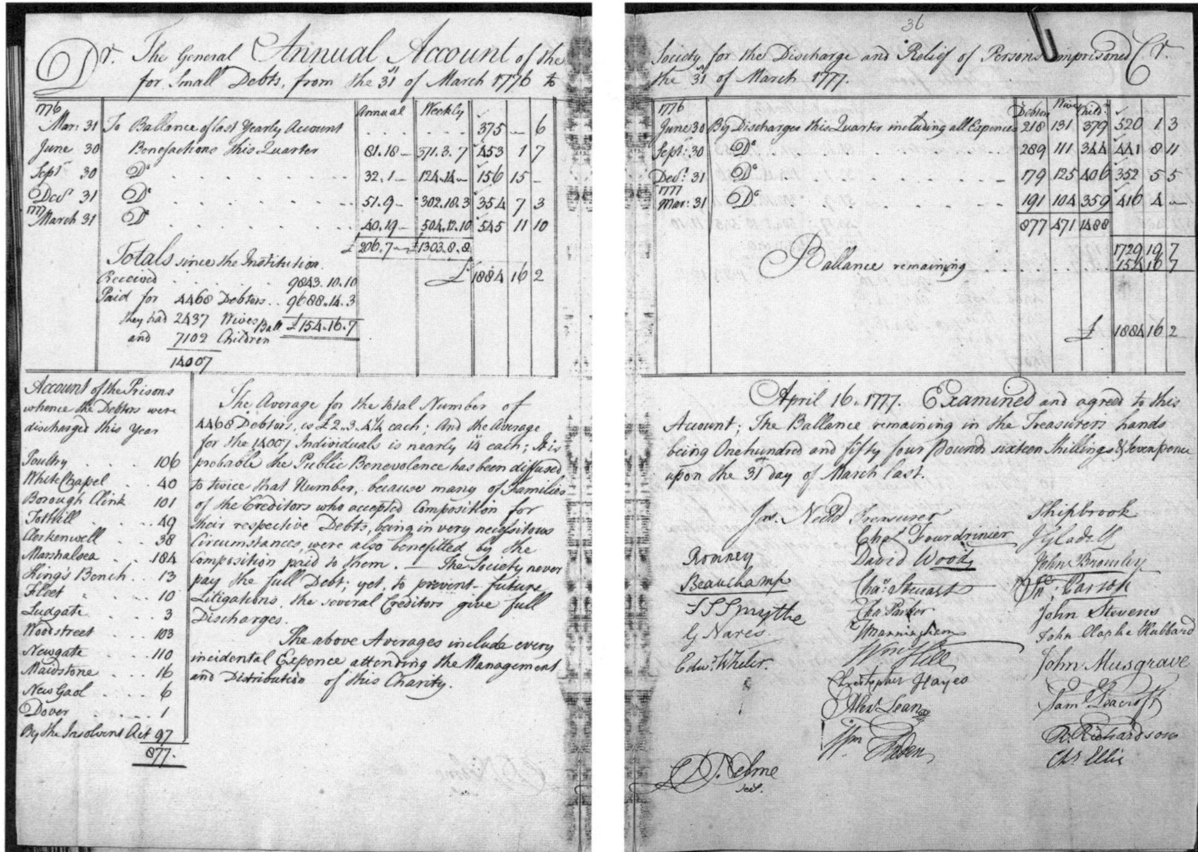

Fig. 4. Account Statement, 1776–1777. Society for the Discharge and Relief of Persons Imprisoned for Small Debts (A/RSD/1/6). London Metropolitan Archives, City of London.

few [are in prison from] . . . a total want of principle and common honesty," "most of them [are there because of] . . . the cruel and unfeeling disposition of their merciless creditors."[81] Samuel Johnson used a similar logic in his essay "Imprisonment for Debt," arguing that imprisoned debtors as an aggregate are generally innocent: "For of the multitudes who are pining in those cells of misery, a very small part is suspected of any fraudulent act."[82] Neild's *Rise, Progress and Present State* provides a similarly vague claim about the average, insisting that "[f]ar the greater number of objects released were manufacturers, seamen, and labourers," and noting that by restoring these objects to industry, the public benefits "from the advantages which it derives to community in general" (25–26). In a newspaper clipping included in the minute books, the Society defends its work through the law of averages: the fact that they had denied twenty-nine petitions that month demonstrates that they are weeding out swindlers; all other imprisoned debtors default to victims of misfortune.[83] How might we interpret the shift from individual names to the law of averages within capital's character of debt? What might it reveal about what debt signified in the latter eighteenth century?

The law of averages, with its assumption that the majority of debtors are honest, animates the often-repeated political argument concerning debt and economic growth. The campaign's most prevalent argument against imprisonment was the utilitarian one about the large economic cost to the nation of the lost labor of imprisoned debtors. In his *Rise, Progress and Present State*, Neild provides the following calculation concerning four manufacturers whose entire families (four wives and twenty-three children), along with themselves, were relieved for "the trifling sum of 15l. 1s. 3d.": "The utility of this charity to the public will appear, from the consideration that every man's labour may be estimated, at an average, to be worth to the community 2s.6d. per day, or 39£. a year: so that the confinement of the four Manufacturers above mentioned, occasioned a loss to the public of the rate of 156£. annually" (n.p.). The nation's net gain, then, is over £140 per year on only four debtors. James Halifax, in his *Sermon Preached for the Benefit of the Society*, cites the same figure of £39 per year as the cost of lost labor. Arguing that the imprisonment of honest debtors deprives the public "of that benefit, which is inevitably lost, by having so many hands bound up in a prison," Halifax takes the total number of prisoners released since the Society began (2,700) and multiplies it by £39 a year to arrive at a total of £105,300 of wealth that the public would gain by not imprisoning these people.[84] Society member Josiah Dornford provides the same calculation, though using a different figure: "If the earnings of each individual may be computed, on the average, at twenty pounds per Ann. what a loss to the Community; since according to Mr. Howards statement in the year 1782, there were 2197 debtors in prison."[85] John Howard's statistical portrait of prisoners in England, which came out five years after the Society's founding, is one of the first examples of quantitative sociology, and his careful recording of statistical information is referenced throughout the campaign (Neild continues this work after Howard's death).[86] Such calculations lead a letter writer in the *Gazetteer* to commend the Society for providing "the most *essential* service to the *commercial interests* of this kingdom, by giving freedom and new life to those useful manufacturers, whose labours are to the community an invaluable treasure."[87]

The argument in favor of relieving debtors that ultimately justifies the Society's work is less about identifying individual cases of misfortune (though many sentimental and illustrative examples are given) than about the systemic economic calculation that imprisoning debtors is bad for business.[88] In fact, the Society boasts that it was "[d]isinterested" and did not care about debtors as individuals but only as "fellow-creatures," that is to say, as part of an aggregate or generalized Humanity; they were strangers helping strangers (Neild, *Rise*, xxxiv).[89] The Society's own challenge in dividing good from bad debt, its appeal to averages rather than individual stories, suggests that the project of disinterested humanism aligns with capital's unfriending of debt. Debt as financial instrument and as innocent misfortune both require anonymous numerical aggregations that divorce economic obligations from the social obligations particular to each debt's history. Thus, when debt becomes a financial instrument, the responsibility for caring for disenfranchised poor debtors is abstracted and divorced from the social collective, from what it means to live together for better or worse. Debt's securitization unfriends debt not only in the financial marketplace but within the philanthropic world as well. In either case, financialized debt allows creditors to *become* strangers and permits those responsible for taking on the original risk to walk away from its costs. In his history of bankruptcy in the United States, Bruce Mann demonstrates how the eighteenth-century practice of assignability "severed the connection between debts and their underlying social relations, thereby making possible a transformation in the relations between debtors and creditors."[90] The severing of the social connection, the estrangement caused by assignability, was all too visible when the collateralized debt obligations (CDOs) crashed in 2008, revealing just how deep financial derivatives can bury risk and hiding, in this case, the millions of social relations between predatory mortgage brokers and working-class homeowners on which the CDOs were built.[91] The severing of debt from its underlying social relation was also the defining event in the life of James Stephen, the radical reformer and prisoner whose 1770 *Considerations on Imprisonment for Debt* initiated the campaign against imprisonment. Stephen was the first writer to directly politicize the issue and to organize against the systemic injustice of capitalism's debt peonage. For that reason, I consider him to be the first debt resistor. His case brings into focus what happens when debt no longer circulates between friends; for Stephen, assignability lands him in jail.

James Stephen and the Politics of Debt

Forgive us our debts as we forgive our debtors.
—Matthew, 4:12 and *A King's Bench Sermon; With . . . a Preface by Mr. Stephen*[92]

Failed entrepreneur, industrious liberal, imprisoned debtor, and political rebel James Stephen provides a fascinating case study for a cultural history of debt. In particular, his story compellingly illustrates how the anonymous circulation of debt contracts in the financial marketplace both launches the entrepreneurial expansion that produces economic growth and works to silence the moral and social obligations at the heart of the way a society divides its resources. The first to argue against the constitutionality of imprisoning people for debt, Stephen articulated a politics of debt forgiveness that in contemporary times would be akin to the Internationalists' response to the 1980s IMF "debt crisis" or to the Occupy movement's Strike Debt campaign with its challenge to austerity agendas. What makes Stephen's argument so radical for the 1770s is that he holds the sellers of credit instruments responsible for the costs of the risk, and rejects the moral assumption that debtors should pay for creditors' mistakes. Like Graeber, he would argue that not all debts need to be repaid. Stephen's volatile business history laid the groundwork for his political activism, and his son's *Memoir*, the source for most of my biographical history, provides us with a window on how capital's new character of debt unfriended families and severed social relations from economic ones.

Stephen, the great-great-grandfather of Virginia Woolf and father of James Stephen Jr. (a leading abolitionist and right-hand man to William Wilberforce), was the son of a Scottish merchant who likely traded in contraband goods.[93] Stephen took up the trading business, and his frequent failures suggest that his ambitions for upward mobility often overstretched his resources and entrepreneurial savvy. His "first failure in business," as his son recalls in his *Memoir*, came when the ship carrying wine Stephen was importing from France to Scotland, shipwrecked off the coast of Poole in southern England.[94] His "second failure in business" involved his brother John, who worked for the East India Co., and like most East Indiamen, John made money, not from his salary, but from financialization or, as Stephen Jr. writes, the "great commercial advantages by loans of capital on respondentia bonds," or loans upon the cargo of a vessel. One of John's respondentia bonds was taken out with Stephen as surety, and the cargo was lost. That would have been the end of it (respondentia bonds were repaid only upon the safe arrival of cargo), but there was "a dispute . . . [with] the creditor," Robert Herries, from whom Stephen had borrowed for his surety.[95] When the enterprise led to a brotherly quarrel, Stephen and John severed relations. At some point in between these two failures, Stephen entered into another family commercial partnership, this one with another brother, William, and a brother-in-law as shareholders.[96] After the business went bankrupt, a family feud ensued, and Stephen never restored relations with either his brother-in-law or William. "Whether they had ventured too boldly upon extensive dealings," Stephen Jr. writes, "I do not know. From my Father's disposition it is not unlikely."[97] James Stephen was known to be a larger-than-life character, both physically and energetically, and his mercantile ambitions seem to have repeatedly outreached his grasp, causing lifelong family feuds and a volatile domestic economy, with his wife working hard to maintain respectability and keep the family among the middling sort.[98]

The business dealing that eventually landed Stephen in debtor's prison is one involving the baronet Sir John Webbe, who convinced Stephen to go into business with him to develop prospective coal deposits on his estate near Poole. Their business contract had Webbe providing the capital and Stephen overseeing the projects. When the coal did not materialize and Webbe became uncomfortable with the expenses Stephen was accumulating, he decided to pull out, thereby causing their rupture. Webbe, via his steward, threatened arrest for rent due, but when Stephen produced evidence that he had paid the rent, Webbe took another tactic: he went to Robert Herries, to whom Stephen owed money on the bond taken out for John's East India deal, and purchased the debt. In Stephen's own veiled description of the affair in *Considerations on Imprisonment for Debt*, it seems Webbe paid Herries £150 for a debt amounting to £340. Webbe then used this debt to arrest Stephen, who remained in the King's Bench prison from August 1769 to March 1771, writing and publishing *Considerations* and *An Address to the Twelve Judges of England* while in jail.[99] In other words, assignability is precisely what severed Stephen's debt from its original social relation and allowed the more powerful Webbe to imprison the less well connected Stephen. Stephen Jr. notes that Herries "afterwards declared to my father that he thought Sir John [Webbe] acted as his friend in the transaction, and that had he known the oppressive purpose he would not have assigned the debt."[100]

In his *Memoir*, Stephen Jr. distills the lesson to take away from his father's checkered business dealings: one should feel "a horror at all partnerships or joint concerns in matters of pecuniary interest between Members of the same family," and he recalls his mother counseling her children to avoid any business dealings with their brothers.[101] Such breakdowns in family relations over money loaned between members was widespread. Margaret Hunt writes that "[t]he image of whole families failing owing to the fact that they had imprudently provided money or security for relatives is one of the master narratives of middling culture. It recurs over and over in letters, diaries and autobiographies of urban non-elites of the period. . . . And it is difficult to find *any* good runs of personal records from tradesmen's families between about 1650 and 1800 that do not record failures."[102] The Stephen family fits in this archive.

How do we interpret this "master narrative"? The trail of family feuds and broken brotherly bonds that followed Stephen's failed enterprises led him to provide an interpretation opposite to the one his son later provides. While Stephen Jr. advises against loaning money to family and friends, Stephen's version of the story is that problems occur precisely when debt is severed from those social relations. His writing argues that when we anonymize debt contracts, we silence the exploitative power dynamics at the heart of commercial life.

Stephen, who used his time in prison to teach himself the law, including the Magna Carta, proclaimed that the common law "gave no power to our creditors over our bodies."[103] On this basis, he took out a writ of habeas corpus, appealing the legality of his confinement to Lord Mansfield's court. Mansfield summarily dismissed the case, prompting Stephen to vent his frustrations by reproducing his legal argument in *Considerations on Imprisonment for Debt*, addressed to Parliament. Though significant, the detailed legal and constitutional argument is dwarfed in the text by the power of Stephen's direct address, the fact that it is not "their" but "our" bodies confined. His clear articulation of the injustice at the heart of debtor-creditor relations comes from his own particular experience. His tracts include the utilitarian argument—"by restoring to the free air such a number of useful subjects," freeing prisoners would be in the best interests of the nation—but he does not dwell on political arithmetic and the law of averages. Instead, he develops a sustained critique of easy credit and queries why poor debtors are carrying the entire risk of economic growth.[104]

In *Considerations*, he first raises the issue of who should have access to credit, and argues that it would be "imprudent to trust" money to people who do not have some kind of solid equity: "[I]f dealers were more cautious whom they trust, it would greatly contribute to the advantage of the trade of Great Britain."[105] "To be in debt is not a crime, nor is the contracting of a debt, an action blamable," as Stephen points out.[106] He goes even further to suggest that the drive for upward mobility is so natural that "[a] man launched into the world with some property, will naturally think of improving it; or if he begins the world with none, his views will tend to acquire some."[107] The problem is not a man's desire to improve but the seduction of easy credit: "Those who have no property to begin with, urged by necessity, enticed by other people's example and success, spurred on by an enterprising spirit, solicit and obtain too easily a credit, which they intend as a means of honestly enriching themselves, and which often is the cause and origin of their ruin."[108]

The credit system further seduces men into ruin through the escalating risks that debtors take once they find themselves in over their heads: "[T]he dread of prison . . . drive men in trade into such destructive connexions [*sic*]" that they seek out credit from "blood-suckers" at higher interest rates, in particular through discounting bills of exchange.[109] Higher-risk credit circulates as traders broker short-term deals in order to survive the next business day, and, instead of returning home to their wives and families, honest traders are forced to cavort with shady dealers. "[T]his fictitious" business of "imaginary credit"—that is, of discounted bills—is carried on until banks are defrauded or the original debtor ends up in jail, or both. "There is a circulation, and not real business," Stephen succinctly states about debt speculation.[110] In the *Address*, Stephen singles out pawnbrokers and bill discounters for the "exorbitant profit" they reap on other people's misery. For example, one discounter, "for a sum of twenty seven pounds, seven shillings and nine pence received by this man, three months and twenty days before it was due, . . . paid six guineas."[111] The discounter's business is legal, Stephen points out, and this so-called "upright and conscientious dealer . . . now keeps in jail for some twenty three pounds, a man with whom he has had dealings . . . for upwards of twenty three years." Over the years he has made "five hundred pounds profit, besides *legal interest*," from this man, but because one bill worth £20 that he bought for £13 was not paid when it came due, he keeps the debtor in jail.[112]

Stephen's argument is precisely the one mounted against those involved in selling the subprime mortgages that caused the 2008 crash: creditors who buy debt only to recirculate it and sell it again for a profit should be held accountable for the risks such speculation introduces. Dealers who give credit "to such as they know very well to be in a tottering way" should pay for their speculations.[113] These dealers, having "acquired by experience a knack at knowing how long they [the traders] will be able to support their credit," get out with a profit before the trader breaks.[114] Stephen provides the example of a young inexperienced man who borrows money from a supposed friend to set up in trade. The "friend" clears a "secret profit" of "above two thousand pounds" through commissions on credit that the trader takes out to set up.[115] When the trader eventually breaks, the "friend" scolds him for neglecting his business and for his extravagant expenses, attributing the debt to consumption. The young trader, in this case, is not the one who is morally responsible, Stephen holds, yet he is the one in jail; the dealer who encouraged the debt in order to profit from the commissions is the one who should pay.

Similarly, Stephen wants to jail the cannibalistic rich manufacturer who preys upon poor laborers through the eighteenth-century version of a payday loan scheme. The manufacturer brags to Stephen about forcing poor, starving workers to sell him goods cheaply on a Saturday evening, knowing they would not otherwise be able to find a buyer until Monday and, in order to eat on Sunday, must sell to him. The sicker or more wretched the worker, the lower the price the manufacturer offers as he profits from other people's desperation. The "anthropophagian tale," as Stephen calls it, is a good example of "money's capacity to turn morality into a matter of impersonal arithmetic, . . . justif[ying] . . . things that would otherwise seem outrageous or obscene," to repeat Graeber's claim cited above.[116] Predatory creditors, and not debtor's profligacy, are the problem, as Stephen sees it. He critiques the discourse that condemns debtors for overspending, noting that "luxury" is so widespread that "we must not blame the unfortunate individuals who are ruined by its baneful influence . . . [and] the facility of obtaining credit."[117] If creditors did not encourage overconsumption with high-risk loans, people would not buy superfine cloth but be contented with what they already own. At the beginning of the financial revolution, Stephen understood that "buy with no money down" arrangements and payday loans were capital's way of indenturing the poor.[118]

Stephen earns the title of "first debt resister" when he translates his political analysis into direct action, organizing debtors in the King's Bench to protest their wrongful incarceration. His *Address* calls on debtors to mobilize and "draw up a petition to Parliament," and he invites them to a meeting.[119] Joanna Innes provides the best account of Stephen's activism, in particular his organized "escape" and the mayhem that ensued. Stephen and approximately forty fellow prisoners "rushed the turnkeys" and walked through the prison gates to protest what they saw as their illegal confinement; they were promptly re-arrested, and Stephen was sent to New Gaol for a brief period. As Innes documents from depositions, the prisoners rioted until the charges against Stephen were dropped and he was returned to the King's Bench.[120] Stephen Jr. describes his father's activism as "rash," "romantic," and a "dangerous enterprise."[121] The prison rebellion was covered in the newspapers, and his campaign garnered significant publicity that in itself registers a certain success.[122] Innes documents that for several months in 1771, the King's Bench prison was largely out of prison officials' control. A later affidavit suggests that the riot was not just for beer (the prisoners had destroyed some beer barrels) but for the rights Stephen mobilized them to claim: "[The prisoners] said they didn't have complaints about the prison," but "their complaint was being illegally confined or against Magna Charta and that they were determined not to suffer confinement in that prison for debt any longer."[123] Shortly after the "insurrection," Sir John Webbe settled his claim and Stephen was freed from prison. But he did not escape financial exigency, and money woes haunted him for the rest of his life. He studied law but was refused a place at the bar; he pursued a career as a conveyancer, a type of solicitor who specializes in buying and selling property, but was never able to make more than a subsistence living. Evil creditors hounded him even on his deathbed, as his son recounts, with his landlord, "a wealthy and unfeeling man," threatening to turn him out of his house as he lay dying. Stephen Jr. ultimately made it possible for his father to die at home by taking out credit to be paid with the goods of his father's estate.[124]

The political debt resistance argument that Stephen introduces, along with its indictment of assignability and easy credit, remains a current through the rest of the century. Though never quite so radically expressed, the question of the creditor's responsibility does not disappear from the campaign, and bill discounting emerges as a particular evil.[125] The writer of *Seasonable Advice . . . Concerning . . . Relief of Debtors* (1775) observes that "it is the general rule to lodge all the blame upon the *debtor*: but this, is only because his spirit is bent to the earth by *obligation*," whereas the writer "would have credit in a great many cases *restrained*."[126] The writer singles out bill discounters and debt speculators, especially those who give loans to young men to be paid when they come into their estates. Experts in the art of "dunning" "compel . . . [young men] to credit" and into luxury spending before they come of age, forfeiting their futures.[127] Creditors who compel should not expect to be paid. The capacity of credit instruments to financialize time and encourage debtors to "forfeit their futures" was the basis of a legal case involving John Spencer (later an earl). Spencer borrowed money on the promise that he would repay double the amount if he outlived his grandmother, the duchess of Marlborough. The duchess dies but he dies shortly thereafter, before he had paid the full amount due. His estate refuses to pay, arguing that the loan was usurious, or above 5%, the legal rate of interest. However, the court ruled in the creditor's favor on the grounds that the double amount promised in payment was a contract, not interest, and a man should be allowed to enter into such contracts.[128] In fact, one *can* sell one's future, and this distinction between a contract and interest has fed the growth of the predatory financial industry from the eighteenth century until today.[129]

Tract writers introduce various ways to combat the problem of calculating debt as a number and a contract, rather than as a social relation. The author of *The Case of the Creditors of Joseph George Pedley* calls on governments to introduce regulations and also stressed the need for a moral accounting beyond the financial one. *The Case of the Creditors of Joseph George Pedley* argues that credit should circulate only within the context of brotherly love, and not among self-interested strangers: "If men in trade . . . possessed that brotherly regard for each other which would lead to their prosperity and happiness, they would be aliens to those misfortunes they otherwise bring on themselves, by the banishment of mutual love and friendship from among them."[130] Commerce, the writer continues, should be governed by the rules of mutual love not, as it is now, by men who "respect only the individual good of themselves" and how they can profit; this is the root of the "gross and vicious maxim now reduced to a proverb, that in trade and commerce there is *no* friendship."[131] Remembering friendship and the social relation behind debt is the first step in debt resistance.

Stephen and the tract writers demonstrate that even in these nascent moments of financial capitalism, people were questioning how it devolved the costs of risk on to the poor and the vulnerable. Samuel Johnson early on posed this question in "Imprisonment for Debt": "Those who made the laws, have apparently supposed, that every deficiency of payment is the crime of the debtor. But the truth is, that the creditor always shares the act, and often more than shares the guilt of improper trust."[132] In his critique of capital's debt regime, *Bonds of Debt,* Richard Dienst analyzes the way neoliberal economic policies have shifted the cost of risk to the public and the poor and away from the financial industry and governments. He refers to this as "the classic contradiction between the privatization of profits and the socialization of risks."[133] The fact that the public pays the cost of environmental damage inflicted by oil and gas companies is the simplest example of the contradiction, but we could add the increasing debt burden placed on the middle and lower classes to finance what used to be government-funded education. The "brotherly bond" that might include a social welfare system has been increasingly eroded by abstractions according to which debt circulates as a commodity among strangers and these strangers and their fortunes easily disappear when the music stops, as it did in 2008. Critics such as Graeber and Dienst, as well as Maurizio Lazzarato, Christian Marazzi, and Susanne Soederberg, trace the disappearing act that has been a repeated strategy of capitalism since the eighteenth century, and they raise larger political questions concerning "indebtedness." In so doing, Dienst argues that it is "a mistake to try to pin down either the concept or the experience of indebtedness in a single definition"; we may feel obligated to pay the bill when it arrives, but it is "impossible to decide where practical calculations end and moral imperatives begin, just as it seems impossible to say where a sense of autonomy and self-sufficiency stops and a recognition of the needs of others begins."[134] In other words, the moral imperative of debt requires the interpretation of its narrative specificity, its context, and the community to which the debt belongs. Who loaned what to whom and under what circumstances is a crucial component in the hermeneutic judgment of determining which contracts should be legally enforceable. Narrative rather than numbers is the only ethical way of measuring creditworthiness.

The latter-eighteenth-century campaign against imprisonment for debt failed to effect juridical reform of the common law, a change that remained at least fifty years in the future. In fact, the campaign, with its emphasis on providing assistance to the "misfortunate debtor" as an accidental casualty of commerce, may have been counterproductive in that it may have fed the nineteenth-century ideological collapse of the fraudulent debtor with the insolvent poor. Margot Finn complicates our understanding of the campaign with her analysis of the newly minted small claims courts that occurred contemporaneously. While the Society, James Stephen, and others were busy defending "honest debtors" against common-law imprisonment, Finn notes, the legislature was busy introducing new summary courts that gave judges the authority to render verdicts without a jury, in the interests of efficiently dealing with larger numbers of debtors, a shift that she argues essentially criminalized plebeian debtors: "Over time, the stock phrases employed in small-claims statutes began to shift from the trope of the 'unfortunate' debtor to depict the insolvent poor as intentionally dishonest economic agents."[135] Since, as dominant nineteenth-century ideology assumes, the market is disinterested, anonymous, and therefore equitable, the poor are poor because they are not working hard enough and are lazily living off debt. The poor, in other words, deserve their fate. By the mid-nineteenth century, Finn shows, the poor were imprisoned in higher numbers than in the eighteenth century and debtors came to be classified as criminals. "A century and a half later," after the eighteenth-century debates and after the introduction of new credit instruments, "propertied insolvents had been supplanted by working-class debtors committed by the county courts. . . . [T]hese penal debtors were now classified—by law as by much public opinion—as culpable agents rather than unfortunate victims of circumstance."[136] Small claims courts took the power of imprisonment away from creditors, but, at the same time, they redefined the justification for imprisonment as penal so as to punish debtors for not paying, a redefinition that effectively criminalized poverty. The practice of imprisoning people who do not pay court fines imposed for not paying debts (often because they *cannot* pay it) continues today.[137]

How does the history of debt that I provide in this chapter help us understand the way fiction novelizes money? What does it allow us to say about downward mobility in the sentimental genre? First, it brings into political relief the slipperiness at the heart of capital's characterization of debt, or the way that the financial instruments that define capitalism circulate to silence the unequal economic conditions at their core. Only those with the power to leverage debt as equity profit from the practice of assignability and the anonymous financial instruments that grease the wheels of commerce and fuel economic growth. This profit comes at the cost of the poor, whose debts remain a sin, with slothfulness added to profligacy, and who remain imprisoned, just under different laws. But the very slipperiness that keeps debt a kinetic Janus-faced character (is it debt? is it equity?), provides the novel with a readymade catalyst; debt, not credit, always has a story to tell. As I show in chapter 2, the circulation of unfriended debt is central to the novel's deployment of characterization. The campaign and the law insist that the determination of good and bad debtors is an ontological one in which some people are essentially creditworthy and others are swindlers and frauds. But once debt is divorced from its original social relations and bought and sold anonymously, it ceases to be about ontological character and becomes a question of temporality and epistemology: when, for whom, and under what conditions are the debts procured? For this reason, the character of debt is different from the character of credit that Deidre Lynch and Margot Finn describe in relation to judging a person's ontological creditworthiness. Debt's character, not credit's, requires a narrative context that financial markets sublimate but that animates fiction, giving it great speculative energy.

Second, this analysis of debt's cultural and social history helps to explain why fictional stories of downward mobility are better poised than nonfiction tracts to narrate debt's slippery character. Before turning to the fictional technique of characterization in the novel, I close with an example from a commercial-conduct book that comes up against the temporal contradiction within capital's character of debt, a tension between debt as ontology and debt as epistemology that is registered when we ask the question: If one should never loan money to family and friends, who, then, are the friends that help each other when commercial networks break down and someone is in need of a loan? Thomas Cooke's *The Universal Letter Writer*, one of the many conduct books providing model letters to help a newly literate and trading populace, contains many sample epistles on topics concerning credit and debt. Taken together, they show the tensions that occur when the social consensus has it that one should never loan money to family or friends. In the moral universe of *The Universal Letter Writer*, sympathetic communities always help friends out when they experience financial exigency. But who is the friend that will help is known only retrospectively, after downward mobility has produced the need. The temporal tension makes visible the inability of the anonymous commercial world to provide moral universals for predicting the future; one can never know in advance whether the friend was creditworthy (awkward verb tense intentional). Only through the retrospective temporality of narrative can conduct literature imagine the world as a sympathetic place where friends help friends out.

Reading Cooke's sample letters regarding financial exigency provides a plot full of the dangers and risks of imperial capitalism. From the loss of a Jamaican-bound ship to a bad London loan, letter writers are in constant financial straits and are writing friends and associates to ask for credit or to bail them out of jail. In the ideal universe projected by the letters, the recipients always happily and positively respond, acting out of brotherly friendship and on the basis of the letter writer's moral character. Accidents happen, and as long as the letter writer can attest, as one insolvent does, that "the whole of my conduct has been consistent with the strictest rules of honesty," correspondents always act as friends and come up with money, extend repayment times, or agree to generous terms.[138] Breakdowns occur, not through the merchant's moral agency but because of *other* people's lack of honesty, never the letter writer's own. A tradesmen in "distressed circumstances" writes to his creditors to plead his case, explaining that "your petitioner . . . having lately trusted goods to a considerable amount, to a person in whom he placed the greatest confidence, he soon after became insolvent."[139] The creditor immediately agrees to offer him an extension and promises not to send him to prison. There is a temporal circularity to the moral bonds of social commerce in these letters in that financial commerce is projected to be built on the bonds of mutual assistance and love—friends help friends out, honest creditors extend assistance to honest debtors—yet friends need help because other friends have let them down. "Never lend friends money" makes sense in the wake of a friend's betrayal, but when the victims of those false friends go to other friends for money, the bonds of friendship require the loan. In other words, the moral imperative moves, circulating through the discourse on debt along with the character that it can never stabilize. Capital requires the moral imperative of brotherly love to be constantly shifting with the debt: sometimes the strangers who loan you money are friends, and sometimes the friends to whom you loan money should be strangers. The logic depends on keeping upward mobility an abstracted promise for all, but accessible only to a few. If you work hard, you will rise; if you fall, you may or may not have worked hard enough, depending on who you are.[140] Downward mobility thus has a more interesting and complicated story than upward mobility in this moment when debt is normalized as a fact of commercial life, and it provides more fertile ground for negotiating the epistemological contradictions at the heart of capital. The novel's narrative sequencing allows ample room to create financial communities where friends become strangers, and strangers friends. In fact, the greater ambiguity in the moral character of debt, the better the story, a formal effect of characterization that I discuss in the following chapter.

Leveraging Fiction
When Debt Becomes Equity

In a 2008 *Guardian* essay, Colin Burrow claims that "debt doesn't figure centrally in fiction today" though it once did, a circumstance he attributes to "[t]he separation of the financial sense of credit from its various moral and social senses."[1] Once credit and debt are expressed as a simple case of numbers, they no longer have a narrative, a story to tell. The historical separation of financial from moral and social debt was traced in the previous chapter, a shift required by capitalism's logic of accumulation and growth. For economies to grow, more money needs to circulate across larger geographical spaces and between a greater number of commercial agents, an expansion that breeds increased risk of failure and requires such failure to be expressed as a simple business matter and not a moral concern. We can trace the redefinition of financial debt as amoral into both the campaign against imprisonment and into the history of the novel. If, as Burrow suggests, monetary debt disappears from literature when it is no longer a moral or social concern, what happens in the latter eighteenth century? In this period, when economic growth begins its regular upward march and when the discursive separation of financial from moral debt is under way, debt has a story that is repeatedly told in the sentimental novel, figuring centrally in this fiction. After overviewing scenes of debt in the sentimental novel, this chapter turns to Henry Brooke's *The Fool of Quality* and Oliver Goldsmith's *The Vicar of Wakefield* and reads their use of characterization as a dynamic akin to the circulation of financial instruments. Debt's shifting characterization—as equity and as profligacy—reframes sentimental characterization as less about normalizing a trust in the creditworthiness of strangers than about divorcing the claims of friendship from the circulation of money.

It is hard to imagine a novel in the period that does not narrate debt. The visit to a debtor's prison is a conventional set piece, one we see in Henry Brooke's *The Fool of Quality* and Sarah Scott's *History of Sir George Ellison*, in which the hero displays his largesse and capacity for sympathy by relieving imprisoned debtors. "[O]f all Mr. Ellison's charities," Scott's narrator observes, "none gave him such exquisite delight as the release of prisoners confined for debt."[2] Embedded tales of misfortune invariably include unfair persecution for debt; for instance, in "A Pupil," a tale-within-a-tale-within-a-tale in Henry Mackenzie's

The Man of Feeling, Edward recounts the story of a prisoner whose jealous rival became master of his trading debts so he could imprison him.[3] Fear of imprisonment for debt—whether by a fair or spurious charge—haunts many novels. In Mackenzie's *Julia de Roubigné*, Julia's family repeatedly hovers on the brink of ruin, and the threat of imprisonment contributes to her decision to marry the man who pays off her family's hounding creditors. Herbert in Frances Brooke's *Lady Julia Mandeville* describes living with debt as living in a constant state of terror, a fear that was often realized in a pre-1869 Britain, where anyone could be arrested for debt at any time on anyone's whim. Clarissa's arrest for a debt she does not owe to the evil Sinclair is one example of many in which using a bailiff's writ with a trumped-up charge allows villains to imprison the innocent. Samuel Richardson had already used the motif in *Pamela* with Mr. B's arrest of Parson Williams. Clement in *The Fool of Quality* feigns an action for debt in an attempt to coerce Arabella into sex. Frances Sheridan's *Memoirs of Sidney Bidulph* includes the motif of an evil seducer laying a spurious charge in the embedded story of the flower seller whose father withers in debtor's prison because he refuses to sell his daughter to his landlord.

For all that the sentimental novel is drowning in debt, the debt imagined is almost always someone else's. George Ellison saves Mr. Maningham from debtor's prison, where he wallows not because of his own extravagance but for the debts he inherited from his father. Earlier in the novel, Ellison saves the merchant Mr. Hammond, whose impending bankruptcy is caused by his overly lenient extension of trading credit to a family that cannot pay. Mrs. Bilson's Griselda-like suffering, narrated in Fielding's *The Countess of Dellwyn*, is caused by her husband's profligacy; the spending habits of spouses also factor into *David Simple*'s portrayal of debt.[4] Mrs. Belville in Lennox's *Harriot Stuart* tells of her time imprisoned for debt because of her sister's refusal to budget for their downward mobility. Perhaps the most painful suffering for someone else's debts is that of Camilla in Burney's novel (though we could equally include *Cecilia* and *The Wanderer* in this list); Camilla pays her brother's debts, a selfless act that leads to her own difficulties, especially when her father is later imprisoned for debts she incurred that include money owed to save a poor family from eviction for debt. Sacrificing oneself for other people's spending habits is proof of one's moral fiber, proof we did not need from the loyal housekeeper Mrs. Jervis in *Pamela* but that Richardson adds to the sixth edition. Jervis in this later edition has been slowly paying off debts amounting to £36 incurred by her profligate children, debts that she is not legally, though she feels morally, obliged to pay.[5] If a character is not imprisoned or suffering because of money borrowed by someone else or because of a spurious charge, debt enters the novel as simple misfortune, money lost on a bad mortgage or payment for the necessities of life, such as what happens to Camilla and Valentine in the former case and David Simple in the latter, both in Sarah Fielding's novel.

Debtors in sentimental novels have two things in common: they are almost always portrayed sympathetically and their debts generate stories. Even—and, I hope to demonstrate below, especially—when debtors are the novel's protagonists, as in Henry Fielding's *Amelia* and Goldsmith's *Vicar of Wakefield*, they are positively characterized and invoke the reader's sympathy. Peter Lineham observes that heroes and heroines in eighteenth-century novels are more likely to be imprisoned for debt than villains, noting that "[s]ympathy was accorded to the debtor, but none was spared for the creditor."[6] The exception to Lineham's rule is Tobias Smollett's novels, which contain diverse renderings of debt, including the unusual portrayal of unrepentant flagrant debtors.[7] We might add the frequent appearance of gamblers in fiction who, while technically in debt, are often villains, though rarely central figures.

How might we interpret the widespread presence of sympathetic debtors as characters in sentimental fiction? What does the narratability of this figure tell us about the character of debt? The presence of debtors as victims of misfortune could be understood mimetically, as a reflection of how they are portrayed in nonfiction, especially within the campaign against imprisonment for debt. Fiction tells stories remarkably similar to the cases narrated in the sermons and tracts discussed in chapter 1. One could also read sympathetic debtors in literature as popularizing the new cultural assumption that being in debt is a necessary and widespread condition of living within a commercial market culture. In this reading, we might foreground how debt is linked to questions of morality, especially issues of reading moral character and judging who to trust and who is creditworthy. Critics have repeatedly aligned debt in fiction with characterization for this reason. In focusing on the question of creditworthiness, critics have noted how such representations negotiate capital's new credit relations, reading for the way novels imagine how to trust the moral character of strangers, given that social and moral bonds give way to the anonymous marketplace. Fictional characters are understood as akin to the self-actualizing individual required by commercial culture, the particular individual of Ian Watt's *Rise of the Novel*; in this interpretation, reading characters and reading individuals are analogous. For Margot Finn, fiction actually allows more room than political economy to explore the limits of individualism and to "expose the social and cultural forces that constrained contractual individualism in English market culture."[8] Novels challenge the anonymous credit market, Finn claims, by remembering how personal credit was often more complicated, entailing gifts and social obligations. Deirdre Lynch's *Economy of Character* also takes issue with an overemphasis on individualism. Character, Lynch persuasively demonstrates, cannot be reduced to the literary representation of the modern individual, complete with psychological interiority; rather, character in early fiction exteriorizes and maps social relations in the new market economy. Both Finn and Lynch read character in the novel for the way it functions like a credit rating, predicting which strangers to trust and negotiating anonymous market relations.

By associating literary character with the character of credit, critics compare the literary interpretive practice of reading character to aggregated credit evaluation, creating fictions of predictability with the confidence that past events determine futures through typology. In her book *Dead Pledges*, on contemporary credit crisis literature, Annie McClanahan, following Lynch and Finn, sees the credit rating of character as central to the history of realism: "Realist fiction taught readers to interpret literary characters on the basis of external details about dress, manners, and appearance; confidence that such details could produce accurate literary judgments produced, in turn, confidence in their economic equivalents." For McClanahan, the relationship between literary character and credit ratings is dialectical insofar as "[t]he practice of credit evaluation borrowed the realist novel's ways of describing fictional persons as well as the habits of reading and interpretation it demanded. And the realist novel, in turn, relied on the credit economy's models of typification . . . to produce socially legible characters."[9]

While I do not dispute the cultural work of literary character to function as a form of credit evaluation, aggregating characteristics in order to speculate on whether the stranger will turn out to be a friend, my own reading of character begins not from the perspective of credit but from that of debt. To query how debt informs literary character is to invoke a different temporality and to spotlight downward mobility. Rather than thinking about the way literary character normalizes a trust in speculative futures and imagines a world where strangers behave in predictable ways, I want to think about how fiction characterizes debt, especially in the moment of insolvency, and how it imagines friendship in the past. Ultimately, I propose that reading character in sentimental literature might be less about learning how to trust strangers in the anonymous marketplace than about teaching readers how not to trust friends, that is, how to negotiate the marketplace as if economic relations were only a matter of financial calculation.

That friends should not loan friends money is a proverb as old as money itself but one that has a particularly prescient role within capitalism, as illustrated by the discussion of James Stephen in chapter 1. The proverb remains a commonsense assumption that mediates social relations today. When I ask both my most radical leftist friends and Google about loaning friends money, they warn against it. Countless nightmare stories exist online of friendships ruined and lives torn apart, as in blogposts with titles like "10 Reasons Why You Should NOT Lend Money to Friends and Family" and "Never Lend Money to a Friend Repeat: Just Don't Do It."[10] Why has loaning money to a friend approached the status of a cultural taboo, not as strong as incest but almost as universal? There is no logical reason why learning to trust strangers with money should also require you not to trust friends; indeed, early credit evaluation methods such as those of the Guardians for the Protection of Trade against Swindlers entail bringing strangers into networks of friendship and warning people precisely which strangers were *not* your friends.

The cultural taboo around loaning friends money brings into focus the unique character of debt within capitalism, namely, the way debt and credit are not two sides of the same coin. To think about credit and debt as mirror images does not account for the way debt instruments are securitized under capitalism to produce the *more* of economic growth, a *more* that requires risk to be displaced from any social obligations—that is to say, from friendship—and requires credit and debt transactions to be "simply" a matter of numbers. Money needs to circulate free from attachments, as "unfriended," to achieve the fantasy of endless profit from circulating capital. The division of finance from friendship through anonymized debt contracts allows financial contracts to be used to leverage equity for profit. Such unfriending makes borrowing money on the equity in my house to invest in mutual funds at a greater rate of return seem the obvious choice, an easy numerical calculation. But who pays for the risk and what generates the profit? The dream of capital is that economic growth absorbs or eliminates the risk and that, in the end, markets produce more profits than losses for everyone, amounting to an aggregated gain. But buying and selling debt contracts manages risk by displacing responsibility onto a future that is not one's own, a process that makes credit and debt under capitalism asymmetrical. The asymmetry is illustrated in the difference between those with the power to leverage—or those with the equity necessary to use borrowed money to make more money—and those without the financial resources to do so who must pay their debts. That is, between the homeowner who is indentured to a high-cost interest-only mortgage and the homeowner who leverages a home equity line of credit to invest for greater returns in mutual funds. Both people are debtors, owing money on their houses, but the similarities end there. Critics such as Maurizio Lazzarato and Alison Shonkwiler argue that, because of this asymmetry, class divisions under global capital have been rewritten from those between workers and capitalists to those between creditors and debtors, those with liquidity and those without, or "those who work for money and those whose money works for them."[11]

Turning debt into a financial contract that can be transferred not only facilitates exchanges between strangers but allows creditors to *become* strangers, to erase the social obligations entwined with the risk, to deny a responsibility to the past. The introduction of increasingly sophisticated debt instruments—from bills of exchange, bonds, mortgages, and stocks at the beginning of the financial revolution to collateralized debt obligations, home equity loans, and redeemable preferred stock today—not only allows strangers to loan strangers money but also makes it difficult, and in some cases nearly impossible, to trace the stranger who owns the risk. Securitization, assignability, and transferability—not anonymity per se—defines debt under capitalism. The ability to make money on the promise of making money in the future—which is essentially what a debt security is—requires the unknown future to be freed from its past. The problem of loaning friends money is that you might need to help them out when the contingencies of the future mean they cannot make a payment. When, as happens in *The Vicar of Wakefield*, a house burns down, you might have to provide shelter to a friend.[12] If strangers loaned money as if they were friends, then James Stephen would not have ended up in jail, wealth inequality today would not be increasing, Lehman Brothers traders would be paying off millions of Americans' mortgages, and taxpayers would not be left cleaning up the environmental damage left by oil and gas corporations.

Thinking about literary character from the perspective of debt relations frames financial exchange in terms not of speculating on the future but of accounting for the past and remembering social relations, especially in moments of insolvency. In this way, characterizing the debtor in literature is similar to what is meant by characterizing financial instruments: *to characterize* is a legal term used to describe how financial instruments are categorized—whether as debt or equity—when a company declares bankruptcy or when calculating income tax; in other words, when it is determined who is paying for the risk. The difference between debt and equity is that a debt has a fixed term of repayment, a set interest rate, and the lender's risk is not tied to how the debtor uses the money; debts are contracts with set obligations. An equity, on the other hand, is more like ownership or stock. It is an investment in something whereby payment is tied to the value of that underlying something; payment is not fixed and the contract does not have a set time limit. Both debts and equities manage risk and time through contracts, as all financial instruments do, but the ways they profit from risk and time differ. Categorizing a security as an equity is not inherently better than categorizing it as a debt or vice versa; the power and profit come from the intrinsic equivocalness of financial instruments and in the magic of rendering the same financial exchange as two entirely different things. This is the power to take the cost of risk—the price of what does not happen in the future—and have it melt into air. The magic of disappearing risk, of certain debts not being repaid, depends on the belief that all economic calculations are purely financial and unfriended.[13]

Perhaps the most famous contemporary example of making risk disappear by exploiting the equivocations in characterizing financial instruments appeared after Enron declared bankruptcy in 2001. Executives and accountants at Enron used what is called mark-to-market accounting to include as equity the promise of future profits from power plants the moment Enron acquired them, thus making it appear on company financial statements as if Enron were not in debt, a practice that kept the company's stock price and executives' bonuses high. The company also hid debt by turning energy into a financial instrument so that it could be traded not as power to light homes in California but as a speculative contract bought and sold for profit. In the infamous Nigerian energy barge exchange, Enron "sold" the barges to Merrill Lynch, then later bought them back through an Enron-created subsidiary in order to erase a large amount of debt from company financial statements, meaning essentially that Enron listed Merrill Lynch's loan (the money it gave Enron supposedly for the barges) as profit. Since bonuses on Wall Street are calculated on profit lines, the incentive to characterize debt and equity in ways that produce the highest profit in the bottom line is huge.

The way a financial instrument is categorized matters significantly in the moment of loss, for this is when liquidation determines value, when the music stops and accounts must be balanced. According to eighteenth-century bankruptcy law, if the loss comes from buying and selling—that is, from equity—then it does not need to be repaid and the investors must assume the cost of the risk. But if it comes from debt, it registers as consumptive excess, as not spending within one's means, and this debt must be repaid. How one tells the difference, as the campaign against imprisonment for debt demonstrates, is a question of perspective. Did James Stephen take risks he should not have? Or was it simply a liquidity problem that his enemies turned against him? The distinction between business debt and consumer debt masks the equivocation that all financial instruments hold no matter their origins. Capital's endless circulation obfuscates this equivocation while profiting from the illusion of stability; for instance, investment companies promise they can predict the future and "manage risk," but at the same time they do not pay for your losses. Economic growth depends on characterization remaining an ignis fatuus, the ever-changing vanishing point where risk evaporates. Capital acts as if the light is really there, that aggregating risk erases the contingency of the future to ensure all exchanges are simple financial calculations, and, simultaneously, it shines the light in the faces of the poor who do not have the power to equivocate.

What does literary characterization have in common with characterizing a debt? And if financial characterization occurs at the moment of insolvency, what might we learn about literary character from narratives that end up in debtor's prison? I argue that literary character circulates in narratives like financial instruments in that character profits from a dynamic of risk and the equivocations of infinitely recirculating value. The interpretation of a character's actions and motivations, both predicting the future and ascribing meaning to the past, is endlessly deferred and is dependent on perspective. At the same time, as James Phelan has demonstrated, characters must contain some predictable behaviors and be logically coherent such that certain characteristics limit or fix a character's future actions. In response to David Lodge's argument that characters are simply a collection of words, which means that a narrator could very well describe a character as "short but tall," Phelan points out that there are constraints on characterization and the same narrator could not later say of this same character that they were "an easy man to pin down."[14] Narrative profits from imagining character as both fixed and variable, as having an ontological stability or coherence (she is trustworthy) while simultaneously subjecting character to epistemological uncertainty (she could betray anyone at any time). Characters evoke greater readerly interest when they produce that uncertainty, when the dynamic between fixed and variable characteristics introduces interpretative enigmas. Thinking about literary character as generated through a dynamic between fixed and variable textual meanings shifts the analysis of character away from properties of individual characters (Is the character "flat" or "round"? Do they change or remain the same? Are they "believable" or "relatable"?) toward the hermeneutic act of reading character, to the interplay between reader and text. My friends who voraciously read detective fiction often tell me that they read "not for the plot but for the character," by which I take them to mean that the hermeneutic enigma that propels them through the narrative does not come from the complexity of predicting story events but from understanding a character. The complexity of reading character, I argue, emerges not from whether a character evolves or is psychologically complex but from what risks a text takes with misinterpretation, with a misunderstanding of character—risks that call for more-complex interpretative strategies. The risks of misinterpretation are often highest with indirect characterization and with the narrator's tone toward a character—for instance, the satiric rendering of Booth in *Amelia* or Primrose in *The Vicar of Wakefield*.

Indirect characterization, whereby knowledge of a character requires the reader to make inferences from contextualizing speech and action, is riskier than direct characterization, whereby the narrator tells the reader who the character is. When Eliza Haywood and Henry Fielding read Pamela's character as that of a prostitute in their satiric rewritings, they do so because Richardson's epistolary first-person form characterizes Pamela indirectly, through her own words, and the risks of such indirect characterization are skepticism and doubt. But the higher the risk, the greater the enigma of character, a quality that Richardson perhaps achieves more successfully with his multiperspectival *Clarissa*. Sentimental novels with direct characterization, such as *The Fool of Quality* and *Sir George Ellison*, hazard little with their central heroes and demonstrate, by contrast, how the risk of misinterpretation pays off in interpretative layers not present in Brooke's or Scott's didactic novels. Direct characterization, however, can also be risky if the tone or the narrator's perspective toward a character introduces enigmas. An ironic tone or an unreliable narrator requires a more complicated interpretation of a character. By introducing the chance for misinterpretation and calling on the reader to infer, judge, and make meaning, texts leverage the narrative dynamic by postponing fixed meaning and circulating character to turn a profit.

Below I contrast *The Fool of Quality* with *The Vicar of Wakefield* to demonstrate how leveraging character—taking on interpretative risk for narrative profit—makes it harder to trace the social obligations that debt relations entail. What does it mean that whereas Harry Fenton in *The Fool of Quality* obsessively balances his books and pays off all debts, including debts that should not need to be repaid, Primrose in *The Vicar of Wakefield* is released from debtor's prison without paying his debts and reaps enormous profits from the risks he takes? The contrast between the two novels reveals something about the narrative energy of capital to produce character. Both *The Fool of Quality* and *Sir George Ellison* risk little with their central heroes, and in both, all debts are paid; they also contain debt within embedded stories of downward mobility. Alternatively, the ironic and indirect characterization of Primrose and Booth introduces greater narrative risks that end up accruing profits for their debtor-heroes as neither is required to pay their debts.

In characterizing debt through the dynamic of character, I argue that the equivocations of risk and time that define financial instruments also generate the interpretative pleasures of reading character. In so doing, the debtors in downward mobility narratives often become the place where sentimental novels configure capital's social obligations; how we read characters—in both the particular and the general sense—becomes the same as how we characterize their debt. Narrative theory's engagement with literary character as a dynamic or dialectic is at the heart of the specific homology between financialized debt and character that is, I posit, central to sentimental fiction.

Narrative theory often begins discussion of character with a statement about the paucity of works in the discipline that delineate its function. Rimmon-Kenan, for instance, claims that "the elaboration of a systematic, non-reductive but also non-impressionistic theory of character remains one of the challenges poetics has not yet met."[15] Alex Woloch refers to character as "the bête noire of narratology," and he identifies the problem as originating in the constitutive "antinomy" between humanist and structuralist definitions of character.[16] Humanist interpretations—such as Forster's conceptualization of "flat" and "round"—understand characters as representing human beings and see the study of character as the study of what it means to be human, ranging from psychological to sociological engagements that explore identification and affect, such as cognitive theory. The popular version of a humanist reading would be the conflation of character with person in order to evaluate a character's "relatability." Structuralists, on the other hand, reject the human quality of character, positing, as Barthes does in *S/Z*, that character is simply a "vulgar bookkeeping" system, a proper name, in which "the person is no more than a collection of semes," of descriptive attributes and personality traits.[17] From A. J. Greimas's "actantial" model to Hélène Cixous's indictment of the humanist model as bourgeois, structuralists counter humanist referential readings with a semiotic mapping of character in a semantic field.[18] In Woloch's dynamic model, reading character as referencing real people and as structure are not mutually exclusive, because, he argues, "the literary character is itself divided, always emerging at the juncture between structure and reference. In other words, a literary *dialectic* that operates dynamically within the narrative text gets transformed into a theoretical *contradiction*, presenting students of literature with an unpalatable choice: language *or* reference, structure *or* individuality." Woloch's own study reads the dynamic of character through minor characters, and he sees the dialectic between structure and reference as "generative of, and integral to, narrative signification."[19] I argue that the dynamic is akin to the dialectic between debt and equity, between fixed structure and variable individuals, or between aggregating character to predict the future and embracing and profiting from particular contingencies. Both are part of how characterization circulates within literary narrative and of how we parse what makes some characters more interesting than others. The greater the risk of misunderstanding, of misinterpreting a character, the greater a character sustains the tension at the heart of narrative signification and interpretative pleasure. The dynamic of character, the interplay between character as predictive of plot and character as open to risk, I argue, is liquidated in moments of insolvency in the sentimental novel in ways that make visible debt's social obligations.

The Sentimental Hero and Debt Forgiveness in *The Fool of Quality*

No one would ever read *The Fool of Quality* for its character. Harry Fenton is fixed and predictable as a sentimental hero with wealth to leverage. Neither he nor his uncle introduce any disequilibrium to generate a narrative; that lack is filled by other people's financial misfortunes told in episodic embedded tales. Sentimental fiction in general is not known for its depth of characterization, and Harry can be compared to Sir Charles Grandison and Sir George Ellison as heroes who are implausibly good-hearted and morally perfect.[20] Deirdre Lynch thinks about such "characterless" heroes in the context of mid-eighteenth-century "fiction of social circulation." She reads Smollett's novels but she could easily have illustrated her argument with *The Fool of Quality*. Lynch defines "fictions of social circulation" as narrating "the education of a gentleman who eventually becomes worthy of the station assigned him. . . . Characterization is conceived of as the medium of this education. Worth accrues to the gentleman-in-the-making in proportion as . . . he samples the world's variety and familiarizes himself with a range of social conditions and degrees."[21] The characterlessness of the protagonist, to Lynch, supplies the disinterested standpoint necessary for the educated gentleman to learn types and judge other people as objects of sympathy or distrust. Thus, the hero who lacks psychological depth maps the typology of creditworthiness through his sampling of the world's characters. Character is here understood as social type, and judging creditworthiness requires a disinterested standpoint, one that contemporary credit ratings agencies argue they perform with their objective calculations.[22] Nick Valvo demonstrates that sentimentalist conceptions of charity also require disinterestedness and are premised on an understanding of individual moral agency that requires anonymity in charity. Stranger benevolence is the only way to guarantee moral virtue because it "purif[ies] humane relationships . . . of instrumental considerations."[23] The greater distance one has from the poor debtor, the purer one's intentions in relieving them. Sentimentalism promotes anonymous acts between strangers in that it sees the absence of previous social obligations as the best proof of the genuineness of feeling. A friend might want something unstated in return for the gift given.

By reading character from the perspective of debt and not credit, however, a different interpretation of the disinterested and "characterless" hero emerges, one that reads Harry's social education in an unfriended world as training him to mediate all relations through financial calculations. Divorced from his family and community, Harry learns to read other people as financial instruments and as possible investments. I argue that the opposite of sentimentalism's disinterested charity is its characterization of money that passes between friends as always already tainted by the instability of ulterior motives and, ultimately, as replacing moral obligations to family and inherited community with a moral calculation that requires anonymized and subjectively aggregated financial transactions, the same calculation that characterizes debt within capitalism. *The Fool of Quality* accumulates moral capital for its hero by participating in a world in which financial exchanges between strangers can be neatly balanced out, with the hero performing the role of double-entry bookkeeper who ensures all debts are paid. But when we read from the perspective of the debtors' characters, another vision emerges, one in which friends do not loan friends money and in which Harry can balance the books only by paying for risks that others should have paid.

The Fool of Quality presents its readers with a challenge in that its episodic nature, self-reflective Stern-like dialogues between author and critic, and embedded moral tracts make it virtually unreadable today. The novel has been variously described as an example of Irish experimentalism, a "children's book," "[a] supremely digressive and eccentric tale," and, by Samuel Coleridge, an "enchanting Daydream Novel."[24] The episodic (non)plot of Henry (Harry) Clinton's education is heavily influenced by the Enlightenment pedagogical theories of Rousseau and Locke, in which subjects are the product of experience, industry, and individual self-discovery (*The Fool of Quality* was, in turn, a major influence on Thomas Day's similarly didactic educational fable *Sandford and Merton*). The plot, such as it is, involves Harry, the neglected second son of the earl of Moreland, whose older brother, Richard, is favored by his decadent aristocratic parents simply because he is heir to the family fortune. The constitutive unfairness of primogeniture in Harry's life repeats a similar dynamic within the previous Moreland generation, in which the earl, also named Richard, inherited the world from his parents while his brother, also named Henry, was apprenticed to a merchant and given a small settlement, a disproportioning of love that translates into the elder Henry's estrangement. The merchant to whom the elder Henry is apprenticed replaces his blood family, a substitution explicitly consolidated through money: "[A]s your Father did not behave like a Father toward you, in the Dividend which he made between you and your Brother, . . . I make you a present of this Note of 12000*l*."[25] Eventually, the merchant offers Henry a full partnership in his firm and marriage to his daughter. After years accumulating enormous sums—sums that, we later find out, are large enough to finance Charles I's expedition from Holland (4:206)—the elder Henry, disguised as an old man named Mr. Fenton, returns to his brother's neighborhood and, seeing the corrupt home life and neglect that the younger Henry suffers, kidnaps him and gives him a sentimental education. Not until adolescence, when they receive the news that Harry's mother and brother have died, does Harry discover Fenton is his uncle, whereupon the two return to the Moreland estate. After a melodramatic reunion scene with the now-remorseful earl, who has learnt the lesson that money does not buy happiness, the earl dies and Harry inherits the estate cured of its degeneracy by sentimental capital.[26]

Debt in *The Fool of Quality*, with its concomitant embedded stories of downward mobility, generates the bulk of the novel's narrative energy, providing the occasion for Harry's moral lessons and allowing him to circulate his wealth for good. Charity contributes to Harry's moral capital at a pace similar to that of Sarah Scott's in *Millenium Hall* and *Sir George Ellison*: paying the debts of the poor repeatedly translates into the expansion of wealth—the individual's, the nation's, and the colony's. *The Fool of Quality*'s unrelentingly optimistic view of capitalism's potential for universal upward mobility and growth is repeated throughout the text. Set piece after set piece illustrates the reciprocal gain theory of trade in which productive industry leads to greater profits for all through the simple circulation of money as capital. Fenton is, in many ways, this capital personified. When he settles in a new neighborhood, he invites all the worthy poor—that is, people whose "character" can be turned into equity—to regular Sunday dinner and gives them each one crown. With the crown, the poor are able to pay off their small debts and invest in manufacturing implements, such as a wheel to spin wool, and "[t]heir wealth increased with their industry" (1:183). Unlike Burney's Cecilia, who sees her wealth as a straight-up "debt to the poor," Harry looks upon his money "to have been already extracted from the earnings of the poor, the poor farmer, the poor craftsmen, the hard-handed peasant, and the day labourer," and upon his debt as owed not to them since they are sufficiently provided for, but to those who are even poorer (5:23).[27] To these poor he owes the capital investment that will turn them into industrious farmers, craftsmen, and peasants. The climax to the plot of reciprocal gain is arguably the extended passage on canal building in volume 5, in which capital investment is portrayed as charity; building the commercial infrastructure of a national waterway to get goods to market cheaper and faster is imagined as the apex of Harry's charitable pursuits ("the greatest of Charities, a charity to Great Britain, a charity to mankind" [5:47–48]).[28]

In this utopic world where circulating capital leads to everyone's needs being met, merchants are portrayed as the ultimate heroes: "[T]he Wealth, Prosperity, and Importance of everything upon earth arises from the TILLER, the MANUFACTURER and the MERCHANT. . . . The merchant, above all . . . furnishes every comfort, convenience, and elegance of life . . . and weaves into one web the affinity and brotherhood of all mankind" (1:103–4). The pillars of society are not the aristocracy, since, Brooke asserts, the gentlemen of landed property would lose nine-tenths of their wealth without Industry and Commerce raising the "products of lands to tenfold their natural Value" (1:105). By circulating capital through trade, merchants unite the world in a sentimental brotherhood of mutual needs. As Mary Peace has noted, "Commerce here is clearly the engine of sentimental affiliation: virtue and commerce, the things of the world and the moral universe, seem quite reconciled."[29] The reconciliation is made possible through Christian benevolence and a Protestant moderation that checks avarice. Not consuming above one's needs is a virtue: Mr. Meekly refuses the earl's money because, with £700 a year of his own, he has no needs that are not met (1:97). Acquiring only that which is useful is another moral rule; as Fenton schools Harry, "[T]hat . . . which you cannot use, cannot belong to you" (1:180), and thus when Harry receives from Fenton the gift of a coat when he already has one, he learns to give it away and, in return, receive "the gift of doing good to poor people" (1:180). The novel does not question or even specify the origins of Fenton's wealth except to make general comments such as "we sent out Ships to the east, and to the west, and wealth came pouring in upon us from all quarters of the globe" (3:45–46). That Fenton begins with wealth to leverage is what allows the fantasy that economic growth occurs through a sentimental circulation of use value, and not through the circulation of commodities as financial instruments or through an M-C-M′ exchange grounded in colonial violence.

Brooke's sunny representation of a capitalism checked by sentimental virtue and founded in the industrious exchange of use values leads him to represent as common sense the assumption that all debts must be repaid. I discuss David Graeber's unraveling of the logic behind this assumption in the previous chapter. Graeber demonstrates how the claim that "all debts must be paid" rests on the historical fallacy that places the origins of money in barter. This false narrative, Graeber shows, has consequences for the ways we imagine the social obligations of debt, and his counter–origin story argues that money's origins lie with debt between friends, not in barter between strangers. Unsurprisingly, *The Fool of Quality* circulates the false origin story during the scene in which Harry and his tutor, Clement, report to Fenton on their visit to debtor's prison. Fenton interrupts their description with a long digressive lecture on the history of law, commerce, and debt:

> Before money became the medium of commerce, the simple business of the world was carried on by truck, or the commutation of one commodity for another. But, when men consented to fix certain rateable values upon money, as a ready and portable equivalent for all sorts of effects, credit was consequently introduced, by the engagements of some, to pay so much money in lieu of such commodities, or to deliver such or such commodities on the advance of so much money; and states found it their interest to support such public credit, by enforcing the performance of said engagements. (3:248)

The story begins with barter, then moves to money to solve the problem of the "double coincidence of wants," and then ends with the introduction of credit to provide the grease for the wheels of commerce and lubricate the ever-expanding networks of wants. As I discuss in the introduction with the help of Graeber's critique, the narrative in which barter precedes credit is likely backward; various systems for recording debts were introduced long before money as currency or a medium of exchange. Positing that debt precedes money makes visible an economic genealogy that remembers debt's roots within nonnumerical economic systems; that is to say, it describes when debt was the way we negotiated our obligations to each other and divided up resources within our communities. Credit systems that calculate debt by counting coins facilitate exchange between strangers, but the problem with the barter origin story is that it leaves out the central role economic systems play in managing what it is we owe each other. An economic system concerns the ethical principles through which we divide shared resources and is not a matter of simple financial calculation; this is what is forgotten in the representation of repaid debts as balancing account books. In other words, the questionable origin story that Brooke narrates in *The Fool of Quality*, that Smith recounts in *The Wealth of Nations*, and that most introductory economic textbooks repeat today masks the way wealth is generated in capitalism, not through a simple exchange of commodities—Fenton buying goods in America on credit to sell them later in England—but through buying and selling debt itself as a commodity, thus initiating a cycle of disappearing risk dependent on economic growth.

In turning to the novel's representation of financial insolvency, and specifically to Harry's visit to debtor's prison, I argue that Brooke's characterless hero—whose moral perfection and pro-merchant propagandizing introduces no interpretative risks—ends up paying the risks of capital that others do not pay. In this way, the novel provides a direct example of how sentimental ideology is the softer side of the same capitalist coin. Reading debt here illustrates the way charity under capitalism takes the form of a subsidy for the rich, analogous to contemporary food banks that provide the costs of the reproduction of labor that the employer's payment of a minimum wage does not. By paying debts that should not be repaid, I argue, Harry is simply paying the real costs of the capital Fenton has accumulated, and thus his generosity is no generosity at all. Charity as capital investment is a theme that emerges over the course of Harry's education as his charitable relief is more like buying stock in the debtors' future than like paying a debt. The same logic used by the Society for the Relief of Small Debts is narrated here: imprisoned debtors represent an aggregate loss of future wages, and relieving them will produce a net gain in the nation's wealth.

The interpretative challenge for the reader of *The Fool of Quality* is not in judging character but in keeping all the novel's characters straight as they proliferate in episode after episode in which strangers narrate debt and Harry and his uncle relieve them. The debtors whose stories are narrated are almost entirely those with plots of downward mobility, those who once had money but now have none. People in debt from everyday structural poverty—because wages do not cover living costs or because an illness leads to unemployment—occasionally appear in the novel but not as characters with stories to tell. Characters' interest, the amount of space their story takes up, is calculated by their past equity.

The fictitious value of Giffard Homely, a beggar introduced in volume 4, is a good fifty pages. Homely enters the novel offstage, as a robber who reportedly stole a loaf of bread. The robber turns out to be a beggar with a wife and seven children who did not steal the bread but was given it by Mr. Niggard's boy as charity. Mr. Niggard, a man whose debts Harry had previously relieved to the sum of £25, refuses his boy's charity and wants Homely arrested for theft. Harry not only pays for extra loaves of bread and gives the boy money to reward his generous spirit, but also forgives Mr. Niggard in the hope that—typecast name aside—he will reform his ways. In return for saving him from prison, Homely tells Harry his story. Debt is characterized twice in the tale as simply a problem of leveraging; Homely defaults on money owed because family or friends to whom he has loaned money have not repaid him, including his brother. Like both Henrys, Homely is the second son and thus was apprenticed to a tanner upon his father's death, while his spendthrift brother burns through the family inheritance. When his brother's creditors "fell upon him, [Homely] became his bail for two hundred pounds" (4:166). His brother absconds without paying, and the bailiffs come looking for Homely; to escape imprisonment, he runs away to Lincolnshire, where he goes to work for another tanner. Though lacking capital, he is industrious and hardworking—merits the tanner recognizes by allowing him to marry his daughter. The tanner wagers that, because of his character, Homely "is richer, in my eye, than a spender with thousands," and the wager pays off when, with the daughter's dowry functioning as capital, Homely builds "a Malt-house, and Wind-mill, and planted a large Orchard, with other profitable improvements that cost [him] . . . eight hundred pounds" (4:174, 176). However, misfortune falls a second time, and Homely's generosity in loaning friends money causes trouble again. His neighbor Freestone Hardgrave, a mean bachelor whose "avarice outgrew even the growth of his wealth," wants to take over Homely's little farm and Homely refuses to sell (4:177). Hardgrave then plots Homely's downfall by appealing to his generosity and acquiring a hefty loan from Homely on false pretenses. Homely gives him 230 guineas he has on hand to pay his rent, and though he asks for a written agreement, Hardgrave defers. The narratively predictable happens when Hardgrave does not return the money and Homely cannot pay his rent. His landlord repossesses "all that I was worth," liquidating it for one-third its value (4:181). He and his family end up homeless, starving and begging for a loaf of bread.

Homely's story is only one of many such tales that expand and fill up the novel's five volumes, at least one of which circulated separately in pamphlet form.[30] The sheer number of plot twists in each story, the countless ups and downs, make it almost impossible to keep the characters and the stories straight, and thus when characters return later, it is hard to remember who they are. The proliferation of unindividuated characters has the effect of producing subjects similar to the Society's aggregated objects of charity: anonymous and undifferentiated but universally sympathetic. Losing a fortune and then providentially gaining another carries little interpretative weight, and the effect is a flattening out of characters and plot to foreground the repetition of a narrative pattern: never loan money to friends. Doing so ends repeatedly in personal disaster.

The narrative exchange here mirrors that of the stories-within-stories I discuss in chapter 3: the act of narrative within narratives often turns strangers into friends. Here, there is an added hitch in that storytelling reveals strangers to actually *be* friends, just friends who have not yet recognized each other. The melodramatic plot twists that have storytellers turn out already to be friends test the limits of verisimilitude but weave complex credit networks of good-hearted people. For instance, Homely's story concludes with an episode in which he saves the life of a nobleman and his wife who nearly drown while crossing a river. The reader instantly recognizes the nobleman as Fenton since he has previously narrated such an incident. Fenton is now able to reimburse Homely for saving his life by righting the wrongs that have been done to him, including providing initial investments "upon good securities" "toward beginning a Fortune" for his three daughters' dowries (4:222). The motif of friends needing to be strangers first in order to recognize themselves as friends serves several functions in the novel: it generates countless melodramatic reunion scenes between long-lost family members; it accentuates the presence of class mobility since what makes friends unrecognizable is their poverty, a poverty easily turned into wealth; and it simultaneously allows bonds of inherited class to remain firm, having been purified of ulterior motives through the process of disinterested charity. The entire frame of the novel—Harry not recognizing Fenton as his uncle but loving him like a father—is structured around this motif. Similarly, the misrecognition of the kidnapped gentry child Ned as a beggar boy whom Harry virtuously befriends lasts volumes, until Ned's true parentage is discovered and he is reunited with his parents, who turn out to be Fenton's friends. There is even a curious "double coincidence of wants" when Fenton's old, loyal servant has money to give but no relations at the exact moment when an old beggar woman tells her story, which leads to the servant and beggar recognizing each other as long-lost husband and wife.

The combination of stories that caution against loaning friends money with stories that lead to the recognition of strangers as friends frees the financial exchange between friends from the taint of interestedness. Narrative coincidence manages to mask the unfriendliness of the financial market's disinterestedness. Harry helps Homely out before it is revealed that Fenton owes him his life, and thus Harry's charity appears disinterested. But this narrative timing also has the effect of dividing financial transactions from social ones, a division at the heart of capital's transformation of debt into a financial instrument. This circulation of money allows what should be an ethical given of a society—that we save each other's lives and help those in need—to be a financial transaction representing an exceptional case and illustrating Harry's individual charitable character. Harry's visit to debtor's prison renders explicit the way that calculating debt as a de-individuated number that must be repaid leads to a culture in which abstract numbers trump contextual judgment in deciding meaning.

Harry and Clement's visit to Fleet prison takes place under a strict financial mandate from Fenton: he gives Harry £1,500 for the pleasure of relieving debtors, £500 of which is to relieve those imprisoned for less than £10, with the remaining £1,000 to "be applied to the . . . Relief of those Prisoners of Note, whose Cases and Calamities call for singular Compassion" (2:231). In other words, rich people who fall demand more resources because they have stories to tell. When Harry returns, he confesses to spending £1,000 over his limit, but Fenton quickly forgives him because "I shall be overpaid and enriched by the narration" (3:227). Stories compensate for the financial expenditure, and only downwardly mobile people with past equity have stories worth telling. Clement explicitly names this narrative accounting when they return, reporting that they released ninety-five prisoners with the £500, but he will not individuate any for they were "journeymen, taylors or weavers . . . [not] a single circumstance of whose story was worth reciting" (3:237). The stories "worth reciting" are those of downward mobility in which debt emerges from complications in social networks, including networks of transferable contracts and circulating financial instruments, and in which, repeatedly, blameless people are imprisoned for the faults of their friends.

The first prisoner's story narrated, contra to what I have just claimed, is a rare tale of an unsympathetic debtor, told not by himself but by the jailer. The story is used to introduce Brooke's expository argument against imprisonment for debt. Sink, a German prince, acts like an early investment broker: his character accrues "unmeasurable credit" and "numbers . . . deposited their substance in his hands, in order to be laid out at interest on securities" (3:239). When he cashes in the money and tries to leave the country, one creditor stops him in time, and then all his other creditors line up to stake their claims. He refuses to give them their money, and they cannot access it through bankruptcy courts, because he has hidden it in a series of bank accounts under fake names. He flaunts his money in prison by living high, flouting the sacred rule that all debts must be repaid. Sink's actions outrage Clement, who wishes that the laws of the Grecians and Romans that allowed for the whipping and forced labor of debtors applied to Britain. But Harry disagrees, citing God's eternal laws of virtue and equity that do not allow the imprisonment of a person's body for a crime against property—an argument commonly made in the campaign tracts as well. In fact, the novel at this point breaks into a tract against imprisonment for debt, and its portrayal of Sink, the recalcitrant debtor, serves the purpose of making the larger argument about the aggregate advantage of forgiving debts since many people contract debts not through vanity and intemperance but through "unavoidable damages by water, by fire, the crush of power, oppressive landlords, and more oppressive lawsuits, death of cattle, failure of crop, [and] failure of payment in others" (3:249).[31] These debtors are "blameless" and their ruin is punishment enough (3:249). After Sink, all the debtors in *The Fool of Quality* are predictable and tell the same "blameless" story of family credit networks breaking down. "Have you ever a pretty story for me?" Fenton asks Harry when the expository section against imprisonment for debt comes to an end (3:252).

The "pretty" stories Harry tells reveal how sentimental charity compensates for the profits of circulating capital by paying debts that should not be repaid. The imprisoned debtor Mr. Stern is a poor orphan who, as a child, was placed with his wealthy uncle to manage his £120-a-year estate, a position he views as insipid dependency, calling it "much harder and more insulting than any service to a stranger" (3:261). When Stern falls in love and marries his uncle's daughter, the uncle disowns him. Years later, after the wife has died, Stern ends up in debtor's prison with his daughter, held because they accepted money that they thought was a gift from a distant relative but turns out to have been a credit trap. The daughter invests the £25 "gift" in a millinery business, but the bailiffs arrive to arrest her on a writ from the aptly named Jonathan Delvil, an evil seducer who uses the debt as blackmail, offering to free them from prison in exchange for the daughter's virtue. Harry immediately pays to free them and gives them £50 to invest in the shop, but the original debt, contracted under false pretenses, should not have been repaid. Delvil intentionally caused the Sterns to default on their business loan and thus he should pay the risk of his investment. Instead, Harry pays, legitimating Delvil's behavior by honoring a contract that should have been declared unethical. In the sentimental novel, however, paying for capital's unfair risks ends up being an investment that reaps huge rewards. When a contrite uncle returns to reclaim the family he disowned, the Sterns emerge richer than ever, aided by a surprise West Indian inheritance, and thus they return Harry's money with a profit and direct him to relieve the debt of another family in prison. Harry then circulates the charitable capital to the Ruth family, whose debt has also been caused by a family feud.[32] Cheated out of his inheritance by an elder brother, Mr. Ruth is eventually seduced into borrowing money from two men, Heartless and Hollow, who pretend to be his friends but who are actually loaning him money they have been given by his brother for the purpose of entrapping Ruth in a debt contract. Debt's transferability—the loan from Heartless is actually a loan from Ruth's brother—is here used as a weapon, and the bailiffs arrive to imprison Ruth. Given that the debt was contracted under false pretenses, paying it would wrongly legitimate heartlessness, but Harry pays it even though doing so puts him over his £1,500 limit for debt relief. Once again, the financial risk of corrupt creditors is paid for by sentimental charity, an exchange that directly represents sentimental narrative's capacity to balance capitalism's ethical accounts. Harry is so pleased with Ruth's story that he persuades him "to repeat it over and over, that I might remember it the better" (3:290).

Brooke's obsessive narration of the financial accounting assumes that the columns of credit and debt can be balanced and a family member's past betrayal can be compensated by a stranger's present benevolence. But by turning a stranger's debt into his moral and social equity, especially debt produced by the fictional equity of downward mobility, Harry repays debts that should not be paid, absorbing the cost of other's risks. Assuming the costs of other people's greed and cruelty, I argue, is the narrative price of the main character's characterlessness: since other characters' debts must generate the story and since the only stories "worth reciting" are those of downward mobility, the novel invests in characters as financial instruments whose past value can be leveraged for narrative progression. *The Fool of Quality* takes a stranger's debt and opens it up to a future in which wrongs can be righted and the *more* of economic growth produces an infinity of wealth and happiness.

Take the case of the earl's friend Meekly, who tells his story in the final volume. When he comes of age orphaned, he draws £700 on his uncle's account to travel to Europe, but then his uncle remarries and he calls in the debt, leading to Meekly's arrest while he is in Holland. A charitable stranger happens upon him and remarks that his "[a]ppearance exacts something more from my inclinations" (5:56); in other words, he looks as if he once was rich and now is poor. The stranger pays off the large sum while simultaneously calling it a "pretended debt" since the uncle morally owes the money to his nephew (5:57). Meekly insists on signing an IOU though the stranger charges that he has been "already repaid with usury, in the opportunity of serving an injured and a worthy man" (5:57–58). A few years later, when Meekly's uncle dies repentant, Meekly inherits a fortune and immediately sends a bill to Holland to repay the anonymous stranger, but his creditor cannot be found. Ever honest, Meekly then lays out the money "on the best securities that I could procure," and in the thirty-five years since, "the principal, with interest upon interest, yearly turned into capital, has amounted to nearly five thousand pounds" (5:65). After he tells his story to Harry, Fenton arrives and we discover that "the stranger" is Fenton, and storytelling once again turns anonymous charity into profit. The narrative never probes where the "interest upon interest" comes from, and the "best securities" likely include other strangers' debts, in particular those whose stories are not "worth reciting." Every debt in *The Fool of Quality* is turned into equity by the hero's charitable investments, but, as I have endeavored to show, by participating in a moral accounting in which "all debts must be repaid," the novel reveals not only sentimental morality as picking up the costs of the anonymous financial market, but also the way narrative progression requires risk. Turning to *The Vicar of Wakefield*, we see a different way of characterizing debt. Unlike those in *The Fool of Quality*, the Vicar's debts do not require repayment—a difference, I argue, of characterization, of the fact that the hero in this case is the debtor, not the one providing relief.

The Vicar of Wakefield and the Bonds of Debt

The Vicar of Wakefield, like *The Fool of Quality*, includes a sentimental scene in debtor's prison, but unlike that in *Fool of Quality*, the hero's visit occurs involuntarily, because he himself is the prisoner. Goldsmith's satiric characterization of his hero, coupled with the Vicar's fiscal misfortunes, produces a very different kind of novel than *The Fool of Quality*, one in which the equivocalness of character and the downwardly mobile plot is exploited for narrative effect. *The Vicar of Wakefield*'s continued popularity in contrast to the relative obscurity of *The Fool of Quality* says something about their distinct interpretive energies. The satiric tone of *The Vicar* calls upon the reader to judge both Primrose and his debts, yet the dialectic of characterization makes easy judgments impossible. The complexity of reading the Vicar's character propels the narrative forward in a way that characterization in *The Fool of Quality* does not. Goldsmith's use of ambiguous and indirect characterization for Primrose mirrors the text's equivocations in characterizing its debts, especially around interpreting what responsibility the Vicar has to pay them. Who is this famously lovable yet willfully ignorant character? Primrose's character is never fixed, and this instability keeps the narrative progressing at the same time that Primrose circulates free from the risks of his past. In some ways, Primrose is the ideal character of capital, circulating among strangers to increase his value (the novel closes with his fortune restored and his children married into wealth), and yet he never pays for the costs of the risks he takes.

The implausible series of coincidences that conclude *The Vicar of Wakefield* and that turn the novel's extreme financial losses into providentially enormous gains, includes a significant plot omission, one that, to my knowledge, has not been noted by other scholars.[33] While other mysteries are explained in detail (for instance, how his daughter Sophia's abductor is identified by his long legs and facial scar), the facts of how and by whom Primrose is released from prison are never provided. The reader is never entirely certain what debt he has been arrested for, whether it is for rent owing or for the unpaid bond given to secure his son George's position in the army.[34] He pays the steward with his cattle, which are then liquidated "for less than half their value," and thus the text points us to the bond as the source of the writ against him (121). Whatever the reason for Primrose's imprisonment, it is effected by a writ that does not originate with Ned Thornhill. Earlier in the text, we learn that Ned transferred the bond for George's commission to his attorney, and thus it is his attorney who owns the debt contract (120). Eschewing responsibility, Ned makes the irrefutable point to his uncle that "[i]f [Primrose] . . . has contracted debts and is unwilling or even unable to pay them, it is their business to proceed in this manner" (155). Debts must be repaid, and even Sir William is forced to accept that " '[i]f this . . . be as you [Ned] have stated it, there is nothing unpardonable in your offence" (155–56). Other of Ned's claims prove untrue—his ruin of Olivia, his attempted seduction of Sophia, his exploitation of George—but the claim that Primrose's imprisonment for debt is legal is never disproved. The bond is never paid, yet Primrose's release is presented as a fait accompli. What is the significance of this plot lacuna?

The omission works in a fashion similar to the one Jonathan Culler notes in *Oedipus Rex:* the witness who was to provide evidence that Oedipus did not kill his father never testifies, a gap Culler reveals to be a requirement of the narrative discourse. While story events could potentially render Oedipus innocent, the logic of signification requires Oedipus's guilt; the story would not be a tragedy if Oedipus did not "accede to the demands of narrative coherence and deem himself guilty."[35] Similarly, the demands of narrative coherence in *The Vicar* require Primrose to be released from prison; the jubilee moment is brought on by "the force of narrative . . . in which event is not a cause but an effect of theme."[36] Primrose is freed because the thematics of his suffering and Ned's lack of moral character cause the event, not because he pays his debts. Focusing on what the lacuna makes visible about the particular narrative coherence established by debt in sentimental fiction, I align Goldsmith's ironic characterization of Primrose with fiction's successful profiting from the equivocations of financial instruments, from the risky space between investing in worlds unknown and selling for a profit. What makes the narrative cohere is a dialectic of characterization that manages the contradictions of a debt system in which only certain debts require repayment. The irony here is that Primrose's debt, from a moral perspective, should not be paid, since Ned's credit was offered with a spurious intent. However, capital's character of debt—that is, Primrose's leveraged equity as an equivocating character—is the condition that makes him able to cook the moral account books.

Financial ironies permeate the novel, not only within the text but also surrounding its conditions of production. Ever since Boswell's *Life of Johnson*, the novel's circulation has been attached to Goldsmith's own financial exigency. According to Boswell, Samuel Johnson received an urgent message from Goldsmith that his landlady had had him arrested for debt, and Johnson bailed him out by selling a manuscript he found in Goldsmith's house to a bookseller for £60. Interestingly, Boswell notes that Goldsmith later bragged he had sold the novel for £400; the specific amount remains undocumented.[37] That a novel whose unknown exchange value bails its author out of debtor's prison also contains a denouement in which the main character is released from debtor's prison presents a metatextual *mise-en-abyme* that keeps literary value circulating. The satiric nature of the novel adds instability, constantly undermining any attempt to judge Primrose's character and, like Fielding's Booth in *Amelia*, the debtor is sympathetic even or especially in moments of culpability when human imperfection is the object of meaning. The interpretative dynamic of reading Primrose's character is complicated by Goldsmith's use of first-person narration, which introduces a tension between what Primrose says and the meaning the reader is directed to confer. The ironic distance of the satire alerts us to the fact that Primrose, as narrator, repeatedly declares certain of his characteristics to be fixed that later events reveal to be variable. For example, he denounces pride on many occasions, claiming to have relinquished it at the same time that he lost his fortune, yet pride is what leads him to agree to the ridiculous family portrait and to send his daughters to London. The narrative disjunction between how Primrose characterizes himself and what the events he narrates reveal about his character presents an interpretative challenge. As James Kim points out, "For nearly half a century, readers of *The Vicar of Wakefield* have puzzled over whether to interpret the novel as satire or sentimentality."[38] The puzzle is precisely where the equivocation between debt and equity lies since it constitutes how the reader understands Primrose's financial exigency.[39] Accidents happen to blamelessly cause losses, yet Primrose is simultaneously incapable of predicting other losses that he should have seen coming. What does the novel gain by Primrose's astonishing failures in risk management? I suggest that the tension between the satiric and the sentimental produces a dialectic of character that is "generative of, and integral to, narrative signification," in that it allows Primrose to get away without paying his debts.[40]

The family's downward mobility is plotted primarily through accidents and misfortunes that befall them without warning. In the middle of negotiations to marry George to the wealthier Arabella, Primrose gets news that the merchant in whose hands he invested all his money—a hefty £14,000—has absconded "to avoid a statute of bankruptcy" (15). Without money for a settlement, the marriage is called off. Primrose's response to the news is neither despair nor anger—both emotions that would lead to further action and investigation—but rather resignation and a disavowal of money as the way to happiness ("we have still enough left for happiness" [16]). He accepts his fate, in part because he is blameless: "no prudence of ours could have prevented our late misfortune," he tells his family (16). Like debt in much sentimental fiction, his loss is imagined as someone else's and he has no culpability as an investor. The lack of specific details about the merchant means the reader has no knowledge by which to determine the soundness of Primrose's judgment in entrusting his fortune to this particular man. We know only that accidents happen and misfortunes occur. The merchant is himself a victim of bankruptcy, though we are never told why his creditors are calling in his debts and forcing him to liquidate. He is ultimately culpable not for the financial loss but for avoiding bankruptcy court by leaving the country, which suggests that he has not lost but has stolen his investors' funds. In either case, Primrose is forced to relinquish his curacy and take up a lower-paying position on Squire Thornhill's estate, leaving with £400 after paying all his debts in the neighbourhood.[41]

The second substantial loss and misfortune to befall the Primroses, and the one that reduces the family's already-reduced livelihood to indigence, occurs when fire destroys their house and all their belongings. Again, Primrose's response is immediately one of resignation rather than rage or sadness; he saves his children but then stands and watches the fire burn everything he has of financial value, including "the notes I had reserved for my daughters fortunes" (113). The loss of the unrecoverable cash raises the question of the responsibility Primrose had to secure his money and whether he is culpable for doing the equivalent of hiding it underneath the mattress. The two accidental losses—from the merchant's bankruptcy and from fire—have the effect of canceling each other out: neither investing in stocks nor storing cash guarantee wealth. What the losses have in common is that Primrose is blameless because he could not have done anything to prevent either—market losses in this sense are like house fires—and both accidents prompt him to disavow wealth as the way to happiness and to proclaim the value of his family (he would not "exchange situations" after the fire for "a thousand worlds," since all his family are about him [118]).

While *The Vicar*'s plot of downward mobility, in which accidental misfortunes cause financial loss, does not assign accountability to Primrose, the novel's characterization forces the reader precisely to resolve the problem of his culpability in not foreseeing other losses, specifically, the loss of Olivia's virtue. In most areas of his life, Primrose seems constitutively incapable of risk management, and the plot queries whether he should show better judgment. He admits that he is "careless of temporalities" for having signed away his curacy instead of saving for a rainy day. The interpretive dynamic in the Vicar's character centers on his naiveté and the fact that he monumentally fails to predict losses that seem obvious to the reader. Though warned about Ned Thornhill's history—that "scarce a farmer's daughter within ten miles" has escaped seduction and ruin (17)—Primrose encourages, and indeed feels proud of, Ned's attentions to and interest in his daughters. The reader immediately recognizes what Primrose does not: that the "two young ladies richly drest" who offer London placements to Olivia and Sophia are molls Ned is using to entrap and ruin the daughters (41). When the London ladies swear and the Vicar blithely misreads this breach of upper-class manners as "the surest symptom of their distinction," the passage registers satirically. Primrose thinks he is being the savvy reader of character in not accepting at face value the lower-class slip, but by mistakenly reading the meaning as other than it appears, he becomes the source of a double-irony and bad judgment (42). The satire reveals Primrose to be a mixed character in his obliviousness to risk at the same time that the events of the plot render Ned entirely culpable for Olivia's ruin. Because Primrose cannot be held responsible for an act that could possibly *not* have happened in the future, he is not at fault, a logic analogous to transferable debt contracts whereby the stockholder who profits from buying and selling a financial instrument that later turns out to be devalued does not pay for that loss.[42]

The most comic yet damning illustration of Primrose's inability to assess risk leads to the loss of his horse at the market. Spurred by the need for money to invest in Sophia and Olivia's chances on the London marriage market (as it was "indispensably necessary that their appearance should equal the greatness of their expectations" [59]), the Vicar determines to sell his horse, his last possession of value. He finds no takers at the fair until he advertises his horse for sale to a "venerable old man" whom he had previously witnessed relieving the distresses of a stranger. In a double coincidence of wants that should have raised Primrose's suspicions, the old man instantly declares he is at the market to buy a horse. So the two "struck a bargain. Nothing now remained but to pay me, and he accordingly pulled out a thirty pound note, and bid me change it" (63). With coinage shortages a frequent problem in the period, it is unsurprising when no change for the note can be found at the fair. Primrose eventually accepts a draught that the old man insists will be paid by Primrose's neighbor Flamborough, exclaiming that a "draught upon my neighbour was to me the same as money" (63). But the joke is on him, since he has mistaken the social relation that gives a financial instrument its credibility. Only later, after Flamborough reveals the old man to be the fraud Jenkinson, does Primrose admit "I had done wrong in taking a draught from a stranger" (63). *The Swindler Detected*, a credit evaluation advice manual, includes a section precisely describing the "mutual friend" swindle and cautions all traders to check with the friend before trusting the stranger, commonsense advice we see Primrose not heeding.[43] This mistake, however, is endearing, since Primrose trusted the old man because of his like-feeling charity to someone in need and since, while the charity was feigned, Primrose's sentimental response to it was not.

Because of the novel's narrative style and sentiment, Primrose's failures at risk management, at not acting in accordance with a future he should have seen coming, never translate into negative judgment. Goldsmith exploits sentimental fiction's episodic rhythm to produce Primrose's ceaseless optimism, and the story is told in a relentlessly future-projected tempo that refuses to draw connections to past events. George Eliot admired the novel precisely for this reason; noting the novel's capacity to capture the unordered "processes of outward and inward life," she writes: "[T]he simple opening of a story with a date and necessary account of place and people, passing on quietly towards the more rousing elements of narrative and dramatic presentation, without need of retrospect, has its advantages, [and] . . . the opening chapters of *The Vicar of Wakefield* are as fine as anything that can be done in this way."[44] Marshall Brown, citing Eliot's remarks, argues that Goldsmith's achievement in the novel was this "easy, consecutive narration without retrospect," a temporality that is key to understanding Goldsmith's "handling of time" and key also, I argue, to the way the novel's dynamic of character maps onto capital's asymmetrical debt relations.[45] Brown writes of *The Vicar*'s narration: "There is no background information to be filled in. . . . Hence *The Vicar* is a narrative without omniscience. It is also a narrative without depth: the pluperfect tense expresses the conditions of the narrated events rather than either remote sources or distance and contrast. There is also no retrospective reflection by the narrator, . . . This is, then a narrative without judgment . . . a first-person narrative in which memory plays no shaping role, and regardless of the verb tense employed time always functions in the form of presence."[46] The advantage of this narrative temporality is that nothing sticks to Primrose's character; from page to page or event to event, life happens with or without its grounding events in a narrative of causal coherence. His character refuses to function like a Lockean individual whose past determines their present or whose agency can change the future, and no reflections shape the individual's life through plot. Primrose exists in the ever-present now of capital's shapeless growth, and his character circulates through the world without history or fixed value; like a financial instrument, Primrose has the capacity to take any event and abstract its meaning from context and history (I discuss the temporality of capitalism's spectacular now in chapter 4). We might read his tendency toward pronouncing in pithy clichés and aphorisms as indicating his logic of abstraction.[47]

The effect of a character telling a story without retrospection is that the narrative's coherence does not emerge from causal connections between Primrose's life events. When accidents happen, plots do not cohere causally, and thus Primrose is not tied to his past. The novel has often been criticized for its overreliance on implausible coincidences and an ending that breaks all rules of verisimilitude. These are the effects of a character who is free of obligations and owes nothing to anybody. Even his family ties are imagined not as a bond to a past but as future equity, a point that I expand upon below. First, however, I read the consequences of this character on the novel's representation of strangers and friends, since a narrative that frees its characters from personal history defines their relations to others as always already like anonymous relations between strangers.

The novel's investment in characters without obligations to a past is exemplified by Burchell, a man who has precisely made himself a stranger in order to circulate free from his economic history as Sir William Thornhill. The motif of the rich man who pretends to be poor in order to test the morals of those around him is a common one in sentimental literature; Oliver Surface in Sheridan's *School for Scandal* is perhaps the most famous example.[48] The motif narrativizes and thus turns into an interpretative problem the fact that, when money mediates all social relations as it does within a capitalist exchange economy, one can never tell the motivation of friends. Money poisons friendship by introducing ulterior motives, and the only way to ascertain a true friend is to entirely remove any financial entanglements from social ones, which means that "[d]isproportioned friendships"—what Primrose calls cross-rank social relations—are impossible because the economic disparity produces a structural entanglement. Primrose repeatedly declares himself against "disproportioned acquaintances" (25): "Unequal combinations are always disadvantageous to the weaker side" because the person of lesser wealth will always be servile to the one above (57).[49] He breaks his own rule with Burchell and brags about his "hospitality" to the "poor man," presenting the friendship as a Christian act of benevolence on his part since Burchell needs him more than he needs Burchell. "I was pleased with the poor man's friendship because . . . I knew he wanted mine" (28). Marriage presents the limits of their friendship, with Burchell's poverty disqualifying him from being a potential husband for Sophia. "[I]t would be even madness," Primrose warns Sophia, "to expect happiness from one who has been so very bad an oeconomist of his own" (59). Their friendship is later destroyed by Primrose's assumption that Burchell's interest in his daughter is mercenary. When Primrose finds a copy of the letter Burchell sent to Ned's prostitutes, warning them that he would expose their ruse, Primrose misreads it because of the structural economics of his friendship. Assuming that Burchell is plotting to marry Sophia for her money (little as there is), Primrose misreads the letter as casting aspersions on his daughters' moral characters when, in fact, Burchell was saving his daughters from ruin. Many ironies are revealed through Primrose's misreading of the letter; for example, that he displaces his own ambition in marrying his daughters up onto Burchell. But the irony of ironies is that Primrose succeeds in marrying Sophia to money precisely because Sophia, against her father's wishes, was "a woman who could find merit in a man that seemed poor" and their pure love translates into a wealthy match (59). Primrose reconciles himself to the marriage as a reward to Burchell for his rescue of Sophia from her kidnappers minutes before Burchell reveals himself to be the very wealthy Sir William.[50] The reconciliation happens with Primrose significantly rewriting the past: "You were ever our friend," he asserts analeptically; "we have long discovered our errors with regard to you" (148). The statement represses Primrose's past break with Burchell, a willful forgetting that Primrose's declarative statement in the relentless narrative present tense enacts.

The presentism of the narrative style, with its rewriting of the past, operates in the novel's representation of the moment when Burchell and Primrose first become friends, and provides a case study in how sentimentality frames strangers as friends. Primrose first encounters Burchell in the middle of a liquidity crisis, and the circulating debt relations provide Burchell's sentimental credit as poor but worthy. After hearing the innkeeper's wife complain of a guest who "wanted money" to pay his bill despite having given an old broken soldier three guineas the day before, Primrose meets the curious gentleman, who is "drest in cloaths that once were laced," that is to say, who was once rich (18). Primrose's immediate response is to offer the stranger his purse to pay his debt to the innkeeper, a payment that stands as moral compensation for the stranger's own generosity toward the soldier. With all debts seemingly repaid by Primrose's benevolence, it seems odd that he turns this act of charity into a debt on the next page, calling Burchell a "money-borrower": "[T]hough he was a money-borrower, he defended his opinions with as much obstinacy as if he had been my patron" (19). Primrose's comment assumes that people should and do treat their friends differently depending on their financial position, and he is surprised when Burchell does not show a deference he thinks appropriate to someone in his financial debt. When Burchell turns out, in fact, to be Primrose's patron as Sir William, sentimental characterization through charity is destabilized once again. Debts signify equivocally in the text, and Burchell's so-called debt to Primrose is ultimately transformed into enormous equity when Sophia marries Sir William.

The temporal slippage in which the novel recharacterizes charity as debt, and then debt as equity, fits into the same financial and sentimental logic through which Sir William frees himself from his own history and circulates anonymously as Burchell. Charity, in Sir William's history, became debt when his own excesses in disproportioned social relations caused him to spend more on poor friends than his estates generated. Sir William is "universally known" to be "one of the most generous . . . men in the kingdom," and this reputation for generosity drains his finances and eventually prompts him to become a stranger (19). With dramatic irony, Burchell describes Sir William to Primrose as someone who "carried benevolence to an excess when young," and this extreme sensibility is represented as an illness (19).[51] He cannot *not* feel for friends in need. Because he is rich, he attracts crowds of fawning flatterers, and thus he has lost "a regard for private interest in universal sympathy," that is, he has lost his capacity to judge that others were using him for his money (19). "He loved all mankind; for fortune prevented him from knowing that there were rascals," and anyone who expresses the "slightest distress, whether real or fictitious," he is "disposed to relieve" (19). When his money runs out, "instead of *money*, he gave *promises*," because he feels too much to deny a request (20). Debt changes his friendships and, when he is unable to meet his promises, his friends disappear. In the description of his loss of faith in the world, Burchell slips into first-person narration, using "I" and forgetting himself when he narrates the discovery that his friends were friends only for his money (20). Disenchanted and with a fortune broken by charity, he leaves for Europe, and by isolating himself from friends without money, he restores his wealth. We are never explicitly told how he becomes "more affluent than ever" by traveling to Europe, but the unnarrated here links financial accumulation to living without friends (20). Sir William's wealth, in other words, is generated by freeing himself from social obligations and circulating anonymously.

If, for Sir William, affluence is the effect of breaking ties and freeing oneself from a past, Primrose's strategy for financial accumulation is the inversion: he turns family ties into equities and risks all on a future payoff. His frequent acceptance of unacceptable risk, his refusal to predict the obvious, originates, I argue, in his earlier claim that his children are his equity, his pension plan, "the supports of my declining age," as he calls them (10). With his children to leverage, he can take huge risks; and, indeed, the futures market of reproduction produces high yields for Primrose when all his children marry into wealth. The first sentence of the novel provides a self-estimation of his reproductive value, grounding it in emerging theories of "political arithmetic": "I was ever of opinion, that the honest man who married and brought up a large family, did more service than he who continued single, and only talked of population" (9).[52] The wealth of a nation lies in its population. The Vicar explicitly characterizes his children as equity when he tells the "famous story of Count Abensberg," who presented his thirty-two children to pay his taxes: "[T]hough I had but six," Primrose remarks, "I considered them as a very valuable present made to my country, and consequently looked upon it as my debtor" (10). The Vicar's children prove a risk worth taking, since, in the final prison scene, he not only gets away without paying his debts and marries three of his children to wealthy spouses, but leverages George for an extra £6,000 profit. When George marries Arabella in prison, he does so without her fortune, which, in that moment, is thought contracted to Ned (it is later revealed that Ned was legally married to Olivia, thus restoring Arabella's fortune). Arabella's wealthy father extracts a promise from Primrose that if Primrose later comes into money, he will settle £6,000 on Arabella. In the relentless present, the promise costs Primrose little; he "readily gave" it because "to one who had such little expectations as I, [it] was no great favour" (162). The day after this promise, the Vicar's fortune thought lost to his merchant's bankruptcy is returned when the merchant is arrested in Antwerp. George forgives his father the £6,000 debt *before* he gives him the news of the returned fortune, though Primrose does not immediately accept George's jubilee. He takes the ethical question to Sir William, who arbitrates in his favor, reasoning "that as [George] was already possessed of a very affluent fortune by his marriage, I might accept his offer [of debt forgiveness] without any hesitation" (167). What seems strange in this extended contemplation of whether Primrose is obliged to pay the £6,000 is that the friend who owns the debt—Arabella's father, Wilmot—is never consulted. Neither George nor Sir William have the authority to forgive a promise given to Wilmot; but, in any case, Primrose never pays.

The fact that not all debts in *The Vicar of Wakefield* require repayment is an effect of the circulation of Primrose's character—as satirically naive, as relentlessly optimistic, as lacking retrospection. The "I" equivocates in the ever-present present of his narrative voice, and the force of narrative coherence demands that Ned's wrongs be righted with Primrose's release even though the debt is not repaid. When Primrose acquired the original bond, he quickly accepted Ned's offer and showed Ned "as much gratitude as if I never intended to pay," meaning that he accepted the debt as if it were charity (105). In the end, the "as if" in the statement disappears and Primrose proleptically characterized his debts. Like *The Fool of Quality*, the novel aligns good moral character with the reward of fortune, but the risks it takes with its unfixed character allow Goldsmith to leverage debt for an interpretively dynamic character. It also provides an unintended critique of finance capital built entirely on contractual law: Primrose avoids paying debts because sentimental narrative allows for a moral coherence divorced from the law. Fiction can imagine a world in which creditors pay for the risks they took, but the novel's circulation of unfriended money is what produces that world.

The comparison of the two novels discussed in this chapter leaves us with a counterintuitive observation: *The Fool of Quality*'s unrelentingly optimistic Whig view that commerce will bring universal upward mobility produces a narrative that does not profit from capital's equivocal and temporally shifting character of debt, and therefore all the debts contracted must be paid; whereas Goldsmith's conservative stance against free trade and anonymous commercial markets, voiced in the novel by Primrose in his conversation with the butler,[53] produces a novel in which characters circulate like Enron stocks, accruing profit from simple temporal progression without paying for the costs of the risk. I could easily have used Sarah Scott's *Sir George Ellison* and Henry Fielding's *Amelia* to make the same comparison. Scott's optimistic view that capitalism can circulate through sentimentalism to produce wealth for all, including African slaves, leads to a hero in Sir George as stultifying as Brooke's Harry. In contrast, Fielding's conservative cynicism and satiric view of human greed end up with a narrative dialectics of character and an interpretative dynamic that free its hero from paying his debts. The bailiff who imprisons Booth insists that "Men must be obliged to pay their Debts," yet the novel suggests otherwise.[54] Booth shares Primrose's future-oriented narrative tense and sees his debts and losses as always already recouped in a future yet to arrive. Like Goldsmith, Fielding had spent time in debtor's prison, yet unlike Goldsmith, Fielding explicitly attacks the legitimacy of imprisonment for debt both in the novel and in the pages of *The Champion*.[55] His impassioned plea against imprisonment might explain the strong presence of predatory creditors in *Amelia*. The predators, including his so-called friend James, entice Booth into debt to blackmail him and seduce his wife. James bails him out of prison by paying his £500 debt, but this transfer of the debt contract is a trap to send Booth to the West Indies to work off the debt, leaving James to prey upon Amelia. A similar credit snare is laid by Trent when, knowing Booth's propensity for gambling, he uses cards to get Booth in his debt. Trent is a paid double agent, befriending Booth only to acquire and then transfer the debt to the Lord, who uses it as ammunition in his seduction of Amelia. Fielding's characterization of Booth's debts repeatedly involves the betrayal on the part of characters who are his supposed friends. *Amelia*, as Cheryl Wanko suggests, "teaches us to question every character," and the infinite questioning of character produces a paranoid reading in which friends are never to be trusted.[56]

This chapter charts how thinking about fictional characters as functioning like financial instruments allows us to read the dynamics and dialectics of character, to detect the way judgments about characters often involve temporal equivocations tied up with sentimental and financial accounting. My reading of the narrative dynamic thinks about characters as hermeneutic enigmas, as engaging what readers know about a character, how they know it, from whom they receive knowledge, and what they predict the character will do. I argue that the greater the risks involved in that interpretative dynamic, the greater the power of the enigma to pull us along through the narrative. In other words, as long as characters keep risking the possibility that they might not be who they say they are in the future, the narrative profits. Inversely, reading literary characters as functioning like financial instruments reveals something about the logic of debt under capitalism. The form character takes under capital is a subject split in time between one who takes risks on an unpredictable future, reinventing oneself in an instant, and one who is determined by the past and held responsible to promises and contracts. This character can take individual form in fictional narrative, but outside fiction, the temporal contradiction divides individuals into those with capital to leverage who can free themselves from past obligations, and those with debts who are indentured to a future of payments without end. As long as debt circulates as pure number, freed from the bonds of friendship, the tension between those with equity and those with debt will keep generating more stories of downward mobility.

What I hope I have shown through reading capital's character of debt in these two novels is that the condition under which debt circulates as capital among strangers requires us to unfriend money, to make financial transactions as if they are not also moral. It also may be the condition for interesting characters in the novel. Downward mobility generates stories by reclaiming that act of unfriending as disinterested charity, and these stories reveal the deep integration of the temporal epistemology of the novel with that of capitalism. Particular novels produce different windows into that cross-fertilization depending on how they characterize their debts and their heroes. In the following chapter, I turn my attention to downward mobility's infinite generation of stories through the narrative technique of embedded storytelling. What circulates in the scenes of circulating stories is the contradictory dynamic of use value and exchange value, a relation of form to capital that is similar to the one I have detailed here concerning the contradiction within securitized debt.

When characters circulate in sentimental novels as hard to pin down, they exploit the new temporal dynamic of capital for full narrative effect. The widespread sympathy shown to debtors in sentimental novels must be read within the context of narrative's temporal equivocations, meaning that the sympathy shown to those in debt might have more to do with managing the tension between debt and equity than with recognizing our moral obligations to help those in need. The equivocations of narrative might function like those of financial instruments, unleashing debt to circulate in ways that hide what it is we owe each other. In both cases, the dynamic of interpretation pushes the judgment of value onto us as readers to interpret who owes what to whom, why, and within what context. One of my favorite plots of debt in *The Vicar of Wakefield* comes early in the novel when Primrose is describing his family's great hospitality, bragging about how they open their doors to any friends and strangers passing through the neighborhood. When a guest turns out to have a "bad character," Primrose gets rid of him by equivocating debt: "I ever took care to lend him a riding coat, or a pair of boots, or sometimes an horse of small value, and I always had the satisfaction of finding he never came back to return them" (10). In this example, whose debt to whom is left unpaid?

Narrative Exchange

The Value of Stories-within-Stories

Why are scenes of storytelling so central to sentimental fiction in late eighteenth-century Britain? Shifts in narrative level, in which a character tells their story—most often of tragic loss—to another character, are as familiar to readers of sentimental fiction as the tears its heroes and heroines shed. Dramatizing the narrative act within the narrative act constitutes one of the sentimental novel's distinguishing formal features. In Henry Mackenzie's *The Man of Feeling*, the main character, Harley, is approached by a woman on the Strand, starving and begging for help. The entrance of a stranger having prompted the narrative desire to hear her story, the novel shifts into her autodiegetic tale: "'[I]f you have patience for the recital of my story, it may palliate, though it cannot excuse, my faults.' Harley bowed, as a sign of assent, and she began as follows."[1] Miss Atkin proceeds to tell a conventional tale of "virtue in distress": seduced and abandoned, she is forced into prostitution to survive. When she finishes her tale of woe, Harley "could not speak" for shedding tears (Mackenzie, *The Man of Feeling*, 92). Similar sympathetic scenes of storytelling can be found throughout all the novels discussed in this book. What function do they serve? Such shifts in narrative level can be explained, on the one hand, by the representational goals of the genre. The dramatized scenes of storytelling model the proper sympathetic emotional response, one that validates sentimentalism's philosophical affirmation of an innate moral sense.[2] The scenes thus display what benevolence, charity, and virtue look like to a world that no longer holds these attributes to be the property of social rank.

The didactic explanation for sentimental scenes of storytelling—that fiction teaches the emerging bourgeois readership how to feel—focuses interpretation on the level of content. This chapter concerns itself with the formal device of embedding and argues that the later-eighteenth-century concern with the morality of capital accumulation can be read on the level of form. I examine the formal device of narrative embedding in a range of novels, including *The Man of Feeling*, Sarah Fielding's *Adventures of David Simple*, Frances Brooke's *History of Emily Montague*, and Sarah Scott's *Description of Millenium Hall*, to demonstrate how embedded narratives negotiate multiple exchanges, both narrative and commercial, and that their frequency can be attributed to the ways that the negotiation positions value. The preponderance of scenes of storytelling is a symptom of the historical tension between an emerging finance economy dependent on the circulation of money as capital and a social morality that censures as avaricious the pure pursuit of profit, of making money out of money. Embedded narratives work to negotiate the tension between the drives for individual profit and for social sympathy by circulating wealth through the accumulation of stories that in turn develop their own exchange economies. My hypothesis is that stories-within-stories of downward mobility in sentimental fiction displace financial exchanges onto narrative ones and that by attending to the formal structure of embedding, we can see how capital's structural contradiction between use value and exchange value generates narrative desire.

Narrative exchange often allows for various symbolic values to accrue that are not present on the content level of sympathetic charity. On the level of form, scenes of storytelling do more than simply model sympathy: they can resolve or uncover ideological contradictions; they can circulate a radical or conservative vision of class hierarchy; they can displace financial exchanges onto social ones and vice versa, moral affect onto money. Attending to the specific form of the story's circulation tells a more complicated tale of the cultural work that sentimentalism performs. Sentimental novels almost always have at least one homodiegetic narrator (that is, a narrator who is also a character in the story), and in this way, they stage social relations as intrinsic to the narrative act.[3] Who is listening to whom, why, and to what effect are questions that circulate in terms of both plot and money. To read the narrative exchanges for the ways they negotiate a sociability grounded in moral virtue with a sociability of the anonymous marketplace reveals the extent to which the formalist device of nested storytelling is itself embedded in an emergent capitalist economy. The first part of this chapter describes the typical structure of embedding found in sentimental novels, and the second half examines narrative exchanges in a range of these novels in order to read the plot of the conflict between virtue and commerce in their "*narrative of a narrative*," as Tzvetan Todorov classically described the self-reflective effect of embedded storytelling.[4]

Stories-within-stories, or the Chinese box effect, are as old as stories themselves. But the popularity of the device has ebbed and flowed, with certain of its features lending themselves to a literary moment and others not. In the early modern period, the collection of tales with a framing device—for example, *The Canterbury Tales* or *Decameron*—was popular, partly because it corresponded to the premodern oral form of storytelling that Walter Benjamin analyzes in "The Storyteller." In postmodern fiction, the ubiquity of embedding can be linked to the era's interest in the discursive conditions of truth. The self-conscious use of the *mise-en-abyme*—the novel that tells the story of a character writing a novel—in texts ranging from Paul Auster to John Barth to the *nouveau roman* seems the perfect formal device to highlight postmodernism's self-reflexivity.[5] Analogously, I argue that the sentimental novel's exchange of narrative is embedded within the period's new models of economic exchange. In making this claim, I distinguish the latter-eighteenth-century novel from its earlier incarnations. Embedding narratives occur in amatory fiction of the early eighteenth century (for example, Haywood's *Love in Excess*), but such novels do not often dramatize the scene of storytelling or change narrators. Scenes of narration are largely absent from early realist novels such as those by Defoe, which are characterized by their autodiegetic narrators, heroines and heroes who tell their own stories but do not shift into another character's voice. Early realist plots often profit from the mobility of a newly emerging global capital to tell optimistic tales of upward mobility such as *Robinson Crusoe.* By the latter eighteenth century, the tension between commercial and moral exchange renders such optimistic mapping of heroic capital accumulation challenging, and embedded stories appear to address that challenge. What circulates in downward mobility stories-within-stories is precisely the struggle between the two forms of circulation—between speculative capital and a reciprocal exchange of use value—a struggle readable, I hope to show, in the structure of embedding.

While I argue that scenes of storytelling circulate in particularly symptomatic ways in sentimental literature, the device is found in many nonsentimental novels in the period as well; for instance, the framed collection of tales was regularly used in early pornography (influenced by earlier amatory fiction), and, most famously, Henry Fielding's comic fiction deploys the digressive tale. What distinguishes sentimental fiction's use of embedding? What are its conventions? The formal classifications of embedding help in drawing more finely tuned distinctions.

The Narrative Structure of Sentimental Embedding

Embedded narratives, as the pioneering work of narrative theorists such as Gérard Genette and Mieke Bal have outlined, share many structural components.[6] Here, I foreground three areas of classification—*level*, *voice*, and *function*—and formulate four propositions to more precisely describe sentimental embedding.

First, *level*: embedded narratives in sentimental novels are almost always distributed vertically but often only to the second level, and they are usually loudly announced, marked by gestures like "she began as follows" in the previous example from *The Man of Feeling.* Narrative level, as John Pier defines it, consists of "the relations between an act of narration and the diegesis."[7] It is the number of Chinese boxes, or of stories the story is framed within. Genette counts seven levels in John Barth's story "Menelaid," and Bal notes eight in *Arabian Nights.*[8] In contrast, sentimental literature does not test the labyrinth very far, mostly nesting to a second or third level. Narrative levels, as Pier further defines them, "are distributed vertically when a change of both (diegetic) level and speaker and/or addressee occurs, and horizontally when no change of speaker takes place."[9] While sentimental fiction contains many smaller horizontal shifts in level (for instance, short character sketches), the most noticeable shifts are vertical ones, involving a shift in narrators. The effects of the heavily marked vertical shift into a secondary tale are to foreground the scene of storytelling within the primary diegesis and to emphasize and strengthen the social relation between teller and told. Narrative exchange not only becomes central to the story but is often a crucial event in the primary plot.

Second, *voice*: one level of a sentimental novel is almost always narrated homo- or autodiegetically. In categorizing voice, or the relation between the narrator and the narrated world, Genette distinguishes between a "heterodiegetic" narrator, who is not a character in the story; a "homodiegetic" narrator, who is present in the world they narrate; and an "autodiegetic" narrator, who is both present and telling their own story. Sentimental literature almost always has at least one narrator who is also a character in their own story, and most often such narrators tell their own stories to the hero or heroine of the main diegesis. *The Man of Feeling* and *David Simple*, for example, include multiple autodiegetic narrators within a heterodiegetically narrated diegesis; Sarah Scott's *Millenium Hall* (1762) effects the opposite with a homodiegetic narrator of the primary narrative and a heterodiegetic narrator of the inset tales. Elizabeth Griffith's *History of Lady Barton* (1771) and Frances Brooke's *History of Emily Montague* (1769) are both autodiegetic epistolary novels that include other autodiegetic narrators in embedded scenes of narration.

Third, *voice level*: insofar as sentimental novels are almost always organized vertically, they include a narrator of an embedded tale who is also a character in the embedding diegesis, a relation I designate as "internal." My use of *internal* and *external relations* to describe whether a secondary narrator is present in the primary diegesis (or a tertiary narrator is present in a secondary diegesis, and so forth) supplements Susan Lanser's distinction between public and private narrators (itself a supplement of Genette's categories for defining the narrative situation). Lanser's categorization focuses on the narratee and whether the story is told to an internal (private) or external (public) audience.[10] My own discrimination between internally and externally related narrators emphasizes not the narratee but the relation *between* two levels, more specifically between the narrator of an embedded tale and the narrated world of the embedding story. A vertical shift requires a change in both level and speaker but does not necessarily stipulate that the speaker be a character in the primary level. Similarly, the homodiegetic-heterodiegetic distinction refers to the relation of the narrator to the diegesis of their narration but does not designate the secondary narrator's relation to the primary diegesis. Internal and external simply notes whether the narrator of a secondary tale (be it a homo-, hetero-, or autodiegetic narrator) is present in the primary narrated world. I use the terms *internal* or *internally related* to designate when the subject of the secondary tale is present in the primary diegesis (or the tertiary narrator is present in the secondary diegesis, and so forth) and *external* or *externally related* when the subject's story is included while they are not; for instance, a found narrative or a discovered letter or, most commonly, a heterodiegetically narrated horizontal tale (in other words, when there is not a dramatized scene of telling). My interest in thinking about internal and external narrators lies in differentiating the relations *between* the levels and how the social relations are transformed by and through the sentimental narrative act.

Eighteenth-century fiction generally uses internal narrators and embeds narratives that are generated out of a social relation within the primary diegesis, even if that social relation is fleeting or tangential. Mr. Wilson, for instance, in *Joseph Andrews* (1742), is a character in the (heterodiegetically narrated) primary diegesis insofar as Joseph meets him at an inn; he is also an autodiegetic narrator of the story he narrates. As in *Joseph Andrews*, the autodiegetic narrators of embedded tales in *The Man of Feeling* are internal, or are characters in the heterodiegetically narrated primary diegesis. With the further calibration of the voice's relation between levels, we can specify that embedding in the sentimental novel almost always involves at least one homodiegetic narrator and nests stories that have internal relations; external ones may also be present but there is almost always at least one internally related narrator. Yet the same could be said for *Joseph Andrews*, which is not a sentimental narrative. Thus, the classification *function* needs to be introduced to formulate the final proposition.

Fourth, *function*: sentimental fiction is particular in that the function of the embedded narrative almost always changes because of the narrative act. *Function*, a more open-ended and interpretative category than the structural ones of level and voice, refers to the discursive relation between the story told and the story in which it is embedded. To what ends do the narrative levels interact? Genette originally defined three "types of relationship": *causal*, when the story explains something in the diegesis; *thematic*, when the story is linked by motif and theme, but not diegesis; and *distraction*, when the story is purely digressive and adds nothing to the main story.[11] For my purpose here, it is useful to note Bal's further differentiation of Genette's causal category into two: those embedded tales that explain something in the primary plot. and those that not only explain but also have a determining effect on events in the primary plot.[12] It is this later distinction that, combined with voice, distinguishes the type of embedding more commonly found in sentimental fiction than in other novels. Sentimental novels have internally related embedded tales whose function *changes* in the course of the narrative situation from one of distraction

(Harley encounters a stranger, Miss Atkin, and wants to know her story) to a story that determines events and actions in the primary diegesis (hearing her story endangers Harley's life when an enraged father mistakes him for the lover who has ruined his daughter). Significantly, many of the actions that take place in the primary diegesis and are caused by the narrative act end up changing the ending of the embedded story (Miss Atkin is reunited with her father). Other examples of embedded stories that cause events in the primary diegesis that then resolve plots in the secondary diegesis include "The Fair Cottager's" tale in *The History of Emily Montague*, in which Emily and Rivers help Fanny, the fair cottager, reunite her dead friend's illegitimate son with his father's family and secure for herself an income; and Mrs. Walter's embedded tale in *The History of Lady Barton*, in which Lady Barton rescues Mrs. Walter from her garret exile.

The spilling over into the primary diegesis of a tale that begins as a distraction is a structure common to sentimental literature and is different from the structure of the tales in *Joseph Andrews* insofar as those remain as plot obstructions in the narrative; the teller disappears once the tale is told and the narrative situation does not require further action in the primary diegesis. Entirely digressive tales are also common in sentimental fiction (for instance, the beggar's tale in *The Man of Feeling*) but, in addition, they contain tales that spill over into the primary diegesis to create bonds between teller and listener. Nonsentimental internally narrated stories can affect the primary diegesis, but they mostly do so without changing the relation between the narrator and the primary diegesis. In this category, we might place the stories told to Squire Allworthy at the end of *Tom Jones* that eventually result in the discovery of Tom's birth; the stories allow for the plot resolution but do not change Allworthy's relationship to the tellers. The distinction I am here making is that in sentimental novels the level and nature of the internal relation and the function of the tale changes *because* of the narrative act. The narrative act *acts* in the primary diegesis to change the internal relation from one between strangers to one between friends. The scene of storytelling is thus integrated into the plot and aims to create affective bonds between the teller and the told. In *David Simple*, for example, Camilla enters the plot as a total stranger whom David meets in a garret and becomes the most intimate person in his life, his wife, after she tells him her story. In this way, we can say that characters in the primary diegesis in sentimental fiction *accumulate* social relations at the same time that the stories accumulate.

How might we interpret the significance of this particular embedding structure for a reading of sentimental fiction? If the sentimental movement can be read as promoting a model for forging sympathetic social bonds within an emerging commercial world in which those bonds have become unmoored from propertied wealth, then embedded stories that forge connections between teller and listener fit sentimentalism's philosophical tenets of fellow feeling. Since embedded tales within sentimental novels are often catalyzed by downward mobility, the plot of the characters' financial exigency provides the occasion for sympathetic displays of charity required by the man or woman of feeling. However, an interpretation focused on a mimetic reading of sentimental fiction—whereby the reader learns to copy the sympathetic listener of the tale—ignores the doubled effects of textual mediation that embedding introduces. On one hand, the dramatization of the narrative situation works to erase the distance between experience and representation by putting the reader in the narratee's shoes. On the other hand, embedded narratives structurally introduce distance since they precisely mediate storytelling. Instead of "the story telling itself"—an effect, we might say, of the formally realist text—the story is once removed and thus the narrative act itself is an event in the plot. We need to read the "*narrative of a narrative*" for the way it mediates the narrative exchange. As Ross Chambers observes, embedded narratives demonstrate how the meaning of the story "derives significance from [its] situation" or the conditions under which it is told.[13] For this reason, he understands narrative as "a transactional phenomenon" since the meaning emerges out of the exchange between narrator and narratee.[14] Embedded tales stage their narrative situation, representing the origins of the story in the primary narrative. "Embedded narrative, unlike nonembedded narrative," Richard Shryock notes, "represents the conditions necessary to generate a narrative discourse."[15] These are the conditions that make any discourse possible; that is, as Shryock suggests, "the very elements that compose social relations within a society and produce that society's view of reality."[16]

What are the conditions that generate stories within sentimental novels? Downward mobility is central to all the novels I discuss below. When Harley takes a tour of Bedlam in *The Man of Feeling*, he observes that "[s]eparate from the rest stood one whose appearance had something of superior dignity," an appearance that elicits his desire to know her story (69). The first thing David Simple notices when he first encounters Camilla and Valentine in the garret is that Camilla is wearing a silk dress that was once quite fine; the spoiled dress signifies a story: David "longed to know their Story" for he "was certain by their Manner, and Behaviour, they could not have been bred in very low Life."[17] When Emily Montague in Brooke's novel encounters the "fair cottager," she instantly recognizes that she "is not in the station in which she was born" and is curious to know her story since, as Emily says, "she certainly has one."[18] In *Millenium Hall*, Mrs. Thornby notes of Louisa Mancel that "she was certain she had not been born for the station she was then in, and begged a particular account of her whole life."[19] Downward mobility signifies a story and is the spark of narrative desire.

Why is economic loss the primary source generating narrative in sentimental fiction? In staging the scene of storytelling, embedded narratives foreground the conditions of production, their narrative situation, and draw the reader's attention to the way stories introduce an exchange between teller and told. Because downward mobility is represented as the origin of many embedded tales, and because the listener most often responds to the story with economic assistance, financial and narrative exchange are often compounded, turning the story into a commodity and challenging the refined feeling of emotional identification. Here we might remind ourselves of Roland Barthes's claim, cited in this chapter's opening epigraph, that every narrative proposes a contract in which the story itself becomes an object of exchange. Every narrative, he argues, raises the questions: "*What should the narrative be exchanged for? What is the narrative 'worth'?*"[20] Embedded narratives narrate the contract within the plot, bringing to the fore the conditions of exchange.

Embedded narratives thus pull texts in two different directions: toward distance, self-reflectivity, and the situational production of meaning *and* toward emotional intimacy, authenticity, and unmediated experience. James Paxson notes that embedding introduces two "hermeneutical situations": "[W]e are faced with two competing readings, two hermeneutical situations pitted against each other in antinomian fashion: narrative embedding as a sign of narrativity's *en abyme* self-reflexivity versus narrative embedding as a sign of narrativity's authenticating pragmatic drive."[21] The didactic reading of embedding in sentimental novels links form to content by moving in the second direction, but does not account for the first, the *narrative of a narrative* that the novels tell. My point in recognizing the two pulls is not to resolve the contradiction, since it is structural and constitutive, but rather to interpret the effect of this dynamic narrative movement. How might we see the push and pull of the two hermeneutical situations working within the sentimental project? Such a reading helps us to understand how sentimental fiction's exchange of stories is intricately connected to the circulation of money within capitalism.

Given that the sentimental novel represents the narrative exchange both didactically (the narratee models benevolence by giving money for the story) and discursively (the story's conditions of production are part of the plot), analyzing what is at stake in both exchanges produces a dynamic interpretation of storytelling's economic effect. I argue that such a reading registers the space where sentimental fiction negotiates the historical tensions between virtue and commerce, in that the tension itself is intrinsic to an emerging capitalist culture and requires a circulation that infinitely defers its resolution. In other words, the tension between how the narrative exchange functions didactically and discursively is generated by the tension between morality and money, one that sentimental novels may resolve on the level of content (for example, virtue rewarded) but that they never resolve on the level of form, since the dynamic between the two hermeneutical situations is structural. The unresolvability of the tension, as well as the dynamic created through its circulation, embodies one of capital's founding contradictions, the one between use value and exchange value. By representing the dynamic of a story's use and narrating its exchange, stories-within-stories can represent commodity exchanges as ones based on use value, the products of a virtuous and reciprocal trade, while exchanging those stories for market profit. Scenes of storytelling in sentimental fiction hold on to the belief that stories can be useful commodities, exchanged to consolidate stable social bonds and teach moral feeling, and they often oppose virtuous charity to the avariciousness of the new commercial world. But the way the stories circulate within the main diegesis often tells a different story of financial and moral exchange. That this tension is not resolved—is, in fact, unresolvable—generates the desire for narrative exchange, for the infinite circulation of stories.

In staging the conflict between virtue and commerce, sentimental literature insists that money does not buy happiness. As we have seen (and as chapter 5 shows), the refrain is so common that the refusal of an interest in accumulating money is a precondition of a character's moral worth. It is not enough not to have money; to be virtuous, one must actively reject wealth, insisting that virtue is its own reward and poverty is preferred to its loss. Richardson's *Pamela* offers the classic example of this refrain. Pamela repeatedly refuses Mr. B's offers of money since to accept it would require her to compromise her virtue; in the end, she is rewarded for her refusal with marriage and wealth. The narrative problem that stories-within-stories help resolve for sentimental literature is the problem that led to the anti-Pamela satires that portrayed the heroine's refusal of money as only a ploy to garner a larger payout. When money rewards virtue, how can virtue circulate free from the desire for financial profit? Embedded stories answer this problem by displacing the circulation of a desire for money through narrative onto the desire for doing good. When money circulates through narrative exchanges within novels, it often accumulates virtue. With Marx's M-C-M′ in mind, we might represent this narrative exchange as M-N-M^V, with *N* (narrative) allowing for M^V, or money that has been cleansed of the taint of self-interested greed, to recirculate wealth as a sign of *V* (virtue).

In hypothesizing that at least one level of a sentimental novel has a homo- or autodiegetic narrator, I demonstrate that where precisely the narrator is located matters significantly to the internal relation between teller and listener and has repercussions for what effect the narrative act has on the tale's function. Below I discuss multiple examples of three different structures of embedding: autodiegetic narrators within stories narrated heterodiegetically (*The Man of Feeling*; *David Simple*); autodiegetic narrators within stories narrated autodiegetically (*The History of Emily Montague*); and heterodiegetic narrators within stories narrated homodiegetically (*Millenium Hall*). Insofar as the *narrative of a narrative* that the embedded stories tell changes with the different relations between the teller and the listener—that is, whether the teller is telling their own story to someone else, who may or may not be the narrator of that story—the narrative exchange produces different circulations of the desire for wealth and virtue and builds different sorts of affective relations.

Autodiegetic Narrators within Heterodiegetically Narrated Stories

By far the most common mode of embedded storytelling in sentimental fiction is the category in which third-person narrators pause the main diegesis and shift to scenes where a character tells their own story to the hero or heroine. This is the structure of embedding in *David Simple.* The novel narrates how David, betrayed by his brother, sets out on a journey to London to find a friend since blood no longer guarantees affective communities. The people he meets along the way tell him their stories, and the social relations that accumulate through the narrative often involve David's benevolence. For instance, the struggling wife he meets prompts in him "a strong Desire to know her Story"; she tells him her sad and tragic tale and, at the end, he reaches into his pocket, gives her five guineas and goes along his way (41). *The Man of Feeling* also uses this embedded structure, with the same chronotope of "the journey" facilitating encounters between strangers. In both novels, the relation of listener to teller is mediated by a financial inequality in which the listener's money provides the solution to the problem presented in the secondary tale.

At the same time that it demonstrates the listener's moral character through the disbursement of money to charity, the narrative situation commercializes the exchange and draws attention to the way the teller trades their story for money. Both *David Simple* and *The Man of Feeling* explicitly mark this conundrum, and neither is able to entirely extricate itself from commodifying stories. However, the more pronounced the internal relation, and the greater the effect the secondary tale has on the plot of the primary narrative, the less such commodification is a problem. By turning the storytellers into friends and adding social bonds to the financial ones, *David Simple* manages to elide financial and affective gain, whereas Mackenzie's more conservative maintenance of class boundaries between teller and listener keeps those affective gains at bay. The function of the embedded stories within *The Man of Feeling,* in other words, does not change as significantly through the narrative act as it does within *David Simple,* and thus the narrative exchange does not as effectively bring virtue and commerce into a balanced reciprocity. Mackenzie's conservatism requires him not to make poor strangers intimate friends, and without the social bonds, stories circulate within the novel as commodities sold in the anonymous commercial marketplace that the novel otherwise critiques.

The Man of Feeling

Many critics have noted the conservatism of *The Man of Feeling*, rooted in its nostalgia for the days when benevolent propertied gentlemen like Harley's ancestors had power, not the mercenary men of commerce, who are unrelentingly attacked in Mackenzie's novel.[22] The new, commercial economy is the cause of all suffering: laborers are displaced so the newly wealthy can build fashionable homes; tradesmen's wives are transformed by new money into vain and monstrous hypocrites; London is infected with schemers who appear to be gentleman but are really greedy cheats; and British merchants are pillaging the globe for riches. The strongest critique of commercial capitalism comes when Harley denounces the British colonization of India as a simple cash grab; what began as an original fair exchange of goods—in which traders "barter[ed] the commodities they brought for others which their purchasers could spare"—has become the theft of the country's wealth (118).[23] The novel's critique of commercial capitalism, however, is complicated by the "narrative of the narrative" in which framing devices ironically undercut the hero. A case in point is the critique of colonization. As Maureen Harkin has argued, the narrator "subverts Harley's position" by satirically entitling the chapter that contains Harley's attack "The Man of Feeling talks of what he does not understand."[24] The novel's mix of satire and sympathy poses the primary interpretative problem of the text.[25] How does the satiric framing shape the meaning of Harley's sentimental journey? Where does the narrative exchange leave the critique of commercial capitalism?

Shifting narrative levels introduce the interpretative challenge of the mixed tone, and each shift presents its own narrative exchange. The multiple disorientating layers of framing begin with the fictional editor's first-person account of saving the manuscript from being used for wadding by his hunting partner, the curate. The editor exchanges his wadding—a copy of the German Illustrissimi—for the manuscript, noting that "[w]e exchanged books; and by that means (for the curate was a strenuous logician) we probably saved both" (49). The narrative situation of this textual exchange first replaces both texts' value as literature with their material value as paper or wadding, and then suggests that the aesthetic value of each is determined by the exchange with the reader. Harley's story has no stable use value as a sentimental tale: the book is assigned a value, a meaning, only in the moment of its consumption, through what the market will bear.[26] When we arrive at the primary diegesis in medias res (since the manuscript exists only in incomplete fragments), Harley's story is further distanced by the discovery that the narrator is not the hero but a man referred to by the curate as "the Ghost" who left the manuscript at a farmer's house and the farmer passed it on to the curate. The reader does not know the relation between Harley and the Ghost, since the opening pages are missing. Why the extra distancing? Why does the author keep the reader, as G. A. Starr notes, "at three or four removes from his hero"?[27] Harley's sentimental innocence is kept at a distance while the narrator is positioned as cynically knowledgeable about the ways of the commercial world, and the combination literally gives Mackenzie the best of two worlds, a past world in which land-based property stabilizes virtue and a present in which value is determined by the market.[28] But the structural distancing also buries the story's affective bonds underneath layers of exchanges and increases the chances for those exchanges to reify the social relations between teller and listener. The stories-within-stories of downward mobility are told by secondary characters to Harley, and they circulate satirically as objects, becoming things that are sold, rather than things that build social relations. In Harley's naive world he can feel his way to reuniting Miss Atkin with her father, but the narrator remains outside that affective space, exchanging the story as part of a larger episodic structure.[29]

The first story-within-the-story in *The Man of Feeling*, the beggar's tale, circulates stories as speculative commodities, gaining value only by being exchanged, without the use value of lasting social relations. The beggar engages Harley's sympathy and Harley listens to his pathetic tale of downward mobility, a consequence of his having lost his job due to illness. Forced to beg in the streets, he realizes that his sad tale does not interest the strangers from whom he solicits money, so he decides to try his luck as a fortune-teller. Instead of his own story of loss, he sells strangers prophetic stories of their happiness. "This I found by much the better way: folks will always listen when the tale is their own" (61). The beggar adapts to consumer demand and learns to approach stories in the same way as the speaker of the filibuster that Genette describes: the content of the story itself is unimportant and empty; its value lies in its exchange, in the act of telling that produces the halfpence.[30] Harley's response to the beggar's admission that his trade is "none of the honestest" is to give the beggar a shilling, perhaps accidentally as the heterodiegetic narrator leaves Harley's action ambiguous. The beggar has succeeded in what he set out to do: profit financially from the narrative situation.

Does his story matter? Either we can read the narrative exchange as endorsing the beggar's market savvy, thus positioning Harley as a naive dupe who simply prefers to buy tales of misfortune over prophecies of happiness, or we can read Harley's charitable instinct to reach into his pocket and to demand the "true" story as the right moral response. The distanced ironic narrator does not provide a clear way through the satire-versus-sentiment conundrum; the loss of "compression" in Harley's fingers, which makes him drop the coin while the beggar's trained dog snaps it up, suspends the reader's judgment, and Harley leaves the beggar to go on his way (61). No affective bond from the secondary level spills into the primary diegesis, and the narrative act does not change the plot of either level.

The narrative exchange of money for stories largely propels the reader forward in an otherwise plotless novel. As G. A. Starr and April London have noted, the novel refuses a progressive plot and distrusts linearity; thus, without character development, the episodic and fragmentary plot requires embedded stories to generate its story.[31] Insofar as the narrative goad or the catalyst to storytelling is downward mobility, the exchange of stories depends for its content upon the greedy capitalist producing new victims. The story would end if Harley lived in the glory years of civic humanism. Indeed, his own journey is prompted by downward mobility: dispossessed of the economic status that his birth once entailed, he hopes to increase his small income by traveling to London to acquire the lease on land adjacent to his reduced paternal estate. "[N]ow-a-days, it is money, not birth, that makes people respected," his aunt observes, and Harley must enter the "now-a-days" world to increase his fortune (122). Like the fashionable trinkets of the vain merchants' wives, the stories told require novelty for them to accrue sympathetic value. The narrative situations demand that the listener is hearing the story for the first time to gain its emotional power. The fallen genteel woman in Bedlam whose story Harley elicits cannot cry for her dead lover, though Harley can, because she knows her story too well and her tears have dried up (70). Similarly, the Ghost interrupts Edwards's autodiegetic tale to observe that while Harley was "bathed in tears," Edwards could drop only one since "the story was grown familiar" (108). Scenes of storytelling may register sympathy, but they can do so only once, which is why when Harley retells Miss Atkin's story to her father, the narrative simply remarks, "[H]e related the treacheries to which she had fallen a sacrifice," without retelling them (93). The novel, then, can generate new stories only if it accumulates new losses.

While the embedded stories get longer as *The Man of Feeling* progresses, Harley does not gain insight or close friends, nor do the stories resolve the problem of his own downward mobility. Until we arrive at Old Edwards, the tales Harley hears are mainly digressive and their function does not shift substantially in the telling. Harley's aid alters the plot of the secondary tale, but the exchange is not reciprocal and no lasting value enters the primary story. In other words, Harley does not accumulate strong social relations as he accumulates stories. He does gain obligations that model a traditional aristocratic social structure, but intimate affective bonds are not sustained. Harley's charity resolves the problem of loss narrated in the old farmer Edwards's tale, and they do return to their neighborhood together to live beside each other within the primary diegesis, but the social bond that accumulates through the narrative exchange is weak.[32] Mackenzie's ironic narration, with its conservative nostalgic construction of Harley as a hero from another time, when virtue and rank were attached, ensures that the internal relation between teller and tale does not cross class boundaries and thus Harley becomes Edwards's benefactor and good neighbor, but not his friend.

The Man of Feeling's accumulation of stories culminates in Edwards's and Harley's return to their childhood neighborhood without having changed its destructive modernity, and all that is left in the novel is for Harley to die, a story event that corresponds to a noticeable shift from a heterodiegetic narration to an increasingly homodiegetic one. At this point in the novel, the Ghost inserts himself into the scene as witness to Harley's benevolence: "I have seen his master at work in this little spot. . . . I have seen . . . the smile of conscious satisfaction on his cheek" (117). As the "I" of the text gets closer to Harley, Harley himself recedes. Only on Harley's deathbed is the "I" individualized as "Charles" (136). The narrator uses "I" no less than eighteen times in the two-paragraph chapter describing Harley's corpse. The social intimacy between the narrator and Harley only confirms that they live in different narrated worlds: Harley must die as a man whose feelings "are too tender to be suffered by the world" for Charles to take material form in a world "in general selfish, interested, and unthinking" (136).[33] The introduction of the narrator's feeling "I" after Harley's death has the effect of locating the accumulation of social relations on the wrong narrative level. The telling of embedded stories has not changed the relation between characters or brought Harley any closer to the reader in the present-tense world, but it has changed relations between narrator and hero and turned a heterodiegetic voice into a haunted homodiegetic voice, one that is internally related to a corpse. An analogous awkward shift in narrative voice occurs when the hunter narrator of the frame reenters the text right before Harley's death to explain that the manuscript has too many gaps to proceed, and thus, as a consumer object, this "novel" will have no value (135). In so doing, the hunter reveals that he literally enters the territory of the "I" of the primary diegesis, and that while Charles is the witness to Harley's death, the hunter has acquired firsthand knowledge "from some inquiries I was at the trouble of making in the country" (135). The narrative shift threatens a metaleptic collapse between the frame and diegetic levels.[34]

The "narrative of a narrative" that *The Man of Feeling* tells is that use value is a thing of the past, realizable only through loss, as death and as downward mobility. Not until Harley is on his deathbed can the wealthy Miss Walton, the love of Harley's life, recognize his value: "I know your worth—I have known it long" (137–38); their wealth inequality can never be overcome for the two to marry within the diegesis ("[in] the conceptions of the world, the love of a man of Harley's fortune for the heiress of 4000 l. a-year, is indeed desperate" [135]).

In some ways, the value of the text for the reader is precisely the circulation of narrated loss and deathbed scenes. The beggar may have found that fortunes of happiness sell better than his own story of misfortune, but Mackenzie's text profits from the circulation of a loss unrecuperable in the narrative of narrative.

David Simple

The Adventures of David Simple has the same structure of embedding as *The Man of Feeling*, with first-person narrators of stories-within-stories embedded within a third-person narrative, but it overcomes the problem of both the commercialization of the narrative exchange and the distance between teller and listener by increasing the extent to which the autodiegetic narrators become characters within the primary diegesis. The relation between the embedded tale's narrator and the hero of the primary tale is reciprocated, and this factor changes the economics of the sentimental dynamic. The stories take on a use value through their strong internal relations; the narrative situation turns strangers into the friends that David seeks. But, as we shall see, stories of loss must continue circulating within an exchange economy in order for this transformation to occur. When David retreats at the end of *David Simple* and takes his family out of circulation, closure arrives and the narrative ends. When the story continues in *Volume the Last* with the narrative of David's own downward mobility, he must circulate his story within an exchange economy to stop the losses, but fails to do so. Without the stories-within-stories, the sequel can produce narrative desire only through death. The tension between a story's use value and its exchange value is never ultimately resolved, but reading Fielding's use of narrative embedding in *David Simple* and *Volume the Last* illustrates the generative narrative desire that that tension puts into play.

The stories David hears—which are, significantly, the stories David desires, the ones he seeks out, the ones that he "long[s]" for—are stories of wealthy characters who have been variously bankrupted, been cheated out of a fortune, or otherwise fallen in social status (Fielding, *David Simple*, 103). The novel provides this book's signature example of the narrativity of downward mobility when David observes the distressed stranger Camilla wearing a silk dress that was once quite fine and observes that he "was certain by their Manner, and Behaviour, they could not have been bred in very low Life," and he "longed to know their Story" (102, 103). The spoiled dress signifies a story. Similarly, David "begged" Cynthia to discover Isabelle's story, because there must be a reason why "a woman of Isabelle's Quality [was] leading a Life so unsuitable to the Station Fortune had placed her in" (152). David's desire to hear the story shifts the novel's circulation of wealth from a desire to accumulate money to a desire to accumulate stories. What propels the reader forward is the demand for more narrative, not the desire for the hero to accumulate wealth, and thus more money may be brought in to resolve a narrative problem, but the desire for that resolution, not for the money, provides the story's momentum.

The stories that circulate through *David Simple* prompt David, like Harley, to address the teller's loss with money. After hearing the frugal wife's tale of her profligate husband, David gives her both "Compassion" and "five Guineas" (44). How is Fielding's exchange of stories for money any different than Mackenzie's? The central difference is the social relations that storytelling builds; David begins as an orphan on a quest for friendship and ends up with a wife, a brother-in-law, a sister-in-law, and a happy family in retreat. Along the way, the novel also registers the conditions of exchange under which such storytelling builds bonds of compassion, and these conditions require both value judgments and money. When David's fortune is restored after his brother's betrayal, the money brings no pleasure because "[t]he only Use he had for Money, was to serve his Friends" and, at this point, he has none (20). What I hope to show is that the inverse is also true: the use value of his friends, the value of their stable love, is readable in the text only through an exchange economy that includes circulating capital.

What is the value of a story in the novel? Whose stories are credible and have the power to build friendships? As Bryan Mangano's discussion of the problem of narrative reliability and friendship points out, Fielding introduces narrative skepticism through false friendship and the problem of knowing who to trust in the new anonymous world of market relations.[35] First-person scenes of storytelling that stage true amity are never entirely freed from the skepticism. From the beginning, we learn that not all stories should be valued equally: the truth of the first stockjobber's story at the Royal Exchange that David hears is brought into question by the second one, and his story is further challenged by the third. Reliability is here determined not by an ontological quality or use value of the character but by how the characters circulate in relation to each other, especially as that relation is monetary: if they have something to gain financially by telling a story of someone else's bad character, their story has no credibility. The story's value accrues through its circulation in a social exchange. The same friendship economy determines the value of the stories told by Mr. Orgueil, Mr. Spatter, and Mr. Varnish shortly thereafter. Each tell David the "real" characters of one another and inform him that each is not what they appear. The introduction of the third man in both series of character vignettes shifts the value judgment from the individual identities to the social relations and marks the way such relations are negotiated through an exchange of virtue and wealth.

Significantly, money needs to enter the exchange in order for stories to become worthwhile, though the amount does not matter. If the value of the shilling depends on how much bread or corn it can be exchanged for, the value of the story is determined by whether it puts money into play to consolidate the social bond. The false incest stories Livia tells compromise social bonds and take money away from Camilla and Valentine and thus are given no value. The stories Ratcliff writes David in response to news of David's bankruptcy—the fable of the dog crossing the river and the anecdote of the Baronet's daughter who could not do needle work—are emotionally devastating because they contain no cash (273–74). Had Ratcliff backed up his moralism with money, the stories would have carried weight. Instead, they are empty trifles, meaningful only in the negative way as signifying his selfishness. Money functions, then, to determine the value of the narrative insofar as the stories produce an affective expenditure that needs to be balanced with a financial one, though the value of the money itself is irrelevant. Thus, circulation of the stories requires the accumulation of friends to separate the money from avarice and attach it to social relations. In this way, the story of stories in *David Simple* mirrors the central plot of David's quest for a friend.

Fielding acknowledges that the dynamic of sentimental narrative exchange introduces a vicious circle in which money guarantees affect at the same time that it compromises the social relation by seemingly buying friendship. When relations between strangers are mediated by money, the novel shows, they can quickly become motivated by self-interest and greed. Cynthia's embedded tale especially foregrounds the way unequal economic power dynamics can change the narrative situation from charity to exploitation and false friendship. After Cynthia, an unhappy "Toad-eater," tells David her story—a long narrative of financial vulnerability and sexual exploitation—David offers her money (88). But Cynthia does not immediately accept it for fear that to do so will simply repeat the story she is trying to extricate herself from, one in which dependency leads to mercenary social and sexual relations. Her past experience of economic obligations has taught her to be leery of the hidden costs, especially to women, of accepting charity, and, indeed, she might be right to doubt David's motives since he later admits to a romantic attachment, offering her his hand in marriage, a plot twist that momentarily collapses the virtuous motivations of David with the lecherous ones of the country gentleman who has previously attempted to buy Cynthia's affections. David's feelings for Cynthia confirm her own observation that "[s]he knew too much of the World, to be easily persuaded that any Man could act as *David* did by her, from *pure Friendship*" (97).

After she rejects the marriage offer and the money, David still insists on helping her financially, and Cynthia ultimately accepts because she realizes that the affective bond she has built with him in the course of the narrative exchange is of "pure Friendship" and it obliges her to do him the favor of taking his money as "he would be very uneasy if she refused him" (97). Fielding transposes the internal relation from one in which David helps Cynthia to one in which Cynthia, the secondary narrator, helps David, progressing the plot of the primary diegesis insofar as her act consolidates their friendship. Through the narrative exchange, David's journey to find a friend is successful, and the two later become in-laws when they each marry one of the impoverished siblings Camilla and Valentine, who tell their own tragic family story. By creating and multiplying the strong intimate internal relations between tellers and listeners, Fielding imagines the new commercial world as one where stories can circulate to build social attachments and can recirculate David's wealth in productive and useful ways.

David Simple closes after the narrative exchanges have built a community of intimate friends who at the end retreat from the world of commercial exchange to live useful lives on David's estate. But when the domestic community is forced by economic need to return to the world of commercial exchange in *Volume the Last*, the narrative exchange tells a different story. The sequel opens with David's legal battles over his inheritance and Camilla's father's loss of £10,000 on "a bad mortgage," which forces the family back into the world and launches Cynthia and Valentine as far afield as Jamaica in their attempt to generate wealth (246). The sequel's stories of loss, however, are not compensated by the accumulation of social relations; in fact, they generate only more unrelenting loss. Camilla and Valentine and later David lose their financial fortunes, and nine out of the family's eleven members end up dead. I argue that because the sequel lacks stories-within-stories, it cannot exchange sympathy with financial compensation in a way that would stop the accumulation of loss. As Betty Schellenberg has observed, the shift from comedy to tragedy from the first to the last volume involves a shift in narrative structure from episodic to linear form.[36] In its linear narration of David's downward mobility, the novel stops circulating stories.

In *David Simple*, David happily accumulates stories of loss, building friendships and dispersing wealth in return. But once David becomes the man with the loss that needs to be narrated, embedded tales cease to circulate. Until the appearance of the beggar near the end, *Volume the Last* is free of digressive interruption. In the sequel, it is David who must tell his story of loss, and in this he miserably fails. As his poverty mounts, he makes known to Orgueil "the utmost Distress of his Circumstances, without the Use of either Rhetoric or Complaint" (279). But without the narrative skill—like the "little Rhetorick" Camilla was "mistress of" in pleading on behalf of Valentine—David's description of want produces no response, no money. Telling a good story is in fact part of the sentimental exchange: "[N]o Man breathing knew better than *David* that the painting your Misery in the strongest Colours, is necessary to raise what is called Compassion in a proud Mind" (279). While his humility will not let him stylistically enhance his material conditions, David's naiveté blinds him from seeing that storytelling is part of the bargain of the sentimental economy; virtuous feeling can validate wealth only when Rhetoric is deployed and the stories keep flowing. David foolishly believes he can fix morality to a stable universal standard devoid of circulation. Cynthia, however, understands the necessity of constantly circulating stories as the way to accumulate sentimental affect, and while David lies dying, she sets out to Bath to tell their story to her future benefactor. Her success in Bath has her returning to David and little Camilla with pleasing "Imaginations" of more stories to come and with money to support them (339). The help arrives too late for David, who dies, but Cynthia's storytelling has provided the payback that allows closure to be reached and the deaths in the family to stop.

Cynthia's survival at the end attests to the necessity of the exchange economy, something *The Man of Feeling* refuses to acknowledge. Like Mackenzie, Fielding tries to establish moral happiness outside the system of exchange by having David and his family retreat to the country and opt out of social and commercial relations. But the sequel registers such retreat as impossible. A capitalist economy requires the constant circulation of money, for only when money is put out does it become capital. Similarly, my reading of narrative exchange in *David Simple* shows that virtue requires a constant flow through strangers' stories to give it sentimental value.

The tension between virtue and commerce, between authentic emotion and interested avarice, use value and exchange value, is less likely to be a problem for first-person-stories-within-third-person-stories when the levels mix in a reciprocal fashion or when the narrative act changes the plot of the primary rather than the secondary diegesis. In the anonymously published *Female Sensibility; Or, The History of Emma Pomfret*, the latter is the case, supported by the fact that the economic inequality between teller and listener is reversed so that Mrs. Dormer, the autodiegetic narrator of a secondary tale, consolidates her sympathetic bond with poor Emma through the scene of storytelling; thus when Mrs. Dormer dies and leaves Emma money, Emma is rescued from indigence and can marry for love. Emma demonstrates her virtue not by telling her own tale of woe but by listening to another's. When the narrative act alters the plot in the primary level and the internal relations between teller and listener are strong, wealth is more likely to circulate productively, not speculatively, with a use value of establishing emotional intimacies that mask wealth's origins in capital's anonymous marketplace.

Heterodiegetically narrated sentimental novels by their very nature introduce a distance between the narrator of the secondary tale and the narratee of the primary one, since the narrative act is not between narrators but between one narrator and a listener who is not the narrator of their own story. This is the textual structure that introduces the problematic ironic distance in *The Man of Feeling*. Novels in which both primary and secondary tales have autodiegetic narrators—and thus, the scene of storytelling is narrated by the listener of the story—bring the narratee into a more intimate setting, since both teller and listener are disclosing the stories of their own lives. Does a different narrative structure of embedding shift the representation of the tension between virtue and commerce?

Autodiegetic Narrators within Autodiegetically Narrated Stories: *The History of Emily Montague*

The second most common shift of narrative levels in sentimental literature consists of one narrator telling their own story to another one doing the same. Goldsmith's *Vicar of Wakefield* and Sterne's *Sentimental Journey* both take this form. In *The Vicar of Wakefield* the embedded tales told to the Vicar include those recounted by intimate family members, his son and his daughter, who narrate tales of misfortune that end up revealing social connections and restoring the Primrose family to wealth. As the narrator of a picaresque tale that deploys the chronotope of "the journey," Sterne's Yorick narrates listening to the stories of strangers; and while the narrative exchanges often involve questions of authenticity—is this stranger's story true or are they scamming him for money?—Yorick's good heart is repeatedly narrativized by the tears he sheds in the dramatized scene. When the person shedding the tears over another character's story is the same as the person telling the main story, the sentimental scene of storytelling is drawn into greater sympathetic focus. Epistolary novels add another layer to this emotional immediacy with their intercalated storytelling, in that they narrate the internal relation with a near simultaneity. Elizabeth Griffith's novels *Delicate Distress* and *The History of Lady Barton* include clear examples of this case, where the primary narrative is told mainly through letters between sisters and each of these letter writers includes stories that have been narrated to them by other women who have experienced tragedies. The narrative exchange between the primary and secondary levels causes the addressee of both levels (i.e., both sisters) to act; and future letters demonstrate how the feeling in one scene of storytelling translates into later events. Louisa Barton, who is the listener of Mrs. Walter's tale of seduction and abandonment, and her sister, Fanny, who is the addressee of Louisa's letter containing the story, join forces to rescue Mrs. Walter, thus doubling the social and affective ties the narrative exchange produces.

The increased circulation that the epistolary form entails, with its combination of immediacy and private narratee, produces complex displacements between the financial and sentimental exchanges. This is particularly the case in Frances Brooke's *The History of Emily Montague*, a multivocal epistolary novel set mainly in Quebec. Its hero and heroine, Rivers and Emily, meet and fall in love in Canada, but they face financial obstacles to marrying and settling in

England. After Rivers inherits a small farm in England, the novel seems to resolve these obstacles and come to a close when they marry and retreat to an idyllic rural life. But almost 20% of the novel's discursive space remains; although they marry on page 330 of the 400-page novel, they do so in reduced circumstances, with no extra money to spare. It is not until the very end that they inherit a "nabob" fortune in the form of Emily's reunion with her long-lost father. All the correspondents disavow financial desire, repeatedly asserting a lack of interest in money with conditional statements such as "[I]f I have your heart, I am richer than an oriental monarch" (330); "I know no pleasure equal to your friendship; nor would I give it up for the revenue of an eastern monarch" (345); "[T]here [is not] a nabobess on earth half as happy as [I]" (348). The story of the "Fair Cottager" is embedded between the marriage and the ending, and I argue that its narrative exchange is generated by the need to resolve the contradiction between use value and exchange value in the novel. The scene of storytelling ultimately allows virtue to be rewarded with capital at the novel's close.[37] The exchange erases the conditional *if*'s and allows for Rivers and Emily to live happily ever after with all the riches of an Eastern monarch.

The Fair Cottager's story introduces the desire for wealth by displacing it to the secondary level. Rivers and Emily encounter a stranger with a child in distressed circumstances. She had "an air of the world, which the plainness of her dress could not hide," and because everything about her suggests "this amiable girl is not in the station in which she was born," her presence "tended to excite the most lively curiosity" (356, 357, 356). The incongruity between the stranger's lowly status and her genteel sensibility, evidenced by her ability to converse about books, prompts not only the desire to hear her story but also, significantly, the desire for money. Rivers notes that "her story, for she certainly has one, should be such as, however it may entitle her to compassion, may make it impossible for Emily to shew it in the manner she seems to wish" (357); "the smallness of [River's] . . . fortune" renders Emily's budget for charitable acts limited (356). The story that the stranger Fanny tells is an extremely clichéd one of seduction and abandonment except for the fact that it is not Fanny but her friend Sophia who is the "victim of ruin" and who leaves Fanny in charge of her illegitimate son after she dies. The drama in the story is not in the story itself, since it reads as if Brooke wrote it in her sleep, but in the narrative exchange that the story puts into play.

The complex "narrative of a narrative" exchange works to separate financial concerns from the sentimental bonds: Fanny tells her story in a letter she sends to Emily that the reader accesses as embedded in a letter Rivers writes to his friend Fitzgerald. The shift in narrative levels displaces the narrative exchange from one between Fanny and Emily to one between Rivers and Fitzgerald, and the shift produces a sexual division of labor whereby Emily's heart opens to

Fanny and Rivers takes charge of the social economics. He sends Fanny's letter to Fitzgerald in London, who happens to know the seducer's brother, Sir William. Fitzgerald encloses Fanny's letter with one of his own to Sir William, who responds with joy at finding the son his brother confessed on his deathbed to having. Sir William settles £3,000 on the boy and, at Fitzgerald's suggestion, gives Fanny an annuity of £100. The narrative exchange not only demonstrates how male social bonds generate financial aid and female bonds emotional aid, but, by intertwining the voices, also registers them as necessarily complimentary, drawing together the economic and the sentimental. The economic is displaced threefold (from Emily to Rivers, Rivers to Fitzgerald, Fitzgerald to Sir William), and each narrative exchange consolidates sentimental bonds and increases the affective circle. River's immediate response to Fitzgerald's success with Sir William, and thus the success of the narrative transactions, is to see the exchange as proving that we are all "united by one common bond" (370). Quoting Pope's "Essay on Man," Rivers exclaims, "There is nothing of which I am more convinced than that, 'True self-love and social are the same'" (370).

Helping others is helping oneself, and the narrative transaction creates a ripple outward whereby the self and the social collapse to bring happiness to all. Fanny lives happily ever after, and as her letter passes from hand to hand, the sentimental merit passes as well, a merit that is ultimately calculated financially. I argue that the want of money, the desire for wealth as a resolution to a narrative problem, also spreads outward; and while Rivers and Emily require no funds to help Fanny, the desire for those funds, for a larger charitable budget, has been introduced by the transaction, and if helping others is helping oneself, then helping themselves can only help them help more others. While Fanny and the boy are on their way to London to stay with Fitzgerald, Colonel Willmott travels to River's estate to offer him a substantial settlement to marry his daughter, whom Willmott has not met. Willmott's plan gives both Rivers and Emily, unbeknownst to each other, one last opportunity to show their love by refusing wealth and declining Willmott's offer. When they discover that Emily is the daughter whom Willmott wants Rivers to marry, love and virtue can be united with colonial capital because now they are compatible. In fact, they end up being the same thing, as the daughter Rivers refuses to marry for money is the daughter he has already married for love. Rivers closes the novel revising his earlier declarations against wealth: "Colonel Willmott has made me just as rich as I wish to be . . . whilst I thought a fortune and Emily incompatible, I had infinite contempt for the former, and fancied that it would rather take from, than add to, my happiness; but, now I can possess it with her, I allow it all its value" (407). Money can buy happiness and does have moral value, but only after it has circulated through a narrative exchange that brings together self-love and social commitment, allowing the desire to give money away to merge with the desire for new money.

Heterodiegetic Narrators within Homodiegetically Narrated Stories: *Millenium Hall*

This final section takes up what is perhaps the least common form of embedding, in which a narrator tells someone else's story to someone they know. In the epistolary novels of Elizabeth Griffith, when the sisters are telling each other the sad life stories of other women they have encountered, they do not do so heterodiegetically. Their letters shift to a third narrative level and include autodiegetically narrated stories; for example, the embedded letter from Mrs. Walters to Louisa in *The History of Lady Barton* that the reader accesses when Louisa includes it in a letter to her sister Fanny. Heterodiegetically narrated secondary tales are rare, partly because the emotional attachment between teller and listener is not one of sympathetic identification. Yet such is the structure of Sarah Scott's utopian novel, *A History of Millenium Hall*, whose narrative exchange, I argue, manages a displacement of virtue onto wealth similar to that in *Emily Montague* and provides the strongest illustration of the way novels can resolve the contradiction between use value and exchange value by circulating money through narrative exchange. Telling stories not only has a use value in the novel but also recirculates colonial wealth as virtue. The novel's shifts in narrative level mean that the violence of a speculative economy is located on a distant third level and the heterodiegetically narrated secondary tales within a homodiegetic narration allow for a stabilization of use value. My reading follows Millenium Hall's money through its circulation in the embedded tales to show how the narrative of narrative allows the novel, like capitalism, to gloss over its constitutive contradictions, in part, through a gendering of plot.

The narrator of the main story participates in the world of the Hall, conversing, observing, investigating, and writing about his visit, a visit that provides the novel's primary space-time. Having returned to England from the West Indies with a fortune but having compromised his health by living a life dedicated to capital accumulation, the unnamed narrator journeys to the countryside where a coach accident lands him at the Hall, coincidently inhabited by his cousin Mrs. Maynard (the narrator is named Sir George Ellison in Scott's sequel). She satisfies his curiosity to know the histories of the women who live in the Hall and narrates them heterodiegetically. This structure produces relations that change the primary narrator but do not cause him to respond to the tales with money, since the embedded histories are not told by the subject of sympathetic identification in the midst of distress but are narrated by another after the subject of the narrative has found their way to the utopian community.

The Hall's alternative political economy, one based on the Christian principles of charity and good works, forms the basis of the heavily descriptive primary diegesis. The novel models a society in which commerce easily joins hands with virtue to provide all in the society with more than what they need while still maintaining class hierarchies. The ladies of the Hall retire to the country precisely to escape the evils of a world driven by greed and self-interest. Many of their charities are founded to address problems brought on by an economic system focused entirely on gain: they employ the unemployable, the disabled, the old, and anyone else whom capitalism deems not worth the wage; they hire only those tradesmen who have been bankrupted or otherwise disadvantaged by the market economy; they open a factory to solve an oversupply of labor in the area; they pay higher wages than the squires who starve their employees; and they provide a refuge for genteel single women without fortune who have nowhere else to go. Benevolence toward the economically disenfranchised is the goal of all the ladies' commercial enterprises but, utopically, the businesses also manage to turn an impressive financial profit, always producing an excess of money. The carpet factory they build to employ the unemployable manages to pay high wages and still accumulate profit. The factory's profit is then recirculated, not only as capital (reinvesting and expanding the business) but also as more virtue: the ladies always "apply all they spend, as to make almost every shilling contribute to the support of some person in real necessity; by this means every expence bears the merit of a donation" (Scott, *Millenium Hall*, 169–70). Capital becomes charity.

How does the Hall manage to produce surplus value and promote benevolence? By imposing a strict economy whereby all financial exchanges are determined by use value and whereby people consume only what they need. The ladies follow the standard attributes of the Protestant work ethic: frugality, industry, living within one's means, and saving money by reigning in excessive desires. Profligacy, luxury, and fashionable consumption cause much evil in the text. Mrs. Morgan's wicked stepmother and Lady Mary's aunt Lady Sheerness fit the description of the woman "who lavishes both her time and money on every fashionable folly," and are corrupt and mean because of it (164). When simple need guides economic decisions and reigns in consuming desires, the world produces enough wealth for all. The neighboring woods, for example, provides the Hall with all the food required to feed its inhabitants—pidgeons (*sic*), rabbits, deer, and hares—because the park's previous owners were "good oeconomists" and did not cut down the trees for quick liquid capital (109). The land's value is imagined not as a commodity-to-be-sold but as use, to produce all "the necessaries of life": "These are indeed our riches; here we have almost every thing we can want" (110). The ladies are able to invest in their charities, precisely because they keep their desires to their needs, consume only to subsist, and do not spend on fashionable trinkets and luxury items: "As they ordered every thing in their own family with great oeconomy, and thought themselves entitled only to a part of their fortunes, their large incomes allowed them full power to assist many, whose situation differed very essentially from theirs" (159). Mary Peace points out the crack in this plan in that the ladies are described as not having "any thing unfashionable in their appearance, except that they were free from any trumpery ornaments" (61).[38] In other words, they are not outside the circulations of fashion and bourgeois consumerism. Their house is tastefully decorated, and their table may not be "expensive" but it is served on china purchased with more than what the pidgeons in the woods could produce.

Another gap in Scott's utopic vision of virtuous capitalism is that the Hall's alternative use-value economy—in which everyone happily labors, consumes solely what they need, despises luxury, and trades goods fairly—is set into motion and only made possible by the ladies' interest-bearing investments. Behind the good works are the capital investments each lady makes when she enters the Hall. We can answer the question of where the Hall's profit comes from very specifically and materially since Scott provides as detailed a financial accounting as any Defoe novel. Nicole Jordan and David Oakleaf point out that the novel provides a more intricate domestic account book than most fictional texts.[39] The final pages of *Millenium Hall* enumerate the ladies' spending: between their various charities and their household expenses, they spend £2,110 per year.

While the primary diegesis accounts for the expenses, the embedded tales provide the Hall's capital. At the end of each history, each heroine inherits a fortune, bringing the story to a close and initiating a new investment in the Hall, a relation made explicit at the end of the final embedded story: "As Mrs. Trentham's fortune made a good addition to the income of the society, they on this occasion established in the parish a manufacture of carpets" (243). The novel specifies the amount of the fortunes as obsessively as it counts its expenses; thus, we can add up the total the ladies invest in the Hall: an impressive £78,000, not including Mrs. Morgan's annuity of £1,400 or Mrs. Maynard's "small jointure" (one of the few sums left unspecified) (242). The £78,000 also does not include the enormous capital investment of the Hall itself, with its furnishings, which Mrs. Morgan inherits. Using the standard interest rate of 3% a year, the ladies investments produce £3,740, a calculation the narrator also performs in his head but does not detail (248). In other words, the difference between their expenses and income has them coming out at least £1,630 in the black every year. When the narrator secretly asks Mrs. Maynard what they do with the surplus, she replies that their "accidental charities were innumerable" (248). If, as Robert Markley diagnoses, the logic of charity is sentimentalism's impasse in that virtue accumulates while pocketbooks empty, why do the Millenium Hall women seem to have bottomless pockets?[40] On the level of monetary economics, the answer in the text is speculative capitalism: they accumulate money through interest by investing their inheritances; that is, they gain from money breeding money and from following the golden rule to never spend the investment's principle.[41] But the moral economy within the narrator's description of the Hall insists on a different circulation, one that seeks profit precisely through investing in losing causes and entering into the world of exchange solely to circulate a solid material use value. The embedded stories of the ladies' histories circulate their tales of downward mobility in such a way that the fortunes they receive to solve the plot problem of "virtue in distress," a problem narrated in all their stories, can be recirculated in other narrative levels freed from the world of capital accumulation.

What the didacticism of the primary diegesis, with its detailing of the Hall's virtuous economics, lacks in narrative interest the embedded stories make up for in plot. The action-packed histories of the ladies—full of dramatic deaths, melodramatic reunion scenes, near seductions, broken off engagements, and failed marriages—provide the novel with its narrative propulsion and literally take over the novel, with the four inset tales constituting 70% of its total discursive space. What prompts their telling? What relation is forged between the narrative levels? The narrator's curiosity to know who the women are who have founded such an unusual community provides the initial impetus for Mrs. Maynard's narration, but it is only his previous intimate relation to her—both discursively, as a homodiegetic narrator, and familiarly, in being her cousin—that allows Mrs. Maynard to break the ladies' otherwise strict modesty and tell their stories.[42] In other words, the internal relation between teller and listener may not be changed in the narrative act, but it provides the conditions of the story's telling. The stories themselves also function to cure the illness of masculine mercantile gain by inoculating it with the Hall's feminized virtuous economy. Insofar as the libertine Lamont reforms and the narrator is restored to health, the telling of the stories-within-the-story resolve the plot of the primary diegesis.

The embedded stories all tell gendered tales of "virtue in distress," and, except for the last story, they begin with downward mobility. Louisa Mancel's tale opens with the death of her parents, leaving her penniless and destitute at the age of ten. Lady Mary Jones's story similarly begins with the downward mobility caused by her father's death after he had mortgaged the full value of his estate. Mrs. Selvyn's father is described as "the younger brother of an ancient family, whose fortune was inferior to the rank it held in the country," and Selvyn is threatened with poverty when she loses his already-reduced income upon his death (199). As economically vulnerable, the women face a number of sexually exploitative scenes, and all are rewarded with inheritances in the end. Since the listeners know how the stories end—that is, that the women end up restored to their rank, finding refuge and economic bounty in the Hall—the reader knows that the narrative situation will not provide the solution to the problem of downward mobility. In a way, the storytelling actually contains the volatility of a speculative anonymous commercial world by narrating the upswings and downswings in the past tense within a secondary diegesis. The stability of the 3% interest rate in the Hall's accounting remains untouched and unaffected by the Providential fortunes and misfortunes within the embedded stories. What the narrated stories do provide, often through their own internal shifts to a tertiary narrative level, is the recirculation of speculative capital as use value.

This narrative circulation is nowhere more evident than in the history of Louisa Mancel, one of the founders of the Hall, whose story begins when she is orphaned and left destitute as a child. After a series of volatile plot moments—a guardian's near seduction, the loss of an income—Louisa is reunited with her mother, whom she thought dead. Louisa becomes a waiting maid to a stranger, and when the new employer solicits her story because "she was certain [Louisa] . . . had not been born for the station she was then in," the narrative exchange shifts in function and produces the discovery that the stranger is in fact Louisa's mother (147). The mother then tells her story in a shift of narrative levels to the third degree wherein Louisa is the narratee and the mother describes her second marriage to a husband who had accumulated a fortune in the American and East Indian colonies. The mother herself dies a few pages later in the second-level narrative and Louisa inherits the £40,000 her stepfather accumulated. The mother-daughter recognition scene caused by storytelling produces a strong internal relation between the second and third narrative levels. Hearing the story changes Louisa's life and forges an affective bond that is not just social but also familial. Strangers become intimates through the narrative act. The third-level narrative also provides the solution to the problem of Louisa's poverty narrated in the second level and then generates the plot of the primary level by providing the initial investment to establish the Hall. Ironically, the money that saves Louisa from indigence and founds the charity originates in the same colonial capitalism that causes the problem that catalyzes the primary narrator's visit to the Hall and his desire to hear the stories. But its circulation through the stories decontaminates its initial, mercenary intent. As Nicolle Jordan observes, "[T]ainted wealth becomes purified by changing hands."[43] The functional relation between the levels recirculates the money, effectively displacing it from the product of an intentional desire for profit to the means to a virtuous end. David Oakleaf likens the circulation of West Indian capital through *Millenium Hall* to "money laundering."[44] The fact that capital's accumulation happens in the tertiary level allows it to act as the providential reward for Louisa's hard but virtuous life in the secondary diegesis, and then to circulate as charitable industry in the primary story. Virtue and commerce need not conflict but can productively join hands to build both a narrative and a virtuous community.

Scott extends the reciprocity between virtue and commercial gain produced by the "narrative of a narrative" in her fictional follow-up to *Millenium Hall*, *The History of Sir George Ellison*. In the second novel, Sir George returns to the West Indies, where he institutes a moral reform of slavery, inspired by Millenium Hall, so that his slaves are treated with humanity and generosity *and* they make him a profit, a fantasy of recirculation mirrored by the novel's embedded tales. Sir George comes across people in dire financial straits who tell him their stories at the exact moment he needs a steward or someone to run his new school, and thus their financial needs and Sir George's are reciprocal. They help themselves by helping each other and vice versa. Scott underscores this reciprocity by citing the same refrain from Pope that Brooke does in *Emily Montague*: "self love and the social are the same."[45] The narrative act brings virtue and commerce into this reciprocal exchange by circulating stories as socially useful while they simultaneously generate surplus value.

This chapter surveys a range of sentimental scenes of storytelling, highlighting the narrative device of embedding to argue that it is the signature narrative structure of sentimental fiction and that its centrality to the sentimental novel emerges from the narrativity of downward mobility. The narrative tension inherent in capital's structural contradiction between use value and exchange value produces the desire to exchange stories of loss. In thinking about the way narrative replaces money as the thing that circulates through systems of exchange, I have read three different forms of embedding systems to demonstrate how each allows for specific circulations of the tensions between self-interest and the social, between financial and moral profit, between the listener's and the teller's desires. The ways by which the relations between the listener and the teller are forged—whether the listener is also a narrator and the teller, the heroine; whether characters from different levels develop lasting social bonds; and whether these relations change the course of the plot—provide different narratives of an exchange economy. Some, like those in *Emily Montague* and *Millenium Hall*, generate reciprocal gains that optimistically represent virtue and commerce working together and ideologically mask the tension between use and exchange value through their narrative embedding. The mask is stronger precisely because telling stories turns strangers into intimate friends, and often reveals strangers to be long-lost family members, for example, through the repeated motif of maternal recognition scenes in *Millenium Hall* (this motif is used frequently in *The Fool of Quality*, as discussed in chapter 2). Stories and the social relations their tellings enact are more quickly commodified in the heterodiegetically narrated *Man of Feeling* and *David Simple*, and while each novel manages the exchange differently, in both the narrative act stages the problem of a world where money has become the primary mode of value. Embedded stories of downward mobility in sentimental novels mediate the tension behind capitalism's new circulation of exchange value, but at the same time they profit from the narrative energy that the tension puts into play. The anonymity and fluidity of capitalism's culture prompts the narrative desire to know the poor stranger's story, "for she certainly has one."

Just as capitalism is built upon the logic of infinite circulation (money is capital only when it circulates to make more money), sentimental fiction is grounded in an infinite accumulation of stories whereby, as long as the tension between virtue and commerce remains in circulation, stories can generate more stories. By representing scenes of storytelling that pose the problem of finding stable moral value in a world governed by the fluidity of capital, sentimental narrative is infinitely catalyzed by capitalism's internal contradictions, and the compulsion to narrate narration may thus have more to do with mediating financial value than the sympathetic value it explicitly stages. In the end, what circulates through these scenes of storytelling—no matter what the novel's explicit politics may be—is the contradiction between use value and exchange value, a circulation that demonstrates how sentimental narrative acts are themselves deeply embedded in the narrative of capital.

The following chapter turns to Burney's *Cecilia* to read how the most basic formal device of narrative—plot—manages capital's structural contradiction of economic growth and how speculative accumulation feeds novelistic plot dynamics. Demonstrating the way plot is a form of risk management in Burney's novel, I argue that plot mirrors the temporal complexity of capital. Whereas this chapter draws analogies between the form of the novel and the form of capital through the ways both similarly circulate the contradiction between exchange and use value, the next chapter makes a case for how the two are linked through their temporal dynamics.

The Plot of Capital I

Cecilia and Risk Management

If capital's form is the novelization of money, plot is where we can see the contradictions of infinite economic growth writ large. This and the following chapter concentrate on plot's temporal dynamics in order to think about how downward mobility unfolds time and aligns individual loss with infinite accumulation. The centrality of plot to capital's story is nicely captured by a 2016 Morgan Stanley advertisement that pitches its financial services to a family of twelve as the solution to the problem of "four generations of plot twists" (fig. 5). The ad promises to help "create a wealth plan that reflects all the complexity of a modern family" by starting with "a Financial Advisor who understands individuals."[1] "Understanding individuals" is the great promise not only of Morgan Stanley's financial advisors but also of the novel. How do these promises overlap? The financial services industry assumes that the individual's relation to the family plot is one of wealth management, of pensions, portfolios, and inheritances, of cashing in while cashing out. If the Morgan Stanley family saved for their future plot twists by hiding money under the bed, inflation would quickly extinguish its value. For pensions to keep up with the rate of inflation, they need to be invested in financial markets, allowing them to continue to accumulate value. While universal infinite compound growth is a collective fantasy based on an unrealizable future, real individuals accumulate capital in a plot that ends for some in retirement, death, and inheritance. How do the two temporalities collide, and how might novelistic plots participate in the fantasy of infinite compounding growth? In other words, is the plot of fictitious capital also fiction's plot?

Why is compounding growth a fiction? As Sir Robert Clayton explains to the title character in Defoe's *Roxana*, the difference between compounding interest ("adding every year the additional interest") versus simple interest (5% annually on the principle) is astronomical.[2] Clayton, whom Defoe based on the real-life Bank of England director, shows Roxana a compounding table to prove his point. Roxana's £1,000 at the standard eighteenth-century rate of 5% becomes £3,481 in twenty-five years when compounded, whereas, in that same time, simple interest on principle would amount to only £1,250. Where does that extra £2,231 come from? And what is it worth? Such growth in savings

Fig. 5. "Four Generations of Plot Twists," Morgan Stanley advertisement. https://morganstanley.com/what-we-do/wealth-management, © 2017 Morgan Stanley Smith Barney LLC. Member SIPC. CRC 1685569 (01/17).

cannot exist without "fictitious capital," that is, without the stocks and securities that generate the M′. As a claim on future money that is realized in the present, speculative capital is not tied to commodities or the production of material value; by buying and selling the promise of future wealth, fictitious capital compounds as long as its circulation does not stop, as long as there is a buyer.[3] As noted in this book's introduction, the "more" generated by financial markets relies on the Ponzi scheme continuing ad infinitum; such schemes may be possible in the world of the imagination, but in a material world with limited resources, compound growth will inevitably compromise environmental sustainability. Fictitious capital is also part of Giovanni Arrighi's cycles of accumulation, in which bubbles inevitably lead to busts, to tragic plot twists and unforeseen downturns. Morgan Stanley promises to shelter individuals from the future's volatility by "managing" wealth through diversification and through hedging, that is, by offsetting one risk with its negative correlate. This plot of wealth management requires aggregated individuals, because it is only through buying a tiny percentage of thousands of larger futures that one family's wealth can be sheltered from the twists and turns in each of those plots. The eighteenth-century version of a hedge fund—the joint stock company—first introduces the idea of risk management through pooled wealth.[4] Sentimental novels, I suggest, tell the story of the risk-managed aggregated individual and thus plot the rise of a financialized subject.

This and the following chapter focus on the dynamics of plot as a way of thinking about how capital's impossible temporality is captured in downward mobility narratives. I read Frances Burney's harrowing novels of female financial failure, *Cecilia* and *Camilla*, to demonstrate how plot manages temporal contradictions. This chapter explores *Cecilia*'s plot as a form of risk management, and chapter 5 turns to *Camilla* to think about how fictional closure is analogous to realizing fictitious capital. Following the way *Cecilia* plots fictitious capital helps to answer the novel's central hermeneutic question: why does the heroine need to lose her money and her mind in order to gain a husband? *Cecilia* seemingly follows a courtship plot, but it is the financial plot that constitutes its central preoccupation and marriage arrives as financial ruin, not happy ending.[5] What does the novel gain through its heroine's economic loss? By placing narrative theory's insights into plot dynamics beside the contradictory temporal dynamics of capital, I hope to show how Cecilia's problem of downward mobility is resolved through a plot of risk management.

Plot Dynamics and the Chronotopes of Capital

In the introduction, I argue that Smith's *Wealth of Nations* cannot capture capital's narrative, because the stories it tells of the origin of money, of reciprocal gain, and of infinite upward mobility fail to plot capital's contradictions. Smith narrates a linear progressive plot of use value, whereas capital's plot must manage the tension between useful commodities and speculative capital. The difference between fictional plotting and Smith's linear narratives helps us define why novels better capture the plot of capital.

Because plot is one of the most basic categories of fiction, we mostly take it for granted as having something to do with an ordered sequence of events. All stories require events, that something happen; but a plot, or so common knowledge suggests, requires a principle of order that unifies the events.[6] For the most part, prior to post-structuralist narrative theory, critics understood this principle of order as causality, as charting what happens next, and thus "reading for the plot" was denigrated for being the simple construction of a timeline.[7] But if we reduce plot to a causally ordered chronology, the interpretative pleasure of reading seems clinical, more like doing sudoku than generating the complex emotions and insights that novels can evoke. Michael Levenson points to plot summaries—from *Soap Opera Digest* to *CliffsNotes* and, we would now add, Shmoop—to demonstrate the paucity of thinking about plot as a causally ordered chronology of events.[8] In contrast, post-structuralist narrative theory redefined plot as a "dynamic," as a process of understanding that is open and fluid, not closed and fixed. Plot is "a sense-making operation or mental configuration."[9] As a dynamic of meaning-making, plot is the "interpretative activity" in which the reader figures out the interplay between part and whole, a synecdochal thinking that emphasizes relations and connections, webs of meaning.

Invoking Barthes's "code of actions," Peter Brooks writes, "Plot, then, might best be thought of as 'overcoding' of the proairetic by the hermeneutic, the latter structuring the discrete elements of the former into the larger interpretive wholes, working out their play of meaning and significance."[10] This configural dynamic means that, as Levenson notes, "the characteristic movement of the novel is not the breathless succession of punctualities recorded in *Soap Opera Digest* but a rhythm of containments. . . . The passage, not merely forward in causal-chronological time, but through an endless nest of embeddings: a kiss within a courtship, a headache within a disease, an epiphany within a coming of age."[11] In other words, plots function more like the semantic web than the Web 2.0, working with relations between things rather than the things themselves, developing nested and overlapping networks of connections and associations, not timelines. And while narrative is linear insofar as we start on the first page and read to the end, its temporality cannot be contained by chronology, nor does closure signify the finality of meaning, for meaning lies not in the text but in the interpretative act.

Plot as a dynamic between reader and text presumes that narrative has a historical component in that readers' metonymic activity of embedding parts into wholes always involves horizons of the possible and the plausible within the represented worldview. The possible paths *not* taken, the events that do *not* appear but are part of a historical and discursive network of possibilities, are important components of plot.[12] Readers' anticipation of what *might* come next, their configuration of possible nestings, involves them in what Paul Ricoeur describes as plot's "temporal dialectic." Meaning emerges, as Ricoeur sees it, in the interplay between chronological and nonchronological time, between "the episodic dimension, which characterizes the story as made out of events, . . . [and] the configurational dimension, according to which the plot construes significant wholes out of scattered events."[13] Plot seeks patterns not only in relations between events but between things, characters, states of being, descriptions, and other elements—the relations, in other words, that give novels their emotional and intellectual depth and texture.

How does plot as dynamic, as configuration and metonymical thinking, help us analyze the plot of capital? The temporal dialectic that constitutes the dynamic maps onto the way capital's time, far from being unitary or teleological, requires different temporal modalities to manage its contradictory circulations. Temporality is central to capital not only in the way capital monetizes time through wage labor, through Benjamin Franklin's notion that "time is money," but because financialization is based on selling time. The endless array of financial derivatives offered by investment firms are all various packages that sell time in relation to risk. Fixed versus variable mortgages, for instance, offer consumers a choice between a stable or unstable future. The "futures market" literalizes the selling of time with contracts that fix prices to secure the future; thus, as critics such as LiPuma and Lee have detailed, such contracts obliterate time, flattening out the future into an always now.[14] But for the future to be sold for profit, money's plot must be imagined through both chronological and nonchronological temporality; time must be fixed *and* fluid. I argue that the novelization of money as capital—the way financial speculation turns money into a narrative that unfolds across time—requires at least four different temporal modalities to narrate the plot of capital: *adventure time*, *linear time*, *cyclical time*, and *infinite time*. These four temporalities need to coexist to make comprehensible the impossible timing of compound growth. The temporality of *adventure* is the time of risk and speculation, of the spontaneous and the accidental, and of social mobility. In his essay "The Temporalities of Capitalism," William Sewell Jr. notes: "At first blush, nothing would seem to be more eventful than capitalism. New business ventures are launched daily; firms go bankrupt; stock exchanges and futures markets oscillate dizzily."[15] Adventure time involves the eventful individual carpe diem in which everything could be lost or won in an instant. At the same time that capital requires time to change in an instant, it also necessitates that it accumulate and progress, so that its passage is *linear*, signifying growing wealth. Linear time is the clock time of the individual we see in Ian Watt or that E. P. Thompson wonderfully analyzes in his classic "Time, Work-Discipline, and Industrial Capitalism."[16] A linear temporal mode sequences events through causality: hard work leads to economic gain. In contrast, *cyclical* time charts the business cycle—the endless repetition of expansion, stagnation, and recession, of oil prices going up and going down—the cycle of boom and bust in which change looks more like stasis. As Sewell notes, "While it is true that the surface appearance of capitalism is one of incessant change, there is something strangely, almost uncannily, repetitive in the changes."[17] Cyclical time charts the indefinite "now" of fashion, the repetition of cycles of novelty and obsolescence. Lastly, capital requires a temporality that is *infinite*, that is, the no time of endless circulation and infinite growth. This is the time in which no future possibility is foreclosed, in which the entire world can have a Western standard of living, and technology will save us from climate change. This modality contains capitalism's incessant optimism, its unceasing belief that "this time will be different" and "tomorrow will be better."[18]

These multiple temporalities plot relations between events quite differently: adventure time's device is coincidence and the accidental; linear time insists on causality; cyclical time relies on repetition and the episodic; and infinite time refuses the closure of a unified sequence of events. Such conflicting modes of time can be rendered through the temporal dialogism of the novel, its ability to add texture to time through plot configurations, feeding off the contrasting paces of stasis and conflict, of repetition and difference, of progression and risk.[19] Before turning to my reading of *Cecilia*, I flesh out these four temporalities by thinking about them through Bakhtin's concept of the chronotope. By adding space to time, I hope to show how capital's plot takes a specific shape in a particular historical moment—how, in other words, the plot of downward mobility in the latter eighteenth century is tied to a specific moment in the history of capital, just as Defoe's upward mobility plots emerge from an earlier series of events.

Chronotopes help because, by spatializing the four temporal modalities, they designate the historical specificity of capital's plot. When adventure time is spatialized on the sea rather than in the real estate market, the historical moment of capital is likely centuries apart. In "Forms of Time and of the Chronotope in the Novel," Bakhtin cryptically defines the chronotope as "the place where the knots of narrative are tied and untied."[20] I take those "knots" to be plot, and chronotopes as delimiting how those knots are tied. "Time," Bakhtin writes of the chronotope, "thickens, takes on flesh, becomes artistically visible; likewise, space becomes charged and responsive to the movements of time, plot, and history."[21] I align the chronotope with what generates the configural process of plot, the space-time materialization that shapes associations and alternative possible events into episodes and sequences, and thus, chronotopes are historically situated. Haydn White describes chronotopes as "socially determining structurations of practices which set limits not only on what can possibly *happen* . . . but also [on] what can be *perceived* and even *imagined* by agents acting within their constraints."[22]

Historical variations in what gives a chronotope its flesh in novels from Defoe to the present make readable the plot of capital. For instance, adventure time in the latter eighteenth century is embedded in a chronotope that emphasizes risk in the new urban public spaces, whereas in Chris Kraus's contemporary *Summer of Hate*, the risk of adventure time is spatialized within the U.S. real estate market, a difference that places Kraus's novel within the hyperfinancialized moment of late capital. In Edith Wharton's *House of Mirth*, adventure is spatialized inside Gilded Age mansions where Lily risks everything by not marrying into new money; like the New York Stock Exchange a few years later, she crashes. In Defoe, on the other hand, the adventure chronotope is shaped by the seas, by mobility and global travel; it structures the rhythm of his novels into an episodic picaresque corresponding to the initial promise of speculative capital. Both in the particular space-time representation and in the variations of the relations between the four temporalities—which ones take precedent, which ones generate the main obstacles, which ones produce happiness, and so forth—one can chart capital's history, and this history produces the sentimental novel's plot of downward mobility and introduces the epistemological necessity of risk management and of diversification.

Let me detail the specifics of the four chronotopes within the sentimental novel to flesh out capital's four temporalities in the latter eighteenth century. I name the chronotopes "risk," "course of life," "fashion," and "tradition" and match them to the four times of capital: adventure, linear, cyclical, and infinite. Each chronotope introduces a particular shape to a narrative sequence, and together they generate the play of contingency and predictability that translates into a plot dynamic in which the heroine must lose her fortune or go into debt in order to marry.

1. *The chronotope of risk.* The time of risk in *Cecilia* is given flesh as modernity's new public spaces. The city street, the public gardens, the road to London provide the expectation of chance meetings, coincidental revelations, and anonymous speculations, all of which involve danger, surprise, and risk. This chronotope makes visible Delvile's mistaken jealousy when he coincidentally runs into Cecilia in Belfield's doctor's doorway, and it gives shape to the *ton*'s incessant speculations after the opera scene that Cecilia must be engaged to Sir Robert. The chronotope of risk surrounds Harrel's gambling, in which fortunes are gained and lost in an instant, and it also permeates the drama of romance in which a chance meeting could bring lovers together or keep them apart forever.

2. *The chronotope of the course of life.* The time of linear progression in the sentimental novel is represented as the time of the individual's coming of age, the time between entering the world and finding one's place in it. Cecilia's own course-of-life plot ends up following a courtship sequence but begins with her "plan of life" for an heiress's independence, a plan for regular reading and useful charitable acts. Cecilia's course is mirrored in the novel by her masculine doppelgänger Belfield's quest to make his way in the world through labor, a project at which he repeatedly fails. The course-of-life chronotope as the linear causal progression of hard work paying off shapes sequences by thrusting the plot toward the ending of individual happiness, represented as a state of calm or equilibrium in either marriage or a self-sustaining way of life.

3. *The chronotope of fashion.* Capital's cycles of accumulation, its drive toward faster ways for money to breed money, is represented as the time-space of the fashionable world in sentimental fiction. Fashion time cycles through the endlessly new; it is the time of consumption and novelty, of Miss Larolles's shopping but also of Cecilia's excitement over attending her first opera or seeing the Pantheon. The West End is its space, exemplified by the Harrels' Portman Square townhouse, with its renovations and masquerade ball. The time-space of the Harrel townhouse is defined by what D. Grant Campbell has called "an

extended caesura between purchase and payment," between credit and debt, a time that forgets the future in which debts must be paid or in which the market will crash.[23]

4. *The chronotope of tradition.* Adding flesh to the temporality of infinite circulation largely entails sequences of inheritance and reproduction in the sentimental novel. In *Cecilia*, tradition is spatialized in the Delvile castle as that which is ancient, connecting past and present through hereditary blood lines that extend into an indefinite future. It is the chronotope in which the individuality of Mortimer Delvile is replaced by his status as heir and in which Cecilia can enter the novel already an heiress. It is significant that the novel's love interest emerges from this space-time as reproduction stands in for infinity with the continuing generation of more heirs.

How do these four chronotopes give shape to the temporal dynamics of plot in *Cecilia*? What do their various embeddings reveal about Burney's relation to capital? My reading of the novel answers these questions by following the money, demonstrating that the reason Cecilia must lose her money to gain a husband lies in the financial market's strategy of risk management.[24]

Cecilia's Bad Timing and the Management of Risk

If we read *Cecilia* as a female bildungsroman in which its heroine matures and progresses over time, then we might say, along with Monckton, that Cecilia needs to learn the "value of money" in order not to lose her fortune.[25] The novel's course-of-life chronotope imagines that Cecilia could stop the flow of her losses through financial literacy, by learning to make better choices and by not loaning Harrel money. I argue that Burney introduces this possible trajectory as an alternative course of events only to demonstrate its impossibility, that far from providing a plot in which individual agency controls both the outcome and her heroine's finances, she embeds chronotopes of risk, fashion, and tradition to reveal the way social relations render individual causality ineffective. What Cecilia needs to learn in order to stop her losses is to manage risk and diversify her portfolio. Not only does she need to "soften her plan," to find her "golden mean" where desires and actions are moderated, but she needs to save up her resources for the inevitable downturn that is to come (131). The chronotopes shape the plot such that the version of capitalism Burney ultimately represents is not one in which hard work pays off or use value wins the day—she is not conservative in that sense. Nor is she conservative in the sense of a nostalgic valuing of tradition or of a precapitalist time. Rather, in her version, market forces rule and the individual circulates within social relations that can never be predicted, a world that severely limits personal agency. Cecilia must either retire from the world or learn to hedge bets, diversify pleasures, and save for a rainy day. "[A]ll the happiness human life seems capable of receiving," the place where the novel ends, comes only through relinquishing moral absolutes, losing a fortune, and not putting all one's eggs in a single basket (941). Contemporary feminist readers may feel unsatisfied with the unappealing, short-tempered, weak-kneed hero that Burney "rewards" her heroine with in the end. Her own contemporary readers Edmund Burke and Samuel Crisp both took issue with the not entirely happy ending, but Burney was adamant that she keep an ending in which "the Hero and Heroine are neither plunged in the depths of misery, nor exalted to *unhuman happiness*."[26] Marriage is not the only game in town and happiness does not arrive with an unquestioning poetic justice that reassures. Far from abandoning the topoi of the new risky urban terrain, Burney's novel dwells in it. With something to lose, Cecilia can be disinvested and can have her economic agency taken away in order to gain the knowledge of when to cut her losses. The plot of downward mobility in *Cecilia*, in other words, provides the justification for mutual funds.

By introducing her heroine as an orphan heiress, months away from coming of age, Burney deviates from the standard courtship narrative that thrives on its heroine's financial and personal vulnerability. A single female orphan without a fortune is the problem that the courtship plot most often poses, from Sarah Scott's *The History of Cornelia* to Charlotte Lennox's *Henrietta* to Frances Brooke's *The Excursion* to Burney's first novel, *Evelina*. But what happens when economic need does not propel the narrative? Cecilia's inheritances—£10,000 from her father and £3,000 a year from her uncle's estate—introduce a different problem through the name clause in her uncle's will, demanding that her husband take the Beverley name. The money changes the plot by interjecting at least three possible endings for the *Memoirs of an Heiress*: the independent single life of useful charity; marriage to a husband who changes his name; or the ending that ultimately occurs, the loss of her uncle's estate with marriage to a husband that refuses her name. The two financial legacies provide this very long novel with distinct halves. In the first, she loses her father's money within a chronotope of fashion; in the second, immersed in a chronotope of tradition, she loses her uncle's estate.[27] The suspense in the second half emerges not from "Will she marry?" but from "Will she keep her uncle's money?" Finances, not romance, provides the plot with its main propulsion. By reading the novel's representation of temporality, I hope to reveal how the plot of an heiress becomes one of risk management.

Time presents the first obstacle to Cecilia's "plan of life" in that she begins the novel a few months short of her coming of age and must journey to London to live with one of her three guardians rather than independently. The social relations that London introduces strain Cecilia's moral compass, and much of the suspense is produced by the conflict between Cecilia's individual desire to live a single moral life and the social customs of the world. The opening chapter, "A Journey," launches the standard adventure chronotope with a young lady's entrance into the world; the risk London poses for the heroine is not the normal one of sexual vulnerability (the money protects her from that) but, as Monckton points out, her being seduced by the corrupting temptations of the "new connections she may form" (17). Belfield dismisses this fear because Cecilia will "regulate her . . . choice of new connections" (17).[28] He is right insofar as Cecilia never wavers in her self-discipline and her faculty of good judgment remains a constant across the changing urban landscape. The problem is that she has little choice in the connections she makes and absolutely no ability to change them. Monckton advises her to "take time" in making new connections and to question appearances, but his hermeneutics of suspicion is challenged by the fact that he himself is the plotting one whom Cecilia needs to be protected against (18). As well, time and knowledge make little difference to Cecilia's entrance into the world. Logical and personal causality is not the principle through which events and people are connected in the urban environment.

From the moment she arrives in London, Cecilia is swept up into the fashionable world of the Harrels' West End society. She literally has not a moment to herself when Mrs. Harrel, after briefly greeting Cecilia, whom she has not seen for three years, immediately leads the heiress into the drawing room where members of the *ton* are "impatient" to meet her (21). The impatient demands of London society set the pace for Cecilia's time in Portman Square. When she tries to slow time down and expresses a desire to spend more time at home without visitors, Mrs. Harrel balks and produces her "catalogue" of events, a calendar in which every day is filled with straight engagements—teas, balls, masquerades, operas, assemblies, and the like. As events "are struck off new ones are made," Mrs. Harrel notes, "and so it is we go on till after the birthday," the only end to the repetitive rhythm of social rounds coming from the king's birthday, which closes the London season (32).

Burney renders the pace of fashion time as both incredibly fast and painfully tedious, a pace that mirrors the uncanny repetitiveness of capitalism's incessant change. Within the chronotope of fashion, society constantly races toward novelty, to being the first to the new. By plotting the "novelty" in a pattern of endless repetition, Burney satirizes emergent consumer culture. The new becomes as predictable as the character "types" that populate the West End and provide much of the novel's humor. The insufferable Mr. Meadows may criticize fashionable life for offering "nothing new, no variety! all the same thing over again!" but his attacks are themselves repetitive and predictable (275). In contrast, Miss Larolles, who puts Meadows to sleep, declares herself "so amazingly surprized" at everything and everyone (140). She arrives in town too late in the season to have a ticket to Lord Darien's famous masquerade, "but," she tells Cecilia, "about ten or eleven o'clock, a young lady of my particular acquaintance, by the greatest good luck in the world happened to be taken suddenly ill; so she sent me her ticket" (24). Later, Larolles is "provoked" because the Parisian lace that she acquired ahead of its arrival at London milliners and that she was planning to "bring . . . out quite new in a week's time" has been worn by Miss Moffat and hers, now, will seem to be "an old thing" (44, 45). Gosport, Cecilia's insider guide to the fashionable world, describes women like Larolles whom he calls "the VOLUBLE" as having "no permanency, no consistency" (62). The *ton* is constantly changing and thus change is the constant. Social relations are entirely superficial, with connections between people forged on the surface of appearances. After only a brief meeting, Larolles treats Cecilia with "the intimacy of an old acquaintance," but when Cecilia does not follow the strict rule to return visits within three days, Larolles snubs her in public (28, 62). The cycles of fashion time-space mean everything and nothing. Miss Larolles says she has "been to twenty places" looking for Cecilia, but we know the places are as empty as her rhetoric (44); she speaks "with no meaning but to be heard" (596). While constantly "out of breath with eagerness" and "never so surprised in [her] life," her timely expressions remain unattached to an object (149, 285). That fashion time passes meaninglessly, as empty rhetoric, is perhaps nowhere more ironized than when Miss Larolles responds to a minor carriage accident by exclaiming, "I declare I dare say I am killed!" (591). The repetition of "I" three times in a logically impossible statement about her own death underscores the narcissism of fashion and its obsession with a "now" that manages even to submerge death into its present. Nothing sticks or adheres or compounds, and time simply cycles from one day to the next without accumulating.

The iterative is thus the favored tense of the fashion chronotope in which multiple events are narrated at once: "Several days passed on nearly in the same manner; the mornings were all spent in gossipping, shopping and dressing, and the evenings were regularly appropriated to public places, or large parties of company" (52).[29] "[E]very day" Cecilia hopes life will be different and "every day" it is the same; thus, she "began to grow weary of eternally running the same round, and to sicken at the irksome repetition of unremitting yet uninteresting dissipation" (53). Even the Harrels' masquerade—the height of their conspicuous consumption and a space conventionally portrayed as eventful and topsy-turvy in eighteenth-century fiction—is represented as boring, with its "wearisome" repetition of people asking "*Do you know me*? *Who are you*?" (106). The iterative of the masquerade has prompted Terry Castle to call the scene "saturnalia by rote."[30]

The fashion chronotope, while representing the speed of the new, often slows down the pace of the linear plot, hijacking the forward momentum of Cecilia's course of life with a dramatic scene in which Cecilia is swept away. The aforementioned masquerade, which Edmund Burke thought "too long," is a good example.[31] I discuss below the effect of the novel's duration; here, I simply note how the thwarted narrative desire, with its clash of temporalities, heightens the contrast between the regulated life of good works in which money is spent on useful projects and a life of fashionable dissipation in which money is wasted on the flashy glitter of the colored lights on the dessert awning, built especially for the masquerade (124). Time may not accumulate in the chronotope of fashion, but "wantonly . . . unnecessary debts" do (103).

The more Cecilia cycles through the London social rounds, the greater her determination to establish her "plan of life," and the contrast between the two punctuates her plan's timeliness. Disgusted when she "arose with the light" to find no one awake in the household except Mrs. Harrel's earnest brother, Mr. Arnott, she decides to spend her mornings "advantageously" in reading (28, 31). Frustrated and "[a]shamed" by the wasted time of life at the Harrels, Cecilia determines to establish what she calls her "scheme of happiness": "She purposed, for the basis of her plan, to become mistress of her own time . . . [and] to drop all idle and uninteresting acquaintance" (55). Socializing only with "the noblest of her society" would leave her leisure to pursue "her favourite studies, music and reading," so that "the occupations of her hours of solitude" would be productive (55). For a brief moment shortly after her resolution, she feels the happiness rewards of her scheme. While Mrs. Harrel's social engagements continue unabated, "Cecilia passed her time greatly to her own satisfaction. Her first care was to assist and comfort the Hills [the carpenter's family to whom the Harrels owe wages]. . . . Her next solicitude was to furnish herself with a well-chosen collection of books. . . . And thus, in the exercise of charity, the search of knowledge, and the enjoyment of quiet . . . passed the hours of Cecilia" (102, 103).

These hours of quiet, of usefulness, and of independence do not last, in part because they are the novel's "unnarratable," the goal to which the plot strives and thus whose arrival would register the story's end.[32] But such hours are fleeting also because Burney shifts the ground under which such a useful temporality can emerge. The conflict between fashion's time-space and Cecilia's course of life, between wasteful and productive time, between ballrooms and private closets, between exchange value and use value, generates a clear moral choice for its heroine, but choosing the latter over the former is not as simple as the novel first suggests. The chronotope of risk shifts the horizon of possible connections and disconnections between people, events, and things and renders Cecilia's path through London unpredictable and financially ruinous. Urban space occasions a seemingly infinite number of coincidental and accidental events whose meanings circulate in ways Cecilia cannot control and that produce the greatest obstacles to her course of life. Everything can change in a moment and the best-laid "plan of life" can be waylaid by speculative gossip or the unintended consequences of a social exchange. An innocent excursion to the opera ends up hatching a whole series of misunderstandings in which everyone, including Delvile, assumes Cecilia is either engaged to Sir Robert or in love with Belfield, neither of which is true. What everyone else "instantly imputed to fondness, [Cecilia's response to the men's fight] proceeded simply from general humanity," but because Cecilia entered the opera's coffee room as "an heiress," everyone infers meanings that her repeated disclaimers cannot subdue (139). With strong judgment and critical awareness, Cecilia forcefully acts to correct the mistake. Unlike Mrs. Harrel, who is "helpless" when they return from the opera, Cecilia, "equally quick in forming and executing her designs," writes to Mr. Harrel to intervene and settle the dispute (142). But solid execution and quick judgment never get Cecilia anywhere; she acts as if she has agency rather than understanding herself as a commodity in the marriage market where her value registers otherwise. Such accidental and speculative encounters in public places increasingly leave Cecilia feeling "infinite vexation" (149). In fact, she is so "vexed" by the coincidences and accidents that befall her that the word *vex*, in both verbal and adjectival forms, occurs twenty-nine times in the first half of the novel, less than *surprise* and *shock* but still more than in most novels.[33] The chronotope of risk permeates the novel with surprise and shock that leads to vexations and ultimately determines the novel's and Cecilia's timing. Risk, I argue, is the chronotope that binds the novel together, working its way through all the others to generate the narrative's eventfulness. Resolving the quagmires that risk introduces requires other forms of time, but these other temporalities emerge to mediate and manage risk.

If the urban world is full of vexations and dangers, keeping Cecilia from fulfilling her plan, why does she not retire from it, stay home, and count the money she saves? Why can she not manage risk by simply refusing to participate in its spaces? For one reason, if she did, she would turn into her guardian Mr. Briggs, whose miserly obsession is a source of repulsion in the novel. A life of parsimony is not a life of happiness, Burney registers, and she matches her satire on the miser with representations of the pleasure and fulfillment social circulation brings. The chronotope of fashion may largely include the novel's satire, but it also contains Cecilia's delight, her curiosity, and her aesthetic pleasure. The masquerade is tedious for the *ton*, but to Cecilia "the novelty of the scene" gives "uncommon satisfaction" and her "expectations of entertainment were not only fulfilled but surpassed" (103, 106). Cecilia's pleasures derive, in part, from the newness of her experiences. She is "enraptured" her first time at the opera "with a sensation not more new than delightful" (65). "[T]he surprize and the pleasure" she receives comes from how "astonished" she is to find live music so different from the sheet music she knows (64). She declares herself very pleased with the Pantheon, having "seen no building at all equal to it" (274). Solitude and retirement are not the answers to her vexations, for she quickly becomes bored of her scheme's social seclusion. After retiring from Mrs. Harrel's rounds and passing "undisturbed another week," Cecilia "sighed for the comfort of society": "To a heart formed for friendship and affection the charms of solitude are very short-lived" (130). Taking herself out of circulation, then, is not the desired course of life and some risk is necessary to live in a social world.

The chronotopes of risk and fashion overlap in the urban space to introduce the horizon of possibility within which Cecilia relinquishes her father's fortune. The biggest threat to Cecilia's "scheme of happiness" comes not just from the *ton* but from the drain on her finances that Mr. Harrel's gambling debts introduce. I analyze Burney's representation of Cecilia's lost fortune because the interplay between expectation and contingency, how the plot combines what can be predicted with what cannot, gets to the heart of Burney's rejection of a causal plot in favor of a plot of risk management.

Harrel's suicide is one of the most original endings to a sequence of events in sentimental fiction. Yet its metonymic nesting within Cecilia's course-of-life plot configures suicide as trite, as unsurprisingly volatile. While death is usually the ultimate ending that confers meaning on life, it does not do so for Harrel. The suicide is expected and predictable, one of "an endlessness of petty disasters," as D. Grant Campbell notes, in a continuum of tedious consumption and debt.[34] Margaret Doody makes a similar observation: "Mr. Harrel tried to provide his own dramatic final climax, which the narrative refuses to acknowledge. His death is not even the end of the chapter."[35] Harrel's debts emerge from the chronotopes of fashion and risk, but because his suicide is an event within Cecilia's course of life, the episode's suspense originates not from whether Harrel will kill himself but in whether Cecilia will lose her money to his gambling addiction. The whole of which the suicide is a part is Cecilia's estate, not his life, so that with the suicide, the reader experiences not the horror of Harrel's death but a certain relief that the drain on Cecilia's finances has finally been stopped.

The tension of the plot of financial loss is built up in this section through repetition, with Harrel asking for money on three separate occasions. Each repetition results in an addition to Cecilia's mounting debt, and the resulting series produces the expectation that she should have known better. As Peter Brooks notes, three is "the minimum repetition to suggest series and process," and by the third time Harrel requests a loan, we know that he will never pay it back, which prompts the interpretative question of why Cecilia keeps giving him money.[36] The first time, she assumes he has property and therefore it is simply a matter of being paid in the future. But she shockingly discovers from Monckton after the second loan that Harrel does not have the equity to back it up; it is in this conversation that Monckton exhorts her to learn "the value of money" (297). In fact, Cecilia seems an expert at understanding how to balance her accounts and match her desires to her pocketbook. As Julia Epstein notes, "[T]he novel dwells with ledger-book particularity on the elaborate specifications of each exchange of funds," and Cecilia calculates these exchanges perfectly.[37] Cecilia's financial accounting, like her "plan of life," takes place within a causal linear temporality in which the present budgets for a future and accounts can be balanced. We see this in the chapter "An Admonition," in which she lectures Mrs. Harrel on domestic management, on the proper way of plotting money with time. Cecilia counsels Mrs. Harrel to "look forward" and spend now only what she can pay, because "if now you live beyond your income, you must consider that in time your income . . . will be exhausted" (193). Cecilia believes that if Mrs. Harrel would simply pause and "reflect for a moment," she would see the error of her ways and "prevent in time so dreadful a catastrophe" (194, 195). Mrs. Harrel cannot foresee the catastrophe, because within the temporality of fashion's cyclical sameness, Mrs. Harrel "*did nothing but what every body else did*" (193 [emphasis in original]).

Knowing the value of money and being able to plot it in linear time do little to stop Cecilia's losses—a point underscored by the fact that she gives Harrel more money *after* she knows that he has no equity to back it up. Why? The sequence of events creates the expectation that Cecilia should have known better, that her money would have been better spent on her charitable endeavors, but the mode through which Burney narrates time configures an individual agency that repeatedly fails to control the circulation of money. Narrative duration helps us chart how Burney produces the plot's vexations and Cecilia's losses. The three scenes in which Cecilia succumbs to Harrel's financial demands are narrated with near isochrony, to use Genette's term for those passages when the time that passes in the story equals as closely as possible the time of narration, usually rendered through dramatic speech. Burney's theatrical style often involves such duration, and the longest chapters in the novel are the ones narrated in "scene" rhythm, all of which are significantly set in the fashionable *ton*.[38] These scenes stretch out the endless "now" of fashion time. If Barthes famously depicted passages of description as those that can be skipped over, in Burney's novels it is often the satiric dialogue scenes that elicit the reader's desire to skip.[39] The flatness of fashion time-space, however, is also what prompts the desire for risk, for something to happen. Since fashion-space overlaps with adventure- or risk-space—both are located in urban social space where an accidental meeting is literally just around the corner—the long passages of dialogue that delay the action locate the desire for eventfulness within the chronotope of risk. We want the white domino to coincidentally arrive in order to produce forward movement. These scenes give rise to such a discomforting combination of suspense and tedium that the sound of Harrel's gun breaks the monotony by releasing Cecilia from the *ton*'s drone.

The chronotope of risk in these passages marks the divide between fashion and Cecilia's course of life. We see this in the way the coincidental mediates between the temporal mode of the fashionable dramatic scene and that of the "pause" of Cecilia's free indirect discourse within her course of life ("pause" is Mieke Bal's term for a section that covers no fabula time).[40] The integration of these temporalities in the sections where Cecilia divests herself of her father's fortune creates a space in which Cecilia is cornered by time and has no choice but to loan the money. Each time she gives, she does so because the immediate claims of social connection trump the financial sense her reasoned reflections contain. The first time she loans money, she is trapped by an obligation she feels toward Mr. Arnott, who cannot refuse his sister's pleas for money though it would mean selling his stocks at a loss. Cecilia offers a loan because the loss to her would be less than the loss to Mr. Arnott. Loss, here, is relative, in relation to and through connection with others, and she gives not to help Mr. Harrel but to save Mr. Arnott. After the decision, Cecilia "reflected" on the danger of the situation and "resolved" to talk to Mrs. Harrel about the domestic management plan, but reflections and resolutions that occur in the pause of free indirect discourse are ineffective outside her solitary thoughts (175).

The immediate and unexpected "now" of risk interrupts West End social relations again in the second scene of Cecilia's losing money to Harrel. She arrives home to discover the house in a state of anxiety: "Frightened and amazed, she stopt short" (263). She finds Harrel "frantic," with "three executions before night," and when he threatens suicide and locks himself in a room, "[h]er terror was *now* inexpressible; she believed him in the very act of suicide . . . her whole fortune, *at that moment*, was valueless and unimportant to her compared with the preservation of a fellow-creature" (264–66; my emphasis). The timing of the scene—the immediate risk of Harrel's suicide—causes Cecilia to promise anything, as the moral choice of a man's life over £1,000 appears unequivocal to a woman like Cecilia. When Harrel revives and agrees not to kill himself, "Cecilia drew back; her recollection returned as her terror abated," and she retreats to her room to "consider what steps she had to take" (266, 267). Withdrawing into free indirect discourse, Burney registers how Cecilia's "heart sunk within her" because she knows giving Harrel money is useless (267). Just then she hears a noise in the hall that announces the arrival of the bailiffs; "finding she had time neither for deliberation nor regret," she is "compelled" to act (268). "Deliberation," "recollection," "consider[ation]," "resolve," and "reflection" register in a narrative arc of causal connections, but in these dramatic scenes Cecilia is pulled along by the "now" of risk, "compelled" to act in the moment.

The last extortion of Cecilia's father's money, when she knows the money will never be returned and when she is alert to Harrel's plot to coerce her, particularly hijacks a causal plot. Cecilia takes every precaution to avoid giving Harrel money. "Luxury has followed luxury," she says to Arnott, and thus *this* time, neither she nor Arnott will give in (378). She warns Arnott to leave town so as not to be subject to his sister's pleas, she tries to remove herself from the house by shifting residences, and she offers to pay in installments if Harrel will retrench expenses by moving to the country, but "however long she had prepared herself for this very attack, *when the moment arrived*, its power over her mind was too strong for resistance" (389; my emphasis). Even though Monckton has anticipated the demands Harrel will make (one year's income, the annuity, and the country house), when Harrel indeed makes them and Cecilia recognizes the plot ("She saw evidently that she was again to be played upon by terror and distress . . . *one year's income* was already demanded"), she still cannot extricate herself (380). Once again, the immediate moral demands of the social take her financial agency away. This time it is not suicide but the threat of violence against Mrs. Harrel that coerces Cecilia: "Cecilia . . . *now* felt her resolution [not to give the money] waver" (386; emphasis mine). Just as Cecilia is justifying why she cannot give the money, "a message came from Mr. Harrel, desiring to see his wife *immediately*" (391; my emphasis). Mrs. Harrel "in great terror" pleads for help; Cecilia, "distressed and trembling," is "wholly overcome" and promises the funds (391). We know she knows better, but the scene is plotted within the chronotope of risk, presenting her with repeated *now*'s and *immediately*'s that shut down the series of events in which saying "no" would be possible. Within the chronotope of risk, social connections, as Monckton has warned, are a danger to Cecilia because you can never know what the moment will bring and everyone may be after your money. If she had not been in the house when the bailiffs arrived, if she could have left and taken refuge at Briggs's or the Delviles', she would have been spared Harrel's coercions and kept her £10,000.

We would be mistaken to think that when Harrel fires the shot that brings relief to Cecilia's finances and shifts the narrative from suspense to a momentary calm, Cecilia's linear time has triumphed over the Harrels' fashion time. While the future does arrive for the Harrels, no accounts are paid and all of Cecilia's resolutions amount to nothing. Suicide is a "great hardship to trade," as one of Harrel's creditors observes, and when Cecilia opens the heavy packet containing Harrel's legacy, she finds nothing but bills (447). As the creditors line up outside Portman Square, Cecilia retreats to the Delviles' and pauses to piece together what happened in those final days, realizing that she has been the equity Harrel borrowed against not just once but twice, to both Sir Robert and Mr. Marriot: Cecilia "saw *now* but too clearly the reason her stay in his house was so important" (435; my emphasis). In these moments of calm, of free indirect discourse, of reflection and taking stock, Cecilia often discovers things belatedly, her insights and knowledge arriving after the point at which they could have made a difference. Her resolutions and determinations either are ineffective because chance events occur that change the conditions, or they arrive too late. The interplay of the temporalities frustrates the reader as, within the pause of Cecilia's free indirect discourse, embedded within the course-of-life chronotope, she is given choices that she does not have within the chronotopes of fashion and risk. Other critics have commented on the claustrophobic nature of Burney's plots, the way her heroines are often trapped in coercive environments; I attribute the claustrophobia to these narrative coercions that deny her her own plot.[41]

With the deployment of the coincidental and the unpredictable, the first half of the novel demonstrates that financial events are not connected through a linear causality wherein individual reasoning pays off. Cecilia's first fortune disappears when events within London's fashionable world reconfigure the plot from one in which her budgeting of life and money are interpretative possibilities to one in which she needs to cut her losses and escape. The future will inevitably arrive and debts cannot be infinitely deferred, but when and where that future will occur cannot be predicted, especially, as the second half reveals, when that future involves matters of love. The romance plot takes over midway through the novel, increasing the pace with which the world of risk connects and determines, plotting nested sequences that further limit Cecilia's choices. Circumstances intervene in chains of events already in motion, foreclosing paths she was otherwise following and stranding her in the middle of a no-man's-land, unable to retreat. Her second fortune falls prey when the coincidental and unpredictable interrupts the aristocratic space-time of Delvile castle to present marriage as a shelter from further loss.

With the notable exception of its patriarch, the Delvile family includes individuals whose moral compass is more attuned to Cecilia's than the Harrels' was, increasing her chances that such social connections will generate happiness. Cecilia's bad timing continues, however, and the obstacles placed by aristocratic and adventure time in the way of her marriage to Mortimer introduce a plot dynamic in which Cecilia has no choice but to relinquish her uncle's estate to the infinity of an old name. As in the novel's first half, the feeling of inevitable loss is prompted by the interplay between Cecilia's free indirect discourse, with its solitary reflection, and her circulation in society, which now involves aristocratic connections. Free indirect discourse alerts us to the way her decision-making processes are based on assumptions—for instance, that the name clause should not bar her from marrying into the Delvile family—that aristocratic society does not share. When Mrs. Delvile speaks with her about Mortimer's marriage prospects, Cecilia assumes she is referring to herself ("The expectations of Cecilia were now again awakened" [498]). Those expectations are then dashed when Mrs. Delvile makes it clear that Cecilia can never be the wife of a son who is "the last of his race" (499). The reader, with Cecilia, reconfigures her possible futures as meaning that she "*now* found her own mistake in building upon her approbation" (501). The romance plot works with the conflicting demands between Cecilia's moral code and society's social codes so that marriage arrives not as a great triumph of love over the obstacles placed by money and tradition, but as the best bet for Cecilia to find happiness.

From the very beginning, the romance plot suffers from bad timing. Cecilia discovers, too late to avoid it, that she has fallen in love and that "her happiness was no longer in her own power" (252). She failed to recognize the signs of love because her two-week stay at the Delvile's residence flew past in a rhythm of calm happiness: "Time with Cecilia now glided on. . . . Easy, gay, and airy, she only rose to happiness, and only retired to rest" (241). In the space of the Delvile's London home, she and Mortimer are entirely in sync ("A sympathy of sentiment so striking impressed them at the same moment with surprise and esteem" [250]) and the familiarity leads to the "involuntary" "choice of her heart" (252). She falls in love with the one man in the novel for whom the name clause in her uncle's will is an obstacle, setting into motion a clash between the chronotope of tradition and Cecilia's scheme of happiness, between custom and individual desire. Cecilia's bad timing continues when coincidental meetings in public lead Mortimer to mistakenly assume she is engaged to Belfield. From the opera to the masquerade to Oxford St. to the Belfield's entranceway, chance keeps bringing Cecilia and Mortimer together only to drive them apart. When Sir Robert "accidentally" enters the drawing room at the Harrels and finds Cecilia alone, she "hastily" retreats but "suddenly" changes her mind; "recollecting that no better opportunity might ever offer for a final explanation with him [of why she will not marry him], she irresolutely stopt" (304). Her determination is forestalled, however, when he "immediately" kisses her hand "at the same moment" the door opens to reveal Mortimer (305). Cecilia's resolutions are no match for the power of coincidental timing.

The misunderstandings that keep the lovers apart draw attention to the conflict of social rank and money that lies at the heart of the novel. As like-minded individuals whose sentiments overlap, Cecilia and Mortimer seem destined to marry but are kept apart by aristocratic prejudice. As with fashion time, the novel represents aristocratic time as a problem that needs to be solved. The pride of thinking that time stops for blue blood, an assumption evident in Mr. Delvile's pomposity and arrogance in thinking his time is more valuable than everyone else's ("my time is extremely precious," he makes sure people know [159]), produces the obstacles to the marriage plot. The aristocracy is running out of money and needs fresh capital to save it from literal and metaphoric "decay" as Burney's symbolic rendering of Delvile castle demonstrates (457). Cecilia is then configured as the solution to the problem posed within the chronotope of tradition in that she has both the money and the morals. But her timing is off; the name clause puts her out of joint with tradition. Indeed, she does not understand the "power of time," of the *longue durée*; Delvile castle, as Gosport points out, "even in ruins, proves its strength by its antiquity: and it teaches . . . the infallible power of time, which defies all might, and undermines all strength" (598).

Coincidental, not aristocratic, time ultimately resolves the tension between the individual and tradition, though it comes at the cost of Cecilia's uncle's estate. Coincidence, as in the *ton*, places Cecilia in positions in which she is compelled to act and in which she has no choice. Delvile castle may represent the "power of time," but it also provides the diegetic space-time in which Mortimer accidentally declares his love. "One evening" Cecilia and Mortimer happen to both be out walking when a "sudden" storm occurs and the ensuing emotional and material maelstrom leads to Mortimer's unplanned revelation of his feelings (471, 473). The spontaneous brings danger but also repeatedly allows characters to speak truths not permitted within normal social conditions; "the moment he was off his guard from surprise, terror, accident of any sort, the moment that he was betrayed into acting from nature and inclination," Mortimer is able to speak his feelings for Cecilia (476). Later, in perhaps the most generative eruption of accidental time into the romance plot, Mortimer happens to arrive at the summer house just as Cecilia confesses aloud to his dog, Fidel, that the Delvile pride and not her lack of feeling stands as the obstacle to their love (546). "Her astonishment" at the sight of him, shocks her into silence, and "unguarded folly" changes the course of the novel (546, 548).

Moments of surprise, shock, and unguarded revelations force the romance forward, but they do so in ways that often feel coercive since they repeatedly go against Cecilia's reflections and deliberations. "Now, therefore" is a common construction within Cecilia's free indirect discourse as she is constantly trying to adjust her plans to match changing circumstances.[42] When Mortimer proposes a clandestine marriage after the accidental summer house meeting, he momentarily makes her believe the problem of the name clause can be overcome and "at length obtained her consent to his plan" (574). But it is a consent that coincidence has coerced and her choice is anything but informed and free: "She considered herself now condemned to refuse Delvile herself" (560). After accidental meetings, Cecilia retreats to reflect, determine, and deliberate but the resolutions come too late. Following the storm, "[l]eft at length by herself, she revolved in her mind the adventure of the evening. . . . That he loved her with tenderness, with fondness loved her, seemed no longer to admit of any doubt. . . . Was the obstacle which thus discouraged him the condition imposed by her uncle's will?" (476–77). She works her way through all the possible obstacles—an affair with Henrietta, a pre-engagement to Euphrasia Pemberton, his mother's wishes—and decides it must be his father's insurmountable pride that keeps him from proposing marriage. She takes two days in deciding that her response to Mortimer's outburst will be a refusal and cold indifference, but when she goes down to breakfast "to meet with firmness" and communicate her decision, she discovers Mortimer is confined to his room with an illness brought on by the storm. "Deep reasoners," as the narrator points out, "when they are also nice casuists, frequently resolve with a tardiness which renders their resolutions of no effect" (482).

Similarly, her "consent" to the clandestine marriage is followed too late by "A Retrospection" when she is "[l]eft now to herself" and regrets her decision (575): "[W]hen at length her recollection more clearly returned," she wants to renege, but it is too late; "to disappoint Delvile so late, by forfeiting a promise so positively accorded," seems morally indefensible to her (577). Since Mortimer has already left for London, launching the series of events that will conclude in their first attempt at a wedding, and since Cecilia does not know where he is staying and thus cannot send him a letter, she decides that the only way to halt the marriage is to travel to London. The resolutions that Cecilia arrives at when left to herself are perhaps at no time in the novel as frustrated by chance occurrences as following her decision to go to London. In the chapter rightly titled "A Torment," Burney torments us with a timing so bad that Cecilia cannot move an inch along the London road without some unfortunate accidental meeting of the *ton* blocking her forward momentum. After stopping at an inn against her wishes to accommodate the frail Mrs. Charlton, "they were *suddenly* encountered by Mr. Morrice" (590; my emphasis). When Cecilia tries to break loose from him, he changes horses and catches up with them. He is riding beside them when *by chance* they come across an overturned chaise that *by chance* turns out to be that of Miss Larolles. Cecilia wants "to drive on with all speed" but, alas, she is stopped when again Morrice catches up to her and forces her to stay (591). Gosport and Aresby "just then" show up and their ridiculous prattle, in scene rhythm, continues for pages (593). For Cecilia "the surprise and vexation of so unseasonable a meeting" produces nothing but despair and stasis (593). She tries to get away, to move forward, but something always inhibits the movement. Morrice, for instance, offers her chaise to the injured Mrs. Mears since, as he says, "I was sure Miss Beverley would not refuse" (593), and indeed, accident after accident makes her unable to refuse or, as the text notes "oblige[s] her to submit" (608).

The torment continues for pages—the chapter is one of the longest in the novel—and the "by chance" pace reaches an absurd level when we have not one but two coincidental accidents befalling poor Miss Larolles's dog, each breaking a different leg. The torment's consequence is to take away Cecilia's ability to act willfully: "[Her] total inability of resistance obliged her to submit, and compelled her to go, stop, or turn, according to their own motions" (608). If she does not arrive that night in London to halt the wedding, she fears she "may be compelled to submit" to Mortimer's terms (611). "Compelled to submit," "obliged her to submit"—these are the outcomes of Burney's use of the chronotope of risk. The torment, in fact, does not really stop when Cecilia frees herself from the *ton*; it continues through her arrival in London, Morrice's appearance at her lodgings, and the mysterious woman's interruption of the clandestine marriage. Cecilia is coerced into the wedding because the chance circumstances—having been seen journeying to London and with Mortimer in her lodgings—require that she marry to save her reputation. A choice she had when she determined to take the journey she no longer has by the end of it, simply because she has circulated socially.

This coercive plotting permeates the novel, configuring the future as infinitely unpredictable. Julia Epstein notes that suspense in the novel originates not in the tension of what will happen next but from "an ambience of continual threat."[43] The future's saturated volatility reroutes the goal of happiness from Cecilia fulfilling her dreams to Cecilia shielding herself from the risk of what might happen next. The pain of uncertainty animates the plot during the protracted marital negotiations. After the storm scene proposal, Mortimer falls ill and Cecilia decides that her uncertainty is the cause, for by not having "the relief he might expect from concluding the affair," he remained in suspense and "she believed his illness and his uneasiness were the same" (482). The anxiety of not knowing the future is worse than knowing, which is why Cecilia resigns herself to Mrs. Delvile's will in breaking the engagement, for, as she thinks, " 'tis suspence, 'tis hope, that make the misery of life" (696). Mortimer, "tortured with suspense," demands a decision, and Cecilia longs to "lessen his inquietude" and "shorten the period" of suspense (646). Every moment in this section "appeared . . . decisive" (680)."[H]ere all is over," Cecilia exclaims, but "all [was] . . . over!" fifteen pages before (650, 637). The repetition of decisive moments—and thus their embedding in the larger sequence in which actions are not decisive—creates a time-space in which calm is simply the lessening of the "inquietude" and "uneasiness," the diminishment of instability. Thus, when the marriage does occur, when the lovers are finally united forever, Cecilia's response is not one of happiness but "fearful anxiety . . . rejoicing that at least all suspense would be over" (830). Cecilia goes from "doubts, apprehensions, and desponding suspense" to "certainty, ease, the expectation of happiness," a space about which the best thing she can say on her wedding day is that "[s]he had nothing left to dread" (833). She is wrong insofar as she has much left to dread: eviction from her home, Mortimer's violence against Monckton, and her own madness. But in that moment, marriage is a risk management strategy that brings an end to volatility.

Why does the novel not end with marriage? That the wedding takes place more than a hundred pages before the novel's close underscores how the plot is not of courtship but of Cecilia's money. The uncertainty that remains is whether and under what conditions Mr. Delvile will accept Cecilia as his daughter-in-law, and thus whether she will keep her fortune. As Catherine Gallagher has wittily pointed out, the marriage literalizes the conditions of Cecilia's life as one of debt as "each hour of her married life puts her deeper in debt" to Eggleston, the next in line for her uncle's estate.[44] When he comes to claim the money before Mortimer has owned her, the chain of events that ensues leads to her losing everything she has left, including her mind and her self. Other critics have analyzed her "mad dash" in depth; suffice it to say here that the tortuous temporality continues until it drives her mad.[45] Her arriving at just the wrong time or arriving a second too late, combined with the near isochrony of the dramatic scene, draws out the suspense until finally "she forgot her situation, her intention, and herself" and she ends up mad in the pawnshop (896). With no possibility of deliberation, reflection, or resolution, and no free indirect discourse since none is available to a character in a coma, Cecilia has arrived at the moment when, with nothing left to lose or to risk, calm arrives.

Her value, in the end, comes not from her status as an heiress but as the insurance policy who guarantees the family's future. Cecilia becomes, in effect, Mortimer's financial advisor, managing their family to produce a profit. I now illustrate how capital's plot dynamic arrives at this moment by turning to the only other time when the novel arrives at a shelter from risk's storms. In the chapter titled "A Calm," Cecilia comes of age, establishes her own house, and for a brief narrative moment lives an independent life. The domestic economics of this "calm" shifts the temporal narrative problem from one of debt to one of savings, a problem that will ultimately require reproduction to be resolved. For one short chapter, Cecilia's dream of an independent life is narratable and, in offering this calm only to take it away, the novel makes visible how *Cecilia* needs to synthesize all four chronotopes to arrive at its final equilibrium. "A Calm" helps us understand how managed risk solves the problem of capital's conflicting temporalities at the same time that it requires Cecilia to give up her fortune. When she finally gains control of her money, Cecilia puts "[t]he system of Her Œconomy" into place (792). With her modest desires, Cecilia lives on a mere £500 of her £3,000 a year, and she decides to dedicate the entirety of the excess to charity projects with Albany: "Her income was very large, and she was wholly without family or connection; to spend it merely upon herself would be something still worse than extravagance. . . . She might save indeed, but for whom? not a creature had such a claim upon her. . . . She would never, she declared, run in debt even for a week, but while her estate was wholly clear, she would spend it without restriction" (795). Keeping her money to her time, balancing her expenses every week, fits the work-discipline time of the course-of-life chronotope but also produces a stagnant time, a regularity, a time in which nothing happens. The chapter's narrative pace makes this evident: whereas "A Torment" takes twenty-one pages to cover one day of the story, "A Calm" narrates an entire winter in a mere seven pages. Without risk, without desire, "without family or connection," there is nothing to generate a plot. The crux of the narrative problem lies in Cecilia's own question: "She might save indeed, but for whom?" Who would she be saving for? That the economic condition of social connection is the need to save and protect oneself against the volatility of the future is the lesson Cecilia learns too late to keep her money. Her mistake, as she tells Mortimer, was that "I have ever thought myself secure of more wealth than I could require, and regarded the want of money as an evil from which I was unavoidably exempted" (808). Only after she has been reduced to nothing is she able to learn that no one is exempt from the insecurity of capitalism's wealth. The realization hits her with force post-marriage, when she is obliged to relinquish her estate to Eggleston and discovers that, though her bills are minimal, the rents she "hoped to receive fell very short of her expectations, for the indulgence she had shewn to her tenants had ill prepared them for so sudden a demand" (866). Cecilia should have saved to cover the contingencies of time and ensure a fluid cash flow.

Like the sympathetic bankrupts I discuss in chapter 1, Cecilia's problem is the innocent one of liquidity, of being cash poor but equity rich. Only when she is "an HEIRESS, dispossessed of all her wealth" does she feel "the capital error she had committed, in living constantly to the utmost extent of her income, without ever preparing . . . against any unfortunate contingency" (869, 873). The contingencies keep money in circulation as capital in the form of a savings account, and keep Cecilia in need of social connections since saving to protect for a future is manifested in a plot dynamic of reproduction. The most obvious answer to the question "Who is she saving for?"—an answer generated by the chronotope of tradition and that signals the novel's final closure—is "her children." Through the loss of her money, the novel, I argue, has shifted Cecilia's ontological state from one of debt (Cecilia remarks early on that "her affluence she therefore considered as a debt contracted with the poor" [55]) to one of saving in which marriage stands in for investment in a safe future. There is an important difference between seeing one's life as always already a debt incurred in the past to living as if one is infinitely in arrears to a future that is to come. The first can be paid off within a course-of-life plot; the second is the existential condition of capital.

The reproductive futurity that emerges from the chronotope of tradition manages the risks of "unfortunate contingency" through inheritance, the past and future meet in an estate that generates infinite wealth if the principal is left alone. Family and tradition add flesh to the temporality of infinite accumulation by prompting the need for saving and investing, for keeping money in circulation. If Briggs had had children, perhaps his money would not have stagnated and there would be logic to his accumulation. Within these terms, Cecilia emerges as the ideal wife because she will not be the fashionable Mrs. Harrel, consuming more than her husband earns; rather, she will be a good domestic manager. Marriage as a safe bet that pays off and aristocratic inheritance as managing the interplay between the predictable and the contingent are confirmed when Cecilia unexpectedly inherits a fortune from Mrs. Delvile's childless sister.

Cecilia loses her money when her future-projected linear-causal "plan of life" is thwarted by the risks, pleasures, and desires she encounters by circulating socially. To live in the world with others requires her to relinquish control of her money, her individual will, and her future to the demands of the free market, in which neither rank nor money guarantee anything. Trying to control the sequence of events leads only to failure. Let us not forget that the biggest plotter in the novel, the person constantly anticipating, countering, and controlling Cecilia's forward momentum from behind the curtain, is Mr. Monckton, who is exposed and discredited.[46] As a response to the risk of the future, never risking anything (Briggs) and overplotting (Monckton) are both bad options. Some risk leads to happiness and some pleasures are worth their novelty. Calm finally arrives when the novel finds a time-space akin to savings bonds: by restricting the potential for gain, one shortens the odds of losing. Moderation is an important budgeting strategy for Cecilia; she eventually finds her "golden mean" (131). When she lived in debt to the poor, she spent indiscriminately on Albany's charitable projects, and thus the poor's infinite needs threatened her resources: "[Albany's] projects are so boundless, that the whole capital of the East India Company would not suffice to fulfil them" (770). The solution to the problem of charity's insatiable demands comes from the existential requirements of saving for a safe and reproductive future; in the closing resolution, Cecilia's "strong spirit of active benevolence . . . was now again displayed, though no longer, as hitherto, unbounded. She had learnt the error of profusion, even in charity and beneficence; and she had a motive for œconomy, in her animated affection for Mortimer" (939). The last words of the novel are narrated from Cecilia's focalization as she finally resigns herself to a world where profits come with losses and there are no moral absolutes: "[S]he surveyed the world at large, and finding that of the few who had any happiness, there were none without some misery, she checked the rising sigh of repining mortality, and, grateful with general felicity, bore partial evil with chearfullest resignation"

(941). *Cecilia*'s play of contingency and predictability makes sense, I argue, within the impossible temporality of capital, in which the reader's desire, like the heroine's, is to find a place of calm where we have "nothing left to dread" (833).

In a recent article on the language of finance capital, Richard Godden describes a derivative as "an instrument for translating volatility into security insofar as it assesses the cost of risk, for a price."[47] The downward mobility plot, I argue, works like a derivative, and the price of translating volatility into security is set by Burney as Cecilia's inheritances and marriage to a compromised hero. Much has been written on the rise of insurance and actuarial science in the eighteenth century, on the new businesses, such as Lloyd's, that profited from securing the future against fire, lost ships, and death.[48] Calculating what one is willing to pay for eliminating risk and developing strategies to hedge against an unwanted future institutes a financialized relation to time that comes with its own cost. Max Haiven notes that the era of financialization has taught us "to manage our lives like individual risk portfolios," which means sacrificing collective futures to our own security and comfort now.[49] As capital increasingly works to free itself from commodity production and as derivatives take up a larger and larger share of market profits, the future is flattened out, as one more thing that rich people can buy in the present. Critics such as Haiven and Slavoj Žižek relate the overwhelming fatalism and cynicism of our contemporary moment to the "no future" instituted by the financial imagination.[50] But in the late eighteenth century, the financial imagination was just developing, and the idea that the future could be secured with money was a relief from more speculative bubbles like the South Sea.

I relate the rise of a temporal dynamic in which risk management makes sense to the novelistic plotting of downward mobility in the sentimental novel. The plot resolution to sentimental loss is to ensure that individuals secure their futures, but the fantasy that risk can be managed comes at the cost of giving over the future to those with the equity to buy time. The long-term temporal problem of derivatives may be approaching its breaking point in our moment of late capitalism; we can now see how the profit reaped from securing individual futures requires the infinite deferral and aggregation of risk, dividing and dispersing payment and responsibility across a sublime number of financial units that render invisible the social and cultural costs of money breeding money. Certain individuals realize vast wealth now, but the cost of risk is ultimately paid by the financially disenfranchised, the debtors who have mortgaged their futures, and by the earth, whose damages are likely irreversible. The temporality required to manage risk through financial derivatives is, then, both a fiction and an ideal plot for fiction and for the novel's individual. *Cecilia* allows us to trace the genealogy of derivatives within the financial imagination and locate in the downward mobility plot the emergence of the individual imperative to manage risk. In *Cecilia*, it becomes impossible to resist the plot of investing and saving for a future, since without it, downward mobility is inevitable.

Frances Burney's biography reveals that she understood the individual need to manage financial risk. As Brian McCrea recounts in *Frances Burney and Narrative Prior to Ideology*, Burney made the leap into the financial imagination, a leap her father could not make. Unlike her father, who kept his money in cash at home, locked up in his armoire, she invested her savings in stocks and, according to McCrea, was "always looking to invest it at the highest, safest rate of return."[51] The D'Arblays' Hoare's bank accounts reveal that almost all of their investments were in government-backed annuities, including navy funds, the safest financial products available in her time.[52] But even government annuities came with risks, a fact we see her managing when the government devalues her navy "fives" (annuities with a 5% return) and she considers whether she should sell out and take the loss. She gathers advice from a number of sources and determines that "not having, unhappily, taken any measures for selling out while stocks were higher, it was *Now* more likely to be advantageous to leave the property untouched, & trust to the good faith of Government in the new 4.s—in which, though unavoidably losers, the 5. stockholder would be less so than in selling out to buy in the 3s."[53] In other words, she, too, knows when to cut her losses and when to hold out for a future that is better.

Capital's time, as I hope this chapter demonstrates, is rife with temporal paradoxes that fictional plots help us to see; they do so not through a causal logic of progression but through a temporal dynamics of chronotopic nesting. Novels can shape time in ways that individuals can only imagine, in part because the end to individual futures is existentially unknowable. The great actuarial science behind life insurance and defined-benefit pension funds depends on some of us dying earlier than others, but individuals cannot reap profits from their own deaths. As the saying goes, "You can't take it with you." Death as the ultimate closure of the individual's plot but not the end of capital's is precisely the temporal dynamic readable in Burney's next novel, *Camilla*. In chapter 5, I turn to the temporal contradiction of realizing capital—how profits from the future accrue in the present—and read this structure into narrative closure. By thinking about closure in the novel through the dynamics of selling out for a profit, I read *Camilla*'s downward mobility plot as registering the cost paid by women of infinite economic growth.

The Plot of Capital II

Camilla, Closure, and the Realization of Capital

How does the plot of capital end? What closure propels the story of infinite economic growth? Could novel endings help us understand what is at stake in thinking about the end of capitalism? The question of capitalism's end currently preoccupies many people, with an increasing interest in whether its end is nigh. The marker "late capitalism" seems to imply an end date. Slavoj Žižek, in *Living in the End Times*, and Wolfgang Streeck, in *How Will Capitalism End?* both see the limits on infinite growth as registering capitalism's impending end.[1] The challenge in answering the question of how capital's plot ends and why it is, as the saying goes, "easier to imagine the end of the world than to imagine the end of capitalism," involves the kinesthetic quality of capital—how, for money to be transformed into capital, it must always be in motion and its story thus belies collective endings.[2] We can imagine the end of an individual plot in capital's realization—selling real estate, cashing out when markets are high, and retiring with secure pensions. But it is far harder to imagine the end to a collective plot that does not entail loss, a buyer left holding the shares when the market falls or the degradation of the earth as we drill ever deeper for ever-greater resource extraction. Recent dystopic fiction that tries to imagine the end of capital often ends up imagining it as the end of the world or at least as the breakdown of civilization, like the slow-burn death that Streeck posits and that many of us feel we are living.[3] We all collectively know the West's consumption levels are unsustainable and yet individual downward mobility, living with less, is not an end we can easily embody. Western middle-class individuals continue to rely on financial investments to support their old age, in part because inflation determines that to afford the future, their pensions must produce compound growth and accumulate more than simple savings. Thus, the Morgan Stanley ad discussed at the beginning of chapter 4 ("Four Generations of Plot Twists") imagines the end of its plot as a stable and secure retirement leading to familial inheritance after death. Passing on wealth to children solves the problem of how infinite economic growth ends in the individual plot: since "you can't take it with you," inheritance provides the impetus for continuing accumulation. But a plot in which "cashing out" is both the realization of profit and reproductive futurity can be only an individual plot and not an epic in absolute time. The narrative arc that ends in the security of infinite wealth cannot be realized by all individuals simultaneously, because, if we all cashed out at the same time, the run on the bank would end in loss and ruin. If I am to sell and realize surplus value, someone has to buy. Individual stories manage to separate out the timing of consuming and saving, whereas buying and selling are necessarily simultaneous within the collective. Thinking about closure in the novel—in particular, the tortuous ending of *Camilla*—helps to make visible the temporal contradiction between the individual and collective plots of capital. This chapter explores downward mobility in Burney's novel to suggest that the heroine's financial losses ensure an ending that recalibrates the disequilibrium between buying and selling, a plot dynamics that manages inflation by making its heroine pay.

Price inflation hides the underlying costs of compounding economic growth by delaying the final accounting and keeping the story moving forward. The problem to which inflation is the solution is the temporal paradox of infinite profits, what David Harvey has identified as "the contradictory unity of production and realisation."[4] Buying and selling, like consuming and saving, are not two sides of the same coin within an economic system grounded in compounding growth—a disequilibrium similar to the one between credit and debt discussed in chapter 2. Harvey argues that capital's two strategies for wrenching ever-greater profit or surplus value out of the world's resources cannot be reconciled. Profits to the seller can be increased either by cutting wages to lower the costs of production or by raising prices of a commodity to realize more value in the sale, but ultimately these strategies lead to a temporal impasse: if you reduce wages, workers have less money to buy and are forced to decrease consumption, but if you raise prices and not wages, your commodity will find fewer buyers.[5] Historically, Harvey argues, this tension has led to cyclical movements between increasing wages and increasing prices, a cycle that renders inflation the norm. This temporal impasse was particularly glaring in the popular press after the 2008 crash when the same newspapers that chided consumers for overspending simultaneously incited them to shop to ensure economic recovery. But how can the same paycheck be deposited in the bank to pay off the mortgage *and* be spent at the mall? This chapter suggests that bourgeois culture's gendering of consumption as feminine is one of the ways the temporal impasse is displaced: women consume extravagantly, while men pay the bills. The difference in time becomes the difference of sex, a displacement we see in the sentimental novel's plots of female downward mobility.

By reading narrative closure as akin to the realization of capital, this chapter explains the tortuous rhythm of *Camilla*'s plot, the disequilibrium between its risks and rewards, by pointing to Burney's desire to write a novel in the "prose Epic Style."[6] When Burney's father criticizes *Camilla* as too unwieldy, as consisting of "detached stories" that needed to be woven "into one story," she precisely rejects a singular or individual plot in favor of an epic with its collective cast of characters.[7] As Elaine Bander notes, *Camilla* is the only one of Burney's novels not to have an orphan heroine and, by embedding the individual woman's plot within the family, the novel demonstrates how reciprocated happiness for the collective is not easily narratable.[8] The novel's domestic economics, in which Camilla goes into debt to meet her ethical obligations to her family, plots the tensions that emerge within communities when speculative capital divorces financial from social relations. In a world where volatile futures are the norm (the plot dynamic seen in *Cecilia*), female downward mobility stabilizes the markets by ensuring that love is untainted by mercenary interest. *Camilla*'s climax arrives when debts produce the heroine's symbolic death, from which Edgar resurrects her. Debt repayment signals the novel's marriage ending insofar as Edgar's first act as a husband "was to clear every debt in which Camilla had borne any share."[9] Marriage, in other words, is the resolution to the financial, not the romance, plot. Burney writes an epic in which Camilla's losses guarantee that the novel's payoff will be reproductive futurity and infinite wealth, and I argue that its tortuous plot rhythms register the costs women pay to maintain the social equilibrium when money circulates unfriended. Female downward mobility in the sentimental novel is the price of a happy ending.

How Money Can Buy Happiness: Closure and the Plot of Downward Mobility

Insofar as novels end on the last page, they form self-contained worlds that function much like a restricted economy in which all expenditures (financial, emotional, social) need to be balanced in a ledger book.[10] Imbalances in a novel's final accounting require readers' interpretation and contribute to their judgment of whether the narrative reaches a satisfying close. Paul Ricoeur delineates the way endings must be "judged 'acceptable after all' "; that is, the reader must be able to look back from the perspective of the whole and see the pattern embedded in the parts.[11] Novels in which we feel "cheated" by an ending—for example, when a deus ex machina glibly solves a problem we have invested in for hundreds of pages—best make the point that most novels, especially realist ones, create a universe in which a balance of expenditure is reached, though never in a way that stabilizes meaning. As narrative theorists, including Peter Brooks, have proposed, endings confer meaning on the story insofar as we project a whole to make sense of a part—"intelligibility, meaning, understanding depend on a fully predicated narrative sentence, on a narrative totality"—but full narrative totality never arrives, since meaning, like the value of a stock, circulates infinitely in the exchange between book and reader.[12] Meaning's realization is the enabling fantasy of narrative, and though it never arrives, its imagined totalities elicit the reader's valuation of the narrative payoff. Was it "worth" it? Is the ending "acceptable after all"? Turning to *Camilla*'s frustrating plot dynamics and its tortuous narrative duration, I wager that its marriage ending constitutes one of the worst payoffs in literary history. The novel's final accounting leaves its reader deep in the red. To use a phrase financial advisors deploy to rate stocks, *Camilla*'s "risk-reward ratio" is extremely low. The disparity between what is risked in the plot's suspense and the reward of its ending has contributed to the novel's long-standing reputation as a "failure," discussed below.[13] I explain the low risk-reward ratio as an effect of sentimental fiction's narrative accounting whereby, in order for love to be rewarded with money, the love of money must first be disavowed. Through *Camilla*'s maddening duration and closure, Burney marks female downward mobility as what buys its community's happiness.

That *Camilla*'s accounts are calculated in a closed or restricted economy is best illustrated by the way its heroine is repeatedly found in situations where she has limited money and has to choose between spending on herself and giving to others. She has a half guinea that she can either spend on the lottery for the locket *or* as charity to the beggar family, but she cannot do both. She needs to buy a dress for the Southampton ball with the same money she requires to rescue the Higden family from bankruptcy. Over and over again, money circulates in the novel around these mutually exclusive choices. Burney's heroine cannot have it all. *Camilla*'s either-or accounting is best summed up by the sentimental equation love ≠ money: to narrate virtue in the historical moment when it separates from commerce, the sentimental novel posits love as readable only through the disavowal or refusal of wealth.[14] The disequilibrium between buying and selling introduced when financial capital circulates between strangers translates into the social problem of determining when love is rooted in virtue and when it is motivated by greed. Is it love or only the love of one's money? Sentimental fiction answers this problem through downward mobility: to arrive at the virtuous life of happiness, characters need first to refuse money.[15] I lay out sentimentalism's moral economy in the introduction, showing that, by the end of the eighteenth century, proclaiming a lack of interest in money had become, paradoxically, a precondition of having money in fiction. The cliché that money does not buy happiness translates into the sentimental plot with a closure that rewards characters with riches only if they have previously suffered financially to prove their virtue. The mutually exclusive choice between acting on love or on financial self-interest introduces a gendered narrative that codes female financial suffering as virtue.

Across the latter eighteenth century, heroines find themselves in Camilla's position: required to refuse money to prove their moral worth, they constantly end up in dire straits. Witness *Clarissa*, in which Richardson's heroine refuses all money that could be construed as compensation for her rape and starves to death to maintain moral purity, an act that Laura Rosenthal refers to as the "suicidal virtue of refusal."[16] Helen Thompson claims that in Burney's last novel, *The Wanderer*, its heroine's "'pecuniary distress' [functions] as a sign of virtue."[17] Penitent prostitutes in Magdalen narratives provide the quintessential love-or-money plots. The heroines, for example, in *The Histories of Some of the Penitents in the Magdalen-House*, repeatedly refuse money from jilted lovers in order to prove their initial fall was for a virtuous love, not a selfish desire for financial gain, a decision that causes their abjection and poverty and leads them to the doors of the Magdalen hospital.[18] From Frances Sheridan's *Memoirs of Miss Sidney Bidulph* to Mary Hays's *Victim of Prejudice*, a pattern appears in fiction in which acting out of virtue is imagined to come at the cost of financial health for women. Virginia Cope's *The Heroine of Disinterest* concentrates on this motif and on "[s]tories of a woman either dispossessed or threatened with dispossession" "who refuse[s] to calculate value in monetary terms" and whose "value, then, is determined not by the property she (may) hold, but by her attitude toward that property—by her emotional rather than her legal relation to the family estate."[19] The disinterested heroine appears alongside capital's plot in sentimental fiction to pay for the risks of circulating money free from ethical obligations. Burney narrativizes the equation love ≠ money around a plot that reveals how women pay for the social risks of capital's inflationary circulation, but in doing so, she produces a novel with one of the most frustrating payoffs and an extremely low risk-reward ratio to its plot.

Ever since the novel's publication, critics have noted that the plot generated by Camilla's coming of age is oddly flat, containing frequent stasis, and that the narrative's forward progression is often suspended in digressive episodes, producing what Andrea Henderson calls its "strange distension."[20] The *British Critic* thought the story "doubtless spun out to an immoderate length; many dialogues, and many adventures, might well be spared."[21] Irrelevant events in the courtship plot—aimless outings in Tunbridge and Southampton, lengthy acts involving secondary characters, tedious conversations among the fashionable set—are narrated in great detail, while a major event such as the breakdown of Edgar and Camilla's engagement constitutes only a few paragraphs, with no attendant tension before or lingering mourning after.

Dissatisfaction with the plot has continued into the present. Describing the nine-hundred-plus-page text as "Burney's most arduous novel," Claudia Johnson diagnoses its problem as one of narrative rhythm: "Working by complicating accretion rather than progression, the narrative flow of *Camilla* . . . is fitful, impeded, constantly breaking down."[22] Critics have come up with various explanations for the novel's unfamiliar pacing: for Johnson, it emerges from the regressive politics of sentimentality in the 1790s; for Henderson, it concerns the working through of new, masochistic forms of desire; for Joyce Hemlow, its origins lie in the novel's status as a conduct book.[23] I read *Camilla*'s tortured narrative rhythm as a product of the dissonance between its romantic closure and its financial plot. The novel's plot follows the money, not the romance, and all the major events are caused by the heroine's mounting debts. Female downward mobility causes the novel's fitful narrative rhythms as well as its anti–romantic climax. As in *Cecilia*, the resolution of the romantic plot happens long before the novel's end, and, in both, the questions raised about the financial and emotional costs of marrying compromised wealthy heroes are never entirely answered.

Why do *Cecilia* and *Camilla*, as well as *The History of Emily Montague*, contain temporal gaps between the resolution of their courtship plots and their final endings? In *Emily Montague*, almost 20% of the novel remains after Emily and Rivers marry; Cecilia and Mortimer marry one hundred pages before the novel's end; and, in *Camilla*, Edgar and Camilla reveal their love and become engaged little more than halfway through the novel. Edgar proclaims, "My heart is all your own," and their single desire for each other never wavers even though the engagement is later temporally broken off (545). For a contemporary reader schooled in the perfectly paced discursive tempo of an Austen novel where the time during which the love story occurs seamlessly equates with the time during which the story is narrated, the tempo in these sentimental narratives feels off. I argue that in novels where the climax to the romantic plot does not signal closure, the delay is caused by a lack of completeness in their economic narratives.[24] Love has not yet shown it is disinterested enough to be rewarded with money—a narrative rhythm that renders the moral purification of financial capital as sentimental fiction's "nonnarratable." *Nonnarratable* is the term introduced by D. A. Miller to designate that which signals a novel's end; if the "narratable" is "the instances of disequilibrium, suspense, and general insufficiency from which a given narrative appears to rise," a "nonnarratable element" occurs when that insufficiency has been filled and thus the novel must end: "What defines a nonnarratable element is its incapacity to generate a story."[25] The nonnarratable of *Emily Montague*, *Cecilia*, and *Camilla* is not the revelation of love and marriage, since there is still more of the story to be told after these events take place. The "more" involves the disequilibrium introduced by financial capital and the need to refriend money.

In *Camilla*, the wealthy Mr. Westwyn, Sir Hugh's oldest friend, voices sentimentalism's narrative lack, or what must be addressed before plots stop generating a story; he delights at the prospect of his son marrying the penniless Camilla, because "[m]oney goes but a little way to make people happy; and true love's not a thing to be got every day" (670).[26] That a wealthy person's "true love" requires, in the same sentence, the denial of mercenary desire points to the way that what makes love narratable in the sentimental novel is the suspicion that all love derives from financial ambition. When wealth is divorced from land and marries capital, the anonymous financial marketplace introduces a hermeneutics of suspicion toward all social relations. Everyone is suspected of having ulterior motives. The nonnarratable, then, is not the fairytale "happily ever after." The ease with which, for example, Pamela's motives in Richardson's novel were reinterpreted as Shamela's demonstrates that rewarding love with money when money circulates as capital requires the balancing narrative of downward mobility. Richardson's straight upward mobility plot required a riskier temporality for the reward of wealth. The nonnarratable of *Camilla*'s aristocratic reproductive futurity arrives only after its female heroine has divested enough to detach her love from all claims on the estate. I argue in chapter 3 that one way the sentimental novel proves that money does not buy happiness is to circulate stories-within-stories of financial loss. Here I argue that Burney uses sentimentalism's nonnarratable—whatever erases all doubt that love is nonmercenary—to show the gendered costs of capital's social relations. She is able to end her plot with love *and* money but only at the cost of her heroine's financial distress.

Camilla and the Social Costs of Economic Growth

If *Cecilia*'s temporality contrasted its heroine's "course of life" with a world of risk, *Camilla*'s temporal dynamics works through the constant interruption of risk into the "now" of consumption. Cecilia's characterization as a planner who reflects on her circumstances underscored her "course of life"; Camilla, in contrast, is characterized by her "vivacity," her overly energetic embrace of the present without a plan for the future (51). Burney's third novel suspends the "now" for nine hundred pages to narrate the time between buying and selling, between Edgar's declared interest in Camilla and the deal being sealed. This duration plots the narrative tension of capital's realization: the suspense is generated by whether Camilla can maintain her value as she circulates socially and whether Edgar will realize that value by marrying her. Given that Edgar sees every social transaction as a potential rip-off that ends with him holding damaged goods, what will make him take the plunge? In extending the scene of consumption, pausing on the infinitely circulating tension between buyer's and seller's remorse, the novel accounts for what we owe to each other and what might be the cost of a win-win exchange economy. In the end, *Camilla*'s moral accounting makes infinite happiness expensive for its heroine. If this were an individual's story, Camilla could realize profits like Defoe's Roxana, but by making this a "prose epic" and embedding her heroine in a family and community, Burney shows precisely how such profits always have social effects.

Consumption, rather than production, is literally front and center in the novel, with Burney's original representation of modern shopping. Many critics have discussed the uniqueness of the Southampton scene, reading Camilla's excursion with Mrs. Mittin to look at goods with no intention of buying as inventing window-shopping.[27] Such a scene repositions the drama of consumption from a social relation between vendors and their neighbors to an anonymous transaction in which the goods themselves must seduce buyers.[28] This shift in shopping culture whereby sellers "market" their goods to strangers complicates the agency of commodity desire by locating it not only in the buyer but in the object as well. Desire for the object, as Burney announces in the novel's opening paragraph, is further complicated by the rule of the heart in which "one thing alone is steady—the perverseness of spirit which grafts desire on what is denied" (7). Heightening demand through denial is one tactic available to the seller, but raising demand is not what eventually seduces Edgar into buying. In sentimentalism's restrictive accounting, the only way Camilla can entice her buyer is through infinite supply, by devaluing herself and relinquishing all her financial resources.

Camilla's plot is catalyzed by financial loss, but it is a perverse downward mobility in that she loses only what she had momentarily gained. Sir Hugh's initial decision to make Camilla his heir and reward her for good behavior is overturned a few pages later when the accident disabling Eugenia causes him to "atone . . . for the ill he had done her, by bequeathing to her every thing he possessed in the world, in estate, cash, and property" (30). What value does the narrative accrue by acquiring and then losing a fortune? What plot does it launch? To begin with, it provides Camilla with the first of many opportunities to increase her moral worth through financial sacrifice. When she hears she is to be an heiress, she is unconcerned since "interest and ambition could find no room in [her] mind" (16). Because of her "instinctive gratitude," the only pleasure she takes in her status as heiress is in the fantasy of giving her future wealth to her family, of buying a coach for her mama, a horse for her brother Lionel, a new bureau for her sister Lavinia (16). Camilla's lack of economic "interest and ambition" feeds Edgar's desire for her, and we are introduced early on to the dynamic in which Camilla's self-denial is what increases Edgar's valuation of her. When Edgar explains that her uncle's reticence toward her after the disinheritance has nothing to do with his withdrawal of love and everything to do with his guilt, Camilla responds with a sentimental outburst: " 'O if that [being disinherited] is all! If my uncle indeed loves me as well as before all this; I am sure I can never, never be so wicked, as to envy poor little Eugenia . . . because she will be richer than I shall be!' " (32). Camilla's lack of disappointment in being disinherited, her rejection of any desire for the money, shifts Edgar's attraction away from Indiana to herself: "[S]he was grown a thousand times more beautiful than Indiana," thinks Edgar (32). Happiness in economic sacrifice is what renders Camilla romantically desirable, an equation Burney plots to its abject extreme.

The second, related plot that "the disinherited Camilla" introduces charts the speculative bubbles within the marriage market. Because she was once, briefly, an heiress, Camilla is repeatedly confused for one and becomes the object of pursuit from mercenary and distasteful men, including the hideous Mr. Dubster and the seamy Major Cerwood. Lionel, Camilla's irresponsible brother, announces to the neighborhood that Camilla became her uncle's heiress at age ten, "only sinking, in his account, the revocation made so soon after in favour of Eugenia" (532). Lionel's false advertising of his sister's worth is discovered by Dubster and Cerwood only when they negotiate to seal the deal. In one of the many repetitive acts in the novel, both Dubster and Cerwood make the same visit to Sir Hugh in order to declare their interests in his niece, and both are left "completely staggered" when Sir Hugh commends them "for a choice so little mercenary, which he looked upon as a mark of a good heart" (533). Neither man has a good heart, as becomes clear with the relief they feel over having their marriage proposals rejected. Not only does financial self-interest code these characters as lacking virtue, but the episodes also mark marital engagement as a moment of realizing value. In these cases, the mercenary suitors find out Camilla is not worth their price.

The nonrealizable collective temporality of realizing capital—that the end of one plot is necessarily the beginning of another—inspires its most tense and revealing dynamics through the story of Edgar and Camilla's romance. We know early on that Edgar wants to buy. He quickly sees through Indiana's shinier façade, deflating the value of beauty over virtue, and he shifts his attraction to Camilla after the raffle when her sacrificial charity, to echo Sir Hugh, gives her "a mark of a good heart" (533). Shortly thereafter, Edgar declares his "irrevocable choice" to his mentor Dr. Marchmont, whose misogyny introduces the obstacle that suspends the romance's resolution, freezing the plot in the moment between desire and satisfaction, between decision and purchase (157). Marchmont's hideous "buyer beware" lecture introduces the skeptical proposition that Camilla may be faking virtue to attract a buyer, and the plot turns on the problem of determining whether Edgar's risk will bring its commensurate reward. Marchmont counsels Edgar to "raise no expectations" by declaring his desire, since "deception is easy" when it comes to evaluating "the worth . . . of her heart" (158). While Edgar wants to stand as "her guarantee," Marchmont convinces him that only time and scrutiny can determine Camilla's value (158). Even though Marchmont agrees that "every possible happiness promises to be yours" (159), the promise can be realized only in a suspended future. Andrea Henderson identifies the "insoluble problem" in this temporality: "[I]f Edgar must be certain of Camilla's value before acting, he will never be able to act—he will be forever inspecting the merchandise."[29] The trouble with the timing of this romantic transaction, as Dubster and Cerwood found out, is that the value of the merchandise is realized only in the moment of its purchase. While sentimental novels such as *Camilla* try to affirm "intrinsic worth," all the narrative's value is realized only in the moment of exchange, requiring a risk that Edgar seems incapable of taking. (*Camilla* includes three assertions that a character has "intrinsic worth," one each for all three Tyrold sisters [477, 723, 784].) In the meantime, Burney dwells in what the seller must do to prove the value of her goods, narrating how the rules of supply and demand are gendered and produce both social inequities and the plot's tortuous rhythm.

That female financial sacrifice is what balances the narrative's accounts and proves Camilla's worth is the painful realization of Burney's novel. Mr. Tyrold, in his "little sermon upon the difficulties and the conduct of the female heart," is blunt in informing Camilla that the decision to marry is not hers, that agency lies rather with the buyer: "[W]here there are two parties, choice can belong only to one of them" (353, 358). Camilla's best hope for happiness is to resign herself to the "self-conquest" of her desires, especially because "[t]he person in question . . . is also rich" and the community will judge her motives to be mercenary if her interest in Edgar was known (359, 361). The fact that Edgar is "heir to one of the finest estates in the country" requires that she not only silence her desire but convince everyone, especially Indiana and Miss Margland, that she is actively disinterested since any desire would be interpreted as mercenary (17). The presumption that the world acts selfishly, that Camilla is out for Edgar's cash, leads to the misinterpretations that lower Camilla's worth. Margland orders her to visit Mrs. Arlbery to prove she is not interested in Edgar, a visit that she has promised Edgar she would not make. When Edgar discovers she went "without waiting for his permission," he is troubled and her value falls in his estimation (168).

Refusing interest and actively rejecting desire are the only actions available to "the disinherited Camilla." In a scene mirroring the ball episode in *Evelina*, the only affirmative decision Camilla can make to the unwanted requests from Dubster and Cerwood at the Northwick dance is to "determine . . . not to dance at all" (90). At the same time that the plot tensions rise with the misinterpretations, so do Camilla's debts. In fact, the negative act of going into debt is what eventually prompts Edgar to risk investing in their shared future. In claiming that *Camilla* plots money, not courtship, I suggest that if we follow the story of her debts, we will see that financial loss, not romantic tension, brings the plot to its climax. The story of Camilla's debt is a prose epic that plots the demands placed on her by merely living in society. If *Cecilia* plotted every day of its heiress's married life as a day she went further into debt, *Camilla* narrates the inverse, in which every day of its dowryless heroine's life on the marriage market requires her to spend money she does not have. She needs to constantly invest in order to ensure that her value stays high and that she does not end up as discounted goods.

As long as Camilla remains with her family at Cleves and Etherington, she has no need for money, but as soon as she ventures into social circulation, financial demands present themselves and cause her to accumulate debt. The raffle for the locket is the first episode that generates the need for money, and it also provides the most insidious example of the novel's restrictive accounting in which virtue is coded as the refusal of consumer desire. Camilla has half a guinea in her pocket to spend either on a raffle for a "mere common bauble," the locket, or in aiding a poor man who is on death row for stealing a leg of mutton to feed his family (93). She instinctively declines the raffle ticket even before she has heard the beggar's story, because she was "totally unused to hazard . . . the little allowance she had been taught to spend sparingly upon herself" (93). Her refusal of desire is immediately met with Edgar's positive attentions: having "observed" her decision, he hunts her down so "that he might express his admiration" (93). But the shame she feels when others buy a ticket and she does not causes her to concede: she "could not withstand" Mrs. Arlbery's "invitation" and so "she gave her half guinea" (94). Edgar's admiration immediately recalibrates to "disappoint[ment]," confirming both that he is the account keeper and that to be in the moral black with Edgar, Camilla must go into the red with Mrs. Arlbery, disappointing her and refusing her invitations (94). Camilla later regrets buying the ticket, because it means she has no money to give after she learns the beggar's story: " 'I was thinking . . . what my dear father would have said, had he seen me giving half a guinea for a toy, and a shilling to such poor starving people as these!' " (98). "[C]harmed" by her moral questioning, Edgar offers to retrieve her half guinea from the raffle (98). When Camilla discovers that she has won the raffle, she is at a loss to explain how since it is "utterly impossible that the locket and the half guinea should belong to the same person"—that is, that charity (sacrificing for others) and consumerism (desiring for oneself) can coexist (123). Unable to refund Camilla's lottery ticket, Edgar had given his own half guinea to the family on her behalf, and the text's confusion over who is indebted to Edgar registers the transformation of financial into moral debt here through the literal displacement of the locket's economic exchange value onto a moral value standing in for the heroine's virtue. Camilla refuses to accept the locket at first, because she believes Edgar is the rightful owner even though his half guinea bought the charity and not the ticket. As Catherine Keohane points out, "[S]he needs to transform something purchased with her own money into a gift, so that the charity, or the right use of money, can be hers."[30] Her rewriting the debt such that she owns the charity, not her commodity desire, is a necessary component to her becoming Edgar's romantic object. Edgar, too, transfers the debt: "It is not you, but those poor people who are in my debt," he tells her (124). By establishing such an absolute division between her consumerism and her charity, between individual desire and self-sacrifice, the text sets up the strict dichotomy that requires her to lose money to gain love. Why can she not have both, especially since she has money to make a few "small purchases" in the haberdasher shop where she awaits the outcome of the raffle (105)? With the beggar's execution imminent and the raffle's deadline having passed, the immediate timing explains why Camilla becomes indebted to Edgar. The simultaneous timing whereby the "now" of social circulation makes financial demands that require Camilla to take on debt produces the narrative's claustrophobia.

Elisabeth Gruner describes *Camilla* as "a courtship novel without suspense, a bildungsroman without visible growth," and, in its middle volumes, the novel's plot seems to be spinning its wheels, cycling around Camilla's lack of action in an ever-tightening financial grip, and watching as others watch her.[31] Her debts increase simply through her living, even as she refuses all financial desire. Burney constantly numerically calculates Camilla's economic life, and the figures show that her debts accumulate not because she spends too much but because she wants so little.[32] Had she wanted more before leaving for Tunbridge, she would have returned debt-free. Sir Hugh gives her a £50 bank note for trip expenses, but "with mingled modesty and dejection" she wants to return "the whole, as unnecessary even to her wishes" (376). Mr. Tyrold does not let her and, "interfering, [he] made her accept twenty pounds" (377). To have wishes that might require money is a prospect she intuits as immodest. Thus, when Lionel shortly thereafter makes his first of many demands for money, she happily loses the lesser £20. Burney once again underscores the sentimental accounting through the story's timing: she meets his request with "pleasure . . . as she opened her pocket-book," telling him, " 'you could never have applied to me so opportunely. I have just got twenty pounds, and I do not want twenty shillings' " (379). The simultaneous arrival and dispersal of the £20 marks Camilla as void of selfishness and generous to her family. Unfortunately, she later discovers that she does need money in Tunbridge to answer living expenses she had not anticipated. A few items at the milliners, subscription tickets to the rooms, and pretty soon her Tunbridge debts amount to £16. Had she taken her uncle's bank note, she would have returned with £34; and, underscoring the point with the numerical calculation, had Camilla only "wanted" the more modest £20, she still would have covered her costs and the plot would end here. Instead, her debts mount. Why?

Camilla goes further into debt not because of the money per se but because of the meaning that gets attached to its circulation. The suspense is an effect of

Camilla's anxiety and shame about the debts being discovered, especially by Edgar. The increasing threat posed by the story of her debts causes the distension in the narrative rhythm, the disequilibrium between the level of suspense and its underlying cause, between the potential damage to her value to Edgar and the actual amounts of her debts. "Financial crises," Julia Epstein notes, "fuel a plot in which, in fact, none of the principals lacks substantial assets."[33] Had Camilla simply asked for the money, or, as Epstein wryly observes, "had Camilla at any point fully unburdened herself" to Edgar, "the novel would not have needed to be written."[34] Financial debt takes on narrative significance not because of its monetary value but because of the ethical value attached to its social revelation. Burney narrates the tension around Camilla's increasing debts to make visible the existential imperative that living comes at a cost, both economically and socially, for women. As her heroine's financial debts mount, so do the misunderstandings that sentimental virtue prevents its heroine from clearing up. Edgar erroneously thinks Camilla's correspondence with Sir Sedley is romantically motivated, when in fact it concerns a monetary transaction made on her brother's behalf and, had she been able to speak about the money, there would be no romantic obstacle. The narrative progresses from her *not* clearing up the misunderstandings and from her remaining silent as others continue to think the worst. The extended postponement of any éclaircissement emerges from the competing ethical and financial demands placed on her, and what results is a plot in which debt is the condition of being attached to others.

The inevitability that a virtuous heroine's cost of living requires her to go into debt is perhaps clearest in Camilla's frustrating relationship with the panderer Mrs. Mittin and the repetitive suspense it involves concerning whether Camilla can stop paying Mittin's inflationary costs of proximity to her. The repetitions suggest Camilla should learn to control Mittin, but while Camilla grows and learns to be more specific with Mittin, it makes no difference to her pocketbook and her debts only increase. As their first shopping foray in Tunbridge illustrates, the problem emerges not from Camilla's consumer desires but from the bourgeois code that dictates she never talk about money in public. To have good manners, Camilla cannot ask the cost of the few small items she purchases at the toy store in Tunbridge; a bill she imagines to be half a crown ends up being one guinea. She then determines "to put nothing apart as a buyer, till she had inquired its price," a maxim similar to the one Marchmont counsels Edgar to take on the marriage market (395). Yet she finds such inquiry impossible. Her next shopping trip, to the milliner's, has her not desiring anything in particular except "to avoid appearing in a manner that might disgrace her party," and she asks the milliner for "what she thought fashionable that was most reasonable" (396). The milliner's interpretation of "reasonable" is three guineas more than her own, but she "was ashamed to dispute" the bill (396). Had she felt no shame in talking about money, she would also have saved herself five shillings by not following Mrs. Arlbery's example and overpaying for her subscription to the Tunbridge rooms (402). Demands for money are an inevitable part of town life, but because of the embarrassment of asking the price in advance and admitting one's funds are limited, she ends up going into debt, first for her ticket to the master of ceremonies ball, then for her ticket to see the monkey, and then for the earring raffle. Camilla risks losing her value to Edgar because that which gives her value—sentimental virtue—requires that she stay silent.

Southampton heightens the dangers she faces from social life, not only by causing the break in her engagement when Edgar misinterprets her window-shopping as desire for another man, but also through the repetition of Mittin's extortions. The plot dramatizes the temporal paradox of realization, the simultaneous impossibility and necessity of knowing the value of the goods before buying. Camilla learns again that one must inspect and determine the price before buying, and yet, again, the timing of the transactions makes it impossible for her to do so. As with the raffle, Southampton presents her with two coinciding demands for her finite resources: she needs a gown for a ball she is attending with the hopes only of seeing Edgar and clearing up the misunderstanding that led to their broken engagement; but she also needs the money to invest in her washerwoman's brother, Higden, whose business is suffering a liquidity problem. Higden's "unmerited" problem is bad timing: he needs Camilla to provide "money or security to the wholesale dealers" in order to acquire the goods to sell to make the profit to pay his bills (711). Camilla allows herself to stand as Higden's security, but problems ensue when Mittin uses the same security as a deposit on material for her gown. Even though Camilla has learned her lesson and gives Mittin an explicit directive only to "make such inquiries concerning the value of the ball-dress uniform"—that is to say, to ask the price but not to buy—Mittin returns having given £15 on security for fabric that, upon inspection, turns out to be spoiled, and Camilla loses her money because the vendor runs off with the deposit (691). Concurrently, accidental timing turns her investment in Higden into a loss when a leaking oil flask ruins his goods; with the family on the brink of homelessness, Camilla gives them £18 to pay the landlord. Camilla learns of the Higden family's near "destruction" as she awaits Mrs. Berlinton to leave for the ball, and Burney brings the obvious opposition to our attention: "She paused—looked now at the pleading group, now at her expensive dress; asked how, for her own hopes, she could risk so much, yet for their deliverance from ruin so little; and with a blush . . . finally consented that the landlord should apply to her the next morning" (714). As with the locket episode, coincidental temporality dramatizes a finite economy in which limited resources pit spending on herself against saving a family from ruin.

If she were not a single woman without a fortune on the marriage market, such choices would not be forced upon her—a point Burney narrates through the ease with which Eugenia navigates the social world. Unlike Camilla, Eugenia is free from money's moral coercions precisely because she cannot take her goods to market. Her deformity disqualifies her from being a romantic heroine, but it also frees her to claim an economic agency Camilla cannot have.[35] With Sir Hugh's money ("a guinea for every pit in that poor face" [30]), Eugenia easily throws the beggar family half a crown even after she has bought her lottery ticket, whereas Camilla has only a shameful shilling (97). When Camilla needs £40 to pay Jacob for the replacement of the horse, Eugenia steps into her own room and quickly returns with £20 (557). When no one else has ready cash to give Lionel as he flees to the continent, Eugenia gives him half a crown (740). Eugenia has easy access to money because it has already circulated through its sentimental cleansing, with her disability exacting the price paid by Sir Hugh to reimburse her for the injury he believes he caused. Camilla has no such cash.

As in *Cecilia*, Burney uses coincidental temporality to place Camilla in impossible and claustrophobic situations; here, the concurrent events highlight the fact that her heroine cannot meet everyone's economic and social needs simultaneously. In the "now," time and resources are not infinite and ethical choices must be made. The temporality enhances the restrictive economy that Camilla finds herself in, where answering one person's demands not only puts her in financial debt but jeopardizes her virtue in the eyes of another, usually Edgar. Sentimental liquidity is explicitly a gendered problem in the novel both because of the nature of female virtue with its strict either-ors and because men have resources that women do not, a point underscored in the contrast between Camilla's debts and those of her male family members. The punishing ratio of risk to reward for women—whereby the anxiety Camilla experiences and the risks to her reputation are out of proportion to the reward of marriage to Edgar—is nowhere more precisely calculated by Burney than in the disequilibrium between female and male consumption. The unbalanced account is a matter of narrative duration with volumes focused on Camilla's anxiety over a paltry debt of £118 9s. as compared to mere paragraphs dedicated to Lionel's and Clermont's debts exceeding £1,700 in accumulated spending (over £500 for Lionel's and £1,300 plus interest for Clermont's). Claudia Johnson calls this pacing "bizarre," noting the attention given to Camilla's "insanely exaggerated sense of guilt . . . while the massive depredations of Lionel and Clermont, legitimate heirs, receive scant mention."[36]

Unlike Camilla, men get away with having financial desires; their sex gives them capital. Lionel extorts money from his uncle under the threat of death, yet, though his actions cause disorder in the family, he himself faces no serious consequences. He laughs off his father's lecture and refuses any moral culpability, claiming that "it was only taking a little of my own fortune beforehand, for I am his heir" (226). Similarly, he sees his sex legitimating taking money from his sisters, for men have needs that women do not: "'[H]ow should she know what it is to be a young man? and to want a little cash, and not know how to get it?'" he complains to Camilla when she hesitates before helping him out (240). Even Sir Hugh laughs off male consumption, quickly opening his pocket-book when Camilla painfully asks him for money on Lionel's behalf: "[W]hat the young boys do with all their money now-a-days, is odd enough" (381). The contrast between male and female consumption produces a dissonant tone when Burney comically narrates Clermont's insatiable and extravagant commodity desires: his request for a newspaper the moment he arrives at the rural Cleves, and his outrageous demand for champagne and Stilton cheese at tea in Southampton. The comic tone is "bizarre" in that both Clermont and Lionel bring their households to the point of tragic breaking. Burney magnifies the disparity when all the accounts come due and we see plainly the costs of the sexual double standard.

As the tension surrounding Camilla's inability to confess her debts mounts, so does her suffering, particularly for the moral duty she feels toward her brother. The main cause of her silence, and thus most of the misunderstandings with Edgar, is not the money she owes for a few books or for her clothes, but her promise to Lionel not to betray his secrets to her father. "The debt he had made her contract with Sir Sedley, the secrecy it exacted, the correspondence it had drawn on, the cruel circumstances it had produced, and the heart-breaking event to which it had, ultimately, led" were all caused by her ethical obligations to family (729). On the verge of releasing herself from the promise and confessing her debts to her father, Camilla is stymied once again by Lionel: "[H]er plan [to confess her debts], though well formed, had fixed upon an ill-timed moment for its execution," namely, the moment her father discovers Lionel's affair; the revelation of Lionel's "wanton calls for money, his culpable connection," postpones her own confession (760, 735). The disclosure of Clermont's debts then replaces Lionel's to continue delaying her confession as Sir Hugh turns to Mr. Tyrold to help finance his own recovery (788).

Burney numerically calculates what male expenditure requires women to sacrifice when she describes the austerity measures Mr. Tyrold inflicts on his family to pay off Lionel's debts. Of his annual £500 salary, he has saved and invested £100 a year, which he planned to divide between Lavinia and Camilla since Eugenia and Lionel have inheritances. But he must now use the money to pay off Lionel's debts: "To take from the little hoard which, with so tender a care, he had heaped for the daughters, so large a share for the son . . . shocked his strong sense of equal justice" (763). This injustice and the burden women bear are doubly emphasized when Lavinia embraces the call for self-sacrifice and austerity and offers "wholly to relinquish . . . her appropriate allowance" (766). Lavinia's "virtuous self-denial," her willingness to forfeit not only present savings but future income, fills Camilla with "agony" because she feels the ethical obligation to do the same yet she cannot because she needs her allowance to pay her moneylender (784, 766). Camilla pays for her inability to sacrifice more when her not offering her future allowance raises Mr. Tyrold's suspicion that she prefers money to love. He is "surprized" that she does not second her sister's sacrifice, and believes it "impossible to suspect her restrained by a greater love of money than Lavinia"; yet he can find no explanation for the absence of her sacrifice (767). The injustice of the first austerity is made worse by the second, putting into play an excruciating rhythm of never-ending demands for women to refuse the "love of money" by giving it away. Camilla went to the moneylender only because both Sir Hugh and her father were struggling to pay off Lionel's and Clermont's first debts and she did not feel she could add her own (smaller) demands to theirs. The dramatic irony in her father's mystified response marks the limit of the family's resources: far from the "love of money," Camilla's inability to give any more comes from her already having given too much. Whereas Lavinia has remained at home, never venturing out into the social world, and can thus naively refuse monetary desires, Camilla's outings connect her to others and embed an individual plot within a world of economic needs and desires. "[T]he demands for wealth are endless and countless," Camilla learns after her stay at Tunbridge, where, even though she denies herself everything, social life comes with both ethical and financial obligations (518).

The limits to Camilla's financial sacrifices register the gendered problem of supply and demand on the marriage market. Choice, as Mr. Tyrold has told Camilla, belongs to the man as the buyer. Camilla earlier tries to raise her value not through an endless supply of charity and sacrifice but by increasing the demand for her affection and making Edgar jealous. Camilla's mentor Mrs. Arlbery encourages this tactic. Widowed and independent, Arlbery can afford the risk of being "utterly careless of appearances" and acting freely on her own desires (194). She raises her own value by devaluing men, increasing their desire through the power of denial. Seeing that Edgar clearly loves Camilla, Arlbery counsels her to make him jealous: "There is but one single method to make a man . . . know his own mind: give him cause to fear he will lose you" (455). Camilla tries this strategy, entertaining Sir Sedley and then later Hugh Westwyn. Reminding herself that "the only way to a lasting accommodation was to alarm [Edgar's] security, by asserting her own independence," she appears gay and lively with other men at public events that Edgar attends (669). But the strategy fails miserably when he interprets her levity as evidence of her innate coquettishness, dropping rather than raising her value in his estimation. Marchmont is right there to remind him not to depend "on the gratitude of your wife after marriage" but to ensure beforehand the endless supply of her affections through her "debt of gratitude" (671). When their engagement is broken, Camilla refuses to accept Edgar's skeptical devaluation of her, querying, "[W]hat is the talisman which can erase from my own remembrance that you have thought me unworthy?" (641). In the end, to bring closure to the novel, the talisman turns out to be a near-death coma that erases all memory of his evaluation of her unworthiness. When saving her life ensures she feels the "debt of gratitude" to Edgar, all obstacles are cleared and virtue is rewarded.

The nonnarratable arrives when Camilla—lost, alone, delirious, and near death—has nothing left to give. The novel's descent into its gothic climax begins when Camilla discovers her father is in Winchester prison for her debt: "[T]he breath of Camilla instantly stopt, and senseless, lifeless, she sunk upon the floor" (823). Already having suffered the blow of Eugenia's kidnapping, she sets out on her mad journey to Winchester. Her "terror" is fueled by shame for her father's imprisonment, and then her imagination inflates her guilt to include the destruction of her entire family—convinced that her mother has disowned her and that Sir Hugh is bankrupt because of her (827). Only her death will be recompense for the "dread forfeiture" (867).[37] The journey is narrated in scene duration, and at times even in slow motion, to heighten its gothic suspense. Wandering the abandoned halls of Cleves at night, she sees ghosts and danger around every corner. Death permeates this section: Camilla's hope is "dead," her heart is "dead to joy," she arrives at Winchester "half dead," her expectations are "wholly dead," and even her letters are dead since they never reach their destination (867, 817, 827, 866). News that an anonymous savior has paid her moneylender and rescued her father only makes Camilla "wish for death, immediate death" (838). "[N]ever was death so welcomed," Camilla exclaims, since her demise will relieve her mother of her daughter's guilt (866). Her death wish converges with the arrival of a corpse at the inn. The body turns out to be Bellamy's (Eugenia's mercenary husband, who, like Harrel in *Cecilia*, dies when confronted with financial insolvency), but before he is identified, visions of his corpse torment her "nearly to delirium" and her imagined death arrives: "Death, in a visible figure, ghastly, pallid, severe, appeared before her, and with its hand, sharp and forked, struck abruptly upon her breast" (874). She proceeds to hear voices from the dead, "by hundreds, by thousands, by millions," pronouncing her "eternal doom" (876).

Self-executed, self-condemned, alone, and dead to the world, she is saved with Edgar's arrival. Burney's use of the locket as the device that explains Edgar's appearance links her symbolic death with the ambiguity between her moral and financial debts, but the locket also underscores the fact that no event has occurred in the romantic plot to bring about their reunion. Edgar is at the inn not on a mission to find the lost Camilla but to refresh his horses, and while there he sees the locket in the maid's hand. Camilla was forced to pawn the locket to pay for her keep at the inn, and Edgar's discovery rescues its sentimental value, reuniting the material object with its romantic symbolism ("[H]ow from the first have I loved—how to the last will I prize it!" Camilla remarks about the locket, though its referent is now firmly merged with Edgar [880]). The reunion extends the novel's dissonant rhythm in that, as soon as Edgar rescues Camilla, and just as expectations are raised for an éclaircissement, he leaves her alone in her sickbed. The resolution to the romance plot actually happens offstage, during the time they are separated. Edgar writes her a letter requesting that she forget everything that has happened in the past near nine hundred pages and remember "our intuitive attachment" (879). Then, after the extended maternal reunion scene and after Eugenia's long explanation of Bellamy's death, a second éclaircissement occurs and, again, Edgar is not in the room. Hovering outside the Tyrold's parlor, he overhears Camilla's admission to her mother that they were kept apart by "[a]ccident" and "deluding appearances," made worse by her own "false internal reasoning" and his "continual misconstruction" (896). He then enters the room but does not immediately embrace her. Camilla, almost "fainting with shame and surprise, . . . gave herself up as disgraced . . . for a short, but bitter half moment" (896). Burney pauses on this "bitter half moment" to reassure us "[i]t was not longer," but the moment is halted nonetheless, as if to underscore that Camilla's abject downward mobility is complete (896). When Edgar does come forward, it is to grab the hand of Camilla's mother and only secondarily does he assist Camilla. Most of the ensuing resolution occurs in a conversation between Edgar and Mrs. Tyrold, his "more than Mother" (896). The climax to the romance plot is stilted and brings no relief, especially in comparison to the relief the reader feels when the family's financial troubles are resolved.

If, as Ricoeur suggests, the reader needs to be able to look back from the perspective of the whole and see the pattern embedded in the parts, the pattern here has nothing to do with courtship, since forgetting the whole thing happened is the best the romantic plot has to offer. Edgar later repeats the plea he made in the letter to wipe the past away, insisting the past is a dream "for which memory must find no place" (897). Indeed, Camilla's claim that she loved the locket from the first to the last is based on her forgetting that she once rejected it as an unwanted bauble. Marriage, in *Camilla*, registers closure only because it arrives as debt relief, to solve the problems in the economic plot: "The first care of Edgar was to clear every debt in which Camilla had borne any share" (910). The novel's final accounting marries off the rest of the family in parallel marriages that keep the money close to home, something that Sir Hugh has desired all along. His "favourite scheme of life" was that all his kin would "live together," that Clermont would marry one of his cousins, and that Edgar would marry one of his nieces and consolidate their neighboring lands. He is thrilled when Camilla does not become engaged to Major Cerwood, whom he considers "a mere stranger" (535). After Eugenia's horrific mercenary marriage to "the poor lad . . . not belonging to any of us," as Sir Hugh describes him, and after Eugenia's willingness to sacrifice her inheritance so that Melmond can marry Indiana, Melmond recognizes her "worth" and the two are united (907, 912). That Eugenia could be loved by him in spite of her lost beauty and not for her money signifies the nonnarratable of her plot: "Eugenia once loved, was loved for ever" (912). Lavinia, whose "self-denial" means she has never had much of a story, emerges as Camilla's surrogate; because Camilla is already taken, Mr. Westwyn suggests his son settle for Lavinia, and Hugh silently agrees (904). Since Lavinia has no dowry, Mr. Westwyn imagines the marriage as repayment to Sir Hugh for loaning him "that thousand pounds . . . when not a relation I had would lend me a hundred" (904). Friends who loan friend's money consolidate bonds through exchanging women, an act that allows their estates to flow risk-free to the next generation.

The multiple marriages bring closure to Burney's "prose epic" story of the family, arriving with all the poetic justice and all the rewards for virtue that its sentimental economics can realize. But the end arrives without a complete payoff, for the problem that the novel has introduced concerning female sacrifice and death is never resolved. Dubster's mercenary approach to marriage defines the existential imperative that Burney's plotting of capital makes visible: he brags about his "luck" in twice marrying "a fortune," especially because he saved money when both his wives died. Complaining that the first "cost me a mort of money to the potecary before she went off," Dubster gleefully boasts about profiting from their deaths (279). In a world where anybody, even a crass wigmaker, can marry a fortune, where money circulates unattached to land, the death of a wife with a dowry is equated with the realization of profit. Sentimental novels counter mercenary marriage with a love that proves its disinterestedness through female loss, but that loss is never compensated and aristocratic capital is what restores the equilibrium. Camilla's symbolic death is the act that brings on the realization of happiness for the family and ensures future wealth through generational inheritance; but its heroine has no future, and thus the novel ends.

This chapter lays out how Burney tortuously narrates the pause between buying and selling to depict, first, how we are all connected, how one individual's investment is another's cashing out, and, second, how women pay the price with bourgeois virtue of resolving the tensions and contradictions of those connections in order for the plot to end. When women are like ticketed goods in the shop, circulating anonymously, they pay the cost for a happy ending in capital's unfriended world. Novelistic closure is akin to secure retirement in that the risks that the future holds have been foreclosed with the accumulation of wealth, but *Camilla*'s closure shows that someone must pay for those risks and that future. When *Camilla* cashes out, poised as the novel has been on the precipice between buyer's remorse and seller's remorse, between "Imprudence and Suspicion," the rewards for its heroine are slim (913). Burney's ambiguous final words underscore the lack of completion in the plot dynamics of female downward mobility: "What, at last, so diversified as man? what so little to be judged by his fellows?" (913) Not only does the novel end with unanswered questions, but those questions acknowledge the infinite complications of social connection, that man diversified means an unknowable future and that infinite wealth is not guaranteed.

It is a fitting conclusion to the story of *Camilla* that its author purposefully sought to make money off its sale by speculating on her value. Burney refused to exchange monetary ambition for aesthetic value and demanded both critical and financial appreciation for her novel. Actively positioning *Camilla* to make herself a fortune, she risked selling it by subscription first rather than going straight to copyright as she had done with her first two novels. The critical response to her decision to publish the novel by subscription, and to her active negotiation of the best financial terms for its publication, demonstrates the challenges facing a woman who does not reject the desire for financial profit. Critic after critic, as Emma Pink has documented, blame the novel's so-called failure on Burney's financial desires, publishing the novel for profit to support her new and growing family.[38] Catherine Gallagher exemplifies this critical response when she argues that the novel is an aesthetic failure because Burney wrote it for money: "She was now completely intent on writing a novel that would sell, and the result was a marked decline in the quality of her work."[39]

The notion that aesthetic value and commercial value cannot coincide is one of the cultural legacies of late eighteenth-century capitalism, similar to the incommensurability in the "love or money" motif. Sara Austin observes that criticism such as Gallagher's "condemns *Camilla* as a mere commodity, written by recipe to increase its profitability. Its length and heterogeneity are understood as attempts to attract buyers by throwing in a little bit of everything."[40] I suggest another reading of its "length and heterogeneity," following its economic plot to claim that Burney narrates the costs of reducing social transactions to "mere commodities" and that attracting buyers is not crass but is a necessary part of living together, especially for women on the marriage market. *Camilla* demonstrates that economics—the domestic organization of shared resources—is about both commerce *and* virtue, money *and* love. The attacks on Burney for being mercenary, then, capture what the novel itself problematizes: that desiring money and desiring love have become mutually exclusive yet are welded together through negative opposition. Since money does not buy love, love cannot come with money—unless the money arrives at the end of a plot of female downward mobility. Significantly, Burney did profit on her novel—as Horace Walpole noted "she has realized about £2000."[41] It outsold *Evelina* and *Cecilia* and allowed her to buy "Camilla cottage." Not only did she ambitiously market her novel, but when it received many lukewarm reviews, she defied the critics in verse: "Now heed no more what Critics thought 'em / Since this you know—All People bought 'em" (xx). Higher risk translated into higher reward for Burney, if not for her heroine.

Epilogue

If this book succeeds in proving its hypothesis that the form of capital and the form of the novel are homologous, what might be the payoff? If the homology allows me to demonstrate that the myth of downward mobility in the sentimental novel helped to make the temporality of infinite economic growth imaginatively real, where does this leave the novel and what might it suggest about downward mobility? Leigh Claire La Berge takes issue with much new economic criticism precisely for the vagueness of its frequent use of the homology between literature and economics, noting that literary critics often leave out labor and materialism when they focus on money as "something that is similar to something else," that is, as similar to literature.[1] In a related criticism, Matt Seybold and Michelle Chihara note that the focus on the formal analogies between money and literature has led some to suggest that literary critics have been seduced by finance in that "[t]he cult of formal difficulty in literature ports easily . . . to a seductive new economy of signs in finance."[2] How is this project different? What is the value of the analogies I have drawn between capital's forms of debt, financial exchange, time, and realizing profit and the novel's formal attributes of character, embedded storytelling, plot, and closure?

First, a historical claim. In tracing the shared genealogy of the novel and capital within the latter-eighteenth-century financial imagination, I provide a historical example of how the stories we tell about money and the economic decisions we make are intricately connected, though not in simple or mimetic ways. The belief that the world can infinitely expand its wealth through global trade is naturalized through the financial and narrative revolutions in the period, but to make the connections between the rise of capitalism and the novel requires an interpretative mind attentive to complexity and form, to infinite specificity and detail, as well as to synthesis and general structures. The historical hypothesis that the democratization of knowledge indexed by the novel's rise shares a genealogy with the normalization of economic growth launched by speculative capital can now be restated more strongly: they not only share historical origins but are two sides of the same coin; one does not emerge without the other. For Hume and other Enlightenment thinkers, it went without saying that "*industry*, *knowledge*, and *humanity* are linked together, by an indissoluble chain."[3] To remember this "indissoluble chain" is to remember that business and the liberal arts grow from the same roots and that our contemporary discursive divide between commerce and virtue has a human history that can and must be changed. I bring the chain back into view for two reasons: First, to register the vital need for humanists to "refriend" the social relations behind the financial abstractions that feed the sophistries of populism, to refuse the rhetoric that high finance is too difficult to understand, and to engage the public, not just ourselves, in connecting the dots and seeing the bigger picture of what it might mean to share resources in more equitable and sustainable ways. Second, I return to the "indissoluble chain" to remind humanists of the imbrication of democracy and capitalism in order to check our impulse to draw firm lines between our ethical scholarship and Wall Street's filthy lucre. If we want to overcome the divide between virtue and commerce, we must realize it goes both ways. We need to reorient our work outward in order to build public confidence in the value of what we do; as Bruce Robbins elucidates, we who make a living in the liberal arts are beneficiaries of a growth economy, and, I suggest, owning that fact requires us to do more than specialized critique.[4]

The second payoff of the homology between capital and the novel emerges from the formalism of my "financial formalism." This book demonstrates *the value of narrative as a form of thinking about capitalism*. I use the remainder of this epilogue to consider this value within our contemporary moment and to speculate on how the insights garnered from reading eighteenth-century novels might speak to the twenty-first century. I do so in part because many critics describe the problem of financialization today as a narrative problem.[5] "Money has lost its narrative quality," a character in Don DeLillo's *Cosmopolis* observes.[6] Joshua Clover defines the challenge of imagining an outside of financialized capital as "the fundamental narrative problem of our historical moment."[7] Max Haiven agrees, and explicitly opposes fictitious capital to narrative, seeing our increasingly granular, abstracted, global financialized world as demanding the connective work of thinking narratively. He writes that "financialization is *both a cause and a consequence* of a broad shift away from narrative and towards metaphor. Financialization forces us to contend with a fragmentary world where narratives no longer seem to hold and where our shared understandings of social and economic processes are increasingly disjunctive and chaotic."[8] Narrative—that complex mode of understanding through which we puzzle out meaning, consider alternative points of view, and make sense of things by configuring large sequences into concrete wholes—counters the mode of understanding that dominates late capitalism by insisting upon meaningful connection. The value of reading narrative lies in the dynamics of interpretation—the act of judging how one thing connects to another, how one person connects to the world. Financialization may resist such narrative thinking, but narrative as a mode of human understanding has circulated throughout all cultures and in all historical periods, which suggests that, except for human extinction, there is no end to narrative, though there may be an end to capitalism. Below I detail the value of narrative thinking in three ways: through the insights that reading literary narratives provides into social inequality; for the antidote that narrative thinking supplies to the deadening temporality of our "end times"; and for the ways contemporary financial fiction charts a path beyond the current impasse of our financialized imagination, a path I illustrate with a brief reading of Chris Kraus's *Summer of Hate*. I end with a reading because it is in the act of interpretation, of thinking *with* novels from the eighteenth century to the present, that the imaginative possibilities of the future lie.

Reading sentimental narratives of downward mobility in the eighteenth century, rather than economic studies measuring growth rates, puts the question of social mobility in a significantly different frame. It shifts the focus away from the endless drive to accumulate more wealth, to make everyone upwardly mobile, and onto a critical analysis of how we distribute the resources we currently share.[9] The myth of downward mobility, I suggest, continues the illusion that more wealth *overall* means more wealth *for all*, and thus it keeps circulating the reciprocal-gain story of capital, with its dangerous idea of compound growth and its silencing of the racial violence of European modernity. My exploration of downward mobility in the sentimental novel shows that the story of loss is, in itself, neither good nor bad but that the interpretative process through which we understand how social relations are exchanged for financial ones, how some people's futures are traded for other people's present, is where the value of the story lies. Over and over, the readings in this book return to the dynamic form of narrative, to the ways narrative parses understanding in relational and metonymic ways. The meaning lies in the reading, not in numbers speaking for themselves, which means that to share resources more equitably, we must also develop shared meanings. Ultimately, my analysis of the myth of downward mobility provides an insight not much different than if the myth of upward mobility had been my subject: both myths often circulate to mystify power dynamics and to provide easy answers to difficult human problems. Reading literary narratives shows us that the answers are far more complicated, that there are multiple perspectives and conflicting truths, that they take time, humility, and curiosity to think through, and that such answers are most meaningful when we put human and ecological relations at the center, which is to say, when we query the relations of power. Who is speaking, to whom, when, from where, and for what gain? These are the questions that emerge from qualitative methodologies and the ones that will help address social inequality. The interpretative judgment exercised in answering such questions, this book argues, requires skills honed by reading novels. My book leaves open the question of whether the future will be one of having less, though it implies that some of us will probably need to embrace downward mobility, to consume in more sustainable ways. But it resists the nostalgic question of whether the next generation of Westerners will make less than their parents in favor of the interpretative analytic that questions growing wealth inequality and thinks about how to distribute resources more equitably among "all our relations," a mode of thinking *with* one another and *with* the land that Indigenous knowledge practices model.[10]

Narrative's relational mode of understanding, the way that stories require readers and listeners to build meaningful connections, can help configure a temporal modality that will allow the world to flourish in "end times." Apocalyptic narratives surround us not only in contemporary film and fiction but also in the dominant feeling of our age, which is one of doom. From climate change to the rise of populism and fascism, from growing wealth inequality to an increase in racist violence, it is hard not to imagine that the end is near. My reading of the temporal dynamics of the novel and of capital unpacks such a feeling and places it within the trajectory of infinite growth and financialization. Reading novels for the ways they configure time makes visible capital's temporal contradictions and shows that the drive toward infinite growth is actually a death drive. As many critical finance scholars explain, the fantasy of never-ending wealth is built on a plot of risk management that mortgages the future and kills the vitality of the present by securing the end.[11] Insofar as "finance is, elementally, the monetized quantification of future uncertainty," it sells the future.[12] This script of financialization works to contract time and to obliterate the moment between M and M′. In seeking out faster and faster ways of breeding money from money, capital has now arrived at a moment when automated high-frequency trading has essentially effaced human temporality, wrenching profits from milliseconds for those with equity. In selling the future, contemporary global capital presents value as an ahistorical financial calculation that is instrumentally fixed, one that does not depend on human judgment, one in fact that explicitly takes so-called prejudiced human bias out of the equation and gives truth over to "analytics."[13] Given the deadening number crunching of our futures by metrics, algorithms, and accounting practices, it is easy to feel that the end of the world is upon us and is out of our control. One of the ways novels help us live lies precisely in their endless circulation of nonfinancial forms of meaning, ones that insist the future is unknown. Mathias Nilges places hope in fiction's art of time to counter capital's deadly temporality, noting that "to narrate finance capital is to engage with the temporal logic that is the foundation for the current crisis of futurity and widespread millennialism. Through narration, we find ways past our inability to think the limits of finance capital."[14] Gary Shteyngart, in his dystopic *Super Sad True Love Story*, literalizes capital's selling of the future with a plot in which the main character works for a corporation that sells eternal life to "High Net Worth Individuals."[15] As *Super Sad True Love Story*'s hyperbolic absurdity stages, the death of death is capital's ultimate dream temporality, one that has been unsatirically claimed by a group of Silicon Valley billionaires who are pouring their enormous fortunes into new technologies that will "make death optional," as one biotech CEO claims.[16] "Why die when you can't take it with you?" could be the company's tag line. This book shows that making death optional would make life meaningless. Narrative's temporal dynamics reminds us that death is where the meaning lies. Since we read as if endings confer meaning, the existential imperative within narrative's mode of understanding means that we can never fix the meaning of our own life's story. In other words, reading novels is a way to remain oriented toward a future that can be different. As long as we keep living in the *as if* of narrative configurations, drawing connections between present acts and future possibilities, we can resist the disabling, demobilizing despair of no-future.

Contemporary fiction contains a wealth of narrative examples affirming the value of human judgment in imagining a future that has not been sold.[17] "If money has lost its narrative properties," Max Haiven and Jody Berland ask, "how can the story of finance be told?"[18] Increasingly, contemporary fiction turns away from postmodernism to realism to find the strategies for representing financialization; in realism's mode of plotting connections, fiction rematerializes finance's deadening abstractions. Alison Shonkwiler observes this return to realism of late: "Classic realism's investment in psychological interiority together with its exterior narrative control is designed to address mismatches between perception and reality" like those that pervade the world of financial abstraction, and thus "[t]he recourse to realism today" can be explained as a way "to examine limitations of understanding in a world more complex than it appears."[19] Mathias Nilges also notes contemporary fiction's reinvestment in realism: "The contemporary turn toward realism and away from the avant-pop sampling, collage-technique and metafiction that characterized postmodernism is a formal example of how the contemporary novel has dealt with the crisis of modern temporal epistemology."[20] Realism is one of the fictional techniques best suited to drawing the connections that financial capital buries in its spectacular now (speculative fiction provides another). The increasing granulation of knowledge into more and more specialized units, as well as the heightened global divisions of labor, works to promote ignorance and to paralyze those trying to make complex connections while simultaneously inflaming conspiracy tendencies. The central narrative thrust of Dickens's *Bleak House*—"What connexion can there be?"—returns in contemporary fiction to plot financial temporality and to interrupt its erasure of time.[21] Chris Kraus's autofictional

Summer of Hate illustrates how current financial fiction uses narrative realism to connect the dots, to demystify the delusion of infinite growth, and to make sense of the violence of financialization. By thinking *with* the novel, we engage the interpretative acts that orient us to an agential humanism in which futures can be different.

The plot of *Summer of Hate* merges real estate speculation with the artist heroine Catt's search for meaning and the ex-convict hero Paul's search for personal freedom. With the profits from selling her assets in overpriced Los Angeles, Catt buys an apartment building in the "under-tapped market in Albuquerque" and hires Paul to help her renovate.[22] Recirculating capital launches the novel and their love affair, and Kraus layers a romance plot into her financial plot—a plot strategy encountered with Frances Burney. Although Catt is a woman with equity, she is not your typical capitalist; like Kraus, she is an artist living on contract faculty wages, is much wealthier and more privileged than Paul, and has a postmodern critical self-reflexivity that self-consciously tries to figure out the plot of George W. Bush's America. Catt is frustrated by the postmodern skepticism and fragmentation that unintentionally led to today's apathetic "everything is subjective" and what we now call the "post-truth" era. "Doubt, the existential disease of the twentieth century," she comments, "trump[s] narrative" (15). And thus she is trying "to place more faith in narrative" (17). In the twenty-first century, however, there is no one grand narrative as there was in Dickens's masterful *Bleak House*, only granulated and multiple narratives. Told in interwoven chapters from Catt's and Paul's points of view, their relentlessly narcissistic voices break through any mystifying and totalizing plot with overparticularized material details of their lives.

Both in its obsession with descriptive detail and in its constant financial accounting, the novel studiously avoids abstracting the world of feeling from the world of things. Paul's original crime was charging $937 to his employer's credit card during an alcohol-fueled joyride; the original $937, however, compounds, and though he is released from prison and is thus "free," the novel plots his debt peonage: he pays $25 a week for parole and $120 a month for the Breath-Safer installed in his car. The interest and penalties on defaulted loans, not to mention the loans themselves, make Paul's life as unaccountable as it is unsustainable. In other words, the novel is structured around the difference between "those who work for money and those whose money works for them."[23] Kraus's juxtaposition of the two individual plots precisely narrates the asymmetrical and irresolvable differences, both financial and affective, between creditors and debtors.

Like Burney in *Cecilia*, Kraus tries and fails to configure capital's temporality within her heroine's linear course-of-life temporality. She nests events not through causality or moral agency but through the Twelve Step Alcoholics

Anonymous program. The novel's twelve chapters trace a narrative trajectory in which Catt's Pygmalion love for Paul could translate into Paul's sobriety and upward mobility, but this future never arrives. The imagined introduction of a possible future, however, allows Kraus to underscore how some futures were always already foreclosed by Paul's debts and his lack of access to capital. After a random police stop on the highway leads to Paul's return to prison (only this time in Joe Arpaio's Arizona), "Paul will replay the day's dissonant string of events and ask himself if there were signs, or maybe causes" (179). But there are no signs, no causes, no secrets that Paul could discover to help him chart a different life.

If *Summer of Hate* refuses causal and monolithic connections, it registers small sequences of change through a narrative duration focused on mapping shifts in the quotidian. Major plot events are relayed in brief, while we pause over intricate descriptions of renovations. When Catt sees a billboard proclaiming "*From Homeless to Harvard—Determination!—Pass it on*," her ever-caustic voice queries: "Couldn't they say *From Homeless to Community College*? Why do you have to win big, in order to win at all?" (208). Smaller, less ambitious narratives open cracks into a future; there are no big climactic moments. Paul, in fact, attends community college, with Catt's financing, and he does improve his economic status. Steps forward, however, are also accompanied by steps back, though not in any logical or symmetrical way. Lacking any arc, the course-of-life temporality ultimately converges with a cyclical temporality in which Catt and Paul's juxtaposed class positions present irresolvable differences. Capital's cyclical temporality does not come from the fashionable world, as it does in Burney's *Cecilia*; rather, here consumerism's 426 TV channels are indistinguishable and flat (25). Nor is cyclical temporality configured around speculative boom-and-bust cycles; in fact, financial markets are tedious and routine. "Money means nothing," Catt explicitly states, and making money for her is stupidly easy (161). The problem of financial capitalism that the novel registers lies with the initial capitalization, with being a person who has equity.

The novel's ending provides a wonderful convergence of the romance plot with the plot of capital in the circularity of infinite regress. Capital's cyclical temporality here is configured in an ending that returns us to the beginning. The ending begins with closure—Catt and Paul break up when he starts a relationship with the needier and less capitalized Amber—but it undercuts that closure in its final paragraph. Amber turns out to be a nightmare and Paul, needing money and single again, dials Catt's number. The novel breaks off with the promise of a future that will be a repetition of the past. Such a plot refuses reproductive futurity: family is here an empty cliché; Paul's fellow prisoners are living for "their kids," but this goal is clearly a delusional fantasy since many of them have restraining orders against family contact (54). The circular ending takes us back to the beginning, which, significantly, opens with Catt's delusion that her BDSM lover is actually trying to kill her and take all her money. The fear of death and the fear of losing her money is where the narrative begins. Overcoming her fear of death through a desire to believe in narrative involves her in the imperative to remember the past: when she tries to narrate for Paul the connection between his Arizona incarceration and global capitalism, she fails because he does not understand what a trade union is; she realizes the problem is that the words "trade union" "refer to things that no longer exist" (220). Stories that connect with the dead, with history, and with the death drive, not with love or family or upward mobility, define where her faith in narrative lies. To Catt, no one is forging the links or forming the sequences in which Paris Hilton's anal sex tape laid the "epistemological groundwork" for the war in Iraq (27). She refuses a guest lectureship at a university because accepting the post is "for people who update their CVs and still believe they are progressing somewhere other than death" (201). Death is the only place we are all progressing to. Love, family, and money are empty signifiers in the novel; instead, meaning is generated through myriad narrative connections in which the reader sees how speculative capital shapes our political and affective relations. Kraus configures *Summer of Hate*'s plot dynamics so that the deadening emptiness of contemporary life is causally linked to capital's mediation of value and, in the interpretative act of connecting her dots, the reader affirms the value of narrative modes of knowing.

If Kraus reaffirms my faith in narrative, she does so because of the complexity of the interpretative act she demands of the reader. My book project's most general contribution may be its vindication of narrative's faculty of judgment, that cognitive act of evaluating, configuring, and rendering meaning out of the world. I hope my readings demonstrate the central importance of the interpretative dynamic in determining what it is we value and where the meaning lies. *Summer of Hate* proves that the act of putting the pieces together to relate Paris Hilton's anal sex tape to the war in Iraq requires far more than instrumental logic. Reading through contradictions, holding together conflicting pieces of evidence, building relations between multiple points of view, are the modes of understanding required to interpret today's financialized world. The value of reading complicated literary narratives lies not in *what* stories they tell but in the complex cognitive acts they train our faculty of judgment to perform, in the way they develop our ability to make sense of large, complex, and often contradictory sequences.

To close with the claim that narrative's interpretative dynamic can challenge the financialized imagination is to affirm literary criticism's hermeneutical function and to resist the pull of surface reading. I agree with Jeffrey Nealon's diagnosis that contemporary literary criticism is almost "anti-hermeneutic" in its resistance to meaning and interpretation. Nealon writes that literary criticism "is no longer literary most obviously in the sense that it's no longer primarily concerned with producing *interpretations* of existing or emerging literary artifacts."[24] Whereas Nealon's resolution is to resist meaning and to focus on the "infinitely molecular," I posit a future for literary criticism in refusing to shy away from interpretation and judging value. Christopher Newfield, in "What Is Literary Knowledge of Economy?" provides a much deeper analysis of the value of reading novels than I offer here, but like Newfield, I stake a claim for the knowledge that novels produce about the economy.[25] Economists may do better at understanding how to make human economies flourish by engaging narrative methodologies. The poverty of our current imaginative skills contributed to the 2008 financial crisis, which devastated the lives of millions. It would be nice to think it was the greed of a few Wall Street traders that got us into trouble, but as one journalist noted "[a]t each link in that chain, there were people aware that something was wrong, but who lacked the ability to put those pieces together."[26] In other words, they needed better narrative skills. I love the story of Bethany McLean, the journalist with a BA in English who first uncovered the Enron scandal. When asked how she was able to penetrate the impenetrable Enron books, she replied, "When you come out of a liberal arts background, you want to know why something is the way it is."[27] That process of asking why, the commitment to a curious mind and the humility not to rest with what you already know, is one of the many things that reading literature teaches us. In other words, without understanding how narrative works in its most complex and capacious forms—including the novel—we may be doomed to live forever in a world with no future.

Introduction

1. For critical accounts of money's transformation into speculative capital in the eighteenth century, see Baucom, *Specters of the Atlantic*; and Baucom and Poovey, "Financing Enlightenment."

2. Watt, *The Rise of the Novel*. This project is informed by the long history of "rise of the novel" criticism, and I am enormously indebted to those literary historians before me who have studied the relationship between the novel's emergence and the rise of capitalism and modernity. The study closest to my subject area is Skinner's *Sensibility and Economics in the Novel*. Skinner provides an important overview of the range of ways economics enters the novel of sensibility and, in that way, provides the groundwork for this more specific study on financial crises. While no monograph addresses downward mobility in the novel, many studies of economics and eighteenth-century literature exist and provide the larger scholarly context for this book: see Bellamy, *Commerce, Morality, and the Eighteenth-Century Novel*; Bowen, *The Politics of Custom*; Brantlinger, *Fictions of State*; Codr, *Raving at Usurers*; Connor, *Women, Accounting, and Narrative*; Kaufmann, *The Business of Common Life*; Lynch, *The Economy of Character*; McKeon, *The Origins of the English Novel*; Nicholson, *Writing and the Rise of Finance*; O'Brien, *Literature Incorporated*; Roxburgh, *Representing Public Credit*; Shapiro, *The Culture and Commerce of the Early American Novel*; Sherman, *Finance and Fictionality in the Early Eighteenth Century*; Thompson, *Models of Value*.

3. Critical finance studies introduces the phrase "financial imagination"—along with "financial imaginary" and "financialized imagination"—to designate how the complexity, breadth, and global influence of contemporary financial markets require new imaginative forms to understand them; a similar imaginative leap was required within eighteenth-century British culture. Max Haiven and Jody Berland introduce their special issue of *Topia*, "The Financialized Imagination," by arguing that "finance has gained tremendous power over the global economy in recent years" and that this new "immaterial, speculative, leveraged wealth" requires each of us to imagine our lives as "risk portfolios and [to] embrace a life of endless speculation." Haiven and Berland, "Introduction," 8, 9. In her book on contemporary fiction, *The Financial Imaginary: Economic Mystification and the Limits of Realist Fiction*, Alison Shonkwiler defines the "financial imaginary" as "the formal project . . . of imaginatively grasping the historical and cultural processes by which the seeming realities of the economy are reconceived as phenomena of virtuality and representation" (ix).

4. Brooks, *Reading for the Plot*, 10.

5. Williams, *Theory and the Novel*, 2.

6. See McKeon, *The Origins of the English Novel*, 171–75. McKeon concentrates on examples of progressive upward mobility and on corrupt aristocrats deservedly coming down in the world but not on the figure of the gentry character who slides into poverty; this is the most common rendering of status inconsistency in sentimental fiction and the one that takes center stage in this book.

For studies of poverty in eighteenth-century literature, see Frank, *Common Ground*; MacKenzie, *Be It Ever So Humble*; Perry, "Home Economics"; Sherman, *Finance and Fictionality*. For an excellent discussion of how the poor are represented in nineteenth-century fiction, see Elaine Freedgood, "The Novelist and Her Poor," *Novel: A Forum on Fiction* 47, no. 2 (2014): 210–23.

7. Charlotte Lennox, *Sophia*, 53.

8. Fielding, *The Adventures of David Simple*, 103, 102.

9. Brooke, *The History of Emily Montague*, 357.

10. Mackenzie, *The Man of Feeling*, 69.

11. Sheridan, *Memoirs of Miss Sidney Bidulph*, 392.

12. Scott, *A Description of Millenium Hall*, 147.

13. Kim, "Mourning, Melancholia, and Modernity," 499. For a reading of the downwardly mobile plot in nineteenth-century American realist novels, see Lawson, *Downwardly Mobile*. Lawson reads novels by writers who experienced downward mobility themselves, especially with the 1837 financial panic, to claim that this experience caused the turn from sentimentalism to realism in the nineteenth century.

14. Kim, "Mourning, Melancholia, and Modernity," 492.

15. Nick Crafts overviews the work on economic growth and revises the rates of growth to 1.4% for 1780–1801 and 0.6% for 1760–80. "The Industrial Revolution," 47. For the major historical studies of economic growth in the period, see Deane and Cole, *British Economic Growth*; Ashton, *An Economic History of England*; Black, *Eighteenth-Century Britain*; Brewer, "The Concept of Growth in Eighteenth-Century Economics"; Broadberry et al., *British Economic Growth*; Crafts, "English Economic Growth in the Eighteenth Century"; Crafts, *British Economic Growth during the Industrial Revolution*; Crafts and Harley, "Output Growth and the British Industrial Revolution"; Daunton, "The Wealth of the Nation"; Mathias, "Risk, Credit, and Kinship in Early Modern Enterprise"; and Rule, *The Vital Century*.

16. Those who argue for the increase in standard of living include Berg, *Luxury and Pleasure in Eighteenth-Century Britain*; Jack, *Corruption and Progress*; McKendrick, Brewer, and Plumb, *The Birth of Consumer Society*; Plumb, *Georgian Delights*; and Woodruff, *Consumption and the Making of Respectability*. Those who argue against it include Black, *Eighteenth-Century Britain*; Crafts, "The Industrial Revolution"; Lindert, "Unequal Living Standards"; Mokyr, *A Culture of Growth*; and Rule, *The Vital Century*.

Malcolm Jack asserts that by mid-century it was clear that standards of living had risen for both poor and rich: "[I]n spite of the new inequalities, the lowest laborers in commercial society were decidedly better off in material terms than the poor of the past societies. By the mid-century no one was willing to condemn the prosperity that underpinned that standard." Jack, *Corruption and Progress*, 186. In contrast, Peter Lindert argues that "workers' living standards showed no clear progress before 1820, but definitely improved from 1820–1850" and that "[m]ost of the economists writing in the late eighteenth and early nineteenth centuries thought that workers' absolute living standards were not improving." Lindert, "Unequal Living Standards," 359, 357.

17. Brewer, "The Concept of Growth," 634.

18. *Financial revolution* is the term first used by P. G. M. Dickson in *The Financial Revolution in England* (1967). For other economic histories of Britain's financial revolution, see Neal, *The Rise of Financial Capitalism*; Ashton, *An Economic History of England*; Brewer, *The Sinews of Power*; Mathius, "Risk, Credit, and Kinship"; and Wennerlind, *Casualties of Credit.*

19. Baucom, *Specters of the Atlantic*, 16. Studies that focus on credit and speculation include Brantlinger, *Fictions of State*; Connor, *Women, Accounting, and Narrative*; Easton, "Cosmopolitical Economy"; Finn, *The Character of Credit*; Lynch, *The Economy of Character Press*; Molesworth, *Chance and the Eighteenth-Century Novel*; Nicholson, *Writing and the Rise of Finance*; O'Brien, *Literature Incorporated*; Sherman, *Finance and Fictionality*; Thompson, *Models of Value*; Wennerlind, *Casualties of Credit*; Codr, *Raving at Usurers.*

20. For general histories of capitalism, see Appleby, *The Relentless Revolution*; and Wood, *The Origin of Capitalism*. There has been a resurgence since 2008 in work on the history of capitalism; for overviews of such work, see Sklansky, "The Elusive Sovereign"; and Jennifer Schuessler, "In History Departments, It's Up with Capitalism," *New York Times*, April 6, 2013, "Education" sec. As well, note Harvard's Program for the Study of Capitalism (http://studyofcapitalism.harvard.edu/), founded in 2009.

21. Harvey, *Seventeen Contradictions and the End of Capitalism*, 7.

22. Bakhtin, "Epic and Novel," 6.

23. Nilges, "Finance Capital and the Time of the Novel," 33.

24. Anna Kornbluh defines *financial formalism* as "a formalism that reads literary form's critical thinking about the historically specific material and conceptual question of finance. Financial formalism esteems figurative language as a mode of thinking about finance, tracking the labyrinth of aesthetic response to intellectual pressures situated in history, but irreducible to it." *Realizing Capital*, 15.

For recent literary scholarship that I would include in this critical school, see McClanahan, *Dead Pledges*; Shonkwiler, *The Financial Imaginary*; Shonkwiler and La Berge, *Reading Capitalist Realism*; La Berge, *Scandals and Abstraction*; "Financialization and the Culture Industry," special issue, *Representations* 126, no. 1 (spring 2014), Peter Hitchcock, "Accumulating Fictions"; Gajarawala, "The Fictions of Finance"; Langenohl, "'In the Long Run We Are All Dead'"; Marsh, "'Paradise Falls: a Land Lost in Time'"; "The Financialized Imagination," special issue of *Topia*; and many contributions in Seybold and Chihara, *The Routledge Companion to Literature and Economics.*

25. For introductions to the concept and study of financialization, see Haiven, *Cultures of Financialization*; Jameson, "Culture and Finance Capital"; Lapavitsas, *Profiting without Producing*; Langley, *The Everyday Life of Global Finance*; LiPuma and Lee, *Financial Derivatives and the Globalization of Risk*; and Martin, *Financialization of Daily Life.*

The percentage of the global economy consisting of financial services, according to *Investopedia*, stands at 16.9%, growing at a compound rate of 6% (http://www.investopedia.com/ask/answers/030515/what-percentage-global-economy-comprised-financial-services-sector.asp). Not only has finance jumped as a percentage of GDP (from 2.8% in 1950, to 4.9% in 1980, to 8.3% in 2006) but profits from the industry are much higher than others (for instance, while only 5% of the GDP, it generated 10% of the profit). Greenwood and Scharfstein, "The Growth of Finance," 3. The growth of the financial industry is matched by the increase of individual Americans who have a stake, however small, in the stock market (often through pooled pension plans or mutual funds), having risen to 51.9% in 2001, up from 25% in 1987 and 3% when Wall Street crashed in 1929 (Langley, *Everyday Life*, 2).

26. Haiven, *Cultures of Financialization*, 1. Arjun Appadurai is one of the few to acknowledge, if only in passing, that "financialization" defined "as the process that permits money to be used to make more money through the use of instruments that exploit the role of money in credit, speculation, and investment" began with the rise of insurance in the eighteenth century. *Banking on Words*, 2. The marginalization of historical analysis is acknowledged by Matt Seybold and Michelle Chihara, the editors of *The Routledge Companion to Literature and Economics*, and they have tried to address it with a section on histories, though the European eighteenth century is not represented.

27. Much could be written about the phrase's origins; it is most often traced to Fredric Jameson's essay "Future City," wherein he attributes it to nobody in particular: "Someone once said that it is easier to imagine the end of the world than to imagine the end of capitalism" (76).

28. Fisher, *Capitalist Realism*.

29. Robert Markley was one of the first to read sentimentalism as promoting early capitalism, arguing that sentimentalism effected the shift of the moral conscience of wealth from aristocratic property to bourgeois culture. "Sentimentality as Performance." Other standard critical accounts of the relationship between sentimental and commercial discourses include Barker-Benfield, *The Culture of Sensibility*; Bellamy, *Commerce, Morality, and the Eighteenth-Century Novel*; Ellis, *Politics of Sensibility*; Skinner, *Sensibility and Economics in the Novel*; and Thompson, *Models of Value*. Stephen Shapiro has described the historical co-emergence of sentimentalism and capitalism as follows: "Sensibility arose as the disenfranchised gentry and nascent middle class appropriated emotion as a tool with which they could contest the *ancien regime*. The nobility might have good blood, but the new elites advertised themselves as having alternative qualities, the audience-oriented sympathetic emotions that were invested in the flesh." "Sentimental Economies," 242.

30. Todd, *Sensibility*, 97.

31. Landry, "Picturing Benevolence against the Commercial Cry," 106. Michael Genovese's " 'A Mixture of Bad in All' " is an exception to the critical consensus that *David Simple* is anti-capitalist. His forthcoming book on finance and feeling in the eighteenth century promises to further complicate a reading of sentimentalism's economics.

32. Denby, *Sentimental Narrative and the Social Order in France*, 88–89. I would also include in this critical current Barker-Benfield, *The Culture of Sensibility*; Bellamy, *Commerce, Morality, and the Eighteenth-Century Novel*; Ellis, *The Politics of Sensibility*; Markley, "Sentimentality as Performance"; Peace, *Changing Sentiments and the Magdalen Hospital*; Shapiro, *Sentimental Economies*; and Skinner, *Sensibility and Economics*.

33. My wording "the novel thrives on capitalism" is an inversion of Chris Kraus's statement that "capitalism thrives on narrative," which she articulated in an interview

about *Summer of Hate*, a novel I discuss in my epilogue that brilliantly unravels the inequalities within contemporary finance capital. Rumsby, "An Interview with Chris Kraus."

34. Richard V. Reeves, in "The Case for Downward Mobility," makes the excellent point that in our discussion of income inequality we should dedicate more resources to analyzing why rich people do not experience downward mobility, rather than concentrating only on why poor people do not experience upward mobility. The difference introduces the importance of distinguishing between absolute mobility and relative mobility, or discerning how people's mobility ranks against their peers versus their parents. Reeves, "The Case for Downward Mobility," *Brookings* (blog), September 30, 2013, https://www.brookings.edu/blog/social-mobility-memos/2013/09/30/the-case-for-downward-mobility/.

35. Lukács, *The Theory of the Novel.* Fredric Jameson's work has been central in scholarly thinking about capitalism and the novel's formal properties. See, especially, "Culture and Finance Capital"; "The End of Temporality"; "Future City"; and *The Political Unconscious.* Joshua Clover cites Jameson's *Singular Modernity* for the claim that "Jameson . . . grows increasingly and formidably certain that capitalism is a narrative category: 'the synchronic and non-narrative 'moments' of the mode of production are in fact 'narrativized' by capitalism.'" Clover, "Autumn of the System," 37. In her introduction to *The Financial Imaginary*, Alison Shonkwiler lays out why she sees narrative realism as remaining the main cultural site for a twenty-first century engagement with finance capital's abstraction of reality (xii–xiii).

36. Harvey, *Seventeen Contradictions*; Arrighi, *The Long Twentieth Century.*

37. Clover, "Autumn of the System," 36.

38. Max Haiven explicitly opposes "fictitious capital" to narrative, arguing that "financialization is *both a cause and a consequence* of a broad shift away from narrative and towards metaphor. Financialization forces us to contend with a fragmentary world where narratives no longer seem to hold and where our shared understandings of social and economic processes are increasingly disjunctive and chaotic." "Metaphoric Wealth," 51.

39. Nilges, "Finance Capital and the Time of the Novel," 44. See note 24 above for a list of critical works on contemporary financial fiction.

40. Shonkwiler, *The Financial Imaginary*, xxv–xxvi.

41. By "new economic criticism" I refer to the body of interdisciplinary scholarship in economics and literature represented by Mark Osteen and Martha Woodmansee's watershed anthology *The New Economic Criticism.* In their introduction to a new, watershed anthology, *The Routledge Companion to Literature and Economics*, Matt Seybold and Michelle Chihara overview the critical importance of new economic criticism, but they also see interdisciplinary work between literature and economics as having moved on, noting that "New Economic Criticism has largely disappeared from the academic lexicon" (7). My own description of new economic criticism is that it takes as its starting point a dissatisfaction with "old-fashioned dialectical materialism" in which aesthetic production is understood as superstructural and determined by a material economic base. Markley, "Recent Studies in Restoration and Eighteenth-Century Literature," 638. Instead, it draws on the methodologies of new historicism and cultural studies and reads far more political economy than Marx. New economic criticism overlaps with critical finance studies but is distinguished from it by its emphasis on "economics," including its

ties to economics as a discipline; critical finance studies concentrates on the dominance of finance capital within contemporary economics. My bibliography of new economic criticism within eighteenth-century studies in particular includes: (1) *Studies of economic themes and events represented in literature*; for instance, Andriopoulos, "The Invisible Hand"; Finn, *The Character of Credit*; McVeagh, *Tradefull Merchants*; Parrinder, "Highway Robbery and Property Circulation in Eighteenth-Century English Narratives"; Wall, "The English Auction"; Weiss, *The Hell of the English.* (2) *The economics of literature*, including print culture studies analyzing literary modes of production; see, for example, Flint, *The Appearance of Print in Eighteenth-Century Fiction*; Frost, *The Business of the Novel*; Ingrassia, *Authorship, Commerce, and Gender*; and Justice, *The Manufacturers of Literature.* (3) *The analogies between symbolic and financial economies*, including Gallagher, *The Body Economic*; Godden, *Fictions of Capital*; Kaufmann, *The Business of Common Life*; MacKenzie, *Be It Ever So Humble*; Poovey, *Genres of Credit Economy*; Purdy, *Literature and Money*; Kathryn Sutherland, "Introduction"; and Tratner, *Deficits and Desires.* My project fits into this last category, what Claudia Klaver, following Mary Poovey, has called "historical epistemology studies," since I am as interested in *how* narrative functions to make coherent economic truths as I am in *what* narratives say about money. Klaver, *A/Moral Economics*, xxi.

42. Goux, *Symbolic Economies*, 2.

43. Ricoeur, "Narrative Time," 170, 177, 171.

44. Ricoeur, "Narrative Time," 178. In reading the novel's temporality as an effect of capital, I seek to read novelistic time back into the world to suggest ways of telling stories that break away from economic growth. In this way, my project intersects with that of Jesse Matz, who, in "The Art of Time, Theory to Practice," argues "that narrative's temporal dynamics, its performance of durations, frequencies, speeds, and other time-schemes, might constitute an 'art of time' through which to practice temporal diversity," and that this practice of temporal diversity will have practical effects (275).

45. Harvey, *Seventeen Contradictions*, ix.

46. Arrighi, *The Long Twentieth Century*, 5. David Harvey's *The Limits to Capital* details the necessity of crisis within capitalism's logic.

47. David Harvey succinctly sums up the contradiction of fictitious capital: "The perpetual tendency to try to realize value without producing it is, in fact, the central contradiction of the finance form of capitalism," "Class-Monopoly Rent, Finance Capital, and the Urban Revolution," 254.

48. Using the large-scale system-histories of Braudel and Wallerstein, Arrighi maps world history in terms of four major "cycles of accumulation" (the Italian, Dutch, British, and US) in which capital begins by circulating through commodity production, then "sets itself free" from commodities through greater financialization, before inevitably suffering a crisis in confidence or value that leads to collapse and a return to a period of commodity production. Arrighi, *Long Twentieth Century*, 6. See also Wallerstein, *The Modern World-System*; Braudel, *Civilization and Capitalism, 15th–18th Century*, vol. 2. Robert Albritton, in "Stages of Capitalist Development," writes of the British stage: "Mercantilism refers to the early development of capitalism in the seventeenth and eighteenth centuries. It is British capital that becomes predominant in this stage, so it is to Britain that we should turn to look for the most characteristic form of capital accumulation" (119).

49. See Harvey, *Seventeen Contradictions*, for a deeper analysis of capital's structural contradictions.

50. Robbins, *Upward Mobility and the Common Good.*

51. Newfield, "What Is Literary Knowledge of Economy?" 21.

52. Leigh Claire La Berge, in *Scandals and Abstraction*, contests economists' self-representation of finance as too hard and too complicated for the layperson to understand, a point expanded upon by Michelle Chihara's review essay "What We Talk About When We Talk about Finance," *Los Angeles Review of Books*, posted September 18, 2015, https://lareviewofbooks.org/article/what-we-talk-about-when-we-talk-about-finance.

53. Shiller, "Narrative Economics." Shiller called for a "controlled experiment to prove the importance of changing narratives in causing economic fluctuations" (2). See also Robert Shiller, "To Fix the Economy, Tell the Right Stories," *Globe and Mail*, May 13, 2009, https://www.theglobeandmail.com/opinion/to-fix-the-economy-tell-the-right-stories/article1344258/; and Akerlof and Shiller, *Animal Spirits*. For a blog post that makes explicit the instrumental use of narrative for financial profit, see Brendan Markey-Towler, "How Storytelling Drives Finance and Economics," *The Conversation* (blog), February 2, 2017, http://theconversation.com/how-storytelling-drives-finance-and-economics-71813.

54. See, especially, McCloskey, "Storytelling in Economics." McCloskey's groundbreaking work in the rhetoric of economics also demonstrates how economists' reliance on models and modeling produces a truth akin to metaphor. Her website contains an excellent annotated bibliography of her contributions to the field: http://www.deirdremccloskey.com. See also Rothschild, *Economic Sentiments*. For other examples of scholarship that reads economics as literature, see Bradbury, "The New Science of Economic Man"; Brown, "Dialogism, the Gaze, and the Emergence of Economic Discourse"; Finel-Honigman, *A Cultural History of Finance*; Goede, *Virtue, Fortune, and Faith*; Glaisyer, *The Culture of Commerce in England*; Heinzelman, *The Economics of the Imagination*; Henderson, *Economics as Literature*; Klamer, McCloskey, and Solow, *The Consequences of Economic Rhetoric*; and Maifreda, *From Oikonomia to Political Economy*.

55. Fernand Braudel takes "Wheels of Commerce" as the title for the second volume in his magisterial *Civilization and Capitalism, 15th–18th Century*. Joel Mokyr argues that the "'Great Enrichment'" of the nineteenth century would not have been possible without the cultural foundation laid in the late eighteenth century that developed the confidence in growth: "The fundamental belief that the human lot can be continuously improved by bettering our understanding of natural phenomena and regularities and the application of this understanding to production has been the cultural breakthrough that made what came after possible." Mokyr, *A Culture of Growth*, xiii.

56. Defoe writes of the prospects of foreign trade: "Here then is an undiscover'd Ocean of Commerce laid open to us, and some specimens are offer'd, which if entred upon . . . would open such new channels of trade among us." Earlier he remarks, "The commerce of the world, especially as it is now carried on, is an unbounded ocean of business." Defoe, *A Plan of the English Commerce*, x, vii. In his "Of the Balance of Trade," David Hume makes extended use of water imagery, portraying trade as the "springs and rivers" and rejecting mercantilists' fears of losing specie by an imbalance in foreign trade with the image that the sea will always even out. Hume, *Selected Essays*, 189. (For a discussion of Hume's water imagery, see Margaret Schabas's "David Hume on Experimental Natural Philosophy, Money, and Fluids.") Like Hume, Adam Smith sees trade in fluid

terms, as "the channel of circulation" that flows in and out, eventually leveling off. Smith, *An Inquiry into the Nature and Causes of the Wealth of Nations*, 293. The imagery occurs in fiction as well: Henry Brooke's *The Fool of Quality* (1767) declares: "[I]ndustry and commerce are the . . . never-failing fountains from whence the wealth of this world can alone be taught to flow" 1:107–8. "Liquid modernity" is the term Zygmunt Bauman coined to capture the global flow of financialized capital of late modernity. Bauman *Liquid Modernity*.

57. Emma Rothschild provides an excellent reading of the *Wealth of Nations* as an epic that begins with uncultivated man and the darkness of feudal Europe and "ends in a new, enlightened society of independent individuals, reasoning and disputing, trucking and exchanging, being fair and deliberate, seeing through their own prejudices, having conversations about vexation and oppression, reflecting on their own sentiments." Rothschild, *Economic Sentiments*, 8.

58. Smith famously claims: "The discovery of America, and that of a passage to the East Indies by the Cape of Good Hope are the two greatest and most important events recorded in the history of mankind." *An Inquiry into the Nature and Causes of the Wealth of Nations*, 2:626 (subsequent citations to Smith, *Wealth of Nations*, refer to this edition). Karl Marx and Frederick Engels echo Smith's charting of the historical plot of capital when they write: "The discovery of America, the rounding of the Cape, opened up fresh ground for the rising bourgeoisie." *Communist Manifesto*, 34.

59. Smith's stadial history is more explicitly outlined in his *Letters on Jurisprudence* but runs throughout *Wealth of Nations*. For an overview of its significance, see Sutherland, "Introduction" xiv–xxi. See also Palmeri, *State of Nature, Stages of Society*.

60. "One man, we shall suppose, has more of a certain commodity than he himself has occasion for, while another has less. The former consequently would be glad to dispose of, and the latter to purchase, a part of this superfluity. But if this latter should chance to have nothing that the former stands in need of, no exchange can be made between them." Smith, *Wealth of Nations*, 37. Thus, money enters the picture to provide a medium of exchange.

61. Graeber, *Debt*, 40.

62. He does add a qualification to his claim that the "discovery of America" was one of the "most important events" in mankind's history: noting the "misfortunes" of violence, he ascribes them to the "accident" that the discoveries happened at a particular time when "the superiority of force happened to be so great on the side of the Europeans." Smith, *Wealth of Nations*, 626.

63. Smith, *Wealth of Nations*, 634.

64. Book 3, chapter 1, explicitly describes trade's constitutive reciprocity: "The gains of both are mutual and reciprocal, and the division of labour is in this, as in all other cases, advantageous to all the different persons employed in the various occupations into which it is subdivided." Smith, *Wealth of Nations*, 376.

65. Douglas A. Irwin traces the "doctrine of universal economy" from the Stoics to classical economics: "The doctrine held that Providence deliberately scattered resources and goods around the world unequally to promote commerce between different regions." *Against the Tide*, 15. The triangular transatlantic slave trade extends this violent logic to a highly profitable triple coincidence of wants. For historical analyses that demonstrate how colonial trade was far from reciprocal, see Findlay and O'Rourke, *Power and Plenty*;

Kenneth Morgan, "Mercantilism and the British Empire"; and Nechtman, "A Jewel in the Crown?"

66. The phrase comes from Christian Marazzi's *The Violence of Financial Capitalism*.

67. Much has been written about the South Sea Bubble. See, for example, Paul, *The South Sea Bubble*. In his classic essay, "The Moral Economy of the English Crowd in the Eighteenth Century," E. P. Thompson documents the riots that occurred throughout the period over price inflation. Julian Hoppit's work on bankruptcy, *Risk and Failure in English Business, 1700–1800*, demonstrates the volatility of prices and the regularity of momentary recessions.

68. Brooke, *The History of Emily Montague*, 389. I analyze Brooke's novelistic portrayal of the "reciprocal gain theory" in my essay "The Failure of Trade's Empire in *The History of Emily Montague*." The novel's embedded storytelling features in chapter 3.

69. I thank Nicholas Hudson for articulating this so succinctly to me in the question period following my paper "The Economics of Plot in Camilla," presented at the *Canadian Society for Eighteenth-Century Studies*, Ottawa, Ontario, November 2009.

70. Fielding, *David Simple*, 64.

71. Richardson, *The History of Sir Charles Grandison*, 2:534. This novel provides a telling example of how money requires a circulation through narrative to make virtue and commerce cohere. Grandison inherits a fortune from his friend Mr. Danby, who has chosen to give his money to Grandison and disinherit his two nephews and niece because they are morally undeserving of his estate. Grandison, in turn, disperses the money back to the nephews and niece, by adding moral lessons and narrating their turn to virtuous productivity: one nephew is apprenticed to a West Indian merchant, and the other to a French wine merchant; the niece receives money to marry the son of "an eminent Turky merchant." Like Levi-Strauss's famous example of yams in the Trobriand Islands in which the act of exchanging a yam for a yam shows that what is being exchanged is not the material good but the social relations, the gift of Danby's estate demonstrates that the point of the exchange is not to reward Grandison with more wealth but to tell a story in which virtue accumulates through its circulation. The story depends on the Danby heirs first losing the inheritance and then regaining it, with virtue accrued (ibid., 1:447–53).

72. Burney, *Camilla*, 670.

73. J. G. A. Pocock's writing provides the most extensive investigation into the debate; while he charts the various redefinitions, he cautions against viewing their divide as a fact of history: "There were innumerable treatments of the tension between virtue and commerce, and innumerable attempts to resolve it, . . . [and] there is no greater and no commoner mistake in the history of social thought than to suppose that the tension ever disappeared." *Virtue, Commerce and History*, 122. What cultural historians call the "luxury debates" were central to the construction of a divide between financial wealth and moral capital. For an overview of these debates, see Clery, *The Feminization Debate in Eighteenth-Century England*; and Berg and Eger, *Luxury in the Eighteenth Century*.

74. Poovey, "Aesthetics and Political Economy in the Eighteenth Century"; see also Poovey, *Genres of the Credit Economy*.

75. Most recent criticism on the "Adam Smith Problem" refutes the critical argument that Smith's two books are contradictory and shows the way Smith's ideas about virtue and self-interest are compatible. For discussion of the Adam Smith problem, see Montes, "Das Adam Smith Problem"; Peace, "The 'Adam Smith Problem' and the Retreat of Senti-

mental Virtue from the World"; and Tribe, "'Das Adam Smith Problem' and the Origins of Modern Smith Scholarship."

76. Bourdieu, "The Forms of Capital," 242. Bourdieu's point is that the "disinterestedness" of artistic appreciation is actually a form of capital that he calls "cultural capital."

77. In his discussion of how sentimental philosophy frames "disinterested" charity, Valvo argues that philanthropy in the period sought "to purify humane relationships . . . of instrumental considerations" by asserting that anonymous charity was disinterested. "Sentimental Disinterest," 412. He writes: "To act economically is to pursue one's individual interests unconstrained by moral or affective considerations. These are two sides of the same coin. If sentimentalism is the attitude that strictly distinguishes the humane from the instrumental in social life, then the economic can be understood as sentimentalism's chiastic mirror image, the attitude that distinguishes the instrumental from the humane" (412).

78. There are many small-scale alternative economic experiments in finance; for instance, the Occupy movement's rolling jubilee or peer-to-peer lending. For a discussion of these alternatives, see Rob Aitken, *Fringe Finance: Crossing and Contesting the Borders of Global Capital* (London: Routledge, 2015).

79. Barthes, *S/Z*, 89. Emphasis in the original; throughout, I comment on such emphasis in quotations only where I have added it.

80. A recession is defined as two quarters of no growth. For longer discussions of the problem of growth, see chapter 15 of David Harvey's *Seventeen Contradictions*, which focuses on the danger of compound economic growth. Wolfgang Streeck's *How Will Capitalism End? Essays on a Failing System* is perhaps the most important recent contribution to thinking through the limits of capital accumulation. As well, see Piketty, *Capital in the Twenty-First Century*; Heinberg, *The End of Growth*; and Rubin, *The End of Growth*. Two well-received books that offer alternatives to growth-based economic models are Tom Jackson's *Prosperity without Growth*, and Kate Raworth's *Doughnut Economics*.

81. The exceptions when Western economies slowed include the world wars in the twentieth century. For contemporary social analyses in which downward mobility in contemporary America is shown to be the rule, not the exception, see Ehrenreich, *Bait and Switch*; and Newman, *Falling from Grace*. Determining whether standards of living are decreasing in the West is challenging, given that income inequality is increasing, skewing the "averages." Some current research suggests that the middle class is not in the dire straits feared, whereas other studies show declining income mobility, especially in the United States. See David Leonhardt, "Upward Mobility Has Not Declined, Study Says," *New York Times*, January 23, 2014. Raj Chetty and other economists at *Opportunity Insights* are dedicated to understanding social mobility in the United States; they show that income mobility (the likelihood that children will make more than their parent) declined from 90% for those born in 1940 to 50% for those born in 1985 (https://opportunityinsights.org/).

The "great transformation" is Karl Polanyi's term for the shift to market societies; *The Great Transformation*. Kenneth Pomeranz uses the idea of the "great divergence" to describe the emergence of Europe as a global power greater than China over the course of the eighteenth century; *The Great Divergence*. Eric Jones calls it the "European miracle"; *The European Miracle*.

Chapter 1 • Fictitious Capital and the Social History of Debt

1. Joseph Stiglitz, "Progressive Capitalism Is Not an Oxymoron," *New York Times*, April 20, 2019. For an extended discussion of his argument about economic growth, see his "Inequality and Economic Growth."

2. "Quarterly Report on Household Debt and Credit," first quarter, 2019, Center for Microeconomic Data, Federal Reserve Bank of New York, https://www.newyorkfed.org/microeconomics/hhdc.html.

3. Muldrew, *The Economy of Obligation*, 274.

4. Mann, *Republic of Debtors*, 5. For historical studies analyzing this shift, see Barty-King, *The Worst Poverty*; Duffy, *Bankruptcy and Insolvency in London during the Industrial Revolution*; Finn, *The Character of Credit*; Geisst, *Beggar Thy Neighbour*; and Muldrew, *The Economy of Obligation*. Finn argues that the shift to modern, anonymous market-based debt relations did not occur overnight, and she describes the personalized credit relations that continued into the eighteenth century. That said, she concurs that the larger shift took place and defines it as follows: "Where early modern debt relations had been predicated on conceptions of mutual trust, modern consumer credit was shaped most decisively by notions of personal character" (*The Character of Credit*, 18–19). Mary Poovey charts a slightly different history of debt in "Demonizing Debt, Naturalizing Finance," in which she reads the shift from a religious to a secular frame as introducing the idea of debt as personal failure. Our histories are not incompatible in that I would argue that the late eighteenth-century ideas of accidental debt are the first stage in the longer history that arrives in the nineteenth century at the demonization of certain people's debts.

5. Dianne Maley, "Financial Facelift," *Globe and Mail Report on Business*, April 23, 2011, https://www.theglobeandmail.com/globe-investor/personal-finance/use-inheritance-to-pay-debt-then-borrow-to-invest/article4262748/. If I had taken the advice and borrowed $100,000 from my 2.4% home equity line of credit to invest in an NEI Ethical Select Mutual Fund portfolio, which has an average rate of return of 5.5%, I would have made at least $38,000 by now. I did not.

6. For a critique of the logic of borrowing to grow, see Ross, "Till Death Do Us Part."

7. Graeber, *Debt*.

8. Graeber, *Debt*, 14.

9. The legal case against Navient, a private corporation hired by the US government to service student loans, for its deceptive practices in getting students to agree to payment plans that benefited the company rather than the students is just one example of many that illustrate today's student debt peonage. For other examples, see the essays collected in Hartlep, Eckrich, and Hensley, *The Neoliberal Agenda and the Student Debt Crisis in U.S. Higher Education*.

10. I take the terms *debt resistor* and *debt resistance* from the Occupy movement, which developed the critical analysis to show how personal debt under capitalism is a political tactic that exploits the poor. For an articulation of this position, see *The Debt Resistor's Operations Manual*, available as a pdf from strikedebt.org. "Strike Debt" is a subcommittee of Occupy, of which David Graeber was a founding member. For a UK counterpart, see Debt Resistance UK (http://debtresistance.uk/). For analyses of con-

temporary debt resistance movements, see Aitken, "Everyday Debt Relationalities"; McKee, "Debt"; and Ross, *Creditocracy and the Case for Debt Refusal.*

11. For the history of bankruptcy and bankruptcy law, see Cohen, "The History of Imprisonment for Debt and Its Relation to the Development of Discharge in Bankruptcy"; Duffy, "English Bankrupts"; Duffy, *Bankruptcy and Insolvency in London during the Industrial Revolution*; Hoppit, "Financial Crises in Eighteenth-Century England"; Hoppit, *Risk and Failure in English Business*; Hoppit, "Attitudes to Credit in Britain"; and Marriner, "English Bankruptcy Records."

Ian Duffy summarizes the change as follows: "[I]t was increasingly accepted that autonomous economic circumstances, and not just fraud or incompetence, could plunge a trader into financial difficulties. Bankruptcy thus came to be viewed as an act of mercy for the innocent victim of the uncontrollable workings of the economy." *Bankruptcy and Insolvency*, 17. Margaret Hunt, in *The Middling Sort*, notes the importance to the lives of middle-class business families of the introduction of limited liability since "business risks were shouldered for the most part by individuals and families rather than banks or investment firms"; she adds that "As a problem in the history of ideas, the rise of limited liability has been relatively little studied; were it to be investigated it would undoubtedly tell us a great deal about the ways capitalist institutions worked their way into British life and British minds" (23). I hope this chapter adds to that project.

12. Blackstone, *Commentaries*, 2:473.

13. Blackstone, *Commentaries*, 2:474.

14. Defoe, *The Complete English Tradesman*, 1:81.

15. Marriner, "English Bankruptcy Records," 357.

16. See Anderson, "Money and the Structure of Credit in the Eighteenth Century"; Hoppit, *Risk and Failure*; Mann, *Republic of Debtors*; and, especially, Carlos, Kosack, and Castro Penarrieta, "Bankruptcy Discharge and the Emergence of Debtor Rights in Eighteenth Century England."

17. Hoppit, *Risk and Failure*, 45.

18. Hoppit, *Risk and Failure*, 51.

19. Hoppit, *Risk and Failure*, 176.

20. Peter Lineham comes to a similar conclusion for imprisonment for debt, that numbers of committals of debtors to prison increases during good economic times and actually decreases during economic depressions: "The number of committals for debt seems to have been greater when credit was more readily available, and when credit was scarce, the rate of arrests diminished proportionately." Lineham, "The Campaign to Abolish Imprisonment for Debt in England," 64. Given the relation of the growth in failure to the growth in commerce, Marriner argues for its importance to history; charting the rise of financial failure, she concludes that the vast numbers who failed "played a crucial role in economic, commercial, and industrial development, and it would not seem unreasonable to expect to learn a great deal from their experiences." "English Bankruptcy Records," 351.

21. Hoppit, *Risk and Failure*, 178.

22. Lepore, "I.O.U."

23. Marriner, "English Bankruptcy Records," 357.

24. 13 Eliz. c. 7, as quoted in Blackstone, *Commentaries*, 2:474.

25. For extensive discussions of the occupations included and excluded, see Duffy,

Bankruptcy and Insolvency; and Hoppit, *Risk and Failure*. Duffy points out elsewhere that one of the main reasons for maintaining the restriction was to protect aristocratic landowners from having their land subject to bankruptcy forfeiture. "English Bankrupts," 300.

26. Hoppit, *Risk and Failure*, 183; Howard, *State of the Prisons*, 35. In his analysis of the demographics of debtor's prisoners in the early nineteenth century, Peter Lineham notes that shopkeepers and merchants constituted a disproportionately high percentage of prisoners: "[T]he Commercial and Industrial classes are out of all proportion to their actual numbers in society. The majority of debtors came from this group, whereas only ten per cent of society fell into this category," "The Campaign to Abolish Imprisonment for Debt in England," 51. See note 80 below for a more extensive breakdown of prisoners by profession.

27. The process was that a creditor took out a writ with the sheriff's bailiff, who then arrested the debtor; the debtor had twenty-four hours at the bailiff's house to try to make bail. "To be bailed out," Lineham explains, "the debtor had to produce two 'respectable housekeepers' each willing to guarantee double the amount of the alleged debt." "The Campaign to Abolish Imprisonment for Debt," 5. If bail was not met, the debtor was sent to prison; the case could take a year or four court terms before the creditor had to prove the debt in court, so a person could spend a year in jail simply on the whim of another person. For an extensive description of how the debtor laws worked, see Innes, "The King's Bench Prison."

28. Innes, "The King's Bench Prison," 261. Lineham, examining committal figures from parliamentary papers in the early nineteenth century, sees numbers increasing even more after 1798, from 3,900 committals in 1798 to 8,625 in 1816: "[Imprisonment for debt] had grown out of all proportion to the growth in population, until by 1813 the only alternative to a permanent Relief Act could be more frequent temporary acts, or else the gaols would be intolerably crowded." "The Campaign to Abolish Imprisonment for Debt in England," 60.

29. Blackstone insisted that "traders" strictly defined were "the only persons liable to accidental losses, and to an inability of paying their debts, without any fault of their own. If persons in other situations of life run in debt without the power of payment, they must take the consequences of their own indiscretion." *Commentaries*, 2:473.

30. Dornford, *Seven Letters*, iii, 7.

31. Dornford, *Seven Letters*, 9.

32. Oglethorpe, *A Report from the Committee Appointed to Enquire into the State of the Goals of England* (1729). Oglethorpe's report documented serious abuses in the prisons, including bribery on the part of bailiffs and turnkeys; as a solution to the problem, he petitioned to found the colony of Georgia with imprisoned debtors. For discussions of Oglethorpe, see Pitofsky, "The Warden's Court Martial"; and Lineham, "The Campaign to Abolish Imprisonment for Debt," 18–19.

33. Lineham, "The Campaign to Abolish Imprisonment for Debt," 14; Johnson, "Imprisonment for Debt."

34. Review of Edward Farley's *Imprisonment for Debt Unconstitutional and Oppressive*, *Monthly Review*, July 1790.

35. The saying "A prison pays no debts" is often ascribed to the prison reformer John Howard (for example, Farley, *Imprisonment for Debt Unconstitutional and Oppressive*, 39,

cites Howard for this truism). Howard, however, cites it as a commonplace in *State of the Prisons*: "It is often said, 'A prison pays no debt'" (20).

36. My summary of the arguments contained in the tracts synthesizes a wide-ranging list of printed sources, including Bevan, *Observations on the Law of Arrest and Imprisonment for Debt: Together with a Short Sketch of a Plan for an Amendment of That Law*; Burges, *Considerations on the Law of Insolvency*; Cross, *The Insolvent Debtor*; Delamayne, *The Rise and Practice of Imprisonment in Personal Actions Examined*; Dodd, *A Prisoner Released*; Dornford, *Seven Letters*; Farley, *Imprisonment for Debt Unconstitutional and Oppressive*; Francklin, *A Sermon Preached at the Chapel in Great Queen Street*; Grant, *The Public Monitor*; Halifax, *A Sermon Preached at the Parish Church of St. Paul*; Howard, *State of the Prisons*; Neild, *An Account of the Rise, Progress, and Present State of the Society for the Discharge and Relief of Small Debts*; Smith, *Mild Punishments Sound Policy*; Stephen, *Considerations on Imprisonment for Debt*; and Stephen, *An Address to the Twelve Judges of England*.

Lineham's discussion in "The Campaign to Abolish Imprisonment for Debt" remains the most comprehensive overview of the campaign; see also Innes, "The King's Bench Prison"; and Finn, *The Character of Credit*.

37. Neild, *Rise, Progress, and Present State*, xii. Further references to this text are cited parenthetically in the text as Neild, *Rise*.

38. Finn, *The Character of Credit*, 152. While Finn emphasizes the continuity in the rhetoric of "misfortune" from the early modern period until the mid-nineteenth century, I argue that the continuity masks the way "misfortune" was qualified in the late eighteenth-century campaign so as to apply specifically to accidental loss associated with commercial trade.

39. Finn provides many examples of such bequests; for instance, Ralph Carter's 1576 will, which included an annual delivery of meat to imprisoned debtors, a bequest still active in 1866. *The Character of Credit*, 126.

40. Burney, *Cecilia*, 586.

41. Cross, *The Insolvent Debtor*.

42. A Liveryman, *Morning (London) Chronicle*, February 23, 1776.

43. *New, Candid, and Practical Thoughts on the Law of Imprisonment for Debt*, 9.

44. Bevan, *Observations on the Law of Arrest and Imprisonment for Debt*, 52; *Considerations on the Laws between Debtors and Creditors*, 12.

45. *The Case of the Creditors of Joseph George Pedley*, 7.

46. Hoppit, *Risk and Failure*, 167.

47. *An Humble Address to a Member of Parliament*, 1.

48. Smith, *Mild Punishments Sound Policy*, 95, 94.

49. Halifax, *A Sermon Preached at the Parish Church of St. Paul*, 8; Finn, *The Character of Credit*, 202.

50. Translator's preface, in *Imprisonment for Debt Considered*, n.p.

51. Hoppit, *Risk and Failure*, 167.

52. Grant (a pseudonym), *The Public Monitor*, vi–vii.

53. Bevan, *Observations on the Law of Arrest and Imprisonment for Debt*, 10, 48. Significantly, Bevan's call still maintained the moral distinction between honest debtors (that is, people involved in commerce) and fraudulent debtors and only the former should

have access to limited liability, 52. Neild's *Account* also proposed a form of universal discharge (lix–lx).

54. It is hard to date the end of imprisonment for debt, though it certainly continues through the nineteenth century. Charles Dickens drew on his father's stint in Marshalsea in his fictional representation of debtor's prison in *Little Dorrit* (1857). The Debtors' Act of 1869 introduced serious limits on such imprisonment in England, but the de facto practice of imprisoning debtors still continues; in many jurisdictions across North America one can be imprisoned for defaulting on court-ordered payments such as fines, child support, and legal charges. See Benns and Strode, "Debtors' Prison in 21st-Century America." *ProPublica* did a brilliant series on debt and bankruptcy in contemporary America; see, in particular, Kiel and Waldman, "The Color of Debt."

55. Haagen, "Eighteenth-Century English Society and the Debt Law," 225.

56. Innes, "The King's Bench Prison," 254.

57. Duffy, "English Bankrupts," 300. Paul Haagen, in "Eighteenth-Century English Society and the Debt Law," concurs with this interpretation of why the law was not changed, arguing that governments were not interested in rationalizing the laws but in maintaining their power and influence within the aristocratic class (234).

58. For background on the rise of public benevolence, including a discussion of how charitable organizations were a product of modern governmentality, see Andrew, *Philanthropy and the Police*. Lynn Festa, in *Fiction without Humanity*, describes how *human* was an elusive category in the period. I further suggest that the people who counted as having human rights did not automatically include poor debtors.

59. The Society held its first meeting at the Thatched House Tavern in St. James Street on February 23, 1772 (because it met in that tavern, the Society is often referred to as the "Thatched House Society") and was active into the twentieth century. Dodd's sermon, entitled "The Prisoner Released," was reprinted and also included in Neild, *Rise, Progress, and Present State*. Neild's entry in the *Oxford Dictionary of National Biography* ascribes the sermon to Rev. Weeden Butler, Dodd's assistant and amanuensis, who took over the Charlotte Street Chapel when Dodd was executed for fraud in 1777 after forging a bond in order to pay off his own debts. James Neild was called to testify at Dodd's trial as someone familiar with Dodd's handwriting. It could be that later accounts ascribing the sermon to Butler were an attempt to distance the Society from Dodd's fraud or that the more famous Dodd was credited at the time with the sermon.

60. After Strike Debt's "Rolling Jubilee" within Occupy Wall Street, where $701,317 was raised to buy up and abolish $31,982,455.76 worth of debt, a journalist for *Forbes* magazine traced the origins of its strategy to The Society. Worstall, "Occupy's Rolling Jubilee Succeeds Partly Because It's Not a New Idea at All." The Society remains a registered charity in the United Kingdom under the name Debtor's Relief Funds Charity. While no longer relieving individual debtors or actively fund raising, it disperses income from investments to other charitable organizations that support young people at risk and prisoner rehabilitation.

61. London Metropolitan Archives, City of London, A/RSD/1. The minute books are in multiple volumes, and I reference the minute volume with date and shelf mark. No extended study of the Society exists.

62. Biographical information on Neild comes from the entry for him in the *Oxford*

Dictionary of National Biography and from Tattam, *A Short Memoir of the late J. C. Neild*. The impetus for Neild's charity work on behalf of imprisoned debtors is often ascribed to a visit he made in 1762 to a fellow apprentice in the King's Bench Prison. Neild was outraged at the prison conditions and started his visitations of prisons thereafter. The visits continued throughout his life, and he published regular reports of their state in *The Gentleman's Magazine* in the early nineteenth century, as well as in book form in 1812, *The State of the Prisons in England, Scotland and Wales*. The Society's work and Neild's initial visitations predate the work of the more famous penal reformer John Howard, who published *State of the Prisons in England and Wales* in 1777.

63. In compounding, or only paying a small percentage of the debt, the Society took a principled position that creditors needed to assume more of the costs of the risk in any composition.

64. Some stewards would charge prisoners for a copy of the form, a fact attesting both to the Society's popularity and to the endemic corruption of jailors (jailors were not paid a salary and thus were always on the lookout for ways to increase the small income that fees generated). The Society's minutes for January 7, 1795, note the resolution that "George Taylor a Petitioner from the Poultry Compter having complain'd that he could not obtain a blank petition without paying for the same. Order'd that the secretary do inquire into and report the same to the Rev Mr Butler previous to the next meeting." The February 4, 1795, minutes record that the steward of the Poultry Compter was found to be charging 1 shilling for a blank petition, and the Society decides that in future the Keeper will be the only person with access to the form, which they must distribute free of charge (LMA/A/RSD/1/9).

Extortion of jailors through charging illegal fees was widespread and a frequent cause for criticism by campaigners against imprisonment for debt. The corruption produced the phenomenon of published handbooks for debtors that circulated to arm prisoners with knowledge on standard fees and the legal process that would help them avoid being taken advantage of by creditors and jailors. See, for example, *The Debtor and Creditor's Assistant*.

65. Innes cites John Howard's statistics, giving the ratio of men to women in prison for debt as nineteen to one in 1779. "The King's Bench Prison," 263.

66. "Rules and orders (1772–1859) extracted from the minute books," LMA/A/RSD/16/001.

67. Minute Book, 1778–82, LMA/A/RSD/1/6. Previous minutes include the occasional reference to approving all petitions, but it is not until April 1778 that they begin to keep regular statistics on rejections.

68. Minute Book, 1772–73, LMA/A/RSD/01/001.

69. Minute Book, 1772–73, LMA/A/RSD/01/001. Both Innes and Lineham provide demographic analysis of prisoners' social classifications. From prison records, Innes reports the following classification by the prisoners themselves from 1795: "8% military or naval; 5% mercantile; 7% manufacturers; 14% mechanics; 20% agriculturians; 19% trade; 25% labourers." Innes notes, "The table . . . suggests the range of the prison population. A category surprisingly not identified, and hard to locate within this table, is that of the professional men—lawyers, clergymen, estate agents, journalists—who seem to have been present in fair numbers." "The King's Bench Prison," 263. Lineham's classification by profession of debtors released in 1821–22 includes 52% from "Industry and Commerce" and 27% from the "Lower Orders," and though the information is incomplete, he concludes

that the research demonstrates "the very wide occupational and social range of the imprisoned debtors." "The Campaign to Abolish Imprisonment for Debt," 51.

70. Minute Book, 1772–73, LMA/A/RSD/01/001.

71. Minute Book, 1774–75, LMA/A/RSD/1/3. The de-individualization of the Society's objects of charity supports Charlotte Sussman's larger historical analysis of who gets to count as a person in the period (and who is literally counted); see *Peopling the World.*

72. The numbers vary but weekly averages are 16 in 1774, 19 in 1775, and 13 in 1776.

73. Minute Book, 1778–82, LMA/A/RSD/1/6.

74. See broadsides in the British Library. "Society of Guardians for the Protection of Trade, Against Swindlers and Sharpers" (1816) provides the most information about the Society. Contemporary scholars who mention it in passing include Olegario, *A Culture of Credit,* 6, 33; and Bennett, *Local Business Voice.*

75. July 1, 1778, and December 31, 1782, Minute Book, 1778–82, LMA/A/RSD/1/6.

76. Copied in Minute Book, 1782–87, LMA/A/RSD/1/7.

77. Minute Book, 1787–93, LMA/A/RSD/1/8.

78. "The Singular Case of Hercules Slade a Boy of 13 Years of Age being imprisoned in the Goal of Newgate for a Debt of *l.*12.12.0 for Board and Education!" Minute Book, 1787–93, quarterly report for June 30 to September 30, 1791, LMA/A/RSD/1/8.

79. Minute Book, 1778–82, LMA/A/RSD/1/6.

80. Francklin, *A Sermon Preached at the Chapel in Great Queen Street,* 7.

81. Francklin, *A Sermon Preached at the Chapel in Great Queen Street,* 8.

82. Johnson, "Imprisonment for Debt," 22, 75.

83. The newspaper clipping pasted into the Society's minute book for October 1, 1788, reads: "By the late advertisements from the Thatch'd House Society, it is observed there was no less than 'twenty nine petitioners rejected,' this marks the judicious conduct of the managers of that excellent institution, who will not suffer an imposition upon the public, by liberating unworthy or improper characters." Minute Book, 1787–93, A/RSD/1/8. Twenty-nine was a particularly high number; normally, the number rejected at a meeting was between two and ten.

84. Halifax, *Sermon Preached for the Benefit of the Society,* 7–8.

85. Dornford, *Seven Letters,* 4.

86. Howard, *State of the Prisons.* Neild toured prisons following Howard's death, and his quantitative research was published as *Account of Persons Confined for Debt in the Various Parts of England and Wales* (1800); a third edition in 1808 incorporated the results of his visits to Scottish prisons. His tours formed the basis of letters to his friend the Quaker physician John Coakley Lettsom, which then were used in his recurring column "Prison remarks," in *The Gentleman's Magazine* (1803–13).

In addition to lost future wages, another calculation repeatedly made in the campaign was the loss to the nation's wealth when debtors flee the country rather than being imprisoned. As Edward Farley put the argument, "a month's imprisonment to a tradesmen is a thousand pounds" and thus it makes sense that debtors would leave the country rather than lose their future income (*Imprisonment for Debt Unconstitutional and Oppressive,* 28).

87. Quoted in Neild, *Rise, Progress, and Present State,* 71.

88. Sherman, in *Imagining Poverty,* examines nonfiction writing about the poor in the

eighteenth century and comes to a similar conclusion about how the poor are abstractions in the "new, impersonal modalities for rendering populations—statistics, cost accounting" (2).

89. The importance of anonymity to disinterested humanism and charitable giving is analyzed by Nick Valvo in "Sentimental Disinterest." The relation of disinterested humanism to anonymously circulating money is concretized in a story repeated in the Society's archive, perhaps originating in an early nineteenth-century biographical sketch of Neild. The writer recounts Neild giving the Society a banknote for £1,000, saying that he had received it anonymously in the penny post. Because it was a banknote, it could not be traced, and it was widely believed that the money was in fact from Neild, who preferred an anonymous bequest. Nichols, *Illustrations of the Literary History of the Eighteenth Century,* 2:696.

90. Mann, *Republic of Debtors*, 4.

91. For an account of the collateralized debt obligations at the heart of the 2008 crash, see Michael Lewis's *The Big Short*. Lewis describes the various speculative schemes in which predatory mortgage brokers loaned money to any poor soul to get their bonuses, knowing that their corporate bosses would quickly repackage and sell those mortgages to someone else. The 2015 movie based on the book includes a wonderful scene in which Steve Carrell's character goes to Florida and interviews mortgage brokers who brag about loaning money to people who clearly do not have the means to pay. The real-life Wall Street investor, Steve Eisman (on whom Carrell's character is based) was one of the few to dig down deep into the tranches of the CDOs and trace their origins in predatory creditors, though he used this knowledge to make his own profits through shorting the market.

92. Stephen, preface to *A King's Bench Sermon*, 25. Campaigners against imprisonment for debt often cite this biblical passage from Matthew included in the Lord's Prayer. Modern translations since at least the Book of Common Prayer replace "debts" with "trespasses," and thus it is notable that *A King's Bench Sermon* insists on using "debt." Stephen later argues that "[f]rom not forgiving those who are our debtors arise the train of evils" that his writing describes. Ibid., 34.

93. James Stephen Jr.'s *Memoir* describes Stephen's father as a merchant who "I fear dealt a good deal in contraband importations. To say, however, that he was a smuggler would be giving too harsh an idea of his character. The fact is that at the time, and to a much later period, no importer of dutiable articles in that part of the kingdom did or could abstain from contraband adventures." *Memoir*, 40. There are entries in the *Oxford Dictionary of National Bibliography* (*ODNB*) for James Stephen Jr., his son Sir James Stephen, and Sir James's sons Sir James Fitzjames Stephen and Leslie Stephen. But there is no *ODNB* entry for James Stephen the debtor. Leslie Stephen's biography of his brother, *The Life of Sir James Fitzjames Stephen*, includes a brief biography of his great-grandfather mainly garnered from material in Stephen Jr.'s *Memoir*. Quentin Bell's biography of Virginia Woolf contains similar stories about Stephen, with the *Memoir* as the source text.

94. Stephen Jr., *Memoir*, 41.While in Poole, Stephen met his future wife, the daughter of the customs agent involved in the recovery operations, but the cargo was largely destroyed and the importing business failed.

95. Stephen Jr., *Memoir*, 46.

96. William was a surgeon who immigrated to St. Kitts and made money buying "refuse negroes" (slaves who were sick and thus discounted in the slave markets), treating them until they recovered, and selling them for a profit. Ironically, William's money and commercial ties in St. Kitts ultimately leads James Stephen Jr. to travel to the West Indies where he develops his political antipathy to slavery and returns home to join the abolition movement, Stephen, *Memoir*, 42. While Stephen Jr.'s *Memoir* is unsure about the bankruptcy, Leslie Stephen's biography of his brother states it as a fact. *Life of Sir James Fitzjames Stephen*, 3.

97. Stephen Jr., *Memoir*, 54.

98. Stephen also got into a dispute with yet another brother, Thomas, that Stephen Jr. describes as "a violent family quarrel" (*Memoir*, 81). Stephen had invested in a brewery in Dorchester that Thomas ran. Stephen warned Thomas that the brewery would not generate enough income for Thomas to marry without a dowry, but Thomas went ahead and married a woman who had no money. Thomas and his wife accused Stephen of not paying them their due, and though he did not keep accurate account books, Thomas claimed his brother owed him a huge amount. After the ensuing quarrel, the brothers parted ways.

99. Innes, "The King's Bench Prison," 291. Though published anonymously, *Address to the Twelve Judges* has been credited to Stephen by Innes. Her essay remains the most authoritative source on Stephen.

100. Stephen Jr., *Memoir*, 81.

101. Stephen Jr., *Memoir*, 54.

102. Hunt, *The Middling Sort*, 34.

103. Stephen, *Considerations on Imprisonment for Debt*, 7. Stephen's autodidacticism may have been spurred by his close association in the King's Bench with fellow prisoners Christopher Smart and the portrait painter William Thompson. Stephen Jr. describes the influence these fellow inmates had on his own education: while he was with his father in prison, Smart and others introduced him to literature, loaning him a steady stream of books, including Plutarch's *Lives*, *Don Quixote*, and *Arabian Nights Entertainments* (*Memoir*, 88).

104. Stephen, *Considerations on Imprisonment for Debt*, 2. In his preface to *A King's Bench Sermon*, he argues that imprisonment "deprives the community of the honest industry of upwards of twenty thousand people" (x).

105. Stephen, *Considerations on Imprisonment for Debt*, 70.

106. Stephen, *Address to the Twelve Judges of England*, 8.

107. Stephen, *Address to the Twelve Judges of England*, 25.

108. Stephen, *Address to the Twelve Judges of England*, 25.

109. Stephen, preface to *A King's Bench Sermon*, xvii; Stephen, *Considerations on Imprisonment for Debt*, 70.

110. Stephen, preface to *A King's Bench Sermon*, xvii.

111. Stephen, *Address to the Twelve Judges of England*, 31.

112. Stephen, *Address to the Twelve Judges of England*, 32.

113. Stephen, *Address to the Twelve Judges of England*, 32.

114. Stephen, *Address to the Twelve Judges of England*, 32–33.

115. Stephen, *Address to the Twelve Judges of England*, 36.

116. Stephen, *Address to the Twelve Judges of England*, 42; Graeber, *Debt*, 14.

117. Stephen, *Address to the Twelve Judges of England*, 45–46.

118. For an analysis of contemporary debt servitude, see Susanne Soederberg's *Debtfare States and the Poverty Industry.*

119. Stephen, *Address to the Twelve Judges of England*, 64.

120. Innes, "The King's Bench Prison," 293.

121. Stephen Jr., *Memoir*, 97.

122. Stephen Jr.'s *Memoir* notes that "[a] fairly full account of the insurrection of the prisoners is given in the *Annual Register* for 1770, Nov 19 and Jan 31 1771" (98). His tracts are repeatedly referred to throughout the campaign literature, and another tract was explicitly published to refute his argument: *An Inquiry into the Practice of Imprisonment for Debt, and a Refutation of Mr. James Stephen's Doctrine* (1773). Although the writer disagrees with Stephen's constitutional argument, he ends up arguing against imprisonment for debt on utilitarian grounds.

123. Thomas Watson's affidavit, quoted in Innes, "The King's Bench Prison," 296.

124. Stephen Jr., *Memoir*, 250–53.

125. In addition to bill discounters, tailors seem to be singled out as particularly pernicious creditors. I am not sure of the origins of the stereotype, but in a recurring motif in the literature, tailors entrap their customers by selling them goods in order to imprison them. Christopher Smart complains to Stephen that he is wrongly imprisoned for a debt owed his tailor. Farley tells the story of a tailor who was in business with a bailiff who had "offered the taylor a guinea for every cause he put in his hands." *Imprisonment for Debt*, 140. The tailor advertised that he sold on credit and then would arrive with the clothes and a bailiff who would arrest the customer if he did not produce ready cash. An earlier text shows the prejudice was long-standing. Philalethes reports that "[i]t is a daily custom in London for taylors to send a bailiff home with the last suit of cloaths to be tried on," and thus, he asserts, "more than one half confined debtors under thirty years of age, are at the suit of taylors." *Observations on Debtors*, 1. Stephen also specifically names tailors as preying upon customers (*Address to the Twelve Judges of England*, 46). The motif of the evil tailor-creditor makes its way into fiction in Haywood's *Anti-Pamela*, in which the protagonist's lover's tailor imprisons him for debt.

126. *Seasonable Advice*, 27, 26.

127. *Seasonable Advice*, 27, 29.

128. Geisst, *Beggar Thy Neighbour*, 113.

129. Maurizio Lazzarato's *The Making of the Indebted Man* lays out the temporality of debt and the promise to pay as one of the ways the poor are always already indebted: "Finance is a formidable instrument for controlling the temporality of action, neutralizing possibilities . . . and 'the line where past and future meet.' It locks up possibilities within an established framework while at the same time projecting them into the future" (71).

130. *The Case of the Creditors of Joseph George Pedley*, 2.

131. *The Case of the Creditors of Joseph George Pedley*, 2, 3.

132. Johnson, "Imprisonment for Debt," 22, 76.

133. Dienst, *Bonds of Debt*, 59.

134. Dienst, *Bonds of Debt*, 6.

135. Finn, *Character of Credit*, 206–7.

136. Finn, *Character of Credit*, 189.

137. See *ProPublica*'s "The Color of Debt" for an explanation of how imprisoning Americans not for debt but for not paying their debt criminalizes poor and African American citizens. The criminalization of debt caused the death of Walter Scott in South Carolina in 2015. Scott, an African American, was shot and killed while running away from police because of a contempt-of-court charge regarding his failure to pay child support.

138. Cooke, *The Universal Letter-writer*, 51.

139. Cooke, *The Universal Letter-writer*, 224.

140. Elsewhere in *The Universal Letter-writer*, we see the abstracted promise of upward mobility through hard work in the imagined correspondence between a young merchant and his mentor, a retired merchant, in which the junior expresses serious anxiety over the accidental risks of financial failure, which seem to him very high and growing: "[Since men of] the fairest characters, daily fail, I am justly alarmed, and my fears continue to increase in proportion to their numbers" (133). "I am filled with horror," he writes, since the curse of accidental loss seems to attend all "mercantile affairs, which the greatest prudence can neither see nor prevent" (134). His mentor, who has a "long acquaintance with the fluctuating state of merchandize" (133), sends him a reassuring reply, insisting that he does have control, and that industry, good accounting, and honest hard work will keep him off the *Gazette* lists: "[T]here are some unforeseen accidents, which even the greatest prudence cannot prevent. But these are extraordinary cases, and seldom happen. If you examine minutely into the nature of those causes which generally occasion bankruptcies, you will find them arising from . . . careless attention to business . . . [and] the vanity of those in trade, living above their circumstances" (135). In other words, those who fail do so for reasons they should be held morally accountable for, which begs the question of why limited liability was introduced for wealthy traders in the first place. The elder insists that the young merchant has moral agency in determining his future, while the younger witnesses many prudent friends who have declared bankruptcy. How can hard work matter when it does not matter for bankrupt friends? The fluidity of accidental probability produces a state of unknowing, whereas insurance believes such future unknowns can be known through aggregation.

Chapter 2 • Leveraging Fiction

1. Colin Burrow, "The Borrowers," *The Guardian*, December 6, 2008, http://www.theguardian.com/books/2008/dec/06/debt. From the perspective of a post-2008 world, Burrow might change his claim. The recent boon in "credit crisis" novels reintroduces debt, though the novels mostly narrate crisis satirically, from the perspective of rich white New Yorkers or Londoners who lose their liquidity. These include Carey, *Debt*; Cartwright, *Other People's Money*; Eggers, *A Hologram for the King*; Faulks, *A Week in December*; Gillmor, *Mount Pleasant*; Haslett, *Union Atlantic*; Lipsyte, *The Ask*; McInerney, *Bright, Precious Days*; Mountford, *A Young Man's Guide to Late Capitalism*; and Sweeney, *The Nest*. Notable are the "credit crisis" novels that experiment with point of view in their narration of debt; for instance, Dee, *The Privileges*; Kraus, *Summer of Hate*; Lanchester, *Capital*; Mbue, *Behold the Dreamers*; McPhee, *Dear Money*; Rahman, *In the Light of What We Know*; Shteyngart, *Lake Success*; and Wayne, *Kapitoil*. Another genre of credit crisis novel is the dystopia; for example, Eggers, *The Circle*; Shriver, *The Mandibles*; and Shteyngart, *Super Sad True Love Story*. For a discussion of contemporary "credit crisis" novels, see McClanahan, *Dead Pledges*.

2. Scott, *The History of Sir George Ellison*, 76.

3. Mackenzie, *The Man of Feeling*, 133.

4. David Simple visits two couples, one with a good wife and the other, a bad one. In both stories, one spouse works hard and the other does nothing but overspend and lead the family into insolvency; the sex of the spouse switches between the stories. Fielding, *The Adventures of David Simple*, 38–39.

5. Richardson, *Pamela*, 3:110–11.

6. Lineham, "The Campaign to Abolish Imprisonment for Debt in England," 77.

7. Cadwallader Crabtree in Smollett's *Adventures of Peregrine Pickle* is one such case as he brags about waiting out his time in debtor's jail until one of the many Acts of Insolvency forgives his debt, a debt he was able but refused to pay. The anti-hero scoundrel in *The Adventures of Ferdinand Count Fathom* is deservedly imprisoned for debt. But Smollett also includes sympathetic portrayals of debtors: Roderick Random spends time in Marshalsea for debt, and Matthew Bramble puts Lismahago's affairs in order by refinancing his debts.

8. Finn, *The Character of Credit*, 26.

9. McClanahan, *Dead Pledges*, 35, 33.

10. Casey Slide, "10 Reasons Why You Should NOT Lend Money to Friends & Family," *Money Crashers*, accessed July 27, 2019, www.moneycrashers.com/why-you-should-not-lend-money-to-friends-and-family/; Jeff D. Opdyke, "Never Lend Money to a Friend Repeat: Just Don't Do It," *Wall Street Journal*, updated July 6, 2003, www.wsj.com/articles/SB105724418093207600.

11. Shonkwiler, *The Financial Imaginary*, xix.

12. As Ian Baucom and others have noted, insurance emerges precisely as the financial instrument that takes on the risk for a social group, turning the consolations and gifts of friendship into a commodity that can be sold. *Specters of the Atlantic*.

13. Margaret Hunt, in *The Middling Sort*, provides a telling example of how financial instruments become unfriended. She recounts the story of Samuel Marriott, who writes about deciding between investing in his brother's hosier business or City Corporation. When he realizes the City is more secure, he invests in it and is disowned by most of his siblings because of his decision (27–28).

14. Phelan, "Functions of Character," 109.

15. Rimmon-Kenan, *Narrative Fiction*, 31.

16. Woloch, *The One vs. the Many*, 14.

17. Barthes, *S/Z*, 191.

18. Cixous and Cohen, "The Character of 'Character,'"; Greimas, *Structural Semantics*.

19. Woloch, *The One vs. the Many*, 17. Alison Shonkwiler notes a similar dialectic that she describes as the "tension of character reading between the allegorical and the representational." *The Financial Imaginary*, 48. She explores how contemporary financial novels revert to an abstract typology of moral character and, in so doing, reveal the inadequacy of allegorical character for capturing within realism the twenty-first-century financial imagination.

20. As a genre, sentimental fiction often eschews "mixed characters" in favor of the didacticism of the exemplary. Sarah Scott explicitly rejects the use of "mixed characters" in the preface to *Sir George Ellison*, arguing that readers need clear, moral characters to properly imitate their virtues (4).

21. Lynch, *The Economy of Character*, 81.

22. Annie McClanahan provides a succinct critique of the objectivity and science of the credit rating industry, which often represents its work as taking individual "bias" out of financial judgment. See McClanahan, "Bad Credit." Pierre Bourdieu, in "Forms of Capital," sees the production of "disinterested" exchange as a codeterminant of capital: "[B]y reducing the universe of exchanges to mercantile exchange, which is . . . oriented toward the maximization of profit, i.e., . . . self-interested, it has implicitly defined the other forms of exchange as noneconomic, and therefore disinterested" (241).

23. Valvo, "Sentimental Disinterest," 412.

24. Edwin B. Dike cites Coleridge in "Coleridge Marginalia in Henry Brooke's *The Fool of Quality*," 152. "Irish" "experimentalism" is from Haslett, "Experimentalism in the Irish Novel," 63; "children's book" is from Scheuermann, *Social Protest in the Eighteenth-Century English Novel*, 42; and "supremely digressive" is from Wetmore, *Men of Feeling in Eighteenth-Century Literature*, 7.

25. Brooke, *The Fool of Quality*, 3:5. Further references to this work by volume and page appear parenthetically in the text.

26. This would be a good place for the novel to end, but it does not. Brooke employs the picaresque episodic structure to expand the novel infinitely, moving from the reunion into an extended Oriental tale of Harry's travels. Significantly, when John Wesley took on the task of abridging the novel, it was not the theology but the unruly narrative he felt required revision. Mary Peace provides an insightful discussion of Wesley's revisions in which she cites a letter Wesley wrote to Brooke's nephew declaring that he thought the novel promoted the "religion of the heart" and that he would not need to change the "sentiments" but would focus on "the structure of the story, which seemed here and there to be not quite clear." Peace, "Sentimentality in the Service of Methodism," 279.

27. Frances Burney writes that Cecilia's "affluence she therefore considered as a debt contracted with the poor, and her independence as a tie upon her liberality to pay it with interest." *Cecilia*, 55. I provide an extended analysis of *Cecilia* in chapter 4.

28. Markman Ellis, in *The Politics of Sensibility*, discusses the political economy of the canal project in *The Fool of Quality*.

29. Peace, "Sentimentality in the Service of Methodism," 283.

30. This was *The History of a Reprobate* (1784), a ninety-page excerpt from volume 3 in which Fenton seeks objects of charity from a disembarking boat of returned Barbary slaves and gives them a second chance in life.

31. The reference to cattle disease reminds us of the tract writer, quoted in chapter 1, whose list of possible accidental misfortunes includes "the mortality amongst the horned cattle." *An Humble Address to a Member of Parliament* (1753), 1.

32. For his satire, Brooke borrows from the feud between the Lilliputs and Blefuscus in Swift's *Gulliver's Travels*. The Ruth family feud is caused by a disagreement over "whether the method of setting an egg on end was originally the invention of Columbus or whether it was communicated to him by some other" (*The Fool of Quality*, 3:285).

33. None of the standard critical texts nor the specific work on economics in *The Vicar* mention the plot *lacunae* of the unpaid debt but I have not read every critical article which, in the case of this novel, would be a lifetime's scholarly work. My list includes Anderson, "Stoic Constructions of Virtue in *The Vicar of Wakefield*"; Bender, "Prison Reform and the Sentence of Narration in *The Vicar of Wakefield*"; Brooks, "Goldsmith's

Commercial Vicar"; Brown, *Preromanticism*; Donoghue, *The Fame Machine*; Durant, "*The Vicar of Wakefield* and the Sentimental Novel"; Dykstal, "The Story of O"; Haggerty, "Satire and Sentiment in *The Vicar of Wakefield*"; Harkin, "Goldsmith on Authorship in *The Vicar of Wakefield*;" Hopkins, *The True Genius of Oliver Goldsmith*; Hopkins, "Matrimony in *The Vicar of Wakefield* and the Marriage Act of 1753"; Kim, "Goldsmith's Manhood"; Paulson, *Satire and the Novel in Eighteenth-Century England*; Quintana, *Oliver Goldsmith*; Skinner, *Sensibility and Economics in the Novel*; and Sussman, "Memory and Mobility."

34. To remove George from being a threat to Ned's avaricious courtship of Arabella, Ned procures him an army commission in the West Indies for £100. Feigning charity, Ned says he wants nothing for performing this service "and as for the hundred pound to be paid, if you are unable to raise it yourselves, I will advance it, and you shall repay me at your leisure." Goldsmith, *The Vicar of Wakefield*, 105. Further references to this work are cited parenthetically in the text.

35. Culler, "Story and Discourse," 194.

36. Culler, "Story and Discourse," 195.

37. Boswell, *Life of Johnson*, 294. Ricardo Quintana's biography questions the details in Boswell's account, and he suggests that Goldsmith had begun to write *The Vicar* in 1760, whereas the episode involving Johnson probably occurred in July 1762 and the bookseller was probably Newberry, who bought only a third of the shares in publishing the manuscript; Goldsmith sold other shares to Collins and Strahan and thus he potentially made more than Johnson recounted. Quintana, *Oliver Goldsmith*, 101–2.

38. Kim, "Goldsmith's Manhood," 22. For a discussion of this tension, see Haggerty, "Satire and Sentiment."

39. Until Ricardo Quintana and other critics in the 1960s suggested that Primrose is an unreliable narrator and that Goldsmith's text is ironic, readers interpreted Primrose's character as naive but with the implied narrator's full sympathies directed toward its good-hearted hero. See also Hopkins, *The True Genius of Oliver Goldsmith*. Narrative theorists Vera Nünning and J. Alexander Bareis both use the novel as evidence that determining a narrator's unreliability is historically specific, since Primrose has not always been read as such. Nünning, "Unreliable Narration and the Historical Variability of Values and Norms"; Bareis, "Ethics, the Diachronization of Narratology, and the Margins of Unreliable Narration." John Bender argues against reading the novel ironically or as split and instead posits a first-person narration with a covert, impersonal omniscience. "Prison Reform and the Sentence of Narration in *The Vicar of Wakefield*," 148.

40. Woloch, *The One vs. the Many*, 17.

41. Why, exactly, Primrose has to resign his curacy of £35 to take up a cure of £15 per year is never made entirely clear in the novel. Critics vary in their reading of this detail. Robert Hopkins argues that he was forced to resign over the Whistonean controversy. *The True Genius of Oliver Goldsmith*, 177. In his notes to the Oxford edition, Robert Mack suggests Goldsmith changed the wording of "I gave" the annuity to the orphans and widows, to "I made over" the curacy in the second edition, suggesting he had signed away his legal right to use of the money (173n12).

42. Insider trading laws are meant to regulate the prediction of future risk through managing who knows what about future events, but such regulations are increasingly weakened under neoliberalism.

43. *The Swindler Detected* describes the problem of "pretended recommendation," where a man pretends to know someone you know. The writer gives the example of a man who approached a tradesman, claiming to be recommended to him by a common acquaintance they knew in the country, giving a recognizable proper name. Based upon the common knowledge of the person, the tradesman provides the man goods on credit and the swindler then runs off and pawns the goods (21).

44. Eliot, "Essays and Leaves from a Notebook," 64.

45. Brown, *Preromanticism*, 167.

46. Brown, *Preromanticism*, 167–68.

47. Both Marshall Brown and David Durant note Primrose's penchant for generalizing statements. Brown notes that Primrose uses aphorisms eighteen times in the first half of the novel, with phrases such as "I was ever of the opinion . . ." followed by a moral proclamation "of dubious relevance and even more dubious validity." *Preromanticism*, 153. Durant discusses how Primrose often begins a passage with a generalized maxim. "*The Vicar of Wakefield* and the Sentimental Novel."

48. Richard Sheridan's mother, Frances Sheridan, may have given her son the inspiration through her use of the motif in *Sidney Bidulph.* Though impoverished, Sidney helps a poor man whom Sir George has refused to help, and when the man reveals himself to be Mr. Warner, a rich cousin recently returned from the West Indies, Sidney inherits his fortune.

49. When Ned first starts visiting the family, he discourages the relation: "Disproportioned friendships ever terminate in disgust. . . . Let us keep to companions of our own rank." Goldsmith, *The Vicar of Wakefield*, 27. But then he ignores his own advice when the prospect of upward mobility is too tempting. Contemporary sociological research on cross-class friendships and social stratification focuses almost entirely on the complex question of how and why we keep our friendships within our class.

50. The engagement scene includes the conventional motif of disavowing financial value to proclaim affective and social value, as Primrose says to Burchell: "[I]f you think her a recompence she is yours. . . . And let me tell you, Sir, that I give you no small treasure, she has been celebrated for beauty it is true, but that is not my meaning, I give you up a treasure of her mind. . . . I know no man so worthy to deserve her as you; and if I could give her thousands, and thousands sought her from me, yet my honest brave Burchell should be my dearest choice" (150). The disowning of money for love is the topic of chapter 5.

51. A footnote to this passage in the Oxford edition notes that "the danger of excessive benevolence" is a constant theme in Goldsmith's writing. See *Collected Works*, 3:176.

52. Charlotte Sussman discusses Goldsmith's demographic argument in "Memory and Mobility."

53. Goldsmith's critique of commerce enters the novel in Primrose's defense of the monarchy, given in the debate about liberty with the Butler, whom he mistakes for the master of the house. Primrose argues: "[I]f the circumstances of our state be such, as to favour the accumulation of wealth, and make the opulent still more rich, this will encrease their ambition. An accumulation of wealth, however, must necessarily be the consequence, when as at present more riches flow in from external commerce, than arise from internal industry: for external commerce can only be managed to advantage by the

rich, and they have also at the same time all the emoluments arising from internal industry: so that the rich, with us, have two sources of wealth, whereas the poor have but one." Goldsmith, *The Vicar of Wakefield*, 86–87. In a commercial state, wealth accumulates to a few people and makes everyone their dependents, thus corrupting the nation.

54. Fielding, *Amelia*, 324.

55. Booth argues in his debate with Bondum that the Magna Carta does not allow imprisonment for debt. Fielding, *Amelia*, 324. Fielding expostulates against imprisonment for debt in *The Champion*, 1:286–88. Marshall Brown provides an intriguing suggestion that Goldsmith may not have attacked the law because prisons had done him well. Commenting on the repeatedly positive place prisons hold in Goldsmith's writings, Brown writes that "[a]n incarceration in 1754 providentially saved him from shipwreck and drowning . . . and facing prison again in 1759 he called it the home of 'true society'. . . . Goldsmith's essays, like *The Vicar*, uniformly treat the prison as an agent of (real or imaginary) good fortune." *Preromanticism*, 156.

56. Cheryl Wanko reads the novel's "distinctive method of characterization," defined by the way the reader is required to suspect everyone of ulterior motives. "Characterization and the Reader's Quandary in Fielding's *Amelia*," 517. A character such as James who is first introduced as trustworthy often turns out not to be so, and the reader is left with a quandary. Amelia is unquestionably good but the novel "teaches us to question every character," and thus we must suspect Amelia's character (521).

Chapter 3 • Narrative Exchange

1. Mackenzie, *The Man of Feeling*, 85. Further references to this work are cited parenthetically in the text.

2. The main critical discussions of sentimental fiction often refer to specific scenes of storytelling as representative of sentimentalism's endorsement of charity, but no critic analyzes why such scenes are conventional in the genre. David J. Denby comes the closest in noting, in his discussion of French literature, the importance not just of the plot of misfortune but of how "onto this narrative structure is grafted a second level of meaning, which can be defined as a structure of observation or perception" through scenes of storytelling. *Sentimental Narrative and the Social Order in France*, 4.

3. I use "almost always" throughout this chapter to qualify general formal claims. While I often cannot come up with a counterexample to disprove the claim (for instance, I cannot name a sentimental novel that does not have a homodiegetic narrator), I have not read every sentimental novel. Also, my argument concerns a general tendency in sentimental fiction that I provide a historical interpretation of, rather than defining an essentialist rule that exists outside the narrative context.

4. Todorov, *The Poetics of Prose*, 72.

5. For critical discussions of embedded storytelling that highlight contemporary fiction, see O'Neill, *Fictions of Discourse*; and Shryock, *Tales of Storytelling*.

6. Genette, *Narrative Discourse Revisited*; Bal, *Narratology*. For other critical investigations of the device, see Chambers, *Story and Situation*; Nelles, *Frameworks*; Rimmon-Kenan, *Narrative Fiction*; Shryock, *Tales of Storytelling*; Todorov, *The Poetics of Prose*; Williams, *Theory and the Novel*.

7. Pier, "Narrative Levels." Gérard Genette introduced the terms *extra-diegetic*, *intra-diegetic*, and *meta-diegetic* to distinguish between levels. *Narrative Discourse*, 228–29. Like

others, I find his terms unnecessarily confusing and prefer the less cumbersome terms *frame*, *primary*, *secondary*, *tertiary*, and the like, because the distinguishing characteristic of narrative level is spatial. The question is: Where, in relation to the primary diegetic tale, is the embedded one positioned?

8. Genette, *Narrative Discourse Revisited*, 87; Bal, *Narratology*, 143.

9. Pier, "Narrative Levels."

10. Susan Lanser defines the distinction as follows: "By public narration I mean simply narration (implicitly or explicitly) addressed to a narratee who is external (that is, heterodiegetic) to the textual world and who can be equated with a public readership; private narration, in contrast, is addressed to an explicitly designated narratee who exists only within the textual world." "Toward a Feminist Narratology," 684.

11. Genette, *Narrative Discourse*, 232–33. Genette later modified the types to add more—predicative, persuasive, and obstructive—but the modified list is not necessary for my purposes (*Narrative Discourse Revisited*, 93–94).

12. Bal, *Narratology*, 144–45.

13. Chambers, *Story and Situation*, 7.

14. Chambers opens with the example of a "faggot" joke to demonstrate the importance of the narrative situation: gay men telling "faggot" jokes to each other produces a very different meaning than if the joke is told between straight men. Chambers, *Story and Situation*, 3. In other cases, the narrative situation is the event, regardless of its content. Genette offers the filibuster speech as an example: the content of the speech is irrelevant; the meaning is in the act itself. Genette, *Narrative Discourse*, 234.

15. Shryock, *Tales of Storytelling*, 14.

16. Shryock, *Tales of Storytelling*, 14.

17. Fielding, *The Adventures of David Simple and Volume the Last*, 103, 102. Further references to this novel and sequel are cited parenthetically in the text.

18. Brooke, *The History of Emily Montague*, 357. Further references to this work are cited parenthetically in the text.

19. Scott, *A Description of Millenium Hall*, 147. Further references to this work are cited parenthetically in the text.

20. Barthes, *S/Z*, 89.

21. Paxson, "Revisiting the Deconstruction of Narratology," 132.

22. Maureen Harkin, in observing that Harley is hostile "to social change," notes that this "places him in an older conservative-reactionary tradition." "Mackenzie's *Man of Feeling*," 325. For a reading of Mackenzie's conservativeness, see Williams, "Deathly Sentimentalism." Williams compares Mackenzie's and Fielding's representations of loss and death as indicating equally conservative visions of the rise of commercial culture. While I agree with him that both David and Harley must die because they have "no place in the modern world," I provide a different interpretation to explain why they are outsiders to urban commerce. Williams, "Deathly Sentimentalism," 180.

23. The passage reads: "They [the British] came there as traders, bartering the commodities they brought for others which their purchasers could spare however great their profits were, they were then equitable. But what title have the subjects of another kingdom to establish an empire in India? . . . They have drained the treasuries of the Nabob, who must fill them by oppressing the industry of their subjects" (Mackenzie, *The Man of Feeling*, 118).

24. Harkin, "Mackenzie's *Man of Feeling*," 326.

25. For discussions of the mix of satire and sentiment, see Benedict, "The Sentimental Virtuoso," 473–99; Csengei, "'I Will Not Weep'"; Lilley, "Henry Mackenzie's Ruined Feelings"; and Stern, "Sentimental Frauds." I discuss a similar mix of satire and sentiment in relation to *Vicar of Wakefield* in chapter 2. James Kim's essays focus on what he calls "sentimental irony" in both novels. See "Goldsmith's Manhood" and "Mourning, Melancholia, and Modernity."

26. In fact, as the editor notes, because the manuscript does not carry the empty status marker of "a Marmontel, or a Richardson," he did not even weep while reading it (Mackenzie, *The Man of Feeling*, 49). Ildiko Csengei interprets the exchange of manuscripts as remarking that "[e]very text . . . has its own reader." "I Will Not Weep," 955.

27. Starr, "Sentimental Novels of the Later Eighteenth Century," 186.

28. Barbara Benedict goes further, arguing that "the double frame of the two narrators . . . allows the author to parody sentimental conventions." *Framing Feeling*, 118–19.

29. James David Lilley, in "Henry Mackenzie's Ruined Feelings," provides a detailed reading of the nostalgic effects in the text and traces them to a commercial economy; his reading overlaps with my own. He notes that Harley "outlines a spectral, other-worldly economy, a system of affective values that appear only to the extent that they have already been lost, already antiqued and consigned to pastoral prehistory. . . . Though such sepia-toned 'regions,' where pure affection is finally accorded its proper value, are part of sentimentality's critique of the world of commerce, they nevertheless possess their own economy—an ethereal yet absolute tyranny of ownership where the affective commodity is all the more 'ours' for its invisibility, all the more valuable for its nonparticipation in the secular world of 'selfish' exchange" (653).

30. Genette, *Narrative Discourse*, 234.

31. Starr argues that the fragmentary episodic nature of the novel originates in sentimental fiction's rejection of the bildungsroman or any empiricist linearity: "since narrative is always threatening to imply progress simply by unfolding in time," the novel resists the standard form of plot. "Sentimental Novels," 182. April London reads the "refusal to subordinate the episodic to the imperatives of plot or to a controlling narratorial presence" as representing "the formal realization of Mackenzie's claim that 'narrative would destroy' the reader's emotional engagement with his work." "Historiography, Pastoral, Novel," 46.

32. Edwards's losses are summarized in his "long tale": he has lived on the farm that has been in his family for generations, and he has been prudent and paid rent, but when his lease is up, the London entrepreneur now running the estate refuses to renew it, because "he did not choose to have any farm under £300 a year value on his estate." Capitalism requires expansion, so Edwards expands and rents more land. After a few unfavorable seasons and after "a considerable corn-factor turned bankrupt with a sum of mine in his possession," he fails to pay his rent. Though poor, he is "not altogether without credit" and moves the family to an even smaller farm, but accidents ensue and ultimately he is press ganged and forced to be part of imperial capitalism in India. Mackenzie, *The Man of Feeling*, 107–12.

33. For readings of Harley's status as too good for the world, see Williams, "Deathly Sentimentalism"; and Skinner, *Sensibility and Economics in the Novel*.

34. Since we know that Charles "sometimes visit[s] his [Harley's] grave," a diegetic

overlap is possible, though the frame has introduced Charles as "the Ghost," who disappeared without a trace (Mackenzie, *The Man of Feeling*, 139).

35. Mangano, *Fictions of Friendship in the Eighteenth-Century Novel.* Mangano notes the vicious circle in the text between trusting the third-person narrator (who says they heard the story from David himself), who tells story after story of false friendship and how we should not trust appearances and then includes narrative situations in which first-person storytelling creates bonds of friendship: "The narrator invites us, as readers, to project onto David a faith in these strangers that we recognize he should not have, a faith available only to our advantaged perspective, which, after further reflection on the novel's framing apparatus, should not be available even to us" (96).

36. Schellenberg, *The Conversational Circle*, 23.

37. The novel's print history suggests another reading of the embedded tale that is not incompatible with the one I give here. Brooke's letters reveal that she thought the fourth and final volume dragged with "so little variety of the story for the length of it" but that she was forced to add the fourth volume for financial reasons: her friends had sold subscriptions to *Emily Montague* as a four-volume novel, while she was planning only three (Brooke to Robert Dodsley, August 29 [1769], British Library, Add MS 29747, f 68). In a letter to her friend Richard Gifford, she acknowledges, "It is spoiled by being in 4 vols. but that is not my fault. My friends in my absences, meaning to make it profitable, proposed it by subscription, and gave out receipts at 1/2 a guinea; I was obliged to their intentions and their zeal, but being honest and proud, determined to make it 4 vols" (Brooke to Rev. Richard Gifford, May 21, 1771, British Library MS. Rp 1012, box 18 941D). Adding an embedded tale is a shortcut strategy to draw out the length, but the story itself takes up only ten pages of those final post-marriage seventy.

38. Peace, " 'Epicures in Rural Pleasures,' " 308.

39. In noting the level of financial detail in the novel, Nicolle Jordan asserts that the novel is "obsessed with the financial histories of the women." "A Creole Contagion," 57. David Oakleaf concurs and provides an extensive description of their finances: "[Scott] knows where the money comes from, and when she counts it she is precise, not fanciful." "At the Margins of Utopia," 125.

40. Robert Markley calls charity "the paradoxical impasse of sentimental morality . . . the more you give, the more virtuous you become, although your actions leave you with less and therefore limit your capacity to keep on demonstrating your virtue." "Sentimentality as Performance," 230.

41. The ladies are very attuned to the way interest works, frequently working it into their accounts. For instance, the toad-eaters' refuge is established entirely through such investment interest income. Interest earnings also constitute part of Mrs. Treatham's fortune.

42. Susan Lanser's feminist narratological reading of the embedding structure interprets the containment of the women's stories within the narrator's male voice as a problem and as registering women's inability to claim a public voice. The women have ostensibly told their stories to Mrs. Maynard in private and Mrs. Maynard re-narrates them within the intimate domestic situation which then, the male listener makes public by re-narrating them in a letter to his publisher. William H. Wandless provides a different reading of the nesting, arguing that the narrator does not appropriate and enclose the private feminine voice but rather "collaborates" with Mrs. Maynard to co-produce the

text. The direction of the nesting, I would suggest, prompts the need for another narrative which becomes *The History of Sir George Ellison* in which the narrator puts the Ladies' lessons into action on his Jamaican plantation. Lanser, *Fictions of Authority.* See also Wandless, "Secretaries of the Interior."

43. Jordan, "A Creole Contagion," 62.

44. Oakleaf, "At the Margins of Utopia," 126.

45. Scott, *The History of Sir George Ellison*, 51.

Chapter 4 • The Plot of Capital I

1. The full copy of the ad reads: "He's got a gift for gymnastics. She's got her eye on a little start-up in the Valley. And he wants to retire early. How do you create a wealth plan that reflects all the complexity of a modern family? Start with a Financial Advisor who understands individuals and knows how to bring families together around both shared and personal goals. Let's have that conversation." Interestingly, the four generations begin with pure blue blood (i.e., white people wearing blue) and ends with a mixed-race fourth generation when an African American spouse is introduced in the third.

2. Defoe, *Roxana*, 167.

3. David Harvey's chapter on the "dangerous contradiction" of "endless compound growth" lays out in more detail why such growth relies on fictitious capital and why, then, it will eventually be unsustainable. The burgeoning levels of personal and public debt might suggest, according to Harvey, that we have already reached that point. *Seventeen Contradictions*, 222–45. See also LiPuma and Lee, *Financial Derivatives and the Globalization of Risk.*

4. Hedge funds, as their name suggests, hedge bets by pooling capital and buying shares using various strategies to offset potential losses; for example, buying shares in solar energy to counter shares in oil. The OED dates the financial management use of the word *hedge* to the seventeenth century, with "to hedge in" used to reference debt. Arjun Appadurai analyzes the aggregated individual of finance capital in terms of the "dividual," a dispersed, disarticulated, and divided subject. See chapter 7, "The Wealth of Dividuals," in Appadurai, *Banking on Words.*

5. Critics most often place the economics of *Cecilia* in a gendered frame, but my own reading follows the money plot to argue that the plot of capital, not courtship, entraps the heroine and requires her to lose her money in order to generate the novel's story. James Thompson, in *Models of Value*, reads Burney's plots as conservative, as maintaining a divide between "economic man" and "domestic woman." "Despite the best will in the world," Thompson observes, "her protagonists get themselves entrapped in financial crises from which they cannot extricate themselves. These financial disasters further the view that women are not fully qualified to participate in the system of needs that constitutes civil society—that they want the protection of a husband. That is, that they are not destined to be 'economic man,' but rather to be 'domestic woman'" (158–59). Margo Finn, among others, challenges Thompson's reading; see *The Character of Credit*, esp. 35–39. Critical engagements with Burney's representation of money and gender that have helped generate my reading include Burgess, "Courting Ruin"; Copeland, "Money in the Novels of Fanny Burney"; Gallagher, *Nobody's Story*, 203–56; Goggin, "Learning Finance through Fiction"; Keohane, "'Too neat for a beggar'"; Klekar, "'Her Gift Was Compelled'"; Smith, "The Haberdasher's Plot"; and Thompson, "Burney's Conservatism."

6. E. M. Forster provides the classic example of causality and plot; he reasons that "the king died and then the queen died" is not a plot, but "The king died, and then the queen died of grief" is. *Aspects of the Novel and Related Writing*, 60. The definition of plot as "ordered sequence of events" led critics to study and deduce recurring plot patterns, producing the categorical typologies of Russian formalist Vladimir Propp's work on folktales or Northrop Frye's study of myths. Plot, under these terms, follows a limited number of ordered sequences: quest, courtship, bildungsroman, comedy, tragedy, etc. The categorical description of such plot analysis relies on a narrative temporality based in chronology, in the clock time of linear progress. Propp, *Morphology of the Folktale*; Frye, *Anatomy of Criticism*.

7. In his important 1984 study of plot, Peter Brooks challenged the definition of plot as causally ordered events, noting that, because we take plots to be as obvious as constructing a timeline, literary criticism has tended to associate "reading for the plot" with a simplistic form of interpretation, even as anti-interpretative, since it somehow promotes absorptive reading, of reading only for "what happens next" (*Reading for the Plot*). Brian Richardson takes Brooks's insights further, noting that "a teleological sequence of events linked by some principle of causation" cannot, in fact, account for the way plots actually represent temporal experience; for example, the modernist experiments with time like *The Waves* and *Ulysses* primarily relate events through simple succession, not connection or causality. "Beyond the Poetics of Plot." In arguing for the explanatory weakness of plot as causality, Richardson lists a number of "nonplot-based forms of narrative progression"; for instance, rhythm (Henry James's triadic structures) or contrast (Tolstoy's light and dark chapters) or alphabetical order.

8. Levenson, "Reading Time." For further discussion of how "Newtonian absolute time" or the clock time of the Fordist factory often fails to capture the way plots actually represent temporal experience, see West-Pavlov, *Temporalities*.

9. Dannenberg, "Plot," 435.

10. Brooks, *Reading for the Plot*, 13, 18.

11. Levenson, "Reading Time," 514. Monica Fludernik would concur with Levenson; she writes, in *Towards a "Natural" Narratology*, that understanding narrative as "sequentiality *per se*, even if it provides cause-and-effect patterns of interpretation . . . is ultimately unable to embody narrative dynamics. *The king died and then the queen died of grief* may be a 'plot' as well as a good story material; . . . as narrative, however, it holds little or no interest" (20).

12. For the status of possible events within plot, see Bremond, "The Logic of Narrative Possibilities." Marie-Laure Ryan, in *Possible Worlds, Artificial Intelligence, and Narrative Theory*, builds on Bremond's insights in thinking about the cognitive importance of "possible worlds" to narrative understanding.

13. Ricoeur, "Narrative Time," 178.

14. See LiPuma and Lee, *Financial Derivatives and the Globalization of Risk*. Mathias Nilges's essay "Finance Capital and the Time of the Novel" explores how novels narrate this obliterated future.

15. Sewell, "The Temporalities of Capitalism," 518.

16. Thompson, "Time, Work-Discipline, and Industrial Capitalism." Ian Watt was the first to link the novel's plot to the economic plot through the time of the individual. He argued that the novel is made possible by "the modern sense of time," understood

through the duration of an individual's life, charted across particular hours and days and linking past to present through causality. *The Rise of the Novel*, 24.

17. Sewell, "Temporalities of Capitalism," 519.

18. In "After the Fall," John Lanchester argues that one of the reasons economists did not see the 2008 crash coming is that they believed "this time it's different." They were overconfident that fictitious capital can be managed, ignoring the "iron law of investment that risks are correlated with returns." Lanchester calls "This time it's different" "the four most expensive words in the world."

19. Novel studies has explored narrative temporality in various ways. Watt's emphasis on the linear and causal time of the individual led him to distinguish the novel from previous timeless narratives. *The Rise of the Novel*, 22. Critical histories of the novel since Watt have challenged his reliance on linear causality. Michael McKeon was perhaps the first, arguing that the novel is dialectical and demonstrates not the dominance of "progressive ideology" but the residual circulation of "aristocratic ideology" and the historical conflict between the two. *The Origins of the English Novel*. Feminist critics also revised Watt's emphasis of empirical causality linked to realism, noting that the adventure time of disguise and coincidence remain popular plot devices in amatory fiction by women. See Spencer, *The Rise of the Woman Novelist*. Jesse Molesworth's study *Chance and the Eighteenth-Century Novel* precisely takes issue with Watt's notion of plot, pointing out the persistence and importance of chance to the novel's rise. Amit S. Yahav, in *Feeling Time*, demonstrates how the novel captures the feeling of time or the emotional experience of duration.

20. Bakhtin, "Forms of Time and of the Chronotope in the Novel," 250. After reading Bakhtin's essay, Michael Holquist notes that readers are often "hard pressed to answer the question, 'What exactly is a chronotope?' " *Dialogism*, 107.

21. Bakhtin, "Forms of Time and of the Chronotope in the Novel," 84.

22. White, " 'The Nineteenth-Century' as Chronotope," 122. White continues: "Unlike the notion of the 'world-view,' conceived as a fact of consciousness, the chronotope directs attention to the effective conditions of possibility of both *thought* and *action*, *consciousness* and *praxis* within discrete milieux, structured as fields of institutional and productive arrangements. The mini-worlds of 'the castle,' 'the highway,' 'the boulevard of the capital,' 'the slums of the industrial city,' 'the colonial outpost,' 'the salon,' are not only socially structured, but also, and above all, imaginary *spaces*, each with a different *possible* experience of time, within which the *bodies* and *psyches* of human agents and the relations they can bear with others, whether indigenous to that space-time or only visitors to it from elsewhere, are rigidly delimited" (122). Critics have noted that Bakhtin wavers between defining chronotopes transhistorically (i.e., "chronotope of the road") and delimiting them to historical genres (i.e., "Greek adventure novel of ordeal"). Like White, I read chronotopes as historically specific.

Michael Riffaterre introduces the chronotope in a similarly limited way in order to understand how readers conceptualize based on associative sign systems, because, for him, "[t]he generative power of the chronotope results from its rewriting time in spatial code and from filling the space thus gained with those signs that further translate chronological time into logical time. . . . We may summarize the backward-forward alternation of presuppositions and entailments by saying that the topoi are filled with past time, while the future is filled with diegetic space." Riffaterre, "Chronotopes in Diegesis," 255.

In a plot, space takes on a temporal force (a Madeleine becomes a childhood memory), and time enters diegetic space as a possible narratable future (Cecilia might keep her uncle's estate and marry).

23. Campbell, "Fashionable Suicide," 136.

24. Joyce Goggin, in "Learning Finance through Fiction," also reads Burney's *Cecilia* in relation to financial logics. Goggin uses *Cecilia* to illustrate that fiction teaches readers how financial markets work, whereas I turn the relationship around and read *Cecilia* as enacting new financial temporalities and epistemologies. Goggin argues that fiction helps "to train people to understand market movements and functions as part of everyday life" (62). I agree, but my interest lies less in the content of fiction than in the form of novelistic plotting.

25. Mr. Monckton chides Cecilia for loaning more money to Mr. Harrel and for believing that Harrel's bonds are backed by the value of his estate: "This is very youthful philosophy . . . but it will not lessen your regret hereafter, when the value of money is better known to you." Burney, *Cecilia*, 297. Further references to this novel are cited parenthetically in the text.

26. Burney, *Diary and Letters of Madame D'Arblay*, 2:136. Burney recounts in her diary her conversation with Edmund Burke; he told her "he wished the conclusion either more happy or more miserable; 'for in the work of the imagination . . . there is no medium.'" Ibid., 2:139. In refusing to amend the novel's ending, Burney wrote to Crisp that if she made it happier by having Cecilia keep her uncle's estate, "the last page of any novel in Mr. Noble's circulating library may serve for the last page of mine." Ibid., 2:195. For a discussion of Burney's correspondence with Samuel Crisp over *Cecilia*, see Hemlow, *The History of Fanny Burney*, 149–50; and Parisian, *Frances Burney's* Cecilia, 8–9.

27. Many have noted what Kristina Straub, in *Divided Fictions*, calls *Cecilia*'s "double plot structure" (110). For Straub the two plots are the romantic and 'course of life' plots. For Edward Copeland, the two plots "follow roughly the outlines of the division in *Evelina*, a love plot and a plot of hard cash." "Money in the Novels of Fanny Burney," 29. I see the 'two plots' as two sides of the money plot which could potentially end in three ways. In this way, I concur with Copeland's observation that "[t]he relationship between the rough-and-ready financial plot where Cecilia is tricked out of her paternal inheritance and the love plot is, I would like to suggest, closer than has been previously recognized" (29).

28. Belfield's and Monckton's ongoing debate over whether individual genius or social custom should take precedence in the world is discussed in the political context of the American Revolution by Megan Woodworth in "'If a Man Dared Act for Himself.'"

29. Genette describes the iterative tense in his chapter on time in *Narrative Discourse*, 116–19.

30. Castle, *Masquerade and Civilization*, 262.

31. Burney, *Diary and Letters*, 2:139.

32. D. A. Miller defines the "unnarratable" as that which is the precondition of the narrative but which cannot itself be narrated; for instance, the life of a heroine after marriage in a Jane Austen novel. Miller, *Narrative and Its Discontents*.

33. Word search on *vex* using Project Gutenberg's electronic edition of *Cecilia*, at www.gutenberg.org. A search of ten random late eighteenth-century novels in the *Chadwyck-Healey Eighteenth-Century Fiction* database, displays six novels that include the word two

or three times, three novels not at all, and the only one that includes a similar number (29 for the entire novel) is *Clarissa*. *Surprise* and *shock* occur 101 and 50 times, respectively, in the first half of *Cecilia*. Burney's influence on Jane Austen might be a factor in the fact that *vex** is a popular word in *Pride and Prejudice* (23) and *Mansfield Park* (32).

34. Campbell describes Harrel's suicide as "pointedly prefigured" and not "particularly apocalyptic; he is simply another small, individual failure. . . . Burney portrays a society which, far from heading towards an end in ruin, seems condemned to an endlessness of petty disasters." "Fashionable Suicide," 140.

35. Doody, *Frances Burney*, 133.

36. Brooks, *Reading for the Plot*, 9.

37. Epstein, *Iron Pen*, 160. Even when she is forced to settle accounts in leaving her uncle's estate and finds herself short, the problem lies not in her ability to calculate: she rightfully matches income to expenses. Her fault lies in her assumption that everyone would pay in a timely manner.

38. "The Masquerade," "Man of the Ton," "A Man of Business" [Harrel's suicide], and "A Torment" are the longest chapters, all over twenty pages. Genette notes that dramatic speech is the closest a narrative gets to "rigorous isochrony." *Narrative Discourse*, 87. Mieke Bal's term for the rhythm of uninterrupted dialogue is "scene," in which the "time of the fabula" as nearly matches the "story-time" as possible, a tempo she calls the "zero-line." *Narratology*, 100. "Scene" highlights the theatricality of this narrative rhythm, and much has been written about the influence of the theater on Burney. See, for example, Marcie Frank's "Frances Burney's Theatricality."

39. Barthes, *The Pleasure of the Text*, 11.

40. Bal defines "pause" as a moment "when an element . . . takes no fabula-time. . . . This is the case in descriptive or argumentative fragments." *Narratology*, 100.

41. Helen Thompson reads *The Wanderer*'s suffocating and "irritating disproportion between . . . manifest content and its apparently endless recursivity" in "How *The Wanderer* Works," 965 (quotation). Andrea Henderson reads Burney's masochistic desire, especially in *Camilla*, in *Romanticism and the Painful Pleasures of Modern Life*, 63–124.

42. The phrase occurs seven times in the novel. For example, after the Fidel incident: "She was now, therefore, called upon to think and act entirely for herself" (Burney, *Cecilia*, 588). In London, on the eve of her first wedding attempt: "She now, therefore, finally employed herself in briefly comparing the good with the evil of giving Delvile wholly up, or becoming his for ever" (ibid., 622).

43. Epstein, *Iron Pen*, 166.

44. Gallagher, *Nobody's Story*, 244.

45. For critical readings of the "mad dash" scene, see—in addition to Gallagher, *Nobody's Story*; Epstein, *Iron Pen*; and Doody, *Frances Burney*—Bloom and Bloom, "Fanny Burney's Novels"; Chan, "The Architectural Subject," 89–143; and Greenfield, "Money or Mind?"

46. Monckton is frequently characterized through his plotting and the language of "design" (Burney, *Cecilia*, 82). While Cecilia is staying with the Harrels, Monckton plots various ways of producing a "chance" solitary meeting with Cecilia (102). His elaborate plot at the masquerade is only one instance in which he tries to control Cecilia's movements and responses (126). He anticipates her moves in London and tries to frame them

with various intelligences that steer her in desired directions, for instance, making her suspect that the Delviles are setting a trap to steal her money.

47. Godden, "Language, Labor, and Finance Capital," 414.

48. Recent interest in the rise of insurance in the period was influenced by Ian Baucom's analysis of insurance and the case of the Zong in *Specters of the Atlantic*. See also Bellhouse, *Life Contingent Contracts and the Emergence of Actuarial Science in Eighteenth-Century England*; and Pearson, *Insuring the Industrial Revolution*.

49. Haiven, "Metaphoric Wealth," 58.

50. Haiven, "Metaphoric Wealth"; Žižek, *Living in the End Times*.

51. McCrea, *Frances Burney and Narrative Prior to Ideology*, 7. McCrea quotes from Burney's *Memoirs of Dr. Burney* about her father's financial behavior: "[He] had as little turn as time for that species of speculation which leads to financial prosperity; and he lived chiefly upon the principal of the sums which he amassed" (18n21).

52. Burney, *Journals and Letters*, 10:960–70 (appendix to "The D'Arblays' Finances").

53. Burney, *Journals and Letters*, 11:337–38.

Chapter 5 • The Plot of Capital II

1. Responses to climate change in the popular press often contain a similar pondering of an end, captured in this *Guardian* headline: "Ending Climate Change Requires the End of Capitalism. Have We Got the Stomach for It?" (Phil McDuff, *The Guardian*, March 18, 2019). See also Greg Jaffe, "The End of Capitalism as We Know It?" *Washington Post*, April 21, 2019.

2. The phrase has been credited to Fredric Jameson, who cites but does not attribute it. See introduction, note 27.

3. See, for example, Atwood, *The Heart Goes Last*; Eggers, *The Circle*; Shteyngart, *Super Sad True Love Story*; Shriver, *The Mandibles*; and Mandel, *Station Eleven*.

4. Harvey, *Seventeen Contradictions*, 79–85.

5. There is a third way to increase surplus value, which is to lower production costs by developing new natural resources or technological efficiencies. Environmentalists and climate change scientists are cautioning us about the limits of exploiting natural resources; others question Silicon Valley's messianism that technology will save us. For a recent popular critique of the economic politics of Silicon Valley, see Giridharadas, *Winners Take All*.

6. Burney, *Journals and Letters*, 3:129.

7. Burney's sister Susan conveyed her father's criticism in a letter: "'My dr Father charged me to urge you to weave into one story of interest & length what you had yet to write—he thinks yr book consists of *detached stories*, and that the Public are all longing for & the booksellers depending on another Evelina or Cecilia.'" Burney, *Journals and Letters*, 3:129n10.

8. Bander, "Family Matters in Burney's *Camilla*."

9. Burney, *Camilla*, 910. Further references to this novel are cited parenthetically in the text.

10. I am using *restricted economy* in a very limited sense informed by Georges Bataille, in "The Notion of Expenditure," as an economy in which all expenditure (financial, emotional, social) becomes answerable "to the economic principle of balanced accounts"

(118). While I invoke Bataille in this limited way, his distinction between general and restricted economy, and the debates his work has spurred around whether there is a loss without return, are not my concern. I use the term simply to refer to an economy in which various forms of productivity, not just financial, are balanced within a ledger book.

11. Ricoeur's larger context reads: "In a sense, the story's conclusion is the pole of attraction of the entire development. But a narrative conclusion can be neither deduced nor predicted. There is no story if our attention is not moved along by a thousand contingencies. This is why a story has to be followed to its conclusion. So rather than being predictable, a conclusion must be acceptable. Looking back from the conclusion to the episodes leading up to it, we have to be able to say that this ending required these sorts of events and this chain of actions. . . . This is the paradox of contingency, judged 'acceptable after all,' that characterizes the comprehension of any story told." Ricoeur, "Narrative Time," 174.

12. Brooks, *Reading for the Plot*, 60. Brooks notes that plot propels "the active quest of the reader for those shaping ends that, terminating the dynamic process of reading, promise to bestow meaning and significance on the beginning and the middle" (19). For extended discussions of closure in fiction, see Frank Kermode's classic *The Sense of an Ending*, as well as Miller, *Narrative and Its Discontents*; Reising, *Loose Ends*; and Torgovnick, *Closure in the Novel.*

13. As early as 1950, Joyce Hemlow noted this critical consensus: "It has been customary to discern in *Camilla* the failure of Fanny Burney's powers as a writer." "Fanny Burney and the Courtesy Books," 759. For an overview of this critical heritage, see Pink, "Frances Burney's *Camilla*."

14. For a more extensive discussion of sentimentalism's restrictive "love ≠ money" accounting, see my "Narrative Exchange in *David Simple*."

15. For an insightful discussion of how the novel shapes the narrative of happiness for modernity, see Vivasvan Soni's *Mourning Happiness.*

16. Rosenthal, *Infamous Commerce*, 153.

17. Thompson, "How *The Wanderer* Works," 981.

18. For a discussion of how penitent prostitutes become the guarantee of nonmercenary love, see my "Whore's Love."

19. Cope, *Property, Education, and Identity in Late Eighteenth-Century Fiction*, 5, 4, 5–6. In *Novel Relations*, Ruth Perry describes what she calls the "great disinheritance" as the way the rise of the bourgeois family was disempowering for women, including financially (38–76).

20. Henderson, *Romanticism and the Painful Pleasure of Modern Life*, 86. For an overview of *Camilla*'s critical heritage, see Pink, "Frances Burney's *Camilla*."

21. *British Critic* 8 (November 1796), 536.

22. Johnson, *Equivocal Beings*, 146.

23. Johnson, *Equivocal Beings*; Henderson, *Romanticism and the Painful Pleasures of Modern Life*; Hemlow, "Fanny Burney and the Courtesy Books."

24. My use of the term *completeness* invokes James Phelan's distinction between two main ways a narrative can signal its end. Phelan argues that stories contain different types of instabilities that keep us turning the page: a narrative can be driven forward either by story instabilities (conflicts between characters, a murder that needs to be solved) or by tensions within its discourse about "value, belief, opinion, knowledge, expectation." "Nar-

rative Progression," 211. A story reaches "closure" for Phelan when it signals the end of its story instabilities; for example, when the murder is solved. But it does not also have to reach "completion," the term he uses to designate the resolution of the discursive or ideological tensions a narrative has introduced. The last page of a novel, then, can bring its reader to closure (in Phelan's more limited use of this term, referring to the end of its story instabilities) without completion, to completion without closure, to no closure or completion, or to both closure and completion. I argue that *Camilla* reaches closure in that the obstacles to the marriage ending are overcome, but it does not reach completion of the ideological questions it raises about female financial sacrifice.

25. Miller, *Narrative and Its Discontents*, ix, 5.

26. Sentimentalism's narrative paradox—that in order to show a lack of interest in money, it must constantly talk about money—is readable in the way Westwyn elsewhere uses money as moral reward and punishment. His declaration that money does not buy happiness is complicated by the fact that he constantly uses money to incentivize his son's virtue. He promises to reward Harry with an increase of £50 to his annual allowance if the rumor be true that he rescued Camilla from the Southampton bathhouse (Burney, *Camilla*, 648). A few pages later, he threatens to "cut him off with a shilling" if the young Westwyn tries to assert his will over his father's (658).

27. See Brunström, "Sex and Shopping with Frances Burney" 86–98; Henderson, *Romanticism and the Painful Pleasures of Modern Life*, 90–93; Keohane, "The 'Web of Gratitude' "; Lynch, *The Economy of Character*, 170–86; and Smith, "The Haberdasher's Plot."

28. Andrea Henderson's discussion of the Southampton scene focuses on this new, anonymous form of shopping. She wonderfully historicizes the scene within the context of the introduction of price ticketing, which transformed the purchase of goods and invented window-shopping. *Romanticism and the Painful Pleasures of Modern Life*, 90–93.

29. Henderson, *Romanticism and the Painful Pleasures of Modern Life*, 94.

30. Keohane, "The 'Web of Gratitude,' " 192.

31. Gruner, "The Bullfinch and the Brother," 19.

32. James Thompson notes Burney's use of explicit numerical accounting: "The story of Camilla's debts . . . is told in remarkable detail; no expenditure is forgotten, and periodically we are treated to elaborate accounts of her mounting debts. Every purchase, every article of clothing, every ticket, and every pet is itemized." *Models of Value*, 164. I read her use of figures as underscoring, in part, the disequilibrium between male and female consumption, not as Thompson does in arguing that Burney suggests women need male help in managing their money.

33. Epstein, *Iron Pen*, 127.

34. Epstein, *Iron Pen*, 130.

35. For a discussion of how Eugenia's disability liberates her from gender constraints, see Haggerty, *Unnatural Affections*. Haggerty notes that "Eugenia must learn to appreciate the freedom that her accidents afford her" (141).

36. Johnson, *Equivocal Beings*, 142. For other critics who have noted how the novel foregrounds the failure of *men*, not women, to be proper economic subjects, see Keohane, "The 'Web of Gratitude,' " 232; and Straub, *Divided Fictions*, 183–84. Margaret Doody points out the disparity as well, noting how "we are invited to calculate Camilla's debts, and to realize that although she was a little extravagant, her money losses were largely the

result of her brother's taking her money from her, as well as of his accepting loans in her name from somebody else." *Frances Burney*, 213.

37. In his letter to Lionel on news of his circumstances, Mr. Tyrold pleaded, "[M]ay a forfeiture so dread [*sic*] not extend to me, also through my daughters" (Burney, *Camilla*, 733). Camilla repeats his words to indicate she is "dead of hope," since her parent's "prognostics fulfilled. *May the dread forfeiture*, said my dearest Father, *not extend through my daughters*!" (867). She has extended the "forfeiture" to future generations.

38. Pink, "Frances Burney's *Camilla*," 51–68.

39. Gallagher, *Nobody's Story*, 255.

40. Austin, "'All Wove into One,'" 275.

41. Horace Walpole to Mary Berry, quoted in Bloom and Bloom, introduction to Burney, *Camilla*, xx. Unfortunately, her financial fortunes later turned and she was forced to sell the cottage.

Epilogue

1. La Berge, *Scandals and Abstraction*, 23.

2. Seybold and Chihara, "Introduction," 5.

3. Hume, "Of Refinement in the Arts," in *Selected Essays*, 169–70.

4. Robbins, *The Beneficiaries*. In calling on humanists to do more than specialized critique, I do not endorse Rita Felski's critique of critique in *The Limits of Critique*. My intellectual tendency emphasizes relational thinking with judgment and perspective: we need critique but maybe not so much predictable critique as has been published recently; we need specialized literary scholarship but maybe not so much of it, thus freeing up resources of tenured faculty to engage in public service, to lobby on behalf of contract teaching instructors within central university administration, to build a larger cultural consensus than the currently narrow ones that exist among people who think alike. Along with Kathleen Fitzpatrick, my vision includes more "generous thinking." *Generous Thinking*.

5. Many scholars discuss the relation of contemporary capital to narrative. For representative articulations, see Clover, "Autumn of the System"; La Berge, *Scandals and Abstraction*; McClanahan, *Dead Pledges*; Nilges, "Finance Capital and the Time of the Novel"; Shonkwiler, *The Financial Imaginary*.

6. DeLillo, *Cosmopolis*, 77. I was directed to this quote by Mathias Nilges's citation in "Finance Capital and the Time of the Novel," 31.

7. Clover, "Autumn of the System," 34. Clover turns to poetry as the form of contemporary capital. Mathias Nilges provides a version of Clover's observations when he writes, "The temporal and structural episteme of finance capitalism also presents itself as a problem of narrative." Nilges, "Financial Capital and the Time of the Novel," 44.

8. Haiven, "Metaphoric Wealth," 51.

9. Pinker's *Enlightenment Now*, with its statistical claims about how the world is getting better and global poverty is shrinking, provides a good example of how methodologies that measure, aggregate, and quantify can lead to the continued confidence that infinite economic growth is possible while doing little to address social inequality. It is unsurprising that Bill Gates blurbs the book and tweets cheerful graphs illustrating the decrease in global poverty. Giridharadas, in *Winners Take All*, provides a scathing critique of Bill Gates–like solutions to world poverty precisely because their solutions never in-

volve systemic change in which elites relinquish wealth or give up power. On the subject of the overall effects of relational inequality and how inequality rather than fixed wealth is a better indicator of social well-being, see Kolbert, "Feeling Low." Kolbert concludes, "It's not greater wealth but greater equity that will make us all feel richer" (31).

10. "All my relations" is a phrase common to North American Indigenous communities and is used to center all decision making and knowledge practices outside the individual and view them in terms of effects on the full range of one's kinship structure. To whom one is responsible, in this perspective, includes far more than the Western genetic-nuclear family and is made up of one's community as well as the land, animals, and plants that sustain life. Redistributing wealth equitably among all our relations will require, among other social justice initiatives, large reparations to be paid to the ancestors of victims of European imperialism, since white settlers continue to benefit from generational inheritances accumulated by stealing land from Indigenous peoples and by enslaving Africans. For an indigenous critique of capital accumulation and what it will take to repair the damage, see Coulthard, *Red Skin, White Masks.*

11. For a sampling, by no means exhaustive, of such critical reflections on capital time, see Godden, "Language, Labor, and Finance Capital"; Jameson, "The End of Temporality"; Langenohl, "'In the Long Run We Are All Dead'"; and Nealon, "Value/Theory/Crisis."

12. Haiven, *Cultures of Financialization,* 177.

13. O'Neil, in *Weapons of Math Destruction,* describes how credit ratings first deployed computer algorithms in order to avoid the racial biases of bank managers and to let the "numbers speak for themselves"; however, she shows that those algorithms—which use data such as zip codes and purchasing history to stand in for specific individuals—reinscribe racial bias in more hidden forms. Safiya Umoja Noble brilliantly unravels this racial logic in *Algorithms of Oppression.*

14. Nilges, "Finance Capital and the Time of the Novel," 33.

15. Shteyngart, *Super Sad True Love Story,* 5.

16. Friend, "Silicon Valley's Quest to Live Forever." The leading company is Calico, whose stated mission is "to harness advanced technologies to increase our understanding of the biology that controls lifespan" (see https://www.calicolabs.com/).

17. See chapter 2, note 1, for a list of contemporary financial fiction.

18. Haiven and Berland, "Introduction," 10.

19. Shonkwiler, *The Financial Imaginary,* xvi.

20. Nilges, "Finance Capital and the Time of the Novel," 39.

21. Dickens, *Bleak House,* 235.

22. Kraus, *Summer of Hate,* 19. Further references to this novel are cited parenthetically in the text.

23. Shonkwiler, *The Financial Imaginary,* xix.

24. Nealon, *Post-postmodernism,* 128.

25. Newfield, "What Is Literary Knowledge of Economy?" Among other, more important claims, Newfield suggests that the value of literary knowledge may inhere in its capacity to unleash economic growth; he points to the growing concern about the "innovation crisis" that economists such as Nobel laureate Edmund S. Phelps have diagnosed (23). According to an increasing number of economic studies, Western neoliberal policies will lead to permanent stagnation of their economies if creativity and the liberal arts are

not valued, see Phelps, "What Is Wrong with the West's Economies?" It would be a harsh but meaningful irony if the liberal arts were saved precisely because of their value in generating economic growth.

26. Neil Irwin, "What 'The Big Short' Gets Right, and Wrong, About the Housing Bubble," *New York Times*, December 22, 2015, sec. "The Upshot."

27. Quoted in Capeloa Gil and Gonçalves da Silva, "Introduction," 9.

BIBLIOGRAPHY

Primary Texts

An Address to the Twelve Judges of England, in Behalf of Insolvent Debtors; Whether in Actual Confinement, Or, in Danger of Arrest. To Which Is Added, an Invitation to the Body of Insolvent Debtors, and a Hint to Gentlemen Eminent in the Law. London, 1770.

Bevan, Richard. *Observations on the Law of Arrest and Imprisonment for Debt: Together with a Short Sketch of a Plan for an Amendment of That Law.* London, 1781.

Blackstone, William, Sir. *Commentaries on the laws of England; In Four Books.* Oxford: 1787.

Boswell, James. *Life of Johnson.* Edited by R. W. Chapman. Oxford: Oxford World Classics, 2008.

Brooke, Frances. *The History of Emily Montague.* Edited by Mary Jane Edwards. Ottawa: Carleton University Press, 1985.

———. *Lady Julia Mandeville.* London, 1763.

Brooke, Henry. *The Fool of Quality; Or, the History of Henry Earl of Moreland.* 4 volumes. London, 1766–69.

Burges, James Bland. *Considerations on the Law of Insolvency: With a Proposal for a Reform.* London, 1783.

Burney, Frances. *Camilla; Or, A Picture of Youth.* Edited with an introduction by Edward Bloom and Lillian Bloom. Oxford: Oxford University Press, 1983.

———. *Cecilia; Or, Memoirs of an Heiress.* Edited by Peter Sabor and Margaret Anne Doody. Oxford: Oxford University Press, 1988.

———. *Diary and Letters of Madame D'Arblay.* Edited by Charlotte Barrett. 4 volumes. London: H. Colburn, 1842–46.

———. *Evelina; Or, the History of a Young's Lady's Entrance into the World.* Edited by Edward A. Bloom. Oxford: Oxford University Press, 2002.

———. *The Journals and Letters of Fanny Burney (Madame D'Arblay).* Edited by Joyce Hemlow, Curtis D. Cecil, Althea Douglas, Patricia Boutilier, Edward A. Bloom, Lillian D. Bloom, Peter Hughes, Patricia Hawkins, and Warren Derry. 12 volumes. Oxford: Clarendon Press, 1972–84.

———. *The Wanderer.* Edited by Margaret Anne Doody. Oxford: Oxford University Press, 2001.

The Case of the Creditors of Joseph George Pedley. . . . With Reflections, Moral, Legal, and Philosophical. Bristol and London, 1783.

Considerations on the Laws between Debtors and Creditors. London, 1779.

Cooke, Thomas. *The Universal Letter-writer; Or, New Art of Polite Correspondence.* London, 1788.

Cross, John Cartwright. *The Insolvent Debtor: A Simple Pathetic Tale, Founded on Facts.* Salisbury, UK, 1793.

The Debtor and Creditor's Assistant; Or, a Key to the King's Bench and Fleet Prisons. London, 1793.

Defoe, Daniel. *The Complete English Tradesman.* Volume 1 (1726). In *The Religious and Didactic Writings of Daniel Defoe.* Volume 7. London: Pickering & Chatto, 2006.

———. *A Plan of the English Commerce.* London, 1728.

———. *Roxana, the Fortunate Mistress.* Edited by John Mullan. Oxford: Oxford University Press, 1998.

Delamayne, Thomas. *The Rise and Practice of Imprisonment in Personal Actions Examined . . . in Aid Both of Debtor and Creditor.* London, 1772.

Dickens, Charles. *Bleak House.* Edited by Stephen Gill. Oxford: Oxford University Press, 1996.

———. *Little Dorrit.* Edited by Harvey Peter Sucksmith. Oxford: Oxford University Press, 2012.

Dodd, William. *A Prisoner Released: Sermon Preached . . . for the Benefit of Unfortunate Persons Confined for Small Debts.* London, 1772.

Dornford, Josiah. *Seven Letters to the Lords and Commons of Great Britain, upon the Impolicy, Inhumanity, and Injustice, of Our Present Mode of Arresting the Bodies of Debtors.* London, 1786.

Farley, Edward. *Imprisonment for Debt Unconstitutional and Oppressive, Proved from the Fundamental Principles of the British Constitution, and the Rights of Nature.* London, 1788.

Fielding, Henry. *Amelia.* Edited by David Blewett. London: Penguin Books, 1987.

———. *The Champion: Containing a Series of Papers, Humourous, Moral, Political, and Critical.* 2 volumes. London, 1741.

Fielding, Sarah. *The Adventures of David Simple and Volume the Last.* Edited by Peter Sabor. Lexington: University Press of Kentucky, 1998.

———. *The History of the Countess of Dellwyn.* London: Printed for A. Millar, 1759.

Francklin, Thomas. *A Sermon Preached at the Chapel in Great Queen Street, Lincoln's-Inn-Fields, On Sunday March 20, 1774, For the Benefit of Unfortunate Persons Confined for Small Debts.* London, 1774.

Goldsmith, Oliver. *Collected Works of Oliver Goldsmith.* Edited by Arthur Friedman. 5 volumes. Oxford: Clarendon Press, 1966.

———. *The Vicar of Wakefield.* Edited by Arthur Friedman. Oxford: Oxford University Press, 2006.

Grant, A. *The Public Monitor; Or, A Plan for the More Speedy Recovery of Small Debts.* London, 1789.

Halifax, James. *A Sermon Preached at the Parish Church of St. Paul . . . May 18, 1775, for the Benefit of Unfortunate Persons Confined for Small Debts.* London, 1775.

———. *Sermon Preached for the Benefit of the Society.* London, 1775.

Haywood, Eliza. *Anti-Pamela.* In *Anti-Pamela and Shamela*, edited by Catherine Ingrassia. 51–228. Peterborough, Ontario: Broadview Press, 2004.

The History of a Reprobate: Being the Life of David Doubtful. London, 1784.

Howard, John. *State of the Prisons in England and Wales with Preliminary Observations, and an Account of Some Foreign Prisons.* London, 1777.

A Humble Address to a Member of Parliament, from the Confined Debtors in the King's Bench. London, 1753.

Hume, David. *Selected Essays*. Edited by Stephen Copley and Andrew Edgar. Oxford: Oxford University Press, 1998.

An Inquiry into the Practice of Imprisonment for Debt, and a Refutation of Mr. James Stephen's Doctrine, To Which Is Added, a Hint for Relief of Both Creditor and Debtor. London, 1773.

Johnson, Samuel. "Imprisonment for Debt," *Idler* #22, Saturday, September 16, 1758. In *The Idler, With Additional Essays*. Volume 1 of 2, pp. 74–77. London, 1800.

Lennox, Charlotte. *Sophia*. Edited by Norbert Schürer. Peterborough, Ontario: Broadview Press, 2008.

Mackenzie, Henry. *Julia de Roubigné*. Edited by Susan Manning. East Linton, UK: Tuckwell Press, 1999.

———. *The Man of Feeling*. Edited by Maureen Harkin. Peterborough, Ontario: Broadview Press, 2005.

Neild, James. *Account of Persons Confined for Debt in the Various Parts of England and Wales*. London, 1800, 1818.

———. *Account of the Rise, Progress, and Present State of the Society for the Discharge and Relief of Persons Imprisoned for Small Debts*. London, 1774, 1783.

———. *The State of the Prisons in England, Scotland and Wales*. London, 1812.

New, Candid, and Practical Thoughts on the Law of Imprisonment for Debt, . . . By a Country Attorney. London, 1788.

Oglethorpe, James. *A Report from the Committee Appointed to Enquire into the State of the Goals of England: Relating to the Fleet Prison. With the Resolutions and Orders of the House of Commons Thereupon*. Dublin, 1729.

Philalethes. *Observations on Debtors, and Imprisonment for Debt*. London, 1740.

Richardson, Samuel. *The History of Charles Grandison*. Edited with an introduction by Jocelyn Harris. Oxford: Oxford University Press, 1972.

———. *Pamela: Or, Virtue Rewarded*. 6th edition. 4 volumes. London, 1742.

Scott, Sarah. *A Description of Millenium Hall*. Edited by Gary Kelly. Peterborough, Ontario: Broadview Press, 1995.

———. *The History of Sir George Ellison*. Edited by Betty Rizzo. Lexington: University Press of Kentucky, 1996.

Seasonable Advice, to the Members of the British Parliament, Concerning Conciliatory Measures with America; and an Act of Perpetual Insolvency, for Relief of Debtors. London, 1775.

Sheridan, Frances. *Memoirs of Miss Sidney Bidulph*. Edited by Patricia Köster and Jean Coates Cleary. Oxford: Oxford University Press, 1995.

Smith, Adam. *An Inquiry into the Nature and Causes of the Wealth of Nations*. General Editors, R. H. Campbell and A. S. Skinner. Textual Editor, W. B. Todd. Oxford: Clarendon Press, 1976.

———. *The Theory of Moral Sentiments*. Edited by Knud Haakonssen. Cambridge: Cambridge University Press, 2002.

Smith, William. *Mild Punishments Sound Policy; Or, Observations on the Laws relative to Debtors and Felons, with an Account of the Frauds practiced by Swindlers, Sharpers, and others; Also Some Clauses Necessary in Any Future Insolvent Act; and a Plan for the Relief of Poor Distressed Families and Others*. London, 1778.

Smollett, Tobias. *The Adventures of Ferdinand Count Fathom*. London, 1753.

———. *The Adventures of Peregrine Pickle*. London, 1751.

"Society of Guardians for the Protection of Trade, Against Swindlers and Sharpers." In *Rules and Orders by the Society of Guardians for the Protection of Trade Against Swindlers and Sharpers*. London, 1816.

Stephen, James. *An Address to the Twelve Judges of England, in Behalf of Insolvent Debtors; Whether in Actual Confinement, Or, in Danger of Arrest, To Which Is Added, an Invitation to the Body of Insolvent Debtors, and a Hint to Gentlemen Eminent in the Law*. London, 1770.

———. *Considerations on Imprisonment for Debt Fully Proving, That the Confining of the Bodies of Debtors Is Contrary to Common Law, Magna Charta, Statute-Law, Justice, Humanity, and Policy; . . . With an Account of the Various Applications to the King and Judges by the Prisoners of the King's Bench, for Obtaining Redress; and Some Remarkable Cases of Prisoners Now Confined There*. London, 1770.

———. Preface to *A King's Bench Sermon, With a Dedication to Lord Mansfield, To Which Is Added a Preface by Mr. Stephen*. London, 1770.

Stephen, James, Jr. *The Memoir of James Stephen, Written by Himself for the Use of His Children*. London: Hogarth Press, 1954.

The Swindler Detected; Or, Necessary Cautions to the Public. London, 1781.

Translator's preface. In *Imprisonment for Debt Considered, With Respect to the Bad Policy, Inhumanity, and Evil Tendency of That Practice*. Translated from the Italian. London, 1772.

Secondary Texts

Aitken, Rob. "Everyday Debt Relationalities." *Cultural Studies* 29, no. 5–6 (September 2015): 845–68.

———. *Fringe Finance: Crossing and Contesting the Borders of Global Capital*. London: Routledge, 2015.

Akerlof, George A., and Robert Shiller. *Animal Spirits: How Human Psychology Drives the Economy, and Why It Matters for Global Capitalism*. Princeton, NJ: Princeton University Press, 2010.

Albritton, Robert. "Stages of Capitalist Development." *Studies in Political Economy: A Socialist Review* 19 (1986): 113–40.

Anderson, B. L. "Money and the Structure of Credit in the Eighteenth Century." *Business History* 12, no. 2 (July 1970): 85–101.

Anderson, Margaret. "Stoic Constructions of Virtue in *The Vicar of Wakefield*." *Journal of the History of Ideas* 69, no. 3 (2008): 419–39.

Andrew, Donna. *Philanthropy and the Police: London Charity in the Eighteenth Century*. Princeton, NJ: Princeton University Press, 1989.

Andriopoulos, Stephan. "The Invisible Hand: Supernatural Agency in Political Economy and the Gothic Novel." *ELH: English Literary History* 66, no. 4 (1999): 739–58.

Appadurai, Arjun. *Banking on Words: The Failure of Language in the Age of Derivative Finance*. Chicago: University of Chicago Press, 2016.

Appleby, Joyce. *The Relentless Revolution: A History of Capitalism*. New York: W. W. Norton, 2010.

Arrighi, Giovanni. *The Long Twentieth Century: Money, Power, and the Origins of Our Times.* London: Verso, 2010.

Ashton, T. S. *An Economic History of England: The Eighteenth Century.* London: Methuen, 1955. Reprinted, London: Routledge, 2006.

Atwood, Margaret. *The Heart Goes Last.* New York: Penguin Random House, 2015.

Austin, Sarah K. "'All Wove into One': *Camilla*, the Prose Epic, and Family Values." *Studies in Eighteenth-Century Culture* 29 (2000): 273–98.

Bakhtin, Mikhail Mikhaĭlovich. "Epic and Novel." In *The Dialogic Imagination: Four Essays,* edited and translated by Michael Holquist, 3–40. Austin: University of Texas Press, 1981.

———. "Forms of Time and of the Chronotope in the Novel." In *The Dialogic Imagination: Four Essays,* edited and translated by Michael Holquist, 84–258. Austin: University of Texas Press, 1981.

Bal, Mieke. *Narratology: Introduction to the Theory of Narrative.* Translated by Christine van Boheemen. 3rd edition. Toronto: University of Toronto Press, 2009.

Bander, Elaine. "Family Matters in Burney's *Camilla*." *Age of Johnson* 22 (2012): 281–97.

Bareis, J. Alexander. "Ethics, the Diachronization of Narratology, and the Margins of Unreliable Narration." In *Narrative Ethics,* edited by Jakob Lothe and Jeremy Hawthorn, 41–55. Amsterdam, Netherlands: Rodopi, 2013.

Barker-Benfield, G. J. *The Culture of Sensibility: Sex and Society in Eighteenth-Century Britain.* Chicago: University of Chicago Press, 1992.

Barthes, Roland. *The Pleasure of the Text.* Translated by Richard Miller. New York: Hill & Wang, 1975.

———. *S/Z: An Essay.* Translated by Richard Miller. New York: Hill & Wang, 1974.

Barty-King, Hugh. *The Worst Poverty: A History of Debt and Debtors.* Bridgend, UK: Sutton Publishing, 1997.

Bataille, Georges. "The Notion of Expenditure." In *Visions of Excess: Selected Writings, 1927–1939,* translated by Allan Stoekl et al., 116–29. Minneapolis: University of Minnesota Press, 1985.

Baucom, Ian. *Specters of the Atlantic: Finance Capital, Slavery, and the Philosophy of History.* Durham, NC: Duke University Press, 2005.

Baucom, Ian, and Mary Poovey. "Financing Enlightenment." In *This Is Enlightenment,* edited by Clifford Siskin and William Warner, 323–56. Chicago: University of Chicago Press, 2010.

Bauman, Zygmunt. *Liquid Modernity.* Cambridge, MA: Blackwell, 2000.

Bell, Quentin. *Virginia Woolf: A Biography.* New York: Harcourt, 1972.

Bellamy, Liz. *Commerce, Morality, and the Eighteenth-Century Novel.* Cambridge: Cambridge University Press, 1998.

Bellhouse, David R. *Life Contingent Contracts and the Emergence of Actuarial Science in Eighteenth-Century England.* Cambridge: Cambridge University Press, 2017.

Bender, John. "Prison Reform and the Sentence of Narration in *The Vicar of Wakefield*." In *Ends of Enlightenment,* 133–53. Stanford: Stanford University Press, 2012.

Benedict, Barbara M. *Framing Feeling: Sentiment and Style in English Prose Fiction, 1745–1800.* New York: AMS Press, 1994.

———. "The Sentimental Virtuoso: Collecting Feeling in Henry Mackenzie's *The Man of Feeling*." *Eighteenth-Century Fiction* 28, no. 3 (2016): 473–99.

Benjamin, Walter. "The Storyteller." In *Illuminations: Essays and Reflections*, edited by Hannah Arendt, 83–110. New York: Schocken Books, 2007.

Bennett, Robert J. *Local Business Voice: The History of Chambers of Commerce in Britain, Ireland, and Revolutionary America, 1760–2011*. Oxford: Oxford University Press, 2011.

Benns, Whitney, and Blake Strode. "Debtors' Prison in 21st-Century America." *The Atlantic*, February 23, 2016.

Berg, Maxine. *Luxury and Pleasure in Eighteenth-Century Britain*. Oxford: Oxford University Press, 2005.

Berg, Maxine, and Elizabeth Eger, eds. *Luxury in the Eighteenth Century: Debates, Desires, and Delectable Goods*. Basingstoke, UK: Palgrave Macmillan, 2007.

Bicks, Caroline. *The History of British Women's Writing*. 8 volumes. Basingstoke, UK: Palgrave Macmillan, 2010.

Binhammer, Katherine. "The Failure of Trade's Empire in *The History of Emily Montague*." *Eighteenth-Century Fiction* 23, no. 2 (January 21, 2011): 295–319.

———. "Narrative Exchange in *David Simple*." *The Eighteenth-Century: Theory and Interpretation* 56, no. 1 (spring 2015): 1–19.

———. "Whore's Love." *Eighteenth-Century Fiction* 20, no. 4 (summer 2008): 507–34.

Black, Jeremy. *Eighteenth-Century Britain, 1688–1783*. 2nd edition. Houndmills, Basingstoke, UK: Palgrave Macmillan, 2008.

Blanton, C. D., Colleen Lye, and Kent Puckett. "Introduction." *Representations* 126, no. 1 (May 2014): 1–8.

Bloom, Lillian D., and Edward A. Bloom. "Fanny Burney's Novels: The Retreat from Wonder." *Novel: A Forum on Fiction* 12, no. 3 (spring 1979): 215–35.

Bourdieu, Pierre. "The Forms of Capital." In *Handbook of Theory of Research for the Sociology of Education*, edited by J. E. Richardson, 241–58. New York: Greenwood Press, 1986.

Bowen, Scarlet. *The Politics of Custom in Eighteenth-Century British Fiction*. New York: Palgrave Macmillan, 2010.

Bradbury, Jill Marie. "The New Science of Economic Man: Prose Literature and Political Economy in Eighteenth-century Britain." PhD dissertation: Brown University, 2003.

Brantlinger, Patrick. *Fictions of State: Culture and Credit in Britain, 1694–1994*. Ithaca, NY: Cornell University Press, 1996.

Braudel, Fernand. *Civilization and Capitalism, 15th–18th Century*, Volume 2: *The Wheels of Commerce*. London: Collins, 1982.

Bremond, Claude. "The Logic of Narrative Possibilities." *New Literary History* 11 (1973): 387–411.

Brewer, Anthony. "The Concept of Growth in Eighteenth-Century Economics." *History of Political Economy* 27, no. 4 (December 1995): 609–38.

Brewer, John. *The Sinews of Power: War, Money, and the English State, 1688–1783*. New York: Alfred A. Knopf, 1989.

Broadberry, Stephen, et al. *British Economic Growth, 1270–1870*. Cambridge: Cambridge University Press, 2015.

Brooks, Christopher K. "Goldsmith's Commercial Vicar: Spectacles and Speculation." *CLA Journal* 41, no. 3 (1998): 319–34.

Brooks, Peter. *Reading for the Plot: Design and Intention in Narrative.* New York: Alfred A. Knopf, 1984. Reprint, Cambridge, MA: Harvard University Press, 1992.

Brown, Marshall. *Preromanticism.* Stanford: Stanford University Press, 1991.

Brown, Vivienne. "Dialogism, the Gaze, and the Emergence of Economic Discourse." *New Literary History* 28, no. 4 (autumn 1997): 697–710.

Brunström, Conrad. "Sex and Shopping with Frances Burney." In *Queer People: Negotiations and Expressions of Homosexuality, 1700–1800*, edited by Chris Mounsey and Caroline Gonda, 86–98. Lewisburg, PA: Bucknell University Press, 2007.

Burgess, Miranda. "Courting Ruin: The Economic Romances of Frances Burney." *Novel: A Forum on Fiction* 28, no. 2 (winter 1995): 131–53.

Carey, Rachel. *Debt.* Los Angeles, Ca: Silver Birch Press, 2013.

Cartwright, Justin. *Other People's Money.* New York: Bloomsbury, 2011.

Castle, Terry. *Masquerade and Civilization: The Carnivalesque in Eighteenth-Century English Culture and Fiction.* Stanford: Stanford University Press, 1986.

Campbell, D. Grant. "Fashionable Suicide: Conspicuous Consumption and the Collapse of Credit in Frances Burney's *Cecilia.*" *Studies in Eighteenth-Century Culture* 20 (1991): 131–45.

Capeloa Gil, Isabel, and Helena Gonçalves da Silva. "Introduction" to *The Cultural Life of Money*, 1–20. Berlin: De Gruyter, 2015.

Carlos, Ann M., Edward Kosack, and Luis Castro Penarrieta. "Bankruptcy Discharge and the Emergence of Debtor Rights in Eighteenth-Century England." May 12, 2015. Available at SSRN, https://papers.ssrn.com/sol3/papers.cfm?abstract_id=2607585.

Chambers, Ross. *Story and Situation: Narrative Seduction and the Power of Fiction.* Minneapolis: University of Minnesota Press, 1984.

Chan, Mary. "The Architectural Subject: Space, Character, and Gender in Four Eighteenth-Century Domestic Novels." PhD dissertation, University of Alberta, 2012.

Cixous, Hélène, and Keith Cohen. "The Character of 'Character.'" *New Literary History* 5, no. 2 (1974): 383–402.

Clery, E. J. *The Feminization Debate in Eighteenth-Century England: Literature, Commerce and Luxury.* New York: Palgrave Macmillan, 2004.

Clover, Joshua. "Autumn of the System: Poetry and Financial Capital." *Journal of Narrative Theory* 41, no. 1 (March 2011): 34–52.

Codr, Dwight. *Raving at Usurers: Anti-finance and the Ethics of Uncertainty in England, 1690–1750.* Charlottesville: University of Virginia Press, 2016.

Cohen, Jay. "The History of Imprisonment for Debt and Its Relation to the Development of Discharge in Bankruptcy." *Journal of Legal History* 3, no. 2 (1982): 153–71.

Cohen, Stanley, and Andrew Scull, eds. *Social Control and the State: Historical and Comparative Essays.* Oxford: Martin Robinson, 1983.

Connor, Rebecca Elisabeth. *Women, Accounting, and Narrative: Keeping Books in Eighteenth-Century England.* London: Routledge, 2004.

Cope, Virginia H. *Property, Education, and Identity in Late Eighteenth-Century Fiction: The Heroine of Disinterest.* Basingstoke, UK: Palgrave Macmillan, 2009.

Copeland, Edward. "Money in the Novels of Fanny Burney." *Studies in the Novel* 8, no. 1 (spring 1976): 24–37.

Coulthard, Glen. *Red Skin, White Masks.* Minneapolis: University of Minnesota Press, 2014.

Crafts, N. F. R. *British Economic Growth during the Industrial Revolution.* Oxford: Oxford University Press, 1985.

———. "English Economic Growth in the Eighteenth Century: A Re-examination of Deane and Cole's Estimates." *Economic History Review* 29, no. 2 (1976): 226–35.

———. "The Industrial Revolution." In *The Economic History of Britain since 1700*, 2nd ed. Volume 1: *1700–1860*, edited by Roderick Floud and Donald McCloskey, 44–59. Cambridge: Cambridge University Press, 1994.

Crafts, N. F. R., and C. K Harley. "Output Growth and the British Industrial Revolution: A Restatement of the Crafts-Harley View." *Economic History Review* 45, no. 4 (1992): 703–30.

Csengei, Ildiko. "'I Will Not Weep': Reading through the Tears of Henry Mackenzie's *Man of Feeling.*" *Modern Language Review* 103, no. 4 (2008): 952–68.

Culler, Jonathan. "Story and Discourse in the Analysis of Narrative." In *The Pursuit of Signs: Semiotics, Literature, Deconstruction*, 188–208. London: Routledge, 2001.

Dannenberg, Hilary. "Plot." In *Routledge Encyclopedia of Narrative Theory*, edited by David Herman, Manfred Jahn, and Marie-Laure Ryan, 435–39. London: Routledge, 2005.

Daunton, Martin. "The Wealth of the Nation." In *Short Oxford History of the British Isles: The Eighteenth Century*, edited by Paul Langford, 141–82. Oxford: Oxford University Press, 2002.

Deane, Phyllis, and W. A. Cole. *British Economic Growth, 1688–1959: Trends and Structure.* 2nd edition. Cambridge: Cambridge University Press, 1967.

DeLillo, Don. *Cosmopolis.* New York: Scribner, 2004.

Denby, David. *Sentimental Narrative and the Social Order in France, 1760–1820.* Cambridge: Cambridge University Press, 1994.

Dee, Jonathan. *The Privileges.* London: Corsair, 2011.

Dickson, P. G. M. *The Financial Revolution in England: A Study in the Development of Public Credit, 1688–1756.* London: St. Martin's Press, 1967.

Dienst, Richard. *The Bonds of Debt.* London: Verso, 2011.

Dike, Edwin B. "Coleridge Marginalia in Henry Brooke's *The Fool of Quality.*" *Huntington Library Bulletin* 2 (1931): 149–63.

Donoghue, Frank. *The Fame Machine: Book Reviewing and Eighteenth-Century Literary Careers.* Stanford: Stanford University Press, 1996.

Doody, Margaret Anne. *Frances Burney: The Life in the Works.* New Brunswick, NJ: Rutgers University Press, 1988.

Duffy, Ian P. H. *Bankruptcy and Insolvency in London during the Industrial Revolution.* New York: Garland, 1985.

———. "English Bankrupts, 1571–1861." *American Journal of Legal History* 24, no. 4 (October 1980): 283–305.

Dufresne, Todd, and Clara Sacchetti, eds. *The Economy as Cultural System: Theory, Capitalism, Crisis.* New York: Bloomsbury, 2013.

Durant, David. "*The Vicar of Wakefield* and the Sentimental Novel." *SEL: Studies in English Literature, 1500–1900* 17, no. 3 (summer 1977): 477–91.

Dykstal, Timothy. "The Story of O: Politics and Pleasure in *The Vicar of Wakefield.*" *ELH: English Literary History* 62, no. 2 (1995): 329–46.

Easton, Fraser. "Cosmopolitical Economy: Exchangeable Value and National Development in Adam and Maria Edgeworth." *Studies in Romanticism* 42, no. 1 (2003): 99–125.

Eggers, David. *The Circle.* New York: Alfred A. Knopf, 2013.

———. *A Hologram for the King.* New York: Vintage Books, 2012.

Ehrenreich, Barbara. *Bait and Switch: The (Futile) Pursuit of the American Dream.* New York: Metropolitan Books, 2005.

Eliot, George. "Essays and Leaves from a Notebook." In *Goldsmith: The Critical Heritage,* edited by G. S. Rousseau, 63–64. London: Routledge & Kegan Paul, 1974.

Ellis, Markman. *The Politics of Sensibility: Race, Gender, and Commerce in the Sentimental Novel.* Cambridge: Cambridge University Press, 1996.

Epstein, Julia. *Iron Pen: Frances Burney and the Politics of Women's Writing.* Madison: University of Wisconsin Press, 1989.

Faulks, Sebastian. *A Week in December.* London: Hutchinson, 2009.

Felski, Rita. *The Limits of Critique.* Chicago: University of Chicago Press, 2015.

Festa, Lynn. *Fiction without Humanity: Person, Animal, Thing in Early Enlightenment Literature and Culture.* Philadelphia: University of Pennsylvania Press, 2019.

Findlay, Ronald, and Kevin H. O'Rourke. *Power and Plenty: Trade, War, and the World Economy in the Second Millennium.* Princeton, NJ: Princeton University Press, 2007.

Finel-Honigman, Irene. *A Cultural History of Finance.* Abingdon, Oxon, UK: Routledge, 2010.

Finn, Margot C. *The Character of Credit: Personal Debt in English Culture, 1740–1914.* Cambridge: Cambridge University Press, 2003.

Fisher, Mark. *Capitalist Realism: Is There No Alternative?* Winchester, UK: Zero Books, 2009.

Fitzpatrick, Kathleen. *Generous Thinking: A Radical Approach to Saving the University.* Baltimore: Johns Hopkins University Press, 2019.

Flint, Christopher. *The Appearance of Print in Eighteenth-Century Fiction.* Cambridge: Cambridge University Press, 2011.

Floud, Roderick, and Donald McCloskey. *The Economic History of Britain since 1700.* Volume 1: *1700–1860.* Second ed. 3 volumes. Cambridge: Cambridge University Press, 1994.

Fludernik, Monika. *Towards a "Natural" Narratology.* London: Routledge, 1996.

Forster, E. M. *Aspects of the Novel and Related Writing.* Edited by Oliver Stallybrass. London: Edward Arnold, 1974.

Frank, Judith. *Common Ground: Eighteenth-Century English Satiric Fiction and the Poor.* Stanford: Stanford University Press, 1997.

Frank, Marcie. "Frances Burney's Theatricality." *ELH: English Literary History* 82, no. 2 (2015): 615–35.

Freedgood, Elaine. "The Novelist and Her Poor." *Novel* 47, no. 2 (2014): 210–23.

Friend, Tad. "Silicon Valley's Quest to Live Forever." *New Yorker,* April 3, 2017.

Frost, Simon. *The Business of the Novel: Economics, Aesthetics, and the Case of* Middlemarch. London: Pickering & Chatto, 2012.

Frye, Northrop. *Anatomy of Criticism: Four Essays.* Princeton, NJ: Princeton University Press, 1957.

Gajarawala, Toral. "The Fictions of Finance." *Dissent* (summer 2015): 7–12.

Gallagher, Catherine. *The Body Economic: Life, Death, and Sensation in Political Economy and the Victorian Novel.* Princeton, NJ: Princeton University Press, 2006.

———. *Nobody's Story: The Vanishing Acts of Women Writers in the Marketplace, 1670–1820.* Berkeley: University of California Press, 1994.

Geisst, Charles R. *Beggar Thy Neighbour: A History of Usury and Debt.* Philadelphia: University of Pennsylvania Press, 2013.

Genette, Gérard. *Narrative Discourse: An Essay in Method.* Translated by Jane E. Lewin. Ithaca, NY: Cornell University Press, 1980.

———. *Narrative Discourse Revisited.* Translated by Jane E. Lewin. Ithaca, NY: Cornell University Press, 1983.

Genovese, Michael. "'A Mixture of Bad in All': The Character of Self-Interest in Sarah Fielding's *David Simple.*" *The Age of Johnson* 22 (2012): 207–31.

Gillmor, Don. *Mount Pleasant.* Toronto: Vintage Canada, 2014.

Giridharadas, Anand. *Winners Take All: The Elite Charade of Changing the World.* New York: Alfred A. Knopf, 2018.

Glaisyer, Natasha. *The Culture of Commerce in England, 1660–1720.* Woodbridge, Suffolk, UK: Boydell & Brewer, 2006.

Godden, Richard. *Fictions of Capital: The American Novel from James to Mailer.* Cambridge: Cambridge University Press, 1990.

———. "Language, Labor, and Finance Capital." *PMLA* 126, no. 2 (2011): 412–21.

Goede, Marieke de. *Virtue, Fortune, and Faith: A Genealogy of Finance.* Minneapolis: University of Minnesota Press, 2005.

Goggin, Joyce. "Learning Finance through Fiction: *Cecilia* and the Perils of Credit." *Finance and Society* 1, no. 1 (2015): 61–74.

Goux, Jean-Joseph. *Symbolic Economies: After Marx and Freud.* Ithaca, NY: Cornell University Press, 1990.

Graeber, David. *Debt: The First 5,000 Years.* Brooklyn: Melville House, 2014.

Greenfield, Susan C. "Money or Mind? *Cecilia*, the Novel, and the Real Madness of Selfhood." *Studies in Eighteenth-Century Culture* 33 (2004): 49–70.

Greenwood, Robin, and David Scharfstein. "The Growth of Finance." *Journal of Economic Perspectives* 27, no. 2 (spring 2013): 3–28.

Greimas, A. J. *Structural Semantics: An Attempt at a Method.* Translated by Daniele McDowell, Ronald Schleifer, and Alan Velie. Lincoln: University of Nebraska Press, 1984.

Gruner, Elisabeth Rose. "The Bullfinch and the Brother: Marriage and Family in Frances Burney's *Camilla.*" *Journal of English and Germanic Philology* 93, no. 1 (January 1994): 18–34.

Haagen, Paul. "Eighteenth-Century English Society and the Debt Law." In *Social Control and the State: Historical and Comparative Essays*, edited by Stanley Cohen and Andrew Scull, 227–47. Oxford: Martin Robertson, 1983.

Haggerty, George E. "Satire and Sentiment in *The Vicar of Wakefield.*" *The Eighteenth Century: Theory and Interpretation* 32, no. 1 (spring 1991): 25–38.

———. *Unnatural Affections: Women and Fiction in the Later 18th Century.* Bloomington: Indiana University Press, 1998.

Haiven, Max. *Cultures of Financialization: Fictitious Capital in Popular Culture and Everyday Life.* Basingstoke, UK: Palgrave Macmillan, 2014.

———. "Metaphoric Wealth: Finance, Financialization, and the End of Narrative." In *The Economy as Cultural System: Theory, Capitalism, Crisis*, edited by Todd Dufresne and Clara Sacchetti, 51–72. New York: Bloomsbury Academic, 2013.

Haiven, Max, and Jody Berland, eds. "The Financialized Imagination." Special issue, *Topia* 30–31 (2013): 7–16.

Harkin, Maureen. "Goldsmith on Authorship in *The Vicar of Wakefield*." *Eighteenth-Century Fiction* 14, no. 3 (2002): 325–44.

———. "Mackenzie's *Man of Feeling*: Embalming Sensibility." *ELH: English Literary History* 61, no. 2 (Summer 1994): 317–40.

Hartlep, Nicholas D., Lucille L. T. Eckrich, and Brandon O. Hensley, eds. *The Neoliberal Agenda and the Student Debt Crisis in U.S. Higher Education*. New York: Routledge, 2017.

Harvey, David. "Class-Monopoly Rent, Finance Capital, and the Urban Revolution." *Regional Studies* 8, no. 3–4 (November 1974): 239–55.

———. *The Limits to Capital*. London: Verso, 2006.

———. *Seventeen Contradictions and the End of Capitalism*. Oxford: Oxford University Press, 2014.

Haslett, Adam. *Union Atlantic*. London: Atlantic Books, 2011.

Haslett, Moyra. "Experimentalism in the Irish Novel, 1750–1770." *Irish University Review* 41, no. 1 (2011): 63–79.

Heinberg, Richard. *The End of Growth: Adapting to Our New Economic Reality*. Gabriola, British Columbia: New Society, 2011.

Heinzelman, Kurt. *The Economics of the Imagination*. Amherst: University of Massachusetts Press, 1980.

Hemlow, Joyce. "Fanny Burney and the Courtesy Books." *PMLA* 65 (1950): 732–61.

———. *The History of Fanny Burney*. Oxford: Clarendon Press, 1958.

Henderson, Andrea. *Romanticism and the Painful Pleasures of Modern Life*. Cambridge: Cambridge University Press, 2007.

Henderson, Willie. *Economics as Literature*. London: Routledge, 1995.

Herrmann, Britta, and Barbara Thums. *Ästhetische Erfindung der Moderne? Perspektiven und Modelle 1750–1850*. Würzburg, Germany: Königshausen & Neumann, 2003.

Hitchcock, Peter. "Accumulating Fictions." In "Financialization and the Culture Industry." Special issue, *Representations* 126, no. 1 (May 2014): 135–60.

Holquist, Michael. *Dialogism: Bakhtin and His World*. London: Routledge, 1990.

Hopkins, Robert H. "Matrimony in *The Vicar of Wakefield* and the Marriage Act of 1753." *Studies in Philology* 74 (1977): 322–39.

———. *The True Genius of Oliver Goldsmith*. Baltimore: Johns Hopkins University Press, 1969.

Hoppit, Julian. "Attitudes to Credit in Britain, 1680–1790." *Historical Journal* 33, no. 2 (June 1990): 305–22.

———. "Financial Crises in Eighteenth-Century England." *Economic History Review* 39, no. 1 (1986): 39–58.

———. *Risk and Failure in English Business, 1700–1800*. 1987. Reprint, Cambridge: Cambridge University Press, 2002.

Hunt, Margaret R. *The Middling Sort: Commerce, Gender, and the Family in England, 1680–1780*. Berkeley: University of California Press, 1996.

Ingrassia, Catherine. *Authorship, Commerce, and Gender in Early Eighteenth-Century England: A Culture of Paper Credit.* Cambridge: Cambridge University Press, 1998.

Innes, Joanna. "The King's Bench Prison in the Later Eighteenth Century: Law, Authority, and Order in a London Debtors' Prison." In *An Ungovernable People: The English and Their Law in the Seventeenth and Eighteenth Centuries*, edited by John Brewer and John Styles, 250–98. New Brunswick, NJ: Rutgers University Press, 1980.

Irwin, Douglas A. *Against the Tide: An Intellectual History of Free Trade.* Princeton, NJ: Princeton University Press, 1996.

Jack, Malcolm. *Corruption and Progress: The Eighteenth-Century Debate.* New York: AMS Press, 1989.

Jackson, Tim. *Prosperity without Growth: Foundations for the Economy of Tomorrow.* 2nd edition. London: Routledge, 2017.

Jameson, Fredric. "Culture and Finance Capital." *Critical Inquiry* 24, no. 1 (1997): 246–65.

———. "The End of Temporality." *Critical Inquiry* 29, no. 4 (2003): 695–718.

———. "Future City." *New Left Review* 2, no. 21 (2003): 65–79.

———. *The Political Unconscious: Narrative as a Socially Symbolic Act.* Ithaca, NY: Cornell University Press, 1981.

Johnson, Claudia L. *Equivocal Beings: Politics, Gender, and Sentimentality in the 1790s.* Chicago: University of Chicago Press, 1995.

Jones, Eric Lionel. *The European Miracle: Environments, Economies, and Geopolitics in the History of Europe and Asia.* 3rd edition. Cambridge: Cambridge University Press, 2003.

Jordan, Nicolle. "A Creole Contagion: Narratives of Slavery and Tainted Wealth in *Millenium Hall.*" *Tulsa Studies in Women's Literature* 30, no. 1 (spring 2011): 57–70.

Justice, George. *The Manufacturers of Literature: Writing and the Literary Marketplace in Eighteenth-Century England.* Newark: University of Delaware Press, 2002.

Kaufmann, David. *The Business of Common Life: Novels and Classical Economics between Revolution and Reform.* Baltimore: Johns Hopkins University Press, 1995.

Keohane, Catherine L. "'Too neat for a beggar': Charity and Debt in Burney's *Cecilia.*" *Studies in the Novel* 33, no. 4 (winter 2001): 379–401.

———. "The 'Web of Gratitude': Women, Charity, and Debt in Eighteenth-Century English Literature." PhD dissertation, Rutgers University, 2001.

Kermode, Frank. *The Sense of an Ending: Studies in the Theory of Fiction.* Oxford: Oxford University Press, 1967.

Kim, James. "Goldsmith's Manhood: Hegemonic Masculinity and Sentimental Irony in *The Vicar of Wakefield.*" *Eighteenth Century: Theory and Interpretation* 59, no. 1 (September 2018): 21–44.

———. "Mourning, Melancholia, and Modernity: Sentimental Irony and Downward Mobility in *David Simple.*" *Eighteenth Century Fiction* 22, no. 3 (May 2010): 477–502.

Klamer, Arjo, Donald McCloskey, and Robert Solow, eds. *The Consequences of Economic Rhetoric.* Cambridge: Cambridge University Press, 1988.

Klaver, Claudia. *A/Moral Economics: Classical Political Economy and Cultural Authority in Nineteenth-Century England.* Columbus: Ohio University Press, 2003.

Klekar, Cynthia. "'Her Gift Was Compelled': Gender and the Failure of the 'Gift' in *Cecilia.*" *Eighteenth-Century Fiction* 18, no. 1 (fall 2005): 107–26.

Kolbert, Elizabeth. "Feeling Low: The Psychology of Inequality." *New Yorker*, January 15, 2018. 28–31.

Kornbluh, Anna. *Realizing Capital: Financial and Psychic Economies in Victorian Form.* New York: Fordham University Press, 2014.

Kraus, Chris. *Summer of Hate.* Cambridge, MA: Semiotext(e), 2012.

La Berge, Leigh Claire. *Scandals and Abstraction: Financial Fiction of the Long 1980s.* New York: Oxford University Press, 2014.

Lanchester, John. "After the Fall: Ten Years after the Crash." *London Review of Books* 50, no. 13 (July 5, 2018): 3–8.

———. *Capital.* London: Faber & Faber, 2012.

Landry, Donna. "Picturing Benevolence against the Commercial Cry, 1750–98; or, Sarah Fielding and the Secret Causes of Romanticism." In *The History of British Women's Writing, 1750–1830*, edited by Jacqueline M. Labbe, 150–71. Houndmills, Basingstoke, UK: Palgrave Macmillan, 2010.

Langenohl, Andreas. "'In the Long Run We Are All Dead': Imaginary Time in Financial Market Narratives." *Cultural Critique* 70 (fall 2008): 3–31.

Langley, Paul. *The Everyday Life of Global Finance: Saving and Borrowing in Anglo-America.* Oxford: Oxford University Press, 2008.

Lanser, Susan. *Fictions of Authority: Women Writers and Narrative Voice.* Ithaca, NY: Cornell University Press, 1992.

———. "Toward a Feminist Narratology." In *Feminisms: An Anthology of Literary Theory and Criticism*, edited by Robyn R. Warhol and Diane Price Herndl, 674–93. New Brunswick, NJ: Rutgers University Press, 1997.

Lapavitsas, Costas. *Profiting without Producing: How Finance Exploits Us All.* London: Verso, 2013.

Lawson, Andrew. *Downwardly Mobile: The Changing Fortunes of American Realism.* New York: Oxford University Press, 2012.

Lazzarato, Maurizio. *The Making of the Indebted Man: An Essay on the Neoliberal Condition.* Los Angeles, CA: Semiotext(e), 2012.

Lepore, Jill. "I.O.U.: How We Used to Treat Debtors." *New Yorker* 85, no. 9 (April 13, 2009): 34–41.

Levenson, Michael. "Reading Time." *Novel: A Forum on Fiction* 42, no. 3 (fall 2009): 511–16.

Levine, George Lewis, ed. *Aesthetics and Ideology.* New Brunswick, NJ: Rutgers University Press, 1994.

Lewis, Michael. *The Big Short: Inside the Doomsday Machine.* New York: W. W. Norton, 2011.

Lilley, James D. "Henry Mackenzie's Ruined Feelings: Romance, Race, and the Afterlife of Sentimental Exchange." *New Literary History* 38, no. 4 (fall 2007): 649–66.

Lindert, Peter H. "Unequal Living Standards." In *The Economic History of Britain since 1700.* 2nd edition. Volume 1, *1700–1860*, edited by Roderick Floud and Donald McCloskey, 357–86. Cambridge: Cambridge University Press, 1994.

Lineham, Peter. "The Campaign to Abolish Imprisonment for Debt in England, 1750–1840." Master's thesis, University of Canterbury, 1974.

Lipsyte, Sam. *The Ask.* New York: Farrar, Straus & Giroux, 2011.

LiPuma, Edward, and Benjamin Lee. *Financial Derivatives and the Globalization of Risk.* Durham, NC: Duke University Press, 2004.

London, April. "Historiography, Pastoral, Novel: Genre in *The Man of Feeling.*" *Eighteenth-Century Fiction* 10, no. 1 (1997): 43–62.

Lukács, György. *The Theory of the Novel: A Historico-Philosophical Essay on the Forms of Great Epic Literature.* Cambridge, MA: MIT Press, 1971.

Lynch, Deidre. *The Economy of Character: Novels, Market Culture, and the Business of Inner Meaning.* Chicago: University of Chicago Press, 1998.

MacKenzie, Scott R. *Be It Ever So Humble: Poverty, Fiction, and the Invention of the Middle-Class Home.* Charlottesville: University of Virginia Press, 2013.

Maifreda, Germano. *From Oikonomia to Political Economy: Constructing Economic Knowledge from the Renaissance to the Scientific Revolution.* Burlington, VT: Ashgate, 2012.

Mandel, Emily St. John. *Station Eleven.* New York: Alfred A. Knopf, 2015.

Mangano, Bryan. *Fictions of Friendship in the Eighteenth-Century Novel.* Cham, Switzerland: Palgrave Macmillan, 2017.

Mann, Bruce. *Republic of Debtors: Bankruptcy in the Age of American Independence.* Cambridge, MA: Harvard University Press, 2002.

Marazzi, Christian. *The Violence of Financial Capitalism.* Translated by Kristina Lebedeva. New York: Semiotext(e), 2010.

Markley, Robert. "Recent Studies in Restoration and Eighteenth-Century Literature." *Studies in English Literature, 1500–1900* 37, no. 3 (summer 1997): 637–72.

———. "Sentimentality as Performance: Shaftesbury, Sterne, and the Theatrics of Virtue." In *The New Eighteenth Century: Theory, Politics, English Literature*, edited by Felicity Nussbaum and Laura Brown, 210–30. New York: Methuen, 1987.

Marriner, Sheila. "English Bankruptcy Records and Statistics before 1850." *Economic History Review* 33, no. 3 (August 1980): 351–66.

Marsh, Nicky. "'Paradise Falls: A Land Lost in Time': Representing Credit, Debt, and Work after the Crisis." *Textual Practice* 28, no. 7 (November 2014): 1181–98.

Martin, Randy. *Financialization of Daily Life.* Philadelphia: Temple University Press, 2002.

Marx, Karl. *Capital: A Critique of Political Economy.* Edited by Friedrich Engels. Translated by Samuel Moore and Edward Aveling. 3 volumes. New York: Vintage Books, 1977.

Marx, Karl, and Friedrich Engels. *The Communist Manifesto.* Edited by David Harvey and Samuel Moore. London: Pluto Press, 2008.

Mathias, Peter. "Risk, Credit, and Kinship in Early Modern Enterprise." In *The Early Modern Atlantic Economy*, Edited by J. J. McCusker and K. Morgan, 15–33. Cambridge: Cambridge University Press, 2000.

Matz, Jesse. "The Art of Time, Theory to Practice." *Narrative* 19, no. 3 (October 21, 2011): 273–94.

Mbue, Imbolo. *Behold the Dreamers.* New York: Random House, 2017.

McClanahan, Annie. "Bad Credit: The Character of Credit Scoring." *Representations* 126, no. 1 (May 1, 2014): 31–57.

———. *Dead Pledges: Debt, Crisis, and Twenty-First-Century Culture.* Stanford: Stanford University Press, 2017.

McCloskey, Deirdre N. "Storytelling in Economics." In *Narrative in Culture*, edited by Cristopher Nash, 5–22. London: Routledge, 1990.

McCrea, Brian. *Frances Burney and Narrative Prior to Ideology*. Newark: University of Delaware Press, 2013.

McInerney, Jay. *Bright, Precious Days*. New York: Vintage Books, 2017.

McKee, Yates. "Debt: Occupy, Postcontemporary Art, and the Aesthetics of Debt Resistance." *South Atlantic Quarterly* 112, no. 4 (October 2013): 784–803.

McKendrick, Neil, John Brewer, and J. H. Plumb. *The Birth of Consumer Society: The Commercialization of Eighteenth-Century England*. London: Europa, 1982.

McKeon, Michael. *The Origins of the English Novel, 1600–1740*. Baltimore: Johns Hopkins University Press, 1987.

McPhee, Martha. *Dear Money*. Boston: Houghton Mifflin Harcourt, 2010.

McVeagh, John. *Tradefull Merchants: The Portrayal of the Capitalist in Literature*. London: Routledge and Kegan Paul, 1981.

Miller, D. A. *Narrative and Its Discontents: Problems of Closure in the Traditional Novel*. Princeton, NJ: Princeton University Press, 1981.

Mokyr, Joel. *A Culture of Growth: The Origins of the Modern Economy*. Princeton, NJ: Princeton University Press, 2017.

Molesworth, Jesse. *Chance and the Eighteenth-Century Novel: Realism, Probability, Magic*. Cambridge: Cambridge University Press, 2010.

Montes, Leonidas. "Das Adam Smith Problem: Its Origins, the Stages of the Current Debate, and One Implication for Our Understanding of Sympathy." *Journal of the History of Economic Thought* 25, no. 1 (March 2003): 63–90.

Morgan, Kenneth. "Mercantilism and the British Empire, 1688–1815." In *The Political Economy of British Historical Experience, 1688–1914*, edited by Donald Winch and Patrick K. O'Brien, 165–92. Oxford: Oxford University Press, 2002.

Mountford, Peter. *A Young Man's Guide to Late Capitalism*. Boston: Mariner Books, 2011.

Muldrew, Craig. *The Economy of Obligation: The Culture of Credit and Social Relations in Early Modern England*. New York: St. Martin's Press, 1998.

Nash, Christopher, ed. *Narrative in Culture: The Uses of Storytelling in the Sciences, Philosophy, and Literature*. London: Routledge, 1990.

Neal, Larry. *The Rise of Financial Capitalism: International Capital Markets in the Age of Reason*. Cambridge: Cambridge University Press, 1993.

Nealon, Christopher. "Value/Theory/Crisis." *PMLA* 127, no. 1 (January 2012): 101–6.

Nealon, Jeffrey T. *Post-postmodernism; Or, The Cultural Logic of Just-in-Time Capitalism*. Stanford: Stanford University Press, 2012.

Nechtman, Tillman W. "A Jewel in the Crown? Indian Wealth in Domestic Britain in the Late Eighteenth Century." *Eighteenth-Century Studies* 41, no. 1 (2007): 71–86.

Nelles, William. *Frameworks: Narrative Levels and Embedded Narrative*. New York: Peter Lang, 1997.

Newfield, Christopher. "What Is Literary Knowledge of Economy?" In *The Routledge Companion to Literature and Economics*, edited by Matt Seybold and Michelle Chihara, 15–26. London: Routledge, 2018.

Newman, Katherine S. *Falling from Grace: Downward Mobility in the Age of Affluence*. Berkeley: University of California Press, 1999.

Nichols, John. *Illustrations of the Literary History of the Eighteenth Century*. Volume 2. London, 1817.
Nicholson, Colin. *Writing and the Rise of Finance: Capital Satires of the Early Eighteenth Century*. Cambridge: Cambridge University Press, 1994.
Nilges, Mathias. "Finance Capital and the Time of the Novel; or, Money without Narrative Qualities." *Topia* 30–31 (2013–14): 31–46.
Noble, Safiya Umoja. *Algorithms of Oppression: How Search Engines Reinforce Racism*. New York: New York University Press, 2018.
Nünning, Vera. "Unreliable Narration and the Historical Variability of Values and Norms: *The Vicar of Wakefield* as a Test Case of a Cultural-Historical Narratology." *Style* 38, no. 2 (summer 2004): 236–52.
Nussbaum, Felicity, and Laura Brown, eds. *The New Eighteenth Century: Theory, Politics, English Literature*. New York: Methuen, 1987.
Oakleaf, David. "At the Margins of Utopia: Jamaica in Sarah Scott's *Millenium Hall*." *Eighteenth-Century Fiction* 28, no. 1 (fall 2015): 109–37.
O'Brien, John. *Literature Incorporated: The Cultural Unconscious of the Business Corporation, 1650–1850*. Chicago: University of Chicago Press, 2016.
Olegario, Rowena. *A Culture of Credit: Embedding Trust and Transparency in American Business*. Cambridge, MA: Harvard University Press, 2006.
O'Neil, Cathy. *Weapons of Math Destruction: How Big Data Increases Inequality and Threatens Democracy*. New York: Crown, 2016.
O'Neill, Patrick. *Fictions of Discourse: Reading Narrative Theory*. Toronto: University of Toronto Press, 1994.
Osteen, Mark, and Martha Woodmansee, eds. *The New Economic Criticism: Studies at the Interface of Literature and Economics*. London: Routledge, 2005.
Palmeri, Frank. *Stages of Society: Enlightenment Conjectural History and Modern Social Discourse*. New York: Columbia University Press, 2016.
Parisian, Catherine M. *Frances Burney's* Cecilia*: A Publishing History*. Farnham, Surrey, UK: Ashgate, 2012.
Parrinder, Patrick. "Highway Robbery and Property Circulation in Eighteenth-Century English Narratives." *Eighteenth-Century Fiction* 13, no. 4 (July 2001): 509–28.
Paul, Helen J. *The South Sea Bubble: An Economic History of Its Origins and Consequences*. London: Routledge, 2011.
Paulson, Ronald. *Satire and the Novel in Eighteenth-Century England*. New Haven: Yale University Press, 1967.
Paxson, James J. "Revisiting the Deconstruction of Narratology: Master Tropes of Narrative Embedding and Symmetry." *Style* 35, no. 1 (spring 2001): 126–50.
Peace, Mary V. "The 'Adam Smith Problem' and the Retreat of Sentimental Virtue from the World." In *Political Economy, Literature & the Formation of Knowledge, 1720–1850*, edited by Richard Adelmanand and Catherine Packham, 159–82. New York: Routledge, 2018.
———. *Changing Sentiments and the Magdalen Hospital: Luxury, Virtue, and the Senses in Eighteenth-Century Culture*. London: Routledge, 2017.
———. "'Epicures in Rural Pleasures': Revolution, Desire, and Sentimental Economy in Sarah Scott's *Millenium Hall*." *Women's Writing* 9, no. 2 (2002): 305–16.
———. "Sentimentality in the Service of Methodism: John Wesley's Abridgment of

Henry Brooke's *The Fool of Quality* (1765–1770)." *Religion in the Age of Enlightenment* 5 (2015): 277–308.

Pearson, Robin. *Insuring the Industrial Revolution: Fire Insurance in Great Britain, 1700–1850*. Aldershot, UK: Ashgate, 2004.

Perry, Ruth. "Home Economics: Representations of Poverty in Eighteenth-Century Fiction." In *A Companion to the Eighteenth-Century English Novel and Culture*, edited by Paula R. Backscheider and Catherine Ingrassia, 441–58. Malden, MA: Blackwell, 2005.

———. *Novel Relations: The Transformation of Kinship in English Literature and Culture, 1748–1818*. Cambridge: Cambridge University Press, 2004.

Phelan, James. "Functions of Character." In *Narrative/Theory*, edited by David H. Richter, 109–22. White Plains, NY: Longman, 1996.

———. "Narrative Progression." In *Narrative Dynamics: Essays on Time, Plot, Closure, and Frames*, edited by Brian Richardson, 211–16. Columbus: Ohio State University Press, 2002.

Phelps, Edmund S. "What Is Wrong with the West's Economies?" *New York Review of Books* 16, no. 13 (August 13, 2015).

Pier, John. "Narrative Levels (revised version; uploaded 23 April 2014)." In *The Living Handbook of Narratology*. Edited by Peter Hühn et al. Hamburg: Hamburg University Press. Accessed August 3, 2019. http://www.lhn.uni-hamburg.de/article/narrative-levels-revised-version-uploaded-23-april-2014.

Piketty, Thomas. *Capital in the Twenty-First Century*. Translated by Arthur Goldhammer. Cambridge, MA: Harvard University Press, 2014.

Pink, Emma. "Frances Burney's *Camilla*: 'To Print My Grand Work . . . by Subscription.'" *Eighteenth-Century Studies* 40, no. 1 (fall 2006): 51–68.

Pinker, Steven. *Enlightenment Now: The Case for Reason, Science, Humanism, and Progress*. New York: Viking, 2018.

Pitofsky, Alex. "The Warden's Court Martial: James Oglethorpe and the Politics of Eighteenth-Century Prison Reform." *Eighteenth-Century Life* 24, no. 1 (winter 2000): 88–102.

Plumb, John Harold. *Georgian Delights*. London: Weidenfeld & Nicolson, 1980.

Pocock, J. G. A. *Virtue, Commerce, and History: Essays on Political Thought and History, Chiefly in the Eighteenth Century*. Cambridge: Cambridge University Press, 1985.

Polanyi, Karl. *The Great Transformation*. Boston: Beacon Press, 1957.

Pomeranz, Kenneth. *The Great Divergence: China, Europe, and the Making of the Modern World Economy*. Princeton, NJ: Princeton University Press, 2000.

Poovey, Mary. "Aesthetics and Political Economy in the Eighteenth Century." In *Aesthetics and Ideology*, edited by George Levine, 79–105. New Brunswick, NJ: Rutgers University Press, 1994.

———. "Demonizing Debt, Naturalizing Finance." *Debt: Ethics, the Environment, and the Economy*, edited by Peter Y. Paik and Merry Wiesner-Hanks, 39–55. Bloomington: Indiana University Press, 2013.

———. *Genres of the Credit Economy: Mediating Value in Eighteenth- and Nineteenth-Century Britain*. Chicago: University of Chicago Press, 2008.

Propp, Vladimir. *Morphology of the Folktale*. Translated by Laurence Scott. Revised by Louis A. Wagner. Austin: University of Texas Press, 1968.

Purdy, Anthony, ed. *Literature and Money*. Amsterdam: Rodopi, 1993.
Quintana, Ricardo. *Oliver Goldsmith: A Georgian Study*. New York: Macmillan, 1967.
Rahman, Zia Haider. *In the Light of What We Know: A Novel*. New York: Picador, 2015.
Raworth, Kate. *Doughnut Economics: Seven Ways to Think Like a 21st-Century Economist*. White River Junction, VT: Chelsea Green, 2017.
Reising, Russel. *Loose Ends: Closure and Crisis in the American Social Text*. Durham, NC: Duke University Press, 1997.
Ricoeur, Paul. "Narrative Time." *Critical Inquiry* 7, no. 1 (1980): 169–90.
Richardson, Brian. "Beyond the Poetics of Plot: Alternative Forms of Narrative Progression and the Multiple Trajectories of *Ulysses*." In *A Companion to Narrative Theory*, edited by James Phelan and Peter J. Rabinowitz, n.p. (online ed.). Malden, MA: Blackwell, 2005.
Riffaterre, Michael. "Chronotopes in Diegesis." In *Fiction Updated: Theories of Fictionality*, edited by Calin-Andrei Mihailescu and Walid Hamarneh, 244–56. Toronto: University of Toronto Press, 1996.
Rimmon-Kenan, Shlomith. *Narrative Fiction*. 2nd edition. London: Routledge, 2002.
Robbins, Bruce. *The Beneficiary*. Durham, NC: Duke University Press, 2017.
———. *Upward Mobility and the Common Good: Toward a Literary History of the Welfare State*. Princeton, NJ: Princeton University Press, 2007.
Roderick, Floud. *The Economic History of Britain since 1700*. 3 volumes. Cambridge: Cambridge University Press, 1994.
Rosenthal, Laura. *Infamous Commerce: Prostitution in Eighteenth-Century British Literature and Culture*. Ithaca, NY: Cornell University Press, 2006.
Ross, Andrew. *Creditocracy and the Case for Debt Refusal*. New York: OR Books, 2014.
———. "Till Death Do Us Part: The Marriage of Debt and Growth." *South Atlantic Quarterly* 112, no. 4 (fall 2013): 818–23.
Rothschild, Emma. *Economic Sentiments: Adam Smith, Condorcet, and the Enlightenment*. Cambridge, MA: Harvard University Press, 2001.
Roxburgh, Natalie. *Representing Public Credit: Credible Commitment, Fiction, and the Rise of the Financial Subject*. London: Routledge, 2016.
Rubin, Jeff. *The End of Growth*. Toronto: Vintage Canada, 2012.
Rule, John. *The Vital Century: England's Developing Economy, 1714–1815*. London: Longman Group, 1992.
Rumsby, Martin. "An Interview with Chris Kraus." *Bookforum*. Accessed November 15, 2017. http://www.bookforum.com/index.php?pn=video&id=7536&mode=large&page_id=0.
Ryan, Marie-Laure. *Possible Worlds, Artificial Intelligence, and Narrative Theory*. Bloomington: Indiana University Press, 1991.
Schabas, Margaret. "David Hume on Experimental Natural Philosophy, Money, and Fluids." *History of Political Economy* 3 (2001): 411–35.
Schellenberg, Betty A. *The Conversational Circle: Rereading the English Novel, 1740–1775*. Lexington: University Press of Kentucky, 1996.
Scheuermann, Mona. *Social Protest in the Eighteenth-Century English Novel*. Columbus: Ohio State University Press, 1985.
Sewell, William H., Jr. "The Temporalities of Capitalism." *Socio-Economic Review* 6, no. 3 (2008): 517–37.

Seybold, Matt. and Michelle Chihara. "Introduction" to *The Routledge Companion to Literature and Economics*, 1–12. London: Routledge, 2018.

———, eds. *The Routledge Companion to Literature and Economics.* London: Routledge, 2018.

Shapiro, Stephen. *The Culture and Commerce of the Early American Novel: Reading the Atlantic World-System.* University Park: Pennsylvania State University Press, 2008.

———. "Sentimental Economies: The World-System of Eighteenth Century Aesthetics and the Reflexive Body." In *Ästhetische Erfindung der Modern? Perspektiven und Modelle, 1750–1850*, edited by Britta Hermann and Barbara Thums, 231–50. Würzburg, Germany: Verlag Köningshausen & Neumann, 2003.

Sherman, Sandra. *Finance and Fictionality in the Early Eighteenth Century: Accounting for Defoe.* Cambridge: Cambridge University Press, 1996.

———. *Imagining Poverty: Quantification and the Decline of Paternalism.* Columbus: Ohio State University Press, 2001.

Shiller, Robert. "Narrative Economics." Presidential address delivered to the 129th Annual Meeting of the American Economics Association, January 7, 2017. *American Economic Review*, 107, no. 4 (April 2017): 967–1004.Shonkwiler, Alison. *The Financial Imaginary: Economic Mystification and the Limits of Realist Fiction.* Minneapolis: University of Minnesota Press, 2017.

Shonkwiler, Alison, and Leigh Claire La Berge, eds. *Reading Capitalist Realism.* Iowa City: University of Iowa Press, 2014.

Shriver, Lionel. *The Mandibles: A Family, 2029–2047.* London: Borough Press, 2017.

Shryock, Richard. *Tales of Storytelling: Embedded Narrative in Modern French Fiction.* New York: Peter Lang, 1993.

Shteyngart, Gary. *Lake Success.* New York: Random House, 2018.

———. *Super Sad True Love Story.* New York: Random House, 2010.

Siskin, Clifford, and William Warner, eds. *This Is Enlightenment.* Chicago: University of Chicago Press, 2010.

Skinner, Gillian. *Sensibility and Economics in the Novel, 1740–1800: The Price of a Tear.* Houndmills, Basingstoke, Hampshire: Macmillan, 1999.

Sklansky, J. "The Elusive Sovereign: New Intellectual and Social Histories of Capitalism." *Modern Intellectual History* 9, no. 1 (2012): 233–48.

Smith, Chloe Wigston. "The Haberdasher's Plot: The Romance of Small Trade in Frances Burney's Fiction." *Tulsa Studies in Women's Literature* 37, no. 2 (fall 2018): 271–93.

Soederberg, Susanne. *Debtfare States and the Poverty Industry.* New York: Routledge, 2015.

Soni, Vivasvan. *Mourning Happiness: Narrative and the Politics of Modernity.* Ithaca, NY: Cornell University Press, 2010.

Spencer, Jane. *The Rise of the Woman Novelist: From Aphra Behn to Jane Austen.* London: Basil Blackwell, 1986.

Starr, G. A. "Sentimental Novels of the Later Eighteenth Century." In *Columbia History of the British Novel*, edited by John Richetti, 181–98. New York: Columbia University Press, 1994.

Stephen, Leslie. *The Life of Sir James Fitzjames Stephen: A Judge of the High Court of Justice.* London: Smith, Elder & Co., 1895.

Stern, Simon. "Sentimental Frauds." *Law and Social Inquiry: Journal of the American Bar Foundation* 36, no. 1 (2011): 83–113.

Stiglitz, Joseph. "Inequality and Economic Growth." In *Rethinking Capitalism: Economics and Policy for Sustainable and Inclusive Growth*, edited by Michael Jacobs and Mariana Mazzucato, 148–69. West Sussex, UK: John Wiley & Sons, 2016.

Straub, Kristina. *Divided Fictions: Fanny Burney and Feminine Strategy*. Lexington: University Press of Kentucky, 1987.

Streeck, Wolfgang. *How Will Capitalism End? Essays on a Failing System*. London: Verso, 2016.

Sussman, Charlotte. "Memory and Mobility: Fictions of Population in Defoe, Goldsmith, and Scott." In *A Companion to the Eighteenth-Century English Novel and Culture*, edited by Paula Backscheider and Catherine Ingrassia, 191–213. Malden, MA: Blackwell, 2005.

———. *Peopling the World: Representing Human Mobility from Milton to Malthus*. Philadelphia: University of Pennsylvania Press, forthcoming.

Sutherland, Katherine. "Introduction." In Adam Smith, *An Inquiry into the Nature and Causes of the Wealth of Nations*, edited with an introduction and notes by Kathryn Sutherland, ix–xlv. Oxford: Oxford University Press, 1993.

Sweeney, Cynthia D'Aprix. *The Nest*. New York: Ecco, 2016.

Tattam, Henry. *A Short Memoir of the late J. C. Neild . . . of Chelsea, etc*. London: privately printed, 1852.

Thompson, E. P. "The Moral Economy of the English Crowd in the Eighteenth Century." *Past & Present* 50, no. 1 (1971): 76–136.

———. "Time, Work-Discipline, and Industrial Capitalism." *Past and Present* 38, no. 1 (1967): 56–97.

Thompson, Helen. "Burney's Conservatism: Masculine Value and 'the Ingenuous Cecilia.'" In *Recognizing the Romantic Novel: New Histories of British Fiction, 1780–1830*, edited by Jillian Heydt-Stevenson and Charlotte Sussman, 99–125. Liverpool: University of Liverpool Press, 2008.

———. "How *The Wanderer* Works: Reading Burney and Bourdieu." *ELH: English Literary History* 68, no. 4 (winter 2001): 965–89.

Thompson, James. *Models of Value: Eighteenth-Century Political Economy and the Novel*. Durham, NC: Duke University Press, 1996.

Todd, Janet. *Sensibility: An Introduction*. London: Methuen, 1986.

Todorov, Tzvetan. *The Poetics of Prose*. Translated by Richard Howard. Ithaca, NY: Cornell University Press, 1977.

Torgovnick, Marianna. *Closure in the Novel*. Princeton, NJ: Princeton University Press, 1981.

Tratner, Michael. *Deficits and Desires: Economics and Sexuality in Twentieth-Century Literature*. Stanford: Stanford University Press, 2001.

Tribe, Keith. "'Das Adam Smith Problem' and the Origins of Modern Smith Scholarship." *History of European Ideas* 34, no. 4 (December 2008): 514–25.

———. *Das Adam Smith Problem and the Origins of Smith Scholarship*. Oxford: Oxford University Press, 2015.

Valvo, Nick. "Sentimental Disinterest." *Eighteenth Century* 57, no. 4 (January 2016): 411–32.

Wall, Cynthia. "The English Auction; Narratives of Dismantlings." *Eighteenth-Century Studies* 31, no. 1 (1997): 1–25.

Wallerstein, Immanuel Maurice. *The Modern World-System.* 3 volumes. Berkeley: University of California Press, 2011.

Wandless, William H. "Secretaries of the Interior: Narratorial Collaboration in Sarah Scott's *Millenium Hall.*" *Eighteenth-Century Fiction* 21, no. 2 (winter 2008–9): 259–81.

Wanko, Cheryl. "Characterization and the Reader's Quandary in Fielding's *Amelia.*" *Journal of English and Germanic Philology* 90, no. 4 (October 1991): 505–23.

Watt, Ian. *The Rise of the Novel: Studies in Defoe, Richardson, and Fielding.* Berkeley: University of California Press, 1971.

Wayne, Teddy. *Kapitoil.* New York: Harper Perennial, 2010.

Weiss, Barbara. *The Hell of the English: Bankruptcy and the Victorian Novel.* Lewisburg, PA: Bucknell University Press, 1986.

Wennerlind, Carl. *Casualties of Credit: The English Financial Revolution, 1620–1720.* Cambridge, MA: Harvard University Press, 2011.

West-Pavlov, Russell. *Temporalities.* New Critical Idiom Series. London: Routledge, 2013.

Wetmore, Alex. *Men of Feeling in Eighteenth-Century Literature: Touching Fiction.* New York: Palgrave Macmillan, 2013.

White, Hayden. "'The Nineteenth-Century' as Chronotope." *Nineteenth-Century Contexts: An Interdisciplinary Journal* 11, no. 2 (fall 1987), 119–29.

Williams, Jeffrey. *Theory and the Novel: Narrative Reflexivity in the British Tradition.* Cambridge: Cambridge University Press, 1998.

Williams, Jonathan C. "Deathly Sentimentalism: Sarah Fielding, Henry Mackenzie." *Eighteenth-Century Fiction* 30, no. 2 (winter 2017–18): 175–93.

Winch, Donald, ed.. *The Political Economy of British Historical Experience, 1688–1914.* Oxford: Oxford University Press, 2002.

Woloch, Alex. *The One vs. the Many: Minor Characters and the Space of the Protagonist in the Novel.* Princeton, NJ: Princeton University Press, 2004.

Wood, Ellen Meiksins. *The Origin of Capitalism.* New York: Monthly Review Press, 1999.

Woodruff, D. Smith. *Consumption and the Making of Respectability, 1600–1800.* London: Routledge, 2002.

Woodmansee, Martha and Osteen, Mark, eds. *The New Economic Criticism: Studies at the Intersection of Literature and Economics.* London and New York: Routledge, 1999.

Woodworth, Megan. "'If a Man Dared Act for Himself': Family Romance and Independence in Frances Burney's *Cecilia.*" *Eighteenth-Century Fiction* 22, no. 2 (winter 2010): 355–70.

Worstall, Tim. "Occupy's Rolling Jubilee Succeeds Partly Because It's Not a New Idea at All." *Forbes*, November 14, 2013. www.forbes.com/sites/timworstall/2013/11/14/occupys-rolling-jubilee-succeeds-partly-because-its-not-a-new-idea-at-all/#66e82b40679e.

Yahav, Amit S. *Feeling Time: Duration, the Novel, and Eighteenth-Century Sensibility.* Philadelphia: University of Pennsylvania Press, 2018.

Žižek, Slavoj. *Living in the End Times.* London: Verso, 2010.

INDEX